# CAMPAIGN IN RUSSIA
## THE WAFFEN SS ON THE EASTERN FRONT

**by Leon Degrelle**

INSTITUTE FOR HISTORICAL REVIEW
1985

*Campaign in Russia:*
*The Waffen SS*
*On the Eastern Front*
By Leon Degrelle

English translation
From the French original,
*Front de l'est, 1941–1945*



Published in the United States
by the Institute for Historical Review
Post Office Box 1306
Torrance, California 90505

Published in U.K. by Crecy Books, 1985

Crecy Books, an imprint of
Cathedral Publishing, Ltd.
96 Queens Road.
Clifton, Bristol BS8 1NS

British Library Cataloguing
In Publication:

Degrelle, Leon
Campaign In Russia: The Waffen SS
On the Eastern Front
1. Waffenschutzstaffel—History
2. World War, 1939–1945—Campaign
—Soviet Union
I. Title
940.54'21 D764 ISBN 0-947554-04-1

Manufactured in the
United States of America

**CAMPAIGN IN RUSSIA**
**THE WAFFEN SS ON THE EASTERN FRONT**

LEON DEGRELLE

# INTRODUCTION

With this translation of Leon Degrelle's *Front de l'est* one of the great men of this or any century begins to tell his story in English. For the first time the majority of English speakers in America, Great Britain, and other English-speaking countries will have the chance to make up their own minds about a public figure who for over fifty years has been in his native country, Belgium, and abroad, one of the most admired as well as one of the most reviled and traduced figures of the century. Publicist, political leader, soldier, Catholic, man of the West, Leon Degrelle compels our attention: long slandered by distortion or omission by the powers which seek to control our thought, now he speaks to us in our own language.

In *Campaign in Russia* Degrelle deals almost exclusively with his service on the German Eastern Front in the great European crusade against Communism in Russia, Ukraine, the Baltic states, and the other territories which then languished, and still languish, under the despotic rule of the masters of the Soviet Empire. A master stylist in French, the author of more than twenty books, with an incomparable breadth of life experience and culture, Degrelle as actor and chronicler of the anti-Soviet epic needs little assistance or elucidation from any chair-bound academic or editor.

Yet a few preliminary remarks are necessary to set the stage for the great drama of the Wallonian heroes in the East. Degrelle's life story is little known in England and America, and the General is often not disposed to enlighten us on many salient details. It was not for nothing that his fellow Walloon volunteers jokingly referred to him as "Modest the First, Duke of Burgundy," on the front. Furthermore, both American and English readers of the present-day have little feel for, or knowledge of, the essentials of Continental history so important for understanding Degrelle and his movement, notwithstanding a vast influx of refugee scholars to American and British universities in consequence of national revolutionary developments throughout the Europe of the 1930's and 1940's.

Leon Degrelle was born on 15 June 1906 at Bouillon, on the French border, in the Belgian province of Luxembourg. His father, Edouard

Degrelle, was a prosperous brewer who had immigrated to Belgium from France five years earlier, provoked by a French "anti-clerical" governments's expulsion of the Jesuit order. (So many of the Degrelles had become Jesuit priests that a friend of the family described the Degrelles as "Jesuits from father to son," ironic indeed in view of Degrelle's future troubles with the Catholic hierarchy of Belgium.)

Degrelle the boy grew up along the banks of the Semois, overshadowed by the great castle of Godfrey de Bouillon, leader of the First Crusade and King of Jerusalem, enjoying a relatively untroubled youth despite four years of German occupation during the First World War. In 1921 he entered the Jesuit college of Notre Dame de la Paix at Namur. His grades were average, for the young Degrelle had, from the age of fifteen, commenced an ambitious extra-curricular work of reading and writing. At that age he published his first newspaper article; many more were to follow. When a friend fell seriously ill, young Leon wrote to Cardinal Mercier, the primate of Belgium, to ask him to administer personally the last rites of the Church. Mercier did so, and entered into a correspondence with the teenager. At seventeen, Degrelle published an article on social justice in *Les cahiers de la jeunesse catholique* (*Notebooks of Catholic Youth*) which so impressed the socialist leader Emile Vandervelde that he published it in his paper *Le Peuple* (*The People*) with the regret that the young writer was not a socialist. (These details and much other fascinating material can be found in Jean-Michel Etienne's *Le Mouvement rexiste jusqu'en 1940*, a relatively balanced account of Degrelle and his political activity before the war, published as Number 165 of the *Cahiers de la fondation nationale des sciences politiques,* Paris.)

In 1924 Degrelle left the college to continue his studies at the Catholic faculty at Namur. During that time, and even before, Degrelle had fallen under the sway of the French writer Charles Maurras, founder and leader of *Action Francaise*, who, together with his close collaborator Leon Daudet, expounded brilliantly on French culture and politics in the newspaper that bore the name of their movement. It is difficult today to convey the impact and influence Maurras exercized over French youth (and French-speaking youth in Belgium and Switzerland). Profoundly conservative, with a sweep of classical culture which easily encompassed Hellas and Rome as well as the French cultural and political achievement, which Maurras, a monarchist, saw as chiefly the work of "forty kings in a thousand years," Maurras played a leading role in the controversies of the day. Reading *Action Francaise* in Paris was *de rigueur* for French intellectuals of all political shades, from Proust and Gide to Bourget and Mauriac.

Like many 19th and 20th-century intellectuals on the side of authority and the West, Maurras was not a believing Christian, although he valued the Catholic Church's historical role and traditions highly. At first this didn't blunt his support among young Catholics, including Degrelle. In

1924 the young student responded to a poll conducted by the *Cahiers de la jeunesse catholique*, which posed the question: "Among the writers of the past twenty years, whom do you consider to be your master?" by campaigning among his fellows for Maurras, who won the poll in a landslide, mortally offending certain shades of Catholic opinion, particularly among the hierarchy, and leading indirectly to the condemnation of *Action Francaise* by Cardinal Andrieu, of Bordeaux, and the placing of Maurras's writings on the index of books prohibited for Catholics.

Young Degrelle, loyal Catholic, complied readily with the prelate's injunction. Continuing his studies at the great university at Louvain, he excelled in philosophy and literature, was less successful at the study of politics and law, by which time he was devoting most of his energies to journalism. In 1927 he assumed the direction of *L'Avant-Garde*, the student newspaper, which Degrelle revitalized to such an extent that its circulation soared to an unprecedented 10,000.

Degrelle's prowess as an editor and a Catholic polemicist attracted much notice in Belgium. In 1929 Degrelle was offered an editorship, at age 23, of the Brussels daily *Le XXe siecle* (*The Twentieth Century*), an offer under the terms of which he would not have to cease his studies. In 1930 he was appointed director of *Les editions Rex*, a publishing house closely affiliated with the Catholic youth movement in Belgium ("Rex" stood for *Christus Rex*, "Christ the King").

The twenty-four-year-old publisher immediately embarked on a strenuous program of Catholic and nationalist propaganda, supervising half a dozen periodicals and churning out a flood of books and pamphlets. In 1931, with help from his family and sympathizers, Degrelle was able to buy the financially precarious publishing house, attaining an increased independence from its official Catholic sponsors.

Soon, thanks to Degrelle's energy and leadership, an intellectual and nascently political movement was beginning to coalesce around Rex. At first Degrelle was determined to renew Belgian life from within the established framework, meaning, at that time, the official Catholic movements and the Church-linked Catholic Party. Unfortunately for Belgium and the loftier ethical purposes of the Church, the Catholic Party was an integral part of the morally corrupt and spiritually exhausted climate which characterized the nation, and so much of the West, then and today.

The Belgium of the 1930's, and the preceding century, was a far cry from the cultural and economic giant it had been in earlier ages, when it had boasted successively a proud chivalry, industrious merchants and entrepreneurs, and brilliant artists and scholars. Throughout its history it had been a land of proudly independent nobles and townsmen jealous of their liberties, a place coveted as the pivot of empire by rulers from the Carolingians to the Habsburgs to Napoleon Bonaparte. Charlemagne, Godfrey de Bouillon, Charles the Bold, Charles the Fifth, the Van Eycks, Bruegel,

Rubens, Josquin Desprez, Roland de Lassus: the list of men who lived and worked in the cities and provinces of what is now Belgium is a roll-call of European greatness.

With the defeat of Napoleon's quest for a united Europe, however, Belgium, an independent state bearing that name for the first time from 1830, drifted into increasing political and cultural stagnation. Its role as Britain's tripwire against French and German "aggression" was established definitively by the Belgian Guarantee Treaty, which in effect made the little country the strategic catspaw of the balance-of-power manipulators and imperialists in London.

Following the First World War, Belgium drifted farther into France's orbit politically, and its three ruling parties, the Catholics, the Liberals, and the Socialists, consolidated the system by which they shared the loot of office, engaging in an endless round of financial peculations to which the mass of the Belgian electorate had long since become insensate.

Degrelle's passionate call to rededication and reform was naturally rejected by the men he came to call the "old bonzes" of political Catholicism, and Degrelle responded with a withering critique of their failings. By late 1934 the breach with the Catholic Party was an accomplished and public fact, and Rex, already a potent force through its publications and its formidable mass rallies, was moving steadily in the direction of formal political activity.

Degrelle and his movement launched a brilliant propaganda campaign against the established parties, whom Degrelle denounced as the *pourris*, "the corrupt," before whose offices broom-welding Rexists gathered to dramatize their call for a national cleansing. The Rexists were able to make great political capital out of the cynical financial manipulations of the parties and their henchmen, the "banksters," in Degrelle's memorable coinage. Degrelle was able to point to the fact, for instance, that 59 Catholic deputies of the national assembly held 245 positions on the boards of banking, industrial, and commercial concerns; that 19 Liberal deputies held 113 such positions; and that 17 Socialists, Marxists to a man, reveled in 53 like plums.

Nor did it escape Degrelle and Rex that Belgium's ruling parties, so cooperative when it came to dividing the private spoils of public life, survived politically only by sedulously fostering political division and strife—economic, linguistic, and religious—throughout Belgium. Degrelle, the foremost Belgian orator of the day, flayed the bourgeoisie for the betrayal of the workers; chastized the Liberals and Socialists for their abandonment of Belgium's religious heritage; and wooed the Flemish-speakers of the north, long estranged by the cultural and political arrogance of the dominant Walloons.

Rex's first venture into the electoral lists in May 1936 was a stunning success: the movement elected 21 deputies and 12 senators, establishing itself in its initial attempt as a serious contender to the established parties. Degrelle followed up this success with a series of political hammer blows against the parties: he greatly increased his potential support among the workers by supporting their aims in several massive strikes which broke out after the election ("To break the neck of Communism will get us nowhere if we do not also break the neck of the social selfishness that gave it birth," he proclaimed), and he struck an agreement with the Flemish nationalists, whose political party was also burgeoning.

For a time it seemed as if Rex might change radically the nature of politics in Belgium, but the forces of the establishment, aware of their peril, united in a solid phalanx against Degrelle. When the young leader opposed Belgium's Premier Van Zeeland in a climactic by-election in Brussels in 1937, "all the forces of conservatism joined against him, from Communist advocates of a moderate (*sic*) Popular Front to the Catholics," in the significant phrase of refugee historian Eugen Weber, no friend to Rex or Degrelle (in *Varieties of Fascism*, p. 128).

The Catholic hierarchy, repeating a mistake it has made many times in the last century, condemned its church's most ardent son in the interests of a specious moderation and conservatism: Catholics were forbidden by the primate of Belgium, Cardinal Van Rooey, to so much as abstain from voting for Van Zeeland, who, backed by the massed artillery of the banksters, the press, all three major parties, and the Church, won in a landslide. (The estimable Van Zeeland was forced from office a year later when Degrelle publicized the details of a particularly ripe financial scandal in which he had involved himself.)

After the by-election Rex's fortunes declined sharply. Although Degrelle was subsequently elected to the national assembly (with the highest percentage of any candidate in the nation), Rexist representation dwindled to a handful of deputies. As war loomed in Europe, Degrelle devoted himself to impressing on his countrymen the need for a principled Belgian neutrality.

When Belgium was sucked inexorably into the vortex of the European war in 1940, Degrelle's enemies had a chance to settle their scores. Germany's advance triggered a panic over the alleged activities of "fifth columnists," (who, as Bradley F. Smith has established in *The Shadow Warriors*, were virtually non-existent in Western Europe), giving a pretext for Degrelle's arrest, in flagrant violation of any parliamentary immunity, on 10 May 1940.

Dragged from dungeon to dungeon across Belgium and France, he was beaten and tortured, and was several times in imminent danger of being killed (Joris Van Severen, Flemish leader and Belgian patriot, was murdered by French troops at Abbeville that May). Given up for dead by his family, Degrelle ended up at a concentration camp at Vernet in southern France, which was commanded by a Frenchman named Bernheim. When German officials sympathetic to the young leader discovered his whereabouts, he was promptly released. On his return to Belgium, he avoided collaborating with the German occupation forces, unlike many of his foes in the pre-war political establishment (most of the government, on the other hand, had fled pell-mell across the English Channel, appropriating as much gold and currency as they could carry).

As German arms triumphed everywhere on the contiment, and an attendant postwar redrawing of the map of Europe seemed likely, Degrelle turned his thoughts to the shape and role of his country in the new order. Conscious of the transitory and conditional nature of the nineteenth-century political construct that was Belgium, Degrelle envisioned a possible new state along the lines of old Lotharingia or historic Burgundy, that ancient buffer zone between Germany and France the claims of which have never been entirely eclipsed in the 1,100 year course of Western European history. When Hitler struck against the Soviet Union in June, 1941, Degrelle made his decision. His offer to raise a volunteer battalion of his Walloons to ensure a place of honor for French-speaking Belgians in Hitler's new Europe was accepted by the Germans.

* * * * *

For the average American, particularly one who didn't live through the 1930's and 40's, a forty-year barrage of incessant and one-sided propaganda requires a real act of historical imagination to enter into the spirit of those days, let alone reconstruct them through historical research.

In the liberal and capitalist West, the 1930's were a time of economic stagnation, its nations still exhausted by the senseless slaughter of the First World War, its leaders and office holders devoid of ideals, its political and moral force on the world stage ebbing rapidly. Communism, despite the severe economic and organizational problems of the Soviet Union, was on the march. Secure in its eight-million-square-mile Eurasian bastion, thanks to the financial and technical aid and political indulgence of its plutocratic enemies, it commanded a world-wide conspiratorial apparatus and fostered a global propaganda, each of which seemed to gain in strength from year to year.

In Germany, at the start of this period, a powerful Communist movement seemed to be readying another thrust at revolution. In Spain the Reds would seize control of an anti-Western revolution which, among other atrocities, witnessed the murder of over 6,000 priests and nuns (including fourteen bishops) and the wholesale liquidation of its erstwhile allies on the left, while a large portion of the European and American political leadership and intelligentsia looked on in sympathy. In France a "Popular Front" was inaugurated, according Soviet agents entree to the highest councils and most secret councils of the nation. As Eugene Lyons demonstrated in his excellent *The Red Decade*, a *de facto* popular front had also come into being in America, the government of which was increasingly infiltrated, to the highest policy-making levels, by Soviet agents and sympathizers, and whose leaders tolerated and often participated in the Red propaganda. The same was true, although to a lesser extent, in a politically played-out Great Britain, where the signal Communist achievement was the recruitment of a number of the nation's most gifted and privileged youth, at its greatest university, to the Soviet spy and terror organization.

Against this audacious assault, carried on within and without the citadels of the West, the men of Europe and America seemed, for the most part, powerless, either lulled by its siren songs or paralyzed by indecision and fear. Even the "conservatives," then as now, had little better to offer than airy and diffuse theorizing, Aesopian talk of "revolts of the masses," or "conservative revolutions," usually light-years wide of the mark and scarcely powerful enough to confound even their own countries' worn-out leftist *literati* or rouse their peoples, let alone blunt the disciplined fury of the Communists.

The only effective opponents of this most deadly peril ever to menace the civilization of the West were those men and women of Europe variously called "Fascist" or "Nazi," words long since converted to mere smears in the opinion mills East and West. Their movements, first in Italy, preeminently in Germany, but active and capable in many European nations, were able to displace a doddering liberalism and smash snarling Bolshevism wherever they triumphed, not so much by police repression, although they didn't shrink from it, as by fearlessly grappling with the salient economic and political issues of the day. Hitler's and Mussolini's crushing of the Marxists was accomplished by real achievements on behalf of the workers, not merely in terms of employment, social security, and prosperity, but by earnestly cultivating these tens of millions of men and women as full-fledged and honorable members of their nation, in marked contrast to the scorn and fear of craftsmen and leaders so deeply engrained in the bourgeois caste which dominated liberal circles.

Germany's assault on the Soviet, launched in mortal necessity, has been to date the only serious attempt to destroy the Communist enemy of Western liberties and conscience, despite an unending series of half-hearted jabs and feints by the capitalist powers since the end of the First World War. It was the mightiest and bloodiest struggle the world has ever seen. For Germany and its European allies, it began with an unbroken succession of victories. Checked by the Russian winter at the very gates of Moscow, the armies of Europe held on and continued their advance to the southeast in 1942. With the turn of the tide in 1943, thanks to the Soviet's almost inexhaustible manpower, lavish aid from Bolshevism's capitalist allies, and the vast spaces of the Russian heartland, the Germans, bolstered by hard-fighting European volunteers in the ranks of the Waffen SS, performed prodigies of heroism to the bitter end, when the Red tide engulfed Europe as far as Luebeck and Trieste, and the soldiers of the plutocratic Mammon and the Bolshevik Moloch clasped hands on the Elbe.

In this heroic, failed crusade Leon Degrelle and his Wallonian volunteers played their role to the utmost measure of their hearts and souls. Of the first 800 Walloons who left for the Eastern Front, three survived the war, one of them Degrelle, who was wounded seven times during the course of his three and a half years of combat. All told some 2,500 Walloons fell against the Soviets, only after enduring desperate, hand-to-hand combats by the hundred, hurricanes of steel by the thousand. Outnumbered and outgunned but never outmanned, the Belgians never wavered and never flinched in a battle that was far less tangibly theirs than that of by far the majority of combatants. For the honor of their country, for the future of their continent, they braved a hundred Alamos, a hundred Thermopylaes, so that it might once more be proclaimed, with full justice: *Fortissimi omnium Belgae sunt.*

It needs be remarked that the Wallonian troops were most of them military novices at the outset of the war. Their organizer Degrelle had been rendered quasi-invulnerable by no protective laving in fire or water; no Cheiron bred him to arms. When he departed for the front in 1941 at the age of 35, he had never fired a gun; although he had been offered high rank he chose to start out as a private, sharing all the burdens of his comrades, and rising by his courage and resolve alone through the ranks to the position of commander of the unit he raised, at last the 28th SS Division "Wallonia." No foreign soldier in the armies of the Reich was as highly honored as Degrelle; none so much merited honor.

For their heroism in defense of the West, Degrelle and his men received nothing but slander and persecution.

The Belgian political establishment, returned from its sojourn in London with breasts glittering from medals and orders of "resistance," hounded the Rexists *and their families* with pitiless ferocity, to humiliation, imprisonment, and even death. This purge, part and parcel of a great bloodbath orchestrated by Red leaders throughout Europe, was abetted, as historian Bradley Smith has established, by help from a perhaps unexpected quarter: with help from the British intelligence establishment a number of officers from Stalin's NKVD were parachuted into Belgium to lend their expertise.

Needless to say, Degrelle's family was marked out for especial cruelty. His brother was assassinated by terrorists, although he played no active role in Degrelle's movement. His wife and parents were arrested, brutally mishandled, and thrown in jail. All of them died there. With a superbly refined inhumanity, the votaries of justice and decency rounded up all of Degrelle's children (seven girls and a little boy) and, after changing their names, dispersed them in orphanages, reform schools, and homes for the retarded all across Europe. Such was the humanity and honor of our Western elite, revealed then as it had been revealed many times before, from Pearl Harbor to Dresden to Teheran to Yalta to the camps where American and British minions rounded up the millions of subjects of the Red empire to hand them over to Stalin, to that leader's boundless stupefaction and rejoicing.

By dint of luck, persistance, and the undying loyalty and friendship of his comrades, Degrelle was able to rescue his scattered children and bring them to Spain, the epic flight to which he describes in these pages and where, thanks to the decency and honor of Generalissimo Francisco Franco, he has been able to build a new life.

Despite his years he remains vigorously and mentally nimble. Sentenced to death in 1944 by the leaders of the land he loved and served so well, he has spent more than half his life in exile. The smug bourgeois, the ecclesiastical Tartuffes, and the bread-and-butter socialists of Belgium still sputter and tremble at his name. He keeps the banners of the Wallonian Division, which he saved; some day, he hopes, they will be exhibited at a war museum in Belgium. Asked by a journalist ten years ago if he had any regrets about the war, he answered, "Only that we lost."

* * * * *

Besides its merits as an unparalleled military memoir of the Eastern Front, *Campaign in Russia* has considerable literary value as an epic of Germany and Europe's crusade against Bolshevism. A superb French stylist and a man of profound culture, Degrelle is fully conscious of his tale's heroic sweep, which constitutes at once a compact *Iliad* and *Odyssey* of modern Western courage and resolve. Alive to the classical tradition of Western letters, Degrelle frequently alludes to earlier champions against the East, from Xenophon to Godfrey de Bouillon to Bonaparte.

His own values emerge clearly in *Campaign in Russia*. Not merely valor and honor, but humanity and compassion, a tender solicitude for the Belgian comrades he led east, a sublime love for beauty, and a forthright candor mark his narrative.

Degrelle is magnanimous even to his Communist foes, paying tribute to their courage, even that of their commissars when the occasion arises, despite the many brutal atrocities the Communist soldiers carried out against his men. How different from victors and the masters of public opinion in our country, who to this day wage a relentless campaign of calumny and slander, an as yet unremitting atrocity propaganda against the defeated and the fallen. And although Degrelle is mercilessly frank in depicting the privation and squalor in which the workers and peasants lived under the Bolshevik regime, as a Christian he feels a great compassion for his fellow Christians. Some of the most moving passages in the book describe the Orthodox services which resumed with the German conquest, and in which Degrelle and the Catholic Walloons took part in true ecumenical spirit.

Love of beauty: time and time again Degrelle paints the splendors of the landscape and the heavens in inspired prose. The soldier who exclaims "Life without beauty is worthless!" has an eye for beauty even amid chaos and death, and his matchless descriptions of the carnage of the front evoke the terrifying splendor of the canvases of Bosch, Bruegel, and Goya.

Degrelle has no qualms about telling hard truths and making hard judgements. He is quick to praise the Germans and their allies when they are worthy, quick to chasten them when they are not. His descriptions of the Italians and the Romanians, of Quisling and the German generals are unsparing portraits of men who must now forever fear the burden of their deeds, for evil and for good. He is not a writer stridulously to carp and blame, however. Unlike so many post-war writers who served on the German side, Degrelle makes no attempt to curry favor with publishers and critics by obligatory condemnations of men like Hitler and Himmler. Unafraid to stand up to them face to face (he insisted that his unit have Catholic chaplains, even after it entered the SS, and he once told the Fuehrer that people often said he [Hitler] was crazy), Degrelle criticizes what he deems their errors with a fine discretion, and pays gracious tribute to their dedication and bravery. Indeed, *Campaign in Russia* is a moving threnody to his chosen allies, the German leaders and the German people: their matchless discipline, their boundless courage, the glory of their flaming cities, the pathos of their defeat and ruin.

But it is his brave Walloons, above all the rest, whom the writer seeks to honor with this book: the bold and self-denying men, young and old, who flocked to the standards of their country's ancient glory, from the mines, from the factories, from the schools and shops and offices and universities of their land, without hope of personal gain—no mercenaries, but gallant patriots like the storied Wild Geese of Ireland, who fought on far-flung battlefields in alien armies for the freedom of their nation. 2,500 of them lie dead, the remainder were proscribed in their native land. Degrelle, always more than able to speak for himself, here speaks for them, those not so able with tongue and pen and those eternally mute.

Always, however, the reader returns to Degrelle, the leader, the fighter, the creator, veteran of a hundred battles in the most titanic struggle in history, author of two dozen books, master of his life and the desperate age he lives in. How foreign to Degrelle is the ethic of the "survivor," the man who lives on at any price, the shallow cult of the "winner," the fair-weather glutton for false profit and tawdry fame! What contrast Degrelle's boundless energy for creation, for heroism, for sacrifice, his ineluctible good cheer and breadth of spirit, offers to the intellectual and spiritual inanition of the men and women of contemporary America!

After all his trials, after all his deeds, Degrelle lives on, still working, still creating, the 20th-century Christian knight, Roland returned in triumph, his honor brighter yet, from the pass at Roncesvalles. Always we see him smiling, not from satisfaction at those obscure workings of fate that bring our "happiness," but in some deeper, enigmatic, joy, the same smile one sees on the faces of the sixth century Greek *kouroi*, so many statues of the Buddha, the incomparable Bamberger *Reiter*: no mere stern-faced warrior is he, content to look Death and the Devil hard in the eye, but a man who marches to the rhythms and laws of God and the universe. If his brave Wallonians teach us how to die, Degrelle will teach us how to live.

—Ted O'Keefe

# PREFACE

In 1936 I was the youngest political leader in Europe. At the age of twenty-nine, I'd already shaken my country to its very core. Hundreds of thousands of men, women, and young people followed me with total faith and passion. Our movement had elected dozens of deputies and senators to the Belgian parliament. I could have been a minister in the government: I had only to say one word to enter into the game of politics.

I preferred to pursue, outside the official cockpit, the hard struggle for order and justice, and against corruption, since I was possessed by an ideal which allowed neither for compromises nor for a division of the spoils.

I wanted to free my country from the dictatorial domination of the moneyed interests which corrupted power, undermined our institutions, tainted our consciences, and ruined industry and labor. For the anarchical regime of the old parties, all of them discredited by leprous political-financial scandals, I wanted to substitute, legally, a strong and free State, well ordered, responsible, and representative of the true energies of our people.

This was not a question of tyranny nor of "fascism." It was a question of good sense. A country cannot live in disorder, incompetence, irresponsibility, uncertainty, and corruption.

I called for authority in the State, competence in public offices, continuity in the enterprises of the nation, a real, living contract between the masses and the government, an intelligent and productive harmony among the citizens who were separated and opposed to one another only by artificial struggles: class struggles, religious struggles, linguistic struggles, all manufactured and fed with scrupulous care since they were the very life of the rival parties which, with an equal hypocrisy, disputed theatrically with one another while sharing the advantages of power.

I swooped down, broom in hand, under the eyes of the corrupt gangs that drained away the vigor of my country. I flogged and flagellated them, I destroyed, before the eyes of the people, the whited sepulchres under which they hid their depravities, their plundering, their lucrative collusions. I caused a breath of youth and idealism to pass over my country; I exalted the spiritual forces and the lofty recollections of struggle and glory of a determined, hard-working people with a passion for life.

The Rexist movement was a reaction against the corruption of an era. It was a movement for political renewal and for social justice. It was especially a fervent impetus toward greatness, an outpouring of thousands of souls who wished to breathe, to shine, to raise themselves above the baseness of a regime and an era.

Such was the struggle up until May, 1940.

The Second World War—which I had condemned—changed everything, in Belgium as elsewhere. Old institutions, old doctrines collapsed like castles made of rotten wood, worm-eaten for a long time.

The Rexist movement was not tied in any manner to the triumphant Third Reich: not to its leader, not to its party, not to any one of its leaders or propagandists. The Rexist movement was fundamentally an intensely national movement with absolute independence. All the archives of the Third Reich have been seized: no one has been able to find the tiniest trace of any attachment whatever, direct or indirect, between Rexism and Hitler before the invasion in 1940. Our hands were clean, our hearts were pure, our love for our country, bright and burning, was free of all compromise.

The German onrush overwhelmed our country.

For 99 percent of the Belgians or the French, the war was over by July 1940; the predominance of the Reich was a fact to which, moreover, the old democratic and financial regime ardently wanted to adapt itself as quickly as possible!

Among those who had insulted Hitler in 1939 were many who would be the most eager to throw themselves at the feet of the conqueror in 1940: the heads of the great parties of the Left, the financial magnates, the owners of the largest newspapers, the Masonic ministers of state, the former government, all of them wanted, sought, begged a smile, an opportunity for collaboration.

Was it necessary to surrender the field to the discredited ghosts of the old parties, to the gangsters of a financial system whose only allegiance was to gold, or to sinister pirates lacking both talent and dignity, eager for the meanest tasks of a valet to satisfy their greed and ambition?

The problem was not only sad: it was urgent. To nearly all observers the Germans appeared to be final victors. It was necessary to make up one's mind. Could we, out of fear of taking responsibility, just let our country drift?

For several weeks, I considered the problem. It was only after having asked and obtained from the Royal Palace a completely favorable decision that I decided to let *Le Pays rêel* (*The Real Country*), the newspaper of the Rexist movement, reappear.

Belgian collaboration, which began at the end of 1940, took, however, an unfortunate direction. From all the evidence, the German authorities were very much more interested in the capitalist forces than in the idealist forces. No one succeeded in finding out exactly what Germany was contemplating.

The King of the Belgians, Leopold III, wanted to see things more clearly and to obtain some precise details. He asked Hitler to receive him. The audience was granted. But King Leopold came back from Berchtesgaden[1] without having succeeded and without having learned anything new.

It was clear that our country was going to be made to wait until peace returned. By that time it would be too late. We had to win, before the war ended, the right to negotiate with Germany on an effective basis. How were we to achieve this?

Collaboration within the country was nothing other than an operation of slow encirclement, of nibbling in bits and bites, of endless struggles for influence carried out against obscure secondary personages. Not only would that work not give any prestige to whoever undertook it, but it could only discredit him.

That was a trap I didn't want to fall into. I watched and waited for a different approach. Suddenly, in June, 1941, I had my chance: Germany had gone to war against the Soviet Union.

Here was the unique opportunity, the opportunity to command the respect of the Reich by means of combat, suffering, and glory. In 1940, we had been the conquered, our king a prisoner king.

All at once, in 1941, we were offered the chance to become the comrades and equals of our conquerers. Everything depended on our courage. We had, finally, the chance to win the position of prestige which would allow us, on the day of the reorganization of Europe, to speak with our heads held high, in the name of our heroes, in the name of our dead, in the name of the nation, which had offered its blood.

Through our struggle on the endless Eastern steppes, we wanted indeed to do our duty as Europeans and as Christians. But, we say this openly—we proclaimed it loud and clear from the first day—we had above all given this gift of our youth in order to guarantee the future of our nation in the midst of a rescued Europe. It was for that, first of all, that several thousands of our comrades fell. It was for that that thousands of men struggled, struggled for four years, suffered for four years, sustained by that hope, driven on by that desire, strengthened by the certainty that they were going to succeed in their purpose.

The Reich lost the war, but it could just as well have won it.

Until 1945, victory for Hitler remained possible.

Hitler as victor would, I am certain, have recognized the right of our nation to live and to be great, a right that it had acquired for itself slowly, with difficulty, by the blood of thousands of Belgian volunteers.

These men endured two years of epic struggle before forcing the attention of the Reich. In 1941, the Belgian anti-Bolshevik Wallonian[2] Legion had

[1] See footnotes beginning on page 349.

gone unnoticed. Our soldiers had to multiply their acts of bravery, to risk their lives a hundred times before raising the name of their country to the level of legend. In 1943, our legion of volunteers had become celebrated all along the Eastern Front for its idealism and its fearlessness. In 1944, it reached the height of its fame, at the time of the odyssey of Cherkassy. The German people, more than any other people, are sensitive to the glory of armed combat. Our moral claim on the German Reich was unique in Europe, far superior to that of any other occupied country.

I saw Hitler at length on two occasions in that year, a soldier's visit, but a visit that showed me clearly that we had won our country. Shaking my hand firmly in his two hands at the moment of my departure, Hitler told me with stirring affection: "If I had a son, I would want him to be like you." How, after all our battles, could he refuse me the right of my country to live in honor? Our volunteers had won their dream: they had, in the event of German victory, resoundingly assured the rebirth and the greatness of our people.

The Allied victory temporarily rendered useless that terrible effort of four years combat, the sacrifice of our dead, the Calvary of the survivors.

After the defeat, the world worked unceasingly to mock the vanquished. Our soldiers, our wounded, our maimed were condemned to death or thrown into unspeakable camps and prisons. Nothing was respected, neither the honor of the warrior, nor our parents, nor our homes.

But greatness is never in vain. The virtues won in sorrow and sacrifice are stronger than hatred and death. Like the sun springing from the dark night, they will shine forth sooner or later.

The future will go well beyond that rehabilitation. It will not only render homage to the heroism of the soldiers of the Eastern Front in the Second World War, but it will also say that they were right: that they were right in a negative sense, since Bolshevism is the end of all values; and that they were right in a positive sense, since a united Europe, for which they strove, was the only—perhaps the last—possibility of survival for a marvelous old continent, a haven of human joy and fervor, but mangled and mutilated to the point of death.

A day will come, perhaps, when people will regret the defeat in 1945 of the defenders and builders of Europe.

While awaiting that day, let us tell truthfully their epic tale—how they fought, what trials they suffered, how they gave their hearts to the struggle.

Through the epic of the Belgian volunteers—one unit among a hundred others—it is the entire Russian front which is going to come into view once more, with the sunny days of the great victories, with the still more moving days of the great defeats, defeats which were imposed by physical circumstances, but which the will did not accept.

Out there, on the endless steppes, lived *men.*

You, reader, friend or enemy—watch them come back to life; for we are living in a period when one must look very hard to find real men, and they were that, to the very marrow of their bones, as you are going to see.

L.D.

# Chapter One
# RUSH TO THE UKRAINE

22 June 1941 began like all the beautiful Sundays of summer. I was absent-mindedly turning the dial of my radio, when suddenly some words brought me up short: the troops of the Third Reich had crossed the European border of the USSR.

The campaign in Poland in 1939, the campaign in Norway, the campaign in the Netherlands, in Belgium and France in 1940, the campaign in Yugoslavia and in Greece in the spring of 1941 had only been preliminary operations or blunders. The real war, in which the future of Europe and of the world would be decided, had just begun. This was no longer a war over frontiers or interests. This was a war of religions. And, like all religious wars, it would be unrelenting.

Before engaging its tanks in the steppes, the Reich had resorted to evasion, like a watchful cat.

In 1939 National Socialist Germany was carrying out a program without precedent. It had rebuilt itself in the midst of such lightning bolts, in the thundering and blinding flashes of such cataclysms, that all Europe and all the world felt the tremors. If all his enemies to the West swooped down on the Rhineland and the Ruhr, and if, at the same time, the Soviets expanded toward East Prussia and Berlin, Hitler seriously risked strangulation. He liked to say, over and over, that Kaiser Wilhelm II had lost the First World War by not having succeeded in avoiding a war on two fronts. He was going to do better. But we were to see, one day, side by side, gawking at the ruins of the Reich Chancellery in Berlin, not only Scots and muzhiks*, but Blacks from Harlem and Kirghiz tribesmen from the deserts of Asia. . . .

* * * * *

In August of 1939, on the eve of the Polish conflagration, Hitler at the last minute had avoided being strangled.

---

* See Glossary beginning on page 347.

Stalin had old accounts to settle with National Socialism; his collaboration with the "democracies" therefore appeared assured in advance. London and Paris, with great fanfare, had sent military missions to the Soviet tsar. During that same period, in complete secrecy, Hitler had succeeded in loosening the noose.

Stalin had, like Hitler, played very skillfully. He had every interest in letting the plutocratic democracies and National Socialism exhaust each other, for he was the enemy of both. The more virulently they sapped each other's strength, the better Communism could in the final account facilitate its task. Stalin carried out his game with Asiatic cunning, the leader of an international gang, sure of his men. He could even ostensibly ally himself with the Third Reich: over the entire world, Communist discipline was absolute.

The effects of that extraordinary solidarity promptly made themselves felt. Britain and France had made it a world war after Hitler invaded Poland. When Stalin did the same thing 15 days later, no one in the Allied chancelleries took the risk of reacting

Thus the Soviet leader was able to stab a vacillating Poland in the back with complete impunity, and annex over a third of that unhappy country. Britain and France, so solicitous of Poland's territorial integrity before, neglected to declare war on the USSR.

That moral and military abdication gave an unshakeable confidence to the Communist bands spread throughout Europe. The democracies were afraid of Stalin! They had recoiled before him! What had been intolerable from Hitler had been tolerated coming from the Soviets!

The "democracies" dispensed with morality, principle, and their own self-respect for fear of consolidating Stalin's alliance with Germany. They feared also the sabotage which the Communist parties throughout Europe were preparing or had already carried out. As always a short-sighted self-interest had prevailed over all other considerations.

In reality, the alleged "just war" had lasted only fifteen days. From September of 1939, the Allies had only one idea: not to offend the USSR, to begin a reconciliation with Stalin, in spite of his aggression against their Polish allies.

Stalin was able to multiply his demands, to put an end to the independence of Estonia, Latvia and Lithuania, to snatch Bessarabia from the Rumanians. One single thing was important to the Allies: to enable the Russians to change sides. In less than two years, that would be achieved.

* * * * *

Germany had, in 1939 and in 1940, won the battles of Poland, Norway and the Western Front. But it had struggled for more than five hundred days without having achieved the essential thing: a victorious landing on English soil.

England, for its part, was likewise unable to set foot on the European continent: Churchill was talking about a preparation lasting several years.

Stalin, therefore, had a clear track. Clear in the direction of the Reich. Clear especially in the Balkans.

The game became more and more cautious.

The Germans had skillfully advanced their pawns toward Bucharest, Sofia, and Belgrade. In March of 1941 Yugoslavia's impulsive act in its breaking a treaty, concluded eight days earlier, with the Reich, led to the decisive event. The Soviets, secret instigators of that action, who saw further than that plaything of British espionage, the young King Peter, publicly wired their sympathy to the Yugoslavian government[1].

To be sure, in two weeks German armor swept through Belgrade, Sarajevo, Salonika and Athens; the paratroopers of Marshal Goering occupied the island of Crete. But the German-Soviet break had been clean. Thus far, the alliance with the Reich had served its purpose. It had brought to the Soviets all that Stalin could have expected: a very bloody piece of Poland, the three Baltic countries, some important positions in Finland, and magnificent Bessarabia.

The Nazi lemon had been squeezed dry. The hour had come to squeeze a second lemon: the democratic lemon. We know what kind of juice that lemon finally gave to the Soviets in 1945: the occupation of territories inhabited by two hundred million Europeans and Asians, the Red Army established in Thuringia, on the Elbe, at the gates of Luebeck, at Petsamo, in Manchuria, in Korea, in the Kurile Islands!

The Yugoslav turn-about, the stated claims of Molotov on the Balkans, the military preparations of the Soviets during the spring of 1941: all these left Hitler no doubt about the ambitions of the USSR. The longer he waited, the more likely he would be attacked. In order to concentrate his forces in the East, he temporarily abandoned his plan to invade England. He tried, by various means, to find a peaceful settlement to the conflict between Germany and the United Kingdom. It was too late for that. The British were no longer disposed to cancel the match; once begun, it could no longer be stopped.

For two years, each country had calculated coldly, according to the age-old law of national egoism and self-interest. In the end, each had arrived at exactly the same conclusions.

The Russians, skillfully pushed by the English and spurred on by new attractions, sooner or later were going to pounce. The Germans, sensing that the die was cast, had to bow to necessity. On 22 June 1941 began a battle to the death between the National Socialist Reich and Soviet Russia: two imperialisms, two religions, two worlds grappled across the steppes in the sands of the East.

England, isolated from Europe by the sea and with its principal riches scattered over distant lands, could not sense exactly the importance of the duel. It reacted by thinking more about its immediate interest—the relief of its island—than about what the fate of Europe would be were the Soviets one day victorious.

By contrast, for us—the peoples of the European continent—that struggle was a decisive struggle.

If National Socialist Germany triumphed, it would be the master, in the East, of a tremendous area for expansion, right on its border, tied to it directly by means of railroads, rivers and canals, open to its genius for organization and production. The Greater German Reich, in complete rebirth, endowed with a remarkable social structure, enriched by those fabulous lands, extending in one block from the North Sea to the Volga, would have such power, would have such force of attraction, would offer to the twenty peoples crowded onto the old continent such possibilities for progress that those territories would constitute the point of departure for the indispensable European federation, wished for by Napoleon, contemplated by Renan, sung of by Victor Hugo.

If, on the contrary, the Soviets prevailed, who in Europe would resist them once the enormous German bastion was dismantled? Poland, drained of its blood? The chaotic Balkans, submerged, decayed, occupied, tamed? A depopulated France, having only speeches to oppose two hundred million muzhiks and the Bolshevik ideology, swollen with its victory? Greece, Italy, talkative and charming, with their poor peoples, squatting in the sun like lizards? The jigsaw puzzle of the small European nations, the residues of a thousand years of civil war, each incapable of paying for more than a hundred tanks? The Soviets defeating the Reich—that would be Stalin mounting the body of a Europe which, its powers of resistance exhausted, was ready to be raped.

* * * * *

Naturally they would attempt, late in the day, to save that three-quarter-Sovietized Europe. The Allies of yesterday would tremble, because the USSR no longer contented itself with prey close at hand, but now extended its greedy hands, the Second World War scarcely ended, toward the Pacific Ocean, China, the Persian Gulf, the Mediterranean, the Suez Canal, menacing the colonies, the raw materials, the great multinational trusts.

But even then the Anglo-Americans did not seek to save Europe for Europe: quite simply, they strove to retain in the West a springboard which would allow them to protect their imperialism and to react against Soviet imperialism—free, if necessary, to transform that springboard, with atomic weapons, into an incredible field of ruins.

We, the sons of Europe, were thinking of the life of Europe. Whatever our judgement about the manner in which the war had started, whatever our regrets about the past, whatever bitterness there might have been at the foreign occupation of our countries, each of us understood that well beyond the pleasant or unpleasant things experienced from 1939 to 1941 by our various countries, the fate of all of Europe was in the balance.

This explains the extraordinary, spontaneous movement which aroused innumerable young men, from Oslo to Seville, from Antwerp to Budapest. They didn't leave their beloved homes in Jutland or in Beauce, in the Ardennes or in the Puszta, in Limburg or in Andalusia to serve the special interests of Germany. They left to defend two thousand years of the highest civilization. They were inspired by the baptistry in Florence and the cathedral at Rheims, by the Alcazar in Toledo and the belfry in Bruges. They died out there, in countless numbers, not for some *Dienststelle** in Berlin, but for their old countries, gilded by the centuries, and for their common fatherland, Europe, the Europe of Virgil and Ronsard, the Europe of Erasmus and Nietzsche, of Raphael and Duerer, the Europe of St. Ignatius and St. Theresa, the Europe of Frederick the Great and Napoleon Bonaparte.

Between that age-old Europe and the Soviet onslaught, its horrible leveling, the overflow of its swarming little tribes, they made their choice at once. A new generation, all over Europe, took its stand. Blond giants from Scandinavia and the Baltic countries, Hungarian dreamers with long moustaches, stocky, swarthy Rumanians, enormous Croats with violet greatcoats; Italians, whimsical and sentimental; Spaniards with jet black eyes; bantering Frenchmen; Danes, Dutch, Swiss: all hastened to the battle for Europe. All the nations were there. We even saw some Englishmen volunteer, a dozen in all, a dozen nonetheless.

* * * * *

Thousands of Belgians enlisted, according to their languages, in a Flemish legion and a Wallonian legion. At first they formed two battalions, then, in 1943, two brigades, lastly, in 1944, two divisions: the Wallonian Division and the Flemish Langemarck Division.

For a period of 46 months I would be one of those volunteers for Europe and would live together with my comrades, the most terrible and grandest of epics; would advance on foot for two years to the threshold of Asia, then fall back unendingly from the Caucasus to Norway; would pass from the ecstasy of the offensives of 1941 and 1942 to the bitter glory of defeat and exile, while, over half of an anemic Europe, there streamed the yellow tide of the Soviet conquerors.

## The Conquered Ukraine

In October of 1941 two to three weeks were required to complete the trip from the frontier of the Reich to the Russian front.

We passed through Lemberg,[2] where the streetcars were decked out with small blue and white Ukrainian flags waving in the breeze. Scarcely had we entered the countryside to the southwest when we were able to judge for ourselves the extent of the military disasters which had been inflicted on the Soviets. Hundreds of armored cars were strewn along the road. Every crossroad was a graveyard of metal.

The spectacle went on for a half hour, then most traces of combat disappeared. We had arrived in the midst of the Ukraine, an undamaged Ukraine with hundreds of gigantic hay stacks as long as zeppelins standing on its immense muddy plains.

Peaceful villages scattered their isbas*, white or pale blue, with roofs thick with straw. Each tiny cottage was isolated among groups of young cherry trees.

The walls were made of mud, but the local artists had carved primitive wooden sculptures of love birds, flowers, arrows, and shells, which framed the small windows. These wooden carvings were painted, like the shutters, in vivid colors. The windows were double windows, hermetically sealed, separated by a board as wide as your hand, on which rested, in cotton wool, small glass wares, oranges or tomatoes made of colored cement.

Big girls with high cheekbones hurried about in front of small farms. Their blond hair was tied up in blue or red scarves. They were dressed in dresses of rough cloth which gave them the appearance of Laplanders. In high boots of the Cossack type they splashed merrily in the mud among the noisy pigs.

The train would stop for a few hours in the middle of the fields or in front of a ruined village. We bought chickens that we cooked in boiling water from the locomotive. Some Ukrainian youngsters showed us with pride their exercises in the German language. In their notebooks we read on the first pages: "Stalin is the greatest man in the world" and then, on the last pages, the phrase reviewed and corrected by the prudent teacher: "Hitler is the greatest man in the world." The children did not appear particularly troubled by this.

* * * * *

Certain encounters gave us an idea of the scale of the victories of September and October 1941: these were with the trains which transported fantastic hordes of prisoners of war toward the Reich.

At each stop, we ran to look at the railway cars. We stood astounded in front of those hairy giants, saffron colored, with small, gleaming, feline eyes. Many were Asiatics. They were standing, 80 or even 100 to a car.

During a station stopover one night, we were awakened by terrible cries. We hurried to open the doors of a car full of prisoners: Asiatics, as hungry as piranhas, fought each other while snatching pieces of meat. That prized meat was human flesh! The prisoners were fighting over the remains of a dead Mongol, who had been cut apart with pieces of tin from cans of food. Certain prisoners had felt cheated by being left out of the distribution, which resulted in the brawl. Gnawed bones had been tossed outside through the bars. They were scattered, bloody, alongside the railway car on the muddy ground.

We learned later on that hundreds of thousands of men, packed together in that way, remained standing sometimes for three weeks, fed when there was food near the tracks. Many of these Asiatics, recruited from their wild steppes, preferred to gnaw a Kalmuk or Tatar rib rather than to run the risk of dying of hunger. In one station, I saw several of them digging in the ground. They extracted some red, wriggling worms, a good six inches long, which they gulped down as they might have gulped down an egg. The Adam's apples of these worm-eaters rose and fell with gusto.

* * * * *

One morning we arrived at the Bug River, the large metal bridge over which lay at the bottom of the river. We had to unload all of our baggage and camp in the city of Pervomaisk.

We were able once more to receive news from the front. The advances were not as stupendous as we had been told by the onlookers along the railway line. On the contrary, the German thrust was slowing down: Moscow had not fallen, nor Leningrad; on the Rostov front the situation was not clear. Optimism was still very great, but one noted that certain things were passed over in silence. The Germans in Pervomaisk made discreet references to the difficulties of divisions hurled forward a thousand kilometers beyond the borders of the Reich.

Looking at the mud, we thought about the sea of mud which separated the armies on the offensive from their former bases. One road left Pervomaisk toward the Dnieper River. Some trucks were stuck there mired to axle level. The mud was black and thick as tar. The strongest engines failed, powerless.

The railway lines were themselves hardly more passable. The tracks must not have been touched since the times of the tsars. The trains advanced with a torturous slowness; nevertheless, the rails rose and fell like seesaws. The traffic was light, although the widening of the tracks had been carried out with an extraordinary haste. The transfers from one train to another made everything worse. After reaching the Bug, it was necessary to descend on foot to the bottom of the valley, then climb up again by way of a muddy detour of several kilometers. The trail was a river: men marched in water up to their knees. With the bridges down, all aid to the armies of the south had to be sent forward in similar fashion.

Driving eastward, the German armies had made a daring gamble. Had

Hitler's bold undertaking achieved a speedy victory, the situation on the Eastern Front could have been consolidated very quickly. The Germans, with their genius for organizing, could have deployed troops to restore communications with the rear, to repair and improve the rail lines, and to rebuild the bridges, all within a few months: that would have forestalled disaster.

Unfortunately for the Reich, the war did not end as quickly as the High Command had foreseen. The divisions tried to slog forward, but the autumn floods made the steppes totally impassable. The munitions, the gasoline, the indispensable reinforcements toiled for weeks across dislocated Russia.

A bogged-down army is a liability. And winter was approaching. In 1812, at exactly the same time of year, Napoleon had had to make the anguishing decision to retreat from Moscow.

The armies of the Reich, however, were going to remain in Russia. Here it was not a case of remaining at an advanced point as it had been for the French Emperor, but rather of maintaining a 3,000-kilometer front running from the White to the Black Sea.

As we looked at the empty stations, the destroyed bridges, the trucks sunk in the mud, we couldn't avoid thinking about the hundreds of thousands of men, committed to the depths of Russia, who were going to try what Napoleon had not dared to try: to maintain themselves in spite of everything in the midst of the steppes, with the enemy in front of them, the desert to their backs, the snow falling from the sky, and the ice gnawing away at their bodies and their morale.

Nevertheless, we all had such confidence in the infallibility of the German High Command that we didn't indulge in such thoughts for very long. The war could still end before the very coldest weather began. If not, everything had been foreseen, this time as always . . .

We boarded another train after crossing the flooded valley of the Bug. The countryside remained calm during the day, but at night the trains were fired upon. One morning we noted the bodies of Soviet soldiers along the track. They had tried an isolated attack. Now their twisted bodies lay there in long violet coats.

The water began to freeze solid, and we had to break the ice in the ditches in order to wash in the morning after the train stopped.

We had been packed in, forty soldiers to a car, for 17 days. On 2 November, very early, we passed large anti-tank trenches cut into the reddish-brown hills.

The train began to descend past the endless walls of charred factories. Then a wonderful sight: a mighty blue stream, a brilliant blue, bathed in the sun, suddenly appeared before our eyes: the Dnieper River, more than a kilometer wide.

## Dniepropetrovsk

There had been scarcely any battles between Galicia and the Dnieper. Once the city of Lemberg was seized, the battle to surround Balta had determined the fate of the marvelous Ukrainian plain, covered with corn and wheat, scattered with large blue and white villages, decked out with thousands of cherry trees. The armor of the Reich had pushed on, without any other incidents up to Dniepropetrovsk.

The battles outside the city had been bitterly fought. One cemetery, near the station, held more than 600 German graves. Entire streets had been burned. Yet the city retained its beautiful appearance. Karl Marx Prospect, immediately renamed Adolf Hitler Avenue, went on without end, as wide as the Champs-Elysées.

The war now crossed the river. The appearance it had presented when the German troops went into the heavily inhabited sections of town was more comical than terrifying. Long rows of men stretched out, dead drunk, alongside gutters through which there flowed in torrents three hundred liters of vodka, escaping from barrels that the Bolsheviks had smashed in their retreat. The drunks had lapped up the alcohol even from the mud; then, overcome with bliss, they had awaited, bellies exposed, the arrival of the conqueror.

At Dniepropetrovsk the Stalin regime had made great efforts in construction. We were at first impressed as we approached the suburbs of the city, where we saw outlined the large masonry blocks of the proletarian housing erected by the Soviets. Their lines were modern. The buildings were huge and there were many of them. Undeniably, the Communist system had done something for the people. If the misery of the peasants was great, at least the worker seemed to have benefited from the new times.

Still, it was necessary to visit and examine the buildings. We lived for six months in the Donets coalbasin. We had plenty of time to test the conclusions that we had reached at the time of our entrance into Dniepropetrovsk. The buildings, so impressive from a distance, were just a gigantic hoax, intended to fool sightseers shepherded by *Intourist** and the viewers of documentary films.

Approaching those housing blocks you were sickened by the stench of mud and excrement which rose from the quagmires surrounding each of the buildings. Around them were neither sidewalks nor gravel nor paving stones. The Russian mud was everywhere, and everywhere the walls peeled and crumbled. The quality of the construction materials was of the lowest order. All the balconies had come loose, and already the cement stairways were worn and grooved, although the buildings were only a few years old.

Each floor had a certain number of apartments that were whitewashed and provided with a minuscule kitchen for the use of several families. The electric wires hung in clusters. The walls were made of mud and cracked as soon as you dared to pound a nail into them.

Generally there was no running water. The proletarian dwellers, not able to use the sanitary facilities, relieved themselves all around the buildings, converted as a result into a vast latrine. Cold weather froze the droppings which, with each thaw, caused a terrible stench. Altogether those apartments turned out to be more uncomfortable than the miserable isbas in which, on the richest soil in Europe, millions of Russian peasants vegetated in the midst of a sordid misery, only tattered clothes on their backs, eating from a common bowl, using spoons crudely carved from bits of wood.

Seventy-five percent of our soldiers were manual laborers. Many among them had been susceptible, once, to Soviet propaganda. They stood with their mouths agape when they saw in what conditions of decay and exhaustion the Russian proletariat existed. They shook their heads, having to look twice at the scene before believing it.

Hitler had tried a dangerous experiment. The hundreds of thousands of German workers mobilized and sent to the Eastern Front could have made dangerous comparisons if the Soviets had actually achieved great things for the working class.

On the contrary, every German thought back to the delightful workers' housing in the Reich, to its comfort, to the family garden, to the clinics and maternity hospitals for the people, the leisure time, the paid vacations, the magnificent cruises to Scandinavia or to the Mediterranean. They remembered their wives, their children, happy, in good health, well clothed. Looking at the ragged Russian people, the miserable isbas, the workers' apartments, gloomy and rickety, they drew clear conclusions.

Never had a workers' group made such a study trip.

Four years later, the comparison worked in the opposite direction: after having looted the watches, the jewelry, the clothes from all of Eastern Europe, the Soviet soldier returned grumbling to the USSR, astonished at the comfort of the non-Communist countries and disgusted with his "paradise" of wooden spoons, tattered dresses, and muddy excrement stretching around his house-barracks.

* * * * *

At the end of three days, we received our new marching orders: in the last hours of the night, we would cross over to the left bank of the Dnieper, thus entering the combat zone.

At six in the evening our legion gathered on a terrace overlooking the river. As the water's great roar rose up to us, I left the ranks to repeat once more to my comrades their duties as Europeans, as patriots and as revolutionaries. A strange emotion overcame us. Who among us would recross that river?

At midnight we formed in columns.

There was only one means of crossing the Dnieper, across a wooden bridge 1300 meters long. It had been cut on several occasions by Soviet artillery and aircraft. A heavy barrage of flak protected our narrow footbridge, the only link to the southern front. The black mass of the river was dotted with hundreds of enormous white ice floes, like the legendary lotuses. The skeletons of sunken ships rose above the water.

We hastened across in silence, moved to have arrived at our rendezvous with war.

## The Mud Front

Whoever does not understand the importance of mud in the Russian problem can not understand what took place for four years on the Eastern Front in Europe. The Russian mud is not only the wealth through which the steppe returns to life: it constitutes also a territorial defense more effective than even snow and ice.

It is still possible to triumph over the cold, to move ahead in 40 degree-below-zero weather. The Russian mud is sure of its sway. Nothing prevails over it, neither man nor matter. It dominates the steppes for several months out of the year. The autumn and the spring belong to it. And even in the summer months, when the fiery sun flattens out and cracks open the fields, cloudbursts flood them every three weeks. The mud is extraordinarily sticky because the soil is permeated with oily residues. The entire region is swimming in oil. The water does not flow, it stagnates; the dirt clings to the feet of man and beast.

Disembarking at the Bug River in the month of October we had already been astonished at the sight of trucks swallowed up by that blackish mire, but we couldn't really gauge the situation until we ourselves entered the quagmire of the southern Ukraine.

* * * * *

From Dniepropetrovsk on, the trains no longer ran. The bridges had been cut; the rails had been blown up.

In the month of October 1941, the German troops had raced at full speed to the Donets Basin, leaving an immense region to their rear: with the beginning of the rainy season, this had been converted into a dead zone, virtually inaccessible. The units which had taken off like a shot had to fight for some months separated from Dniepropetrovsk by that three-hundred-kilometer-long swamp.

Stalin escaped disaster by about 15 days. Given 15 more days of sun, the supply trains of the conquerors could have reached the front. But Stalin, tottering at the brink of defeat, was saved by that all-powerful glue, which brought about what his troops and his guns had not been able to accomplish.

Hitler had routed millions of Soviet soldiers, had wiped out their air force, their artillery and their tanks, but he could do nothing against the blows that fell from the sky, soaking the huge oily sponge which sucked at the feet of his soldiers, the tires of his trucks, the treads of his tanks. The greatest and the most rapid military victory of all time was stopped in its final stage by the mud; nothing but the mud, the primal mud, as old as the earth, impassable, more powerful than strategies, than gold, than the minds and the pride of men.

* * * * *

Our legion had arrived in the Ukraine just in time to fight—or more exactly to struggle—against that enemy.

A struggle without glory; an exhausting struggle; a struggle bewildering and disgusting, but one which gave courage to thousands of Soviet soldiers, thrown in all directions by the waves of German tanks which had roared through two or three weeks earlier.

At first they, like the French in June 1940, had believed that all was lost. Everything indicated it. They were afraid, so they went into hiding. Then the rains came. From the poplar groves and the thatched roofs of the isbas in which they'd hidden, the partisans could observe that those marvelous troops of the Reich, who had so much impressed them, were no longer invincible: their trucks were beaten, their tanks were beaten. They heard the drivers, powerless, swear at their engines. Motorcycle drivers unable to free their trapped machines wept with rage. Little by little, the fugitive Soviets regained their confidence.

Thus it was that the resistance sprang from the respite given by the mud, reinforced by the spectacle of the German Army's vulnerability, unthinkable only weeks before, when its long armored columns gleamed in the sun. The mud was a weapon. The snow would be another. Stalin could count on these unexpected allies. Nothing else decisive would take place for six months. Six months of reprieve, after his shoulders had almost been pinned to the mat. . . . It would be enough, until May of 1942, to contain the forces of the Reich which, overwhelmed by the elements, wanted no more than to hibernate in peace. The partisans were already organizing behind the German divisions, harassing them like mosquitos in a swamp, striking quickly, leaving quickly, immediately after the sting.

We had dreamed of dazzling battles. Now we were to know the real war, the war against weariness, the war of the treacherous, sucking mire, of sickening living conditions, of endless marches, of nights of driving rain and howling winds.

We arrived at the front after the summer offensive had ended; when Hitler's armies struggled in monstrous swamps; when partisans appeared from every grove of hazel trees and set their traps everywhere.

It was the partisans we fought, just after leaving Dniepropetrovsk. In theory, the front was located 200 kilometers east of Dnieper. In fact, it was a mere 50 meters from the road. Only a few kilometers from the Dnieper, thousands of partisans had settled in a grove of firs straddling a river called the Samara. By night the bridges in the vicinity were blown up, isolated soldiers were killed, ten mysterious fires had broken out. On the evening of our arrival in the big labor center of Novomoskovsk, the garage where 90 of our Wehrmacht trucks were sheltered was burned, lighting up the entire region.

These cunning assailants had to be caught and wiped out. Our legion received the order to proceed to the areas west, southwest, and south of that forest, the thickly wooded lair of the enemy.

* * * * *

Crossing the belt of mud which separated us from the woods was a devilish ordeal; every meter of mud was an obstacle, exacting effort and suffering.

The entire countryside was pitch black, with water everywhere. Not one farm lamp flickered. We fell into mudholes, dropping our weapons, then groping for them. The water rose to mid-thigh level. The holes were so dangerous that we had to tie ourselves together in groups of three so that we could quickly pull out anyone who stumbled in.

We spent nearly 20 hours crossing those hellish kilometers. After falling we rose soaked from head to toe. All our equipment and baggage had to be abandoned in the water. At last we finally collapsed in some abandoned isbas. We made makeshift fires out of straw and planks from the walls. All our clothes had to come off. We were sticky from a putrid slime that covered our entire bodies; our skin was the gray color of seals.

We rubbed ourselves down for a long time with hay and, in a disgusting stench, as naked as jaybirds, we waited for the return of daylight, amidst the billows of acrid smoke.

* * * * *

So it was that hundreds of thousands of soldiers struggled, like human frogs, along a 3,000-mile front of muck and slime.

With minds troubled, bodies drained of strength, we had to confront an enemy in front of us, behind us, on our flanks. The mud squelched our spirits. Our weakest broke down, exhausted.

During this first phase of combat, one of our men collapsed in the mire, his head blown open. His courage at an end, he had shot himself in the mouth with his rifle.

The land also has its defenses. The old Russian earth, trod upon by foreigners, used its eternal weapons; it defended itself, avenged itself.

It had taken its first revenge, in the dripping autumn of 1941, when we saw that puddle of red blood in the black mud, slippery, impervious.

## A Village

The village of Karabinovska, where we spent nearly three weeks keeping the partisans under control, was, like all Russian villages, crossed by an endless country road, 50 meters wide, lined with isbas, hedgerows, plank fences,and cherry orchards.

The scattered straw huts, weighed down by their heavy roofs of reeds, were nearly all the same, except for the color of the paint. They were entered through a dark little vestibule, or directly into the common room. A stifling heat welcomed us, a smell of dirt, of tomatoes, of breathing, and of urine from the young animals which, during the winter, slept scattered among the people.

Throughout winter, the Russians hardly left the small bench and the rickety wooden stools of the isba. For the most part, the adults got up only to go to the other end of the house to take care of the pig, the cow or an ox. They would return with a load of corn or sunflower stalks, which they used to feed the fire.

The fireplace fulfilled all functions: cooking, central heating, and bed for the entire family. An imposing cube of bricks and mud, it occupied a third or a half of the room and rose, in two stages, up to half a meter from the ceiling. Two or three times a day someone threw a bunch of reeds or a little underbrush into the fireplace. In the evening the entire family climbed up to the upper level of the stove. Father, mother, children, tangled together, curled up, slept right on the lukewarm mud, covered with cheap clothes and a few red quilts, from which emerged a line of bare feet, flat and dirty. Like monkeys on top of a barrel organ, the youngsters spent six or seven months of the winter on top of their fireplace. Their sole piece of clothing was a waist-length shirt. They were dirty and squalid; their noses ran. In Russia, infant mortality was enormous: selection took place in the early years, without mercy.

An entire corner of the isba was reserved for the icons. Certain of them, particularly beautiful, dated from the 15th or 16th centuries. The backgrounds of these miniatures were ravishing: castles in green and white, gracefully leaping wild beasts. Often they depicted St. George slaying the dragon, or the good-natured, bearded St. Nicholas, or the Virgin, dark-complected, with almond-shaped eyes, holding a Christ child painted in the style of the Italian Primitives.

The icons were enthroned among garlands of green or pink paper. The peasants made the sign of the cross twenty times a day as they passed in front of them. Sometimes they still had a very old, dirty, dog-eared prayer book, several pages of which they read with inspiring fervor in the evening, by the glimmer of a flickering oil lamp.

Those people never quarreled with one another, but looked off into the distance, blue or gray-green eyes full of dreams.

Winter plants crowded the isba. They had large oily leaves, and rose to two meters in height, almost to the ceiling, lending a jungle atmosphere to the stinking hovels.

The isbas generally had a shed for the animals, built on as an annex. The better-off peasants, the kulaks, had left for Siberia by the millions a long time ago, there to learn to scorn the goods of this world.[3] Those who had escaped deportation contented themselves with one brown cow, one or two pigs, a dozen hens, and a few pigeons.

This was all the property they had. They brooded over it with zealous care. The calves and the piglets were taken into the warmth of the single family room at the time of the first frost.

The *kolkhoz,** where everyone had to serve the regime, shipped out almost all the wheat, corn, and oil of the region. Thanks to that plundering, Stalin was able to manufacture armored vehicles and cannons to prepare the world revolution. For the peasant, after having sadly devoured his supper of potato casseroles or his onion dishes, all that remained was to pray before his icons, fatalistic, his eyes pure, his will empty.

* * * * *

The autumn passed. The air lost its humidity; the evenings were dry. After a few days, the mud hardened. Then it snowed. It froze. So began the great Russian winter. The shrub-like trees glistened, speckled with a thousand snowflakes. The sky was painted blue, white and pale gold. The sun was soft above the willows that bordered the lakes. One morning, the entire population of the village went down to these nearby lakes.

The lakes were choked with thousands of rushes, like spears, three meters tall, topped with brown and pink plumes. The ice had embraced the gray stalks. The peasants tested the strength of the dark ice, powdered with snow. Finding it solid, they all went off to search for their baskets and scythes.

It was a strange harvest. Under the cold November sun, the villagers cut the tall rushes as they cut the wheat in July. The rushes were destined to cover the roofs of the ochre-colored isbas.

The harvest fell in magnificent waves. Thousands of small, plump sparrows chirped and rolled over and over on the shore. In three days, the ice-ponds were swept bare. The villagers then went home and closed their doors for the winter.

Now was the time for burrowing in, for hibernation. Hail fell, encrusting the mud walls of the isbas, shattering the branches of the cherry trees.

# Chapter Two
# WINTER IN THE DONETS

The Soviet "partisans" formed military units of a special sort. They were nowhere, yet they were everywhere. During the day, crouching in a thicket, lurking inside a haystack, peeking from the attic window beneath the skylight of an isba, their lookouts silently observed the enemy's every step. They noted our supply sheds and equipment, learned our trails and pathways, spied on the advance work of the engineers.

One night they dynamited a bridge and set some trucks on fire. Strong bursts of fire came from a slope. We ran, but were too late. In the vicinity we found an old lined *shapska,* * some tracks of felt boots. Nothing else. The forest had noiselessly absorbed the fugitives.

With only one company, we had to cover several kilometers of the highway from Dniepropetrovsk to Stalino, as well as few kilometers on the edge of the forest, separated from our village by two kilometers of hilly land where groves of shrubs rustled in the wind.

Our posts were located three hundred meters beyond the isbas. We mounted a guard there, our noses white with snow, our hands chapped. The cold had become biting, and we lacked the least bit of winter equipment.

It was not enough to lie in wait in our foxholes. The Russians slunk like cats between our posts at night. Once they had gotten past them, they could carry out their evil work at ease. Half of our forces thus had to patrol constantly in the pasture, from the village up to the forest.

We went forth to camouflage ourselves in the snowy trenches, on the lookout for the least sign of life, our ears to the wind.

We stumbled into holes covered with snow. Our teeth chattered, tormented by those interminable hours of playing hide and seek. We returned frozen to the bone. Our icy weapons steamed for a long time near the sunflower-stalk fires.

From day to day, our grip around the pine grove tightened.

On two occasions, we made deep incursions into the woods. The snow squeaked beneath our feet. Everywhere we discovered tracks of felt-covered boots. But not a branch moved, not a shot was fired. The war the partisans fought was a war of cunning blows, of avoiding set battles.

German troops on our right would make contact with the enemy during these dry, star-spangled nights. Then the black frames of the burning isbas would stand in silhouette against the golden flames, and the Reds would try to flee in our direction.

One night they came around eleven. Lying in the snow, we fired our machine guns. The tracer bullets' paths bloomed like a bouquet of flowers. For an hour, the steppe seemed streaked by blazing arrows. At last, sensing the density of our barrage, the Reds returned to their lairs.

* * * * *

At the northwest edge of the forest, on the right bank of the Samara, the Reds had built solid bunkers.

Our men were ordered to attack the enemy positions across the frozen river. They came under heavy fire as soon as they reached the near bank. Our unit had to advance across 25 meters of glassy ice, without cover, through the withering fire. We took some bloody losses that day, but the bunkers were taken, and the Reds fell in the snow or took to their heels.

The Russian earth received our dead. How many others were going to fall, in the ice, in the mud, or under the golden sun, in the Donets or on the Don, in the Caucasus and in Estonia? Those first crimson drops, scattered like petals on the snow of the Samara, had the unforgettable purity of the first gifts, the first lilacs, the first tears.

* * * * *

It was necessary for us to leave their graves behind, for now we had to join a division which had rushed to a salient on the front line, in the depths of the Donets Basin. At the end of November, without gloves, without winter hats, without fur coats, as the icy blasts of winter swept through our thin uniforms, we began a 200-kilometer advance.

## Roads of Ice

At the end of the autumn of 1941, the ice had completely transformed every road in the Donets. The river of mud was now a river of bumpy lava. The mud had solidified as our hundreds of trucks continued to slash it and grind it. It had hardened like stone into a network of rocky ridges, a half meter high, like black marble, which, fifty or a hundred feet wide, dipped and heaved, gashed by long ruts.

It was useless to try and send ordinary autos into those ruts. A passenger car's gas tank would be smashed after the first few kilometers. Only heavy trucks and cross-country vehicles, with particularly high axles, could take a chance on that glazed frost. They alone could straddle the crevasses.

For the infantrymen the march was miserable. We almost didn't dare to pick up our feet. We could only slide them. Falls were painful, since the ice was as hard as iron.

We had to keep our weapons ready for combat at the slightest warning. At that time a rifleman's equipment consisted of more than thirty kilos of metal, not to mention some three days of rations for the march and all of the usual pack. The effort needed to keep our feet inflamed our tendons. We had to split the backs of our heavy, hard boots with our knives in order to make them a little looser. Each of us clenched his teeth to endure the pain. Sometimes a man fell, his nerves broken by the effort. Gasping, his face against the ice, he was hoisted into the first truck that passed, onto a pile of bread or some ammunition cases. Then the column would resume its wobbling path across the black-glazed frost.

* * * * *

Nevertheless, the country was still pleasant to see. The great white steppe was cross-hatched with hundreds of thousands of gray sunflower stalks. Clouds of sparrows, like little balls of fleece, fluttered madly aloft. The sky, especially, was admirable, as pure as crystal, pale blue, so clear that each tree's bare branches were outlined against the horizon with a sharpness worthy of the Acropolis in Athens.

The peasants sometimes showed us a plane tree or a row of old birches, the last vestiges of a lord's domain. From the buildings of former times, there remained not a board or a stone, not even the trace of the former foundations. Everything was razed to the ground, leveled, covered once more with vegetation.

It had been the same with most of the churches. Some of them were still in existence, desecrated long ago, now used as garages, storage places, meeting halls, stables, or powerhouses, the beautiful green and gold onion dome still gleaming above the white walls. Sometimes we discovered the smashed wainscoting or one or two paintings that the whitewasher had not been able to reach at the peak of the ceiling. Apart from that, the floors were strewn with corn or horse manure. Those church-stables, those churches for cars, for sunflowers, or for meetings of the local Soviet were, however, extremely rare. Over a period of two years we traveled more than two thousand kilometers on foot, from Dniepropetrovsk to the threshold of Asia: we were able to count on our fingers the number of churches encountered en route, all desecrated.

* * * * *

At the beginning of December we passed through Pavlograd. Then we settled down in some completely empty hamlets. The storm raged. Departures took place at four or five in the morning, as the blasts of snow howled around our faces, lashed us, blinded us. We spent hours bringing our large metal carts, loaded with supplies, up to the road. The horses fell on the glazed frost, breaking their hooves. The poor beasts would snort vainly in the whistling snow, pant, get halfway up, then fall again, thrown into a frenzy.

The snow fell so heavily that the path and the steppe were completely indistinguishable from one another. There was not yet any straw covering the high stakes between which the Russians, familiar with their country, mark out their roads when winter levels those vast spaces.

The arrows pointing out directions were covered with piles of snow. The troops soon became lost.

To compound the difficulty, the places we were looking for had generally changed their names two or three times during the past 25 years: the old maps showed a tsarist name; the 1925 maps showed a name as Red as the blood of a bull, the result of the Revolution; the maps of 1935 showed the name of a Soviet boss, in imitation of Stalingrad and Stalino. Sometimes, however, the boss in question had, in the meantime, gotten a bullet in the nape of his neck, deep in the cellars of the GPU: thus, a fourth, new name![1] On the other hand, fifty or a hundred villages on the Russian steppe would bear the same names, the names of wives or daughters of the tsars, adopted out of sloth, preserved by sloth.

During the leg of our march which was to lead us to Grichino, we went around and around, for a whole day, in the blizzard: we reached the settlement only after having travelled 53 kilometers. Even so, that Grichino was not our Grichino. Not only had the place received three different names in 25 years, but there were two Grichinos: Grichino Station and Grichino Village, seven kilometers apart! All typically Russian complications! We didn't arrive at the right Grichino until morning, after wading through snow almost waist deep.

Our company was the first there. It was 48 hours before the others arrived except for one which remained lost, wandered about for fifteen days, saw all its horses die and rejoined us at the front itself, on Christmas Day, escorting a medieval-looking column of large white oxen hitched to its gray trucks.

Unfortunately, the odyssey was not just a matter of daily changes in transport.

The countryside through which the storms buffeted us bristled with Soviet mines. The snow had blanketed them, just as it had the warning stakes placed here and there by the first crew of German scouts.

Lost among blasts of wind which drifted the snow as much as three meters high, one of our companies blundered into a Soviet mine field. The young commander, a former captain in the Belgian army who bore the lovely country name Dupre, was riding ahead when his horse stepped on one of those terrible devices. The horse shot two meters straight up in the air and landed, his guts scattered, while the rider lay helpless in the red snow, his legs torn to shreds.

The howling steppe shrieked its victory. Our soldiers had to brace his shattered limbs with two pieces of wood and then transport their ill-fated captain on some fir tree branches. After several kilometers they reached a deserted isba.

It took twenty-six hours before an all-weather ambulance could come to the aid of the dying captain. He had eleven fractures. Smoking a cigarette in quick, avid puffs, he said his good-byes to his men. Great beads of sweat poured down his face as he silently endured his agony. He died without a word of regret, while taking one last drag on his cigarette.

* * * * *

After the Grichinos there came the Aleksandrovskas. There are one or two hundred Aleksandrovskas in the USSR, of which we wandered through all those in the Donets.

At last we reached the industrial cities. We had reached our goal. A sudden thaw brought us a last stretch of mud. At the end of the muddy fields, we saw shining the mushy glazed frost of Cherbinovka, a coal center with 40,000 inhabitants. They stood motionless, silent, along the walls. Many of them gazed at us intently, sharp-eyed, scowling.

The Bolshevik troops had withdrawn into the steppe, three kilometers farther east, but we sensed that, behind us, communist operatives would be lying in wait.

## Christmas at Cherbinovka

The Eastern Front, in December 1941, was constantly shifting, like the outlines of a beach. Each army of the Reich had brought its wave as far as possible. Each unit had found itself bogged down, at the end of October, in a treacherous mire, flanks unguarded left and right, able only vaguely to guage the situation and intentions of an enemy which had fled before the Germans at top speed, in a disorder often reminiscent of vaudeville.

With the help of the mud, the Reds had shown a certain ability to counterattack; they had reconquered Rostov, which, lacking fuel, the Germans had had to abandon, burning hundreds of trucks there.

Emboldened by this local success, the Soviets had resumed nibbling away to the east of the Donets, on the left wing of our sector. From Slavyansk to Artemovsk, they carried out violent attacks.

The Soviet pressure made itself felt principally about twenty kilometers to the northeast of our bunkers. In front of our positions at Cherbinovka, the enemy roused himself little, at first. He was trapped, just as we were, in a terrain which melted as if it had been dipped in a hot spring.

Our resupply took fifty hours or more to negotiate the twenty kilometers which separated us from the storehouses in Constantinovska. No more motorcyclists could cross. The horses died en route, exhausted, their muzzles sunk in the mud.

* * * * *

Cherbinovka had become absolutely filthy. Everywhere thawed excrement fouled the air with a noisome stench.

The dirtiness and the misery of the city illustrated tragically the Soviet regime's failures in the great proletarian centers. The coal installations still used the equipment of 1900 or 1905, acquired at the time of easy French loans. The mine shafts, dynamited by the retreating Bolsheviks, were no longer usable.

So it was with all of the industrial equipment of occupied Russia. Systematically, with diabolical skill, teams of Soviet specialists had destroyed the factories, the mines, the warehouses of every industrial center, large or small.

Scorched earth! Scorched underground!

They had killed even the horses, down in the coal pits. The nauseating smell of the rotting animals spread throughout the entire area, since the air ducts of the coal mines vented directly onto the streets. These air shafts were sloppily sealed with loose planking, through which carbon dioxide gas and the asphyxiating stench of the rotting carcasses wafted continuously.

* * * * *

The Soviets had carried away or destroyed all of the provisions in the city. The people ate anything they could find. The choicest dishes were scraps from the dead animals which lay in the mud. The population quarreled over them violently, bitterly.

We had had to kill one incurable horse, horrible to look at, completely covered with disgusting pustules. We hadn't even had time to go to look for a cart to take its carcass out of the city. Twenty people had thrown themselves on the unspeakable remains, tearing at the skin, grabbing at the still steaming flesh.

In the end, there remained only the intestines, still more disgusting than all the rest. Two old women had thrown themselves on the stomach and on the bowels, each pulling in opposite directions. The belly burst, covering the two women with a yellow-green puree. The winner of the lioness's share fled without even wiping her face, fiercely clasping her prey to her breast.

The billeting of our troops was of a piece with these prodigies. When we returned from our positions, it was to huddle together in the school buildings recently built by the State: three long buildings, called modern, exactly in the style of all we had seen since Dniepropetrovsk. The first soldier who tried to drive a nail to hang up his weapons split the wall with one blow of his hammer. The floor was constructed of disjointed boards between which the air rushed in. Under the makeshift floor there was nothing, since the building rested only on pilings.

Between the three buildings there was an open space, so muddy that we had to build wooden-plank walkways, supported by heavy trunks, which ran from one building to the other. Around the school the smell of $CO_2$ rose constantly, inducing headaches and nausea.

On about 20 December, the snow and ice returned. We suddenly found ourselves once more at 20 degrees below zero. We shivered on our disjointed board floor, each curled up under a single blanket.

The holidays arrived—holidays for other men.

On Christman Eve we attended midnight Mass at a church reconsecrated by our chaplain. A Russian choir sang in shrill, heart-rending tones. Outside the snow fell in large flakes. Lying behind their machine guns, several of our soldiers occupied combat positions at the four corners of the building.

But our spirits were chilled from having lazed through those drab weeks, in a silence in the depths of which our dreams floated aimlessly.

* * * * *

The European legions, popular in the newspapers of the Reich, had been greeted with scepticism at the front in 1941. Certain German generals feared an intrusion, among their elite divisions, of troops sent to the East solely to make propaganda. They did not always take into account the amount of enthusiasm and good will which our volunteer units embodied.

Such misunderstandings weighed on us.

We eagerly awaited the arrival of an opportunity, even a crisis, which would enable our idealism to be valued at its true worth. That hour was slow to come. Meanwhile, unknown and misunderstood, we squandered our talents in petty, galling duties.

We spent Christmas and the New Year joylessly, holed up in our smoky rooms. A manger scene, drawn in charcoal on the mud mall, recalled for us December in our own homes. A few poor votive lamps smoked. Stretched out on the straw, we stared into space. At the top of the hill, on wooden crosses, the steel helmets of our dead wore clumps of snow, like chrysanthemums fallen from heaven.

## Italians in the Donets

Non-German units were very numerous on the anti-Soviet front.

To the south were ranged the legions from Central Europe and from the

Balkans. Singular legions, consumed by rivalries. The Hungarians and the Rumanians were always ready to tear each other's eyes out for the sake of a grove of beech trees in the Carpathians or for ten meters of lucerne field in the Puszta.[2] The Croats, more Slavic than the Ukrainians, were divided between Muslims and Catholics.

In 1941 the Italians were the largest foreign unit on all the Eastern Front. Sixty thousand of them had come, divided into three divisions and into numerous detachments of specialists. One saw them everywhere, from the Dnieper to the Donets, small, swarthy, funny-looking in their two-pointed forage caps, or looking like birds of paradise under their bersagliere helmets from which projected, amidst the gusts of the steppe, a stately crop of rooster and pheasant feathers!

The Italians' rifles looked like toys. They used them with great skill to kill all the chickens in the region.

We had made their acquaintance as soon as we arrived in Dniepropetrovsk. We soon formed a very high opinion of their spirit of initiative and of their craftiness. They had gathered round an enormous cask which sat, unguarded, on a railway car. It was brimful with Chianti wine. In the side of this mighty tun the Italians had drilled a tiny hole from which the wine gushed through a hollow straw.

The invention proved quite a success with our topers, who went back time and time again to that wondrous fount, worthy of the Burgundian weddings of Charles the Bold or of Philip the Good! The Italians, sure of their supply—it was a 2,000-liter cask—amicably traded places with us. From that moment on, the Walloon volunteers were extremely enamoured with Italy and were delighted with the collaboration it provided on the Eastern Front!

* * * * *

The front was not a single, continuous line, but a series of strong points. Our posts in Cherbinovka had only snow to their left and right. To reach the closest Italians, whose sector extended to the south toward Stalino, we had to march for two hours across the steppe.

We used to go to chat with them during lulls in the fighting. Obviously, their lemons and their Chianti were of some importance. But their charm also drew us.

The complication was that they detested the Germans. The latter, in turn, couldn't abide the Italians' light fingers or their ardent armours in the ruined isbas. Neither could they tolerate the Italians' whimsical demeanor and quaint Latin carefreeness, so full of irreverence, indolence, persiflage, and natural grace, so different from Prussian stiffness.

By contrast, the Italians bridled whenever they saw a German snap to attention or cry out orders. That didn't fit in with having their hands in their pockets, wearing their russet plumes, and performing their merry escapades.

Their brand of nationalism was also different. The Italians loved Mussolini and over and over cried out "Du-ce! Du-ce! Du-ce!" until they were hoarse. Such outburts were only of a sentimental kind, however. Mussolini's dreams of imperial grandeur did not reach them. They were as proud as peacocks, but without ambition.

One day when they insisted on their desire to have peace again at any cost, I had retorted:

"But if you do not struggle to the very end, you are going to lose your colonies!"

"Bah!," they answered, "what good is it to kill yourself for some colonies? We are happy at home. We don't need anything. We have the sun. We have our fruits. We have love . . ."

As a philosophy it had its counterparts. Horace had said the same thing, but less frankly.

Likewise, they found it absolutely useless to work too hard. Our idea of human labor left them bored. Why work so much? And again they would take up their soft, alluring, sing-song litany: the sun, the fruits, love . . .

"After all," I continued, "work is a joy! Don't you other nations love to work?"

Then an Italian from the South, with princely grace, offered me this reply, magnificent in its artlessness and its solemnity:

"But sir, what good is work?"

What good is it? When the Germans heard such answers, they choked for a week and very nearly had attacks of apoplexy.

* * * * *

For the Italians, to their misfortune, the day and night watches provided some "good," as did the thankless duty in the snow and ice.

Often their gregarious sentries left their posts to bask in the warmth of an isba, where they chattered, jested, mooched, and studied very closely the attributes of the local beauties.

The Russians finally took their measure with a low blow. Our pleasant comrades from across the Alps paid dearly for their Latin nonchalance.

One night, in the southern part of the sector, strong detachments of Cossacks glided on their high-strung horses across the deep snow. At dawn, they were easily able to encircle three villages occupied by the Italians, but unprotected by the guards, who were busy sleeping or making love. They were taken completely by surprise.

The Soviets particularly detested the Italians. They hated them even more than they did the Germans, and on the Eastern Front they always treated them with an extraordinary cruelty. In the twinkling of an eye they seized the three villages. No one had the time to react. The Italians were then dragged to the coal pits, where they were completely stripped of their clothes. Then the torture began. The Cossacks brought large buckets of icy water. Roaring with laughter, they emptied them on the bodies of their victims in cold which hovered 30 to 35 degrees below zero centigrade. The poor wretches in the three villages all died, frozen alive.

No one escaped, not even the doctors. Not even the chaplain, who, stripped like a Roman marble, also suffered the torture of water and ice. Two days later, the three villages were recaptured. Naked bodies lay everywhere in the snow, twisted, contorted, as if they had died in a fire.

From that time on, the Italian troops of the Donets were reinforced by German armor. All along their lines heavy German tanks, painted entirely white, engines throbbing, lurked in the deep snow.

* * * * *

That was a necessity.

The Reds became more and more active. To our left, to our right, they struck violently. Day and night, the steppe shook with gunfire. Soviet airplanes appeared. Their bombs dug large gray craters around us.

The cold became ever more penetrating. In mid-January, the temperature dropped to 38 degrees below zero.

Our little horses' snouts were all white with ice. From their nostrils, wet with blood, spattered, drop after drop, on the trail, hundreds of spots, like pink carnations.

## The Howling Steppe

Life had become unbearable in our lairs at Cherbinovka.

Using straw, we had more or less filled up the holes in the windows, half the panes of which had been broken by the Red troops when they made their retreat. But the icy blasts of winter persisted, rushing in, whistling between the floorboards. For sleeping we put on all of the poor equipment that we had, then thrust our feet into the sleeves of our overcoats. But what good were overcoats, light blankets, and a few bits of straw against the winds which howled through our huts from the cursed steppe?

We broke the margarine, the sausages, and the bread, hard as rocks, with an axe. The few eggs that our resupply operation delivered reached us frozen, nearly gray.

Such were our hours of relaxation.

Our advanced positions were located three kilometers from Cherbinovka. We went there in squads, across snow which was generally 40 to 50 centimeters deep, in temperatures varying from 25 to 35 degrees below zero.

Certain companies had dug their small bunkers into the sides of the slag heaps of the coal fields. The others were positioned out in the middle of the steppe.

The snow was nothing. It was the storm which was atrocious. It barked; it meowed with long sharp whistles, throwing into our faces thousands of little darts that tore us like a stream of pebbles.

We finally received some winter caps which covered our necks and ears, and some very thin knitted gloves, which hardly protected us at all. But we still had neither fur coats nor felt boots.

Anyone who took off his gloves for a moment immediately had his fingers frozen. We wore our winter caps pulled up to our noses; our breath, passing through them, was frozen into large tufts of ice, at the level of our mouths, and into long white moustaches fastened to our eyebrows. Our tears themselves froze, becoming large pearls which painfully welded our eyelashes together. We separated them only with great pain. At any moment a nose or a cheek might become pale yellow, like the skin of a drum. In order to avoid frostbite, we had to rub the flesh vigorously with snow. Often, it was already too late.

* * * * *

The dizzying storms gave the Soviet shock troops an obvious superiority.

The Russians were used to that weather. Their skis, their dogs, their sleighs, their high-strung ponies helped them. They were dressed to resist the cold, padded in cotton-wool jackets, shod with felt boots which resisted the snow, as dry as crystal powder. They inevitably benefited from the unspeakable suffering of thousands of European soldiers thrown by a bold offensive into the snows, the winter wind, and the ice, without proper equipment and without adequate training.

The Reds infiltrated everywhere. Their spies, disguised as civilians, crept between our posts, reached the worker centers, and found accomplices there. The great majority of the peasant population was completely ignorant about Communism, except for its demands; but in the industrial centers Soviet propaganda had reached the young workers. It was to them that the spies of the Red Army, dedicated and courageous leaders, addressed themselves.

I was part of an execution squad charged with shooting two of them, who had fully confessed before the military tribunal.

When we reached the middle of the steppe, we lined up in a row. The two condemned men, their hands in their pockets, did not say a word. Our volley knocked them down. There was an extraordinary moment of silence in which the shudder of the rifle shots floated skyward. One of the two communists moved, as if he wanted to summon up a last remnant of life. His right hand left his pocket and rose, fist clenched tightly, above the snow. And we heard a cry, a last cry, shouted in German so that it would be understood by all: "Heil Stalin!"

The dead man's clenched fist fell back to his side.

Those people also had their idealists.

Generally, the Russians who had been condemned to capital punishment accepted their fate with fatalism, their arms at their sides, their faces blank.

To avoid upsetting their troops and to strike the popular imagination, the Germans had decided to hang captured spies. The condemned Russians approached, depressed, eyes vacant, then climbed up on a chair, which itself was perched on a table. They waited there, without protesting, without asking anything. Above them hung the rope. It was tied around their necks. Thus it was, thus it was. They let it happen. A kick upset the chair and ended the tragedy.

One day, the Germans had to carry out the sentences of five condemned men all at the same time. One of the hanged men broke his rope and fell to the ground. He picked himself up without uttering a word, put the chair back on the table, got back up on it and waited, with the greatest naturalness, while a new rope was installed.

In the depths of those hearts there was an oriental fatalism, a childlike innocence and, also, a long habit of taking blows and suffering. They did not rebel against death. They passively accepted death as they had accepted everything else, the filthy isba, the knout of the aristocrats, and the slavery of Communism.

The second half of January 1942 was much busier. Large numbers of Red troops were on the move. Soviet airplanes attacked three or four times per day.

We were still unaware of what had taken place.

Soviet elite units, brought in from Siberia, had crossed the frozen Donets River, to the north of our industrial basin. They had flanked the German defenses and reached important railway lines, notably the Kiev-Poltava-Slavyansk line. They had pillaged a number of supply depots and then moved westward. The Russians and Siberians subsequently made a very deep thrust in the direction of the Dnieper. They threatened to cut off the whole Army of the South. They had already passed the Samara River. Some spearheads of Cossacks had even gotten as far as 12 kilometers from Dniepropetrovsk.

The German commander hastily gathered his available forces for a counteroffensive.

A counteroffensive when the thermometer read between 35 and 40 degrees below zero!

We had little doubt about what awaited us when an urgent order put us in a state of alert.

That very night we were relieved. At four in the morning, we trudged behind our carts in the midst of a stupendous storm which roiled the snow in fury, leaving us utterly blind.

We were completely unaware of our destination. However, the hour for blood and glory had arrived.

## Cossacks

If I remember correctly, it was 26 January 1942.

We did not know exactly how much progress had been made, either by the Siberian troops, gliding on their dog sleds, or by the Cossacks, mounted on high-spirited little horses which stood up to everything.

The enemy could not be far away. That was all that we had been able to learn. We, the simple soldiers of the line, knew few things, nor did I know anything more than my comrades, since I was then an ordinary soldier, living strictly the life of the troops and having no contact with the upper echelon of my company.

Our known objective was, for the second time, the area around Grichino, located sixty kilometers to the northwest of Cherbinovka. Doubtless we would be near the enemy forces throughout the entire march. For the first stage, we had orders to occasionally take some shortcuts.

It took four hours for our column to get ready to move off into the snowstorm. We could see no more than ten meters in front of us. When we arrived in the countryside, the storm tormented us from all sides. The road rose and fell across the low, steep hills. We dragged along with us some *Stahlwagen,* metal wagons weighing hundreds of kilos, excellent for the paved or asphalt roads of Europe, but completely impractical in the snow and ice of the steppe. The Russian peasants themselves used only sleds or wooden vehicles, light, with narrow, very high wheels. Our enormous hearses came clattering down at a mad speed on the downgrades, in spite of their brakes. Some horses tumbled over; some wagons turned over. On the upgrades, we had to push the vehicles, twenty men at a time. At the end of a few hours, several *Stahlwagen* were bogged down or overturned in the snow along the steep paths.

Although the first leg of the march was only twelve kilometers long, we had to toil throughout the night. It was not until six o'clock the next evening that all our supplies arrived. Reaching a village, we encountered four Siberian troops, whom we killed in a brief skirmish.

* * * * *

At five o'clock in the morning we resumed our advance. The whirlwinds of snow had ceased, but the ice had become even fiercer. Overnight it had hardened on the hilly path, which was as slippery as a skating rink underneath the snow. The horses could not move forward. Several broke their hooves. By noon, we had covered little more than one kilometer.

Ahead of us lay a secluded valley, which the storm had filled with phenomenal quantities of snow. Our entire battalion had to set to work digging a corridor fifty meters long and three meters deep. Pulling our *Stahlwagen* up the steep slope was a terrible operation. Not until nine o'clock that night did we reach the mountain top with the first one. In sixteen hours we had made only three kilometers!

We stabled our teams of horses in a shed. Only a few men could find a place next to them. A peasant informed us the existence of a hamlet about four kilometers away, on one side of a small valley. We got back on the road by moonlight. In its deepest points the snow came up to our waists. At last we reached some isbas, more miserable than any we had ever seen.

At ten o'clock we settled down on the hard, packed earth, in the single room of one of the huts, filled with civilians who undoubtedly had been hiding and waiting for the Siberians. A pregnant girl, as red as a lobster, went around from muzhik to muzhik, by the light of an oil lamp. She was dressed solely in a long shirt which went down to her waist. She chattered vulgarly, constantly, continuing her housework until her rounds were completed.

Then she waddled back up to the top of her oven and made some loud remarks, but the men, their work done, were already snoring. Some of the animals stirred. The stench was sickening.

At six in the morning, returning to our carts, we plunged into the snow again. From the top of the plateau we could see the company that had bogged down the night before, wearing itself out pushing its metal vehicles. The climb certainly would last until nightfall.

I was sent on patrol, in search of billeting space, in the direction of a *sovkhoz** that had been pointed out to us, some four or five kilometers to the east. We left at three o'clock, using a troika we had found in a shed.

The *sovkhoz* was there all right, swarming with muzhiks. The living quarters, with the ever-present earthen floor, were overrun by young calves, which sheltered near the family stove, away from the cold. Since the familiar pan always arrived too late, they continually doused the ground. That made for yet another smell.

One of my companions left again with the sled, in order to guide the troops. The squad member who stayed with me was a mine worker from the Borinage,[3] with a thick, sing-song accent, and a first and last name reminiscent of epic poetry: Achille Roland. The civilians kept cool heads. A few Soviet airplanes flew over the *sovkhoz,* dropping handbills announcing the imminent arrival of the Red Army. Our natives scanned the ridge-line and the sky.

At about two in the afternoon, the silhouettes of several horsemen could be seen. The muzhiks gave each other brief, knowing looks. They looked us over, sneakily, squinting through almond-shaped eyes.

* * * * *

At four in the afternoon, none of our comrades had arrived.

We expected to see the Cossacks bolt from cover at the edge of the farm. I had set up my machine gun in the entry way. The weapon would do some damage. We wore strings of grenades at our belts, with which we could quickly restore calm behind us if the muzhiks of the *sovkhoz* tried to attack us.

They kept quiet, very much impressed. A beautiful young Ukrainian girl, who knew some words of German, had sided with us. She was sixteen years old, with beautiful hair with glints of brown and gold in it. She had watched the doings of our squad and secretly given us some supportive glances. She had generously put us on the same level of the oven as the family's small calves and served us, like them, a thick milk, smooth as her skin.

Outside, the storm had begun howling once more. From time to time I went to inspect the area, grenade in hand. It seemed clear that our comrades would no longer be able to make their way to our positions. Besides, where were they? Had they been put out of commission by an attack of the Cossacks or the Siberian infantry, on the plateau where they were laboriously dragging up their metal vehicles?

Night fell. Seven o'clock. Eight o'clock. No one came. The muzhiks were still waiting. Obviously, they would have very much liked to slit our throats, but the belts of cartridges, feeding into our machine gun, discouraged them. They finally lay down on the ground among the young cattle, the pan within their reach.

The wind howled, and with a crash it threw open the wooden door which led to the corridor, throwing clumps of snow on us. We asked ourselves what would happen when we got up.

As a last resort, my companion decided to reconnoiter in the direction of our company. In the darkness, my watch seemed to show 5:00 A.M. The intrepid Achille vanished into the storm.

He reappeared in an hour, transformed into a Santa Claus beneath a cubic meter of snow. Straying in the storm, he had floundered helplessly through the snow. "Are you quite sure of the time," he asked. "It's still so dark out there!"

We looked. It was only 1:30 in the morning! We had confused 5:00 and 12:25. Poor Achille snorted, then went to warm himself a little bit against the dried-mud stove. There, stretched out near the machine gun, we waited for the real break of day.

It came, but that was all that came. The storm was so fantastic that we could no longer imagine that the infantrymen would still be able to catch up with us. One day passed, two days passed. When the fury of the steppe calmed, the Cossacks could cut the road. Suddenly, at eleven in the morning, a sled turned sharply in front of the door, kicking snow up to the thatched roof. A Walloon non-commissioned officer, my former gardener in Brussels, had charged through the storm behind four horses which he had whipped to the point of death. One horse expired no sooner than it had reached the farm.

Readjusting the reins, we started the team off at a gallop. The Russians, in spite of the whistling snow, had run up to the threshold of the *sovkhoz,* their eyes flashing. But the pretty little Ukrainian girl, behind the backs of those wretches, blushingly threw us a kiss. That would have been worth ten such adventures.

One hour later, we rejoined our squad, still blocked at the top of the hill. When a man tried to negotiate that bare ridge, he found himself hurled to the ground by the storm. The men had all crowded together in the barn up against the horses, one as chilled as the other. There was nothing else to do. It was necessary to wait. The steppe was more powerful than we were.

We waited.

* * * * *

Next morning the wind subsided, and we sent several platoons out to the road. A meter of snow covered the ground, but we couldn't stay where we were any longer.

Our column was forming for the departure when some gray dots appeared on the horizon. A half-hour later, we were approached by an extraordinary procession: our commander, coming to meet us, had, since the previous night, driven 180 Russians before him. Using their shovels they had cut a passageway in the vast ocean of the steppe. By that means we were able to cover twenty kilometers, using our bayonets to break the clumps of snow that continually formed under our boots. By dawn we had traversed a corridor four meters deep, to a place called Ekonomiskoye.

There we had hardly any rest: at midnight, 300 Cossacks were spotted. We had to take up our positions in the snow, at the foot of a wonderful mill, its large black vanes glimmering in the moonlight. The steppe was a blue and white expanse of sparkling crystals. Millions of stars lit up the night. They formed a smooth lining undulating across the sky. It was so beautiful that we nearly forgot the cold which pierced our bodies with its darts.

At noon, after having covered about fifteen kilometers, we entered Grichino.

For several days the city had undergone aerial bombing of a kind that the Russians had never before carried out. All of the squares were smashed to smithereens. Cossacks and Siberians were at the gates of the city. If they seized it, one of the largest road and railway junctions of the Donets would be lost.

We had to prepare for the impending battle. We made our billets in a school hall, of which only one window remained intact. The two thin blankets each of us carried afforded little protection against the 40-below-zero temperatures.

One cannot imagine what it is like, in such cold, to rest in a completely open building. It was impossible for us to sleep for a moment. It was not even possible to remain seated.

Nevertheless, we were left with little time to philosophize about our misfortunes. At one o'clock in the morning, they formed us in companies: we were rising to the counteroffensive.

## Rosa-Luxemburg

The winter of 1941–1942 was the most terrifying winter that Russia had experienced in 150 years.

A certain number of German units, billeted in relatively calm sectors, adapted themselves, as best they could, to those frightfully cold temperatures and to the lack of fur clothes. Other units received violent shocks when they found themselves in the path of attempted breakthroughs. They lived through some extraordinary odysseys, often cut off, resisting in small groups, leading heroic counterattacks which lasted for weeks.

The Donets sector was one of the most bitterly contested. There the Soviets threw magnificent troops at us, making a deep penetration. It was checked, then pushed back, only at the cost of exhausting efforts. But one large Soviet pocket remained in the midst of the Donets. It would be mopped up only at the end of May of 1942, at the time of the battle of Kharkov.

At the beginning of February of 1942, the crisis reached a peak. The Russians had advanced to within a few kilometers of the Dnieper. The German counteroffensive had to be carried out with a fierce energy. It was.

The High Command rushed its troops to the assault by every means of transport at its disposal.

There were few enough ways to travel that February, however.

Thus it was that, on 3 February, we left for combat in several railway cars pulled by a snow-plow. The snow was so deep that it slowed down our advance. The rail line had not been demolished after all. We were going after the enemy, pulled along in cattle cars!

* * * * *

For provisions we were given each a large, round loaf of bread which we tied, as best we could, to our packs or against our chests. We had to carry all our wordly goods, including weapons and ammunition, on our backs. No horses or carts could accompany us, nor could we look forward to hot meals. We brought nothing more than we could carry on our own backs. For a machine-gunner like me, that meant a load of more than forty kilograms, of which thirty was for the machine gun and the cartridge boxes.

Getting the snow-plow started and then advancing twenty kilometers took fourteen hours. The cars, of course, were unheated. The floor was as bare as a rock. The cold intensified; that morning it was 42 degrees below zero. Forty-two degrees! So as not to succumb to the cold, we were obliged to run continuously, one behind the other, inside the car.

Everyone was close to exhaustion from having done this ridiculous dance for several hours; however, our lives depended on it. One of our comrades, exhausted, dropped out of the race. He stretched out in a corner. Thinking that he was sleeping, we shook him; he was frozen. At a stop, we were able to gather up some snow. We rubbed him with it from head to toe, for fifty minutes. Then he came back to life a little, letting out a frightful moan, like a cow being slaughtered. He was confined to a hospital for a year and a half, as toothless as an armadillo.

The locomotive thrust aside masses of snow more than two meters deep. At last it stopped in front of a veritable wall of ice, impassable. Besides, the Bolsheviks were only three kilometers away.

When we leaped out onto the steppe, we believed that we were all going to die. The whirlwinds slapped us in the face, knocked us over. Officers and men fell in the snow.

The faces of several of our men were hideous: mottled, empurpled, eyes bloodshot. I couldn't slap my cheek, which froze instantly, for my hands were full gripping my machine gun, cartridge cases, and ammo belts. Others suffered frostbitten feet, which later decomposed into long, blackish strips. Some men's ears froze, soon resembling large apricots, from which oozed an orange pus.

The most unfortunate of our comrades were those who had their sexual organs frozen. Unspeakable suffering for those poor boys. They were dragged from hospital to hospital throughout the entire war, all in vain. The flesh, frightfully swollen, had been burned deeply during that terrible afternoon.

The village to be occupied lay in front of us. It bore the name of the famous Berlin Jewish political figure, Rosa Luxemburg.[4] The Russians must have been as cold as we were because from the moment we came near they trussed up their possessions without asking us for long explanations. We suffered only one dead, our youngest volunteer, aged 16, who took a machine-gun blast in the middle of his stomach. At five o'clock, we occupied the first isbas, while a stupendous sun, bright red, appeared suddenly in the west and sank immediately into the swirling steppe.

* * * * *

It was necessary to pitch camp as best we could.

My group occupied two isbas, which were only huts. One of them was inhabited by two women and seven children. The youngsters defecated in the middle of the room, right on the ground. The mothers would casually push the droppings against the mud wall, then scoop up some handfuls of sunflower seeds from the oven, chewing and spitting them out tirelessly.

We spent the second half of the night on the steppe, at our lookout posts. A return to the offensive by the Russians was possible. How would we react? My machine gun was completely jammed with the ice which formed at 40 degrees below zero. There was no longer any way to make any of our firearms work. The only possible defense remaining was close combat with knives and grenades.

At six o'clock in the morning, a dazzling dawn arose, spreading across the sky: gold, orange, purple, reddish purple with some soft mauves, bordered with clear silver. As I looked at the sky with rapturous eyes at that breathtaking tableau, Aurora's violet bounty festooned above the empty steppe, I cast aside my sufferings and felt love! The most important thing is beauty, at any cost! I saw, above me, the most beautiful lights in the world. I had once contemplated the sky in Athens; my emotion, my joy were even greater as I looked at the sumptuousness and clarity of that Russian sky. My nose was frozen. My cheek was frozen. My machine gun was all ice. But all of my feelings were on fire. In that multi-colored dawn at Rosa-Luxemburg, I was happier than Alcibiades looking at the wine dark sea, from the height of the terraces of the Acropolis.

Two days later, a new spring toward the east.

The cold was relented, but a reddish pus ran from our faces, which were chapped by the ice.

The troops advanced along two hills, very distant from one another, deployed in the manner of the armies of Louis XV. It was a beautiful sight. In front of us, the Panzers broke through the positions of the Soviets. Progress was easy.

We made a stop in a village as dirty as the others, but inhabited by a tribe of Gypsies. The women, perched on the oven in the isba, their legs crossed in the Turkish manner, puffed silently on large pipes. They had black hair, almost blue, wore ragged petticoats, and spat with a vengeance.

On the next day, we arrived at the city of Blagodach, where a furious vanguard battle had just ended. Just in front of us, the ammunition supply of a Soviet cannon had taken a direct hit. A naked body lay there, headless. In place of its neck there was an enormous, blackish, cracked hole. The fat of the thighs had burned, opening long white cracks.

I looked around for the torso's head. Suddenly I saw, stuck to a metal plate, an extraordinary human mask. The explosion had scalped the poor wretch, stripping the skin, the eyes, and a shock of hair from his face. The terrible cold had immediately frozen the grisly mask, which had kept its exact shape and color: the eyes, very blue, were staring straight ahead. The tuft of blond hair fluttered in the wind. It was so real that I almost cried out in fright.

A few Germans had been able to force their way, firing heavy machine guns, into the village. The Russians had fought back, launching a counterattack on three sides at once, like children. Some wonderful

Cossacks had charged from one side, dressed in splendid blue uniforms, waving their eagle-hilted sabres. They galloped in, seated proudly on the aluminum and willow saddles of their agile horses. All of them were mercilessly swept aside. The horses fell dead, their forelegs twisted beneath them; the handsome Cossacks rolled in the snow, in all directions, or were frozen solid by the cold on their saddles, united in death with their mounts.

The Siberian infantry had rushed to the attack as naively as the Cossacks, storming down two hills and then across the steppe. None had been able to come closer than thirty meters from the houses. The bodies of several hundred Siberians lay scattered in the snow. All of them were magnificently equipped, dressed in thick flannels of American make under a thin uniform, which in turn was covered with a heavy cotton uniform, a cloak and a white great coat.

They had been well armed against the cold, at least.

They were nearly all Asiatics, with hair as strong as the bristles of a wild boar. The ice had preserved them at the very moment they fell. One of them had had an eye put out of its socket by a bullet that had entered the center of his forehead. The eye had frozen instantly. It had moved forward, as long as a finger, under the arch of the eyebrow, like a terrifying optical instrument. The pupil stared at us, as lifelike as if the Mongol still breathed. The eyes of the dead, in those forty-below-zero freezes, retained an extraordinary sharpness.

* * * * *

The village was in a pitiful state. We spent the night among young cattle that had escaped the massacre. In our rooms, along with a small calf and some chickens, there were a dozen gentle pigeons which cooed, indifferent to the passions of humankind.

When we got up, a new surprise awaited us: the thaw! Complete thaw! The village splashed about in twenty centimeters of water.

The footsoldier fights in all kinds of weather. We set out again toward the enemy amidst bodies which floated on the roads, like boats set adrift.

## Thaw and Freeze

The Russian thaws take place with extraordinary speed. At the beginning of February 1942, it was forty-two degrees below zero. Four days later, the roads were rivers thirty centimeters deep.

We climbed, with great difficulty, a corpse-littered hill over which the road out of Blagodach led east. Behind us trailed some sleds we had found in the isbas, drawn by several old horses which we had found wandering in the snowy fields. We had neither harnesses, nor traces, nor halters; we hitched up the animals by means of red telephone wires which broke a hundred times and were repaired as often.

We passed a Soviet sledge whose horses and driver had been killed in the same explosion: the soldier, a stocky Mongol, nut brown in complexion, quite stiff, stared at the road from eyeless sockets. Beside him sat an enormous green bottle, filled with a good twenty pounds of tomato juice. The horses and the Mongol were dead, the bottle was intact.

As we marched downhill again, we found ourselves in the midst of a flood. The fields were melting, the water running out through a thousand little channels which drained into the road. The ice refused to melt, so water rose higher and higher. We marched through those icy rivers, soaked to our knees.

We stopped to spend the night in a tiny hamlet, consisting of exactly two isbas. Eighty Croatian volunteers were jammed into the single room of each isba, shoulder to shoulder, with no room to sit down.

It was impossible for one more person to get into those two human rabbit hutches. The two small pigsties likewise were crammed with a mass of chilled soldiers, unable to dry out.

All we could do was to climb up into the hayloft, to the small space which separated the ceiling and the thatched roof. At the peak of the roof that space was one meter high. We had to inch forward from beam to beam, in some danger of falling through the dried mud ceiling onto the backs of the 80 Croats below. More than a hundred of us crawled over to the corners of the roof and then settled down helter-skelter on perches in those dark holes. It was necessary to stay curled up or crouched down. That position was exhausting. Our feet were chilled, our heavy boots filled with icy water. Since the morning we had eaten nothing more than a hunk of our old army bread, if that. Many no longer had even a crust.

* * * * *

At nine o'clock that night, an electric light shone through the trap door from the top of a small ladder. "Get up! We're leaving!"

Leaving! In the middle of the night, along roads streaming with icy water! We had orders to follow right on the heels of the retreating Reds and to occupy, before daybreak, a large *kolkhoz** farther to the east.

None of us could so much as make out the person next to him. We advanced blindly through the water. The fickle weather had made the road a real trap. Beneath water from the melted snow lay a sheet of ice on which our men fell constantly. I had my turn as did the others, sprawling face down with my machine gun. Then I slipped on my heels, and fell backward, gulping down mouthfuls of the road. Soaked to our skins, we struggled through such damp and gloom that we stumbled across the Samara River, meandering over the ice and spreading out over 25 meters wide, without a single soldier noticing that he had crossed a stream! About 1:30 in the morning, we finally arrived at the entrance to the *kolkhoz*. A dozen large dead horses lay in piles of melting snow. There no longer remained a single inhabitable resting place, except for three stables, which were very small and filled with horse manure.

* * * * *

We stationed ourselves, a group of forty men, in one of those.

From the remains of an old flour chest, we made a fire. When the flames rose from it, I hastened to hold out toward it my underwear and my shirt, using a poker. With my usual clumsiness I did things so well that my clothes burst into flames, illuminating the stable magnificently! With only a jacket and a threadbare pair of old trousers, I was through with combat until the end of the winter offensive.

We had no nourishment but the smell of horse manure until the evening of the next day in that evil *kolkhoz*. It was there that, inspecting the slope that went downward toward the Samara, I believed that I could make out a body in the melting snow. I went down to have a look. To my horror, I discovered a young German whose legs the Russians, especially sadistic, had sawed off at the knees. The job had been done with a butcher's saw, unquestionably by an expert. The unfortunate German had been part of a reconnaissance patrol which had disappeared two days earlier. It was obvious that after his mutilation he had still dragged himself fifteen meters, with the desperate will of a young man who didn't want to die.

* * * * *

The ice returned as quickly as the thaw had come. In one night, the temperature plummeted to 20 degrees below zero. On the next day, the Samara was again completely frozen.

The road along the valley was transformed into a horrifying skating rink, horrifying because the bodies of the Russians which had been floating in the water two days before had been frozen in place. Out of the ice there would emerge a hand, or a boot, or a head.

The sleds slowly eliminated those obstacles, grinding down noses and cheeks, which crumbled like sawdust. At the end of a few days, everything was leveled, except for some half-hands and some half-faces which remained level with the white ice, like monstrous fish near the glass of an aquarium tank.

* * * * *

As soon as the ice was hard enough, we continued our advance.

Russian airplanes machine-gunned us heavily. After two kilometers, we found ourselves close to the Samara. The crossing was slow. Meanwhile, a squadron of Soviet airplanes swooped down on us as relentlessly as wasps.

They dove, turned, came back again. Together with some comrades I ran to free a heavy munitions wagon stuck in the middle of the road, an easy target which could go up at any moment. I pushed with all of my strength to move it up to the protection of an embankment. The planes swooped down again, and the vehicle tipped, pinning me. Everything went black.

I awoke again a half hour later, lying in a hut. My eyes could distinguish only great swirls of mauve, like orchids. My left foot had been fractured in two places.

I understood that they wanted to send me to a hospital. That woke me up completely. The ambulance men who had brought me in had at their disposal a horse and a narrow sled. I had them lay me out on that. Then across the dead bodies encrusted in the ice, I started the animal out in the direction of the east.

After an hour I caught up with the company. Stretched out across three planks, I entered Novo-Andrievska, where the Russian fighter planes still harrassed us. They killed one man and wounded several others. Despite the strafing, the Wallonians held the village that night.

* * * * *

We had to go further. My foot looked like a black calf's head. Searching in the snow, a comrade had found one of the enormous felt boots that the tank drivers pulled over their usual footgear. It was even a boot for the left foot. They put it on my wounded foot, which fit into it perfectly. Lying stretched out on my small sled, I set out again with my company.

For the third time, we had to cross the ice covering the winding Samara River. The Soviet airplanes had already resumed the hunt for us. As we crossed the frozen river, they skimmed over us, machine guns chattering, then dropped three large bombs on us. The bombs fell from so low that they did not have time to assume a vertical position and skidded into our ranks like three large gray dogs.

We reached the east bank, but not before several Walloons fell.

We had orders to seize the heights overlooking the valley, which formed the region's water shed. Who held that high ground commanded the Samara Valley.

On 17 February, at 11:00 A.M., we reached the plateau. There a village scattered its isbas along both sides of long, icy ponds. As we crossed the frozen ponds, the Russians, to the east, opened up on us with an extremely fierce artillery barrage.

The troops had been able to run up to the isbas to get a little cover. Flattened at the bottom of my sled, incapable of taking a step, I heard the shrapnel ricocheting on the sides, against the planks. A Croat who ran up, his arms extended, had just fallen on me; he had a monstrous red hole, as large as two fists, where his eyes had once been.

So it was that we entered the village of Gromovaya-Balka, where we were to lose half of our legionnaires, killed or wounded.

## Days of Hell

At Gromovaya-Balka, as everywhere else, there was no continuous front. To our left extended an open space of seven kilometers. On our right friendly forces—Waffen SS of the Viking Division—occupied a small village three kilometers away.

The Russians had massed the bulk of their troops a few kilometers to the east, but their advance posts were positioned quite close to us, inside the haystacks which raised white humps on the steppe.

Since the village of Gromovaya-Balka was built in a slight depression, we set up our positions on the ridge. We weren't able to dig in—the soil was hard as granite—so we constructed our defenses from large blocks of frozen snow, hewn with axes.

Secondary positions were constructed farther back, near some isbas. By preference, our volunteers had cut them into the strawy manure heaps, which were easier to chop through. That won us some unexpected comforts, because our soldiers found amid the dung two magnificent cases of French cognac, buried hastily by the retreating Russians.

Unfortunately, that was the only consolation, for our men were going to spend ten days of hell at Gromovaya-Balka.

* * * * *

For suitable lodgings we had at our disposal only two or three isbas per company. Nearly all of the windows had been broken by the time of our arrival. The Bolsheviks, as usual, had massacred the animals. Their bodies lay inside or at the thresholds of the cottages. One horse had died while lying across one of our two little windows; he blocked three quarters of it. Two other dead horses were stretched out in the cattle shed.

Since the enemy probed us day and night, one half of our men had to constantly occupy positions in the snow. Because of the cold, the companies were split in two to relieve each other every two hours.

Throughout those ten days our soldiers were never able to sleep more than an hour and a half at a time. It was necessary for them to wake up a quarter hour before their guard duty. On their return, it took them another quarter hour to settle down again. Besides, if more than half of the men had been able to rest at the same time, it would have been impossible to get them into the single-room huts, so tiny were they. The twenty-five men who returned for their two-hour rest couldn't even stretch out on the ground. They had to remain standing or squat on the ground. The cold rushed in, unabated, through the broken windows, which we were unable to seal completely.

I myself, with my broken foot, was able to remain stretched out only on a kind of bench attached to the wall, one meter above the floor. It was on that perch that I, day and night, frozen and powerless in my plaster cast, witnessed the departure and the return of my unfortunate comrades.

The resupply of food was as simple as possible. The sleds took forty to fifty hours to reach us. The enemy artillery implacably carried out their evil work on the white foundation of the road for the last kilometers if the supply people risked the trip during the day. If they tried to reach us at night, they got lost in the steppe and would stumble onto one of the Soviet posts.

We received only just enough so that we did not lose strength: some bread, which we cut with our bayonets, and some cans of meat, frozen at the factory and refrozen in masterly fashion on the troikas.

The lack of sleep was killing to the men. Cold is terribly exhausting, and requires a struggle by the entire body. Our companies had to stay in holes in the ice, twelve hours out of every twenty-four, without moving a meter. The men stood on ice. If they tried to lean on something, they leaned on ice. It was 20 to 25 degrees below zero at all times. The short rest in the isba allowed them neither to warm themselves up again—it was nearly as cold there as it was outside—nor to regain their strength. They were unable to stretch out on the ground, nor even to have their minds at peace, since, at every instant, a volley of shells fell, damaging the cottages, flattening some of the walls.

In the space of a few days, the Soviet artillery lobbed us several thousand shells. Some isbas caught fire. Others, hit on the roofs, had their thatch strewn over an area of twenty meters. Our casualties were heavy.

One of our heavy machine guns, hit directly, was thrown four meters into the air along with the gunner; he fell back untouched, still holding the handle of the weapon; the other two members of the crew were mangled.

One shell came right through the window of an isba where a dozen of our comrades were resting. It was a scene out of a slaughterhouse. One soldier was missing among the heap of the dead and wounded who were dragged out of the destroyed cottage; the next day they found some fragments of flesh and bones, the consistency of porridge, stuck to the rubble, all that remained of our companion. He had taken the shell in the middle of his chest.

* * * * *

Our telephone lines were continually cut.

The forty men who maintained communications between the companies and the battalion command post, and then between the battalion and the division, had suffered terribly since the beginning of the offensive. Each night during our advance, in weather as cold as 40 degrees below zero, across veritable rivers created by the thaw, they had to unreel kilometers of telephone wire. They came back from the steppe with severe frost bite on their hands, their cheeks, their noses, their ears.

At Gromovaya-Balka, they spent their days and nights crawling on the snow and ice, in the midst of machine-gun fire, along their damnable wires, which the Reds cut three or four times an hour.

Maintaining communications was absolutely vital, for those wires were the arteries of the battalion. Many of our little telephone men died for those wires.

There was among them an old man, with white hair, always the first on duty. He too was hit. He still had the strength to take a little Bible from his pocket and to recite two or three short lines from a psalm before he died.

* * * * *

The state of utter misery in which we found ourselves was aggravated by other afflictions, of a more intimate kind.

We were, for the most part, covered with mysterious sores that the soldiers of the Eastern Front called "the Russian plague."

The illness began with incredible itching on the feet and the calves. It was almost impossible not to scratch them. But, if you began scratching, the complications were not long in coming. Bluish sores formed, as irritating as if they were being eaten by salt and pepper. They bled and most of all ran with pus. This was disgusting to see. It was necessary not to scratch, but men's nerves snapped as a result of being held back. If during the day you had the energy to resist the biting of that venom, at night, while sleeping, your hands unconsciously went to your feet and calves, and your fingernails dug into those corrosive spots, going deep, bleeding. We had to keep our boots on, while asleep, so as not to be overcome by that terrible itching.

Thousands, tens of thousands of soldiers on the Eastern Front were removed from the line because those flowing wounds proved so stubborn. At Gromovaya-Balka, some of our comrades were affected down to the bone itself. Three quarters of the troops, at least, covered their bloody calves with dirty rags. But, in spite of the bandages, the violet holes of the wounds, eaten by unknown acids, tempted their fingers, lured their nails, night and day.

* * * * *

Swarms of fleas devoured us.

We had waged the entire counteroffensive in the Donets without a single change of underwear. Each of the unspeakable huts where we were quartered had sheltered, before us, hordes of Mongols, Tatars, Siberians, teeming with vermin. Our straitened circumstances, with forty or fifty men crammed together in squalor, made us easy prey for the greedy, merciless vermin.

A number of soldiers, running out of strength, did not want to lose yet another hour of their scant sleep by indulging in useless flea hunts. Even if you eliminated your fleas, your neighbor did not kill his. At the moment he woke up, half of his supply moved to your territory. And how could we organize a general delousing amidst those crowded conditions with soldiers curled up, incapable of even stretching out or moving?

We had only to thrust our hands under our arms or between our thighs; we brought back handfuls of hideous fleas. Some were small, lively and whitish; some long, with bodies like darts; some round, with red stomachs the size of a pinhead. Their colors were amazingly adapted to the color of our clothes.

The fleas took pleasure in sucking at wounds. They found their way in large numbers beneath dressings. I felt them swarming constantly along my wounded foot. There was nothing to do, just let them eat you alive, your nerves held sternly in check.

* * * * *

Each day the Soviets became more aggressive.

For more than a week, we hardly slept at all. Even when the men came back for their two hours of rest in the isba, grenades and shells came clattering down in such abundance that everyone threw himself to the ground, confused, expecting a shell to land in the middle of the room at any moment.

There were no cellars, nor had we any other shelters.

Beginning on 25 February, the Soviet tanks came at nightfall. They would approach to within several hundred meters of us; each time, they fired a few rounds, then disappeared into the darkness.

Our patrols engaged in some bloody hand-to-hand battles with the Russian forward posts.

The Soviet troops carried out a plan of elementary simplicity: they set themselves to eliminating all obstacles, one by one. First they struck in full strength at the village held by the SS to our right. If that redoubt fell, we would be isolated, the sole defenders of the path to the Samara, the objective toward which the Soviets had chosen to drive with all available forces.

The SS were around two hundred in number. They were real heavyweights. Our men who kept contact with their command post could not get over their coolness under fire. The Russians were within thirty meters machine-gunning them from house to house. In one day the SS withstood ten assaults by an enemy twenty times more numerous. They resisted, immovable, playing cards at each respite.

At the end of a week they held only a narrow passageway, a hundred meters wide, leading to the west. Three-fourths of those courageous men had fallen in the struggle.

On 28 February 1942, at five in the morning, several thousand Reds pounced on the fifty or so survivors. The Germans suffered an hour's savage massacre. Only a few managed to escape. We saw them running toward us across the snow, followed closely by the Bolsheviks.

They came just in time to help us, for, even as the Viking's village was being overrun, hordes of Soviet troops, which had massed to the east of Gromovaya-Balka the night before, flooded towards us.

At six o'clock in the morning, two regiments, consisting of four thousand men, attacked us, supported by fourteen tanks.

There were barely five hundred of us; we had a single tank.

## Gromovaya-Balka

Throughout that night, our battalion had been in a state of alert. Our patrols had spotted important enemy movements. We could tell that the attack was imminent.

The fall of the village held by the SS had isolated us in the middle of an open space fifteen kilometers square. The Reds were eager for revenge and they longed to pour down into the valley of the Samara, from which our forces had chased them two weeks before.

They spared no effort to make their suc~ess decisive. Their artillery, massed on the heights, loomed above us, and their observers relayed our every movement in the village, already reduced to a heap of rubble.

Our soldiers looked like ghosts.

At midnight, a first alert had been sounded. At six in the morning, a new alert sent our companies to combat positions. Almost immediately a hail of machine-gun fire began to fall on all sides.

* * * * *

I was stretched out on two planks in our isba, forty meters behind our ice forts, which faced east. I listened anxiously to the din of battle. Suddenly the roof crackled with flames: the thatch was on fire.

Hopping on one foot, I reached the window: a tremendous mass of infantry was advancing in close order.

I thought at first that they were the Croatian volunteers: they had on nearly the same purplish-blue cloaks. Shells fell all around them; the German artillery, which was reinforcing us, was firing nearly point blank at those thousands of men.

They had emerged from a ravine and were marching toward the center of the village, taking the positions of our companies from behind. One would have thought that they were taking part in a training exercise, so unconcerned were they. They spread out only when they had advanced to about one hundred meters from my isba, the first one to the northeast. I then caught sight of the 14 Soviet tanks which roared straight ahead.

My company, overwhelmed, fell back to the second isba.

I couldn't hold back any longer. My metatarsals had had two weeks to mend. Kicking off the splint which encased my foot, I limped forward, with my rifle as a crutch, across the open ground to join my squad.

* * * * *

My pain forgotten, I took my post at my machine gun once again. There were twelve of us, pinned down twenty meters in front of the second house. I wedged myself between two large, dead horses, hard as rocks, against which the bullets smacked with an odd sound.

The enemy had fanned out from the east to the northeast, facing the two lines of isbas in the village. At the same time they attacked us they fell on our comrades in the 2nd Company, who were defending the huts on the other side of the pond.

The men of the 2nd performed incredible feats of bravery in their defense, but their forward post fell before the onslaught. Together with their superb NCO's they fell almost to the last man, blunting the Red pack's momentum with their stand.

To the northeast, Soviet troops, Russian and Asiatic, penetrated beyond the first isbas. Our brave soldiers and the savage Reds slaughtered one another in brutal hand-to-hand combat.

One of our old Rexist songs wafted above the battle. At that time, early in the war, our troops conserved a few uses from a bygone age: they sang as they leaped to the attack. The survivors from the 2nd Company counter-attacked, probing the Russians. Their commander, First Lieutenant Buyds, a manufacturer from Brussels, rushed forward, a machine gun in his hands. His re-formed company, behind him, at the corners of the houses, reached its former positions in the snow.

But each of our men had to deal with a bunch of Reds. The Soviet tanks flattened all the focal points of the struggle. Lieutenant Buyds continued firing his machine gun, until the Russians were within a few paces; then he caught a bullet in the upper chest and died, his head slumped over his weapon.

The Reds retook the first thatched cottages to the northwest. We saw their tanks roar after our wounded, catch them, then crush them under their iron treads.

Our situation was scarcely any better. The Bolsheviks now occupied the smoking rubble of the first isba and had overrun several neighboring out-buildings. From the northeast, several of their Maxim machine guns raked us with fire. An open shed lying between us and the enemy had its roof tiles swept off in the firing. They scattered like a fallen house of cards.

Our men fell, struck by explosive bullets that made tremendous holes in them. One of my comrades fell in front of me, his head no more than a gruesome doughnut-shaped mass; his eyes, his nose, his cheeks, his mouth had disappeared, blown away by the impact.

The Reds were no longer only in front of us. The isbas on our left flank had already fallen; now, the Soviets held our former positions on the eastern ridge. From there they poured into the heart of the village.

Our soldiers were beset by small, fierce knots of Reds, who fought savagely, refusing to give ground.

We fought mainly with our rifles, using our ammunition carefully, felling a Bolshevik with each shot. The enemy advanced with mule-like unconcern. A beautiful golden sun had risen over the snow, behind our attackers. The Russians who occupied our positions in the ice presented, in silhouette, perfect black targets. Each head that dared to rise for a moment above our former icy outposts caught a bullet.

But we, too, suffered heavy losses.

After an hour, I was the only one left from my small group, wedged between the carcasses of the two frozen horses, real rocks of protection. Bullets richocheted everywhere. One of them had cut, near my cheek, a six-inch groove in the butt of my rifle. Some Russians had outflanked me on the left, and there were at least thirty of them ten meters in front of me. It was then that I felt myself pulled from behind by my good foot. A young corporal from my squad, named Henri Berkmans, seeing me lost, had crawled up to me and thus hauled me away on my stomach, as if he were dragging a sled.

After twenty meters of that unexpected exercise, I reached the threshold of the thatched cottage where the rest of our company was defending itself. My heroic rescuer, alas, had less luck than I: a volley of grenade bursts deeply slashed the soles of his feet; he died after suffering terribly.

It was perhaps nine o'clock in the morning. The Soviet tanks which had invaded the northwest sector now found themselves several hundred meters behind us. They carried out a monstrous man hunt, wheeling around the isbas, amusing themselves by crushing our comrades one by one, whether they were unharmed or wounded or dead. We realized perfectly well that we were going to be surrounded and pulverized in our turn by those mastodons, all the more since the southeast sector was by then bearing the brunt of the Soviet troops swarming from the village where they had exterminated the last pockets of SS defenders.

We were the object of frenzied gunfire. The ice around us flaked off in hundreds of little dancing puffs. Each of us took cover as he could, behind some peasant sleds, or flush with the balustrades of the windows.

An old soldier from the First World War, named Steenbruggen, was especially eager for combat. Hit with a bullet in the nape of the neck, he collapsed, but, his right hand raised, cried out: "Goodbye, comrades, Rex will win!" We thought he had died. Fifteen minutes later, a corpse sat up again: "But, in the name of God, I am not dead!" It was our old soldier, come back to life! He was alive in spite of the bullet in his head! He was able to drag himself to a first aid post; having been born with an unusually thick neck, he recovered from his wound.

Our luck was short lived, however. A Soviet tank, determined to seal our fate, rumbled across the ice-topped pond, headed straight for our isba.

* * * * *

The tank aimed its cannon. We only had time to throw ourselves to the floor of the isba. Three shells, aimed perfectly, completely destroyed the front wall. We were buried by the rubble from the plaster walls. The thatched roof was on fire. Some of the men were streaming with blood; one of them had had his left arm cut off.

Luckily one of the three shells had opened a breach in the wall at the back of the dwelling, one meter high. We were able to pull our wounded through the hole, and then crawl out ourselves, one after the other.

In order to reach the next house, we had to cross a space of some thirty meters. The men who ran it all in one stretch were mercilessly mowed down. To confuse the enemy trying to take aim, it was necessary to cross at most five meters, then throw yourself to the ground, then run for four or five more meters, and throw yourself to the ground once more. The enemy marksmen, confused each time by such tactics, then looked for a less mobile target.

One of our young soldiers had taken cover next to a body. Panic-stricken, he wasn't looking. Suddenly he saw, right beside him, the corpse's slate-blue eyes, staring blankly. The dead man was his father, a brave tailor from Brussels.

* * * * *

We took shelter in a neighboring isba. In turn, its roof flamed above our heads. We set our backs up against the threshold of the house, behind a bank of ice, very yellow with frozen urine.

The tanks were overrunning us. Hundreds of Russians machine-gunned us at almost point blank-range. Right behind us, the thatched roof fell in like an enormous, fiery torch.

The tanks had almost ended their sweep behind us. We did not fire our rifles anymore, since we knew the value of each cartridge. The end was drawing near. Our company commander put his hand on mine: "If you die," he told me simply, "I will not survive you . . ."

Neither of us was about to die, however. All at once, we heard the roar of engines overhead. Red tanks were blowing up! Isbas were exploding! Whole bunches of Reds were tossed in the air like ragdolls!

The Stukas* had arrived!

With incredible precision, they hit the Soviet tanks dead center, and flattened the attackers, stupidly crowded together in bunches as usual. The enemy tanks fled in great haste to escape the diving planes' cannon fire. The infantry took off right behind them.

Our battalion commander immediately threw the last forces that he had into a counterattack. Their wave surged past us. By noon, the Wallonian Legion had completely retaken Gromovaya-Balka, reconquering even the first isbas, on both sides of the pond. Russian bodies lay everywhere. We took a large number of prisoners, Mongols, as ugly as monkeys, Kirghiz, Siberians, all astounded at having been bested with such spirit. They constantly repeated: "Belgiski, karoch! Belgiski, karoch!" ("Belgians, famous!") while squinting their little yellow eyes.

Unfortunately, all of our wounded were dead, deliberately crushed by the Soviet tanks or killed with bayonet thrusts.

After having carried out their providential attack, the German Stukas had left. The Russians regrouped, and their tanks started to move again. Everything was going to start over again.

We were powerless against their tanks. At that time, the panzerfaust* did not yet exist, nor did we have any anti-tank guns. We even lacked mines.

From the beginning of this impossible struggle, the German 100th Division, on which we depended tactically, had promised to help. A Panzer column had been dispatched toward our village, but it was intercepted by a group of Red tanks. The ensuing battle on the steppe, which lasted several hours, barred the 100th's reinforcements from coming to help.

Our men had to fight once more a defensive battle, isba by isba, barn by barn, slope by slope. At three in the afternoon, they stood, their backs to the walls of the last houses, before the cherry orchard to the southwest of the village. If they were forced out of those last redoubts, they would be thrown out onto the steppe, flat, without a bush, where the deep snow extended for many kilometers.

We had to react so as not to be pushed to that fatal extreme. Our commander, Captain Pauly, gathered together the remains of all of the companies and, grenade in hand, was the first to rush to the counterattack, shouting our old cry: "Rex will win!" Everyone in the battalion still fit for service followed him, including the armorers, the cooks, the couriers, the truck drivers. It was a frenzied scramble. Reds and Walloons killed each other, even in the huts, where, firing revolvers through cracks in the doors, they shattered one another's skulls at point-blank range.

The Russian tanks, running short of shells, rumbled about trying to crush our soldiers, who darted from isba to isba. The Soviet infantrymen, panicked and exhausted, first hesitated and then began to give ground. In the thick of the hand-to-hand combat, some German infantry reinforcements appeared in the snow to the west. The enemy rout was then complete. For a third time, the village was retaken.

The Reds again devoted themselves, for some time, to chasing after our men. But our tanks, winners in the battle of the steppe, showed up in their turn on the hillside. A half-hour later, the Soviet armor and infantry had disappeared in the blue snows to the northeast.

Night was about to fall. The bodies of seven hundred Reds lay across the snow, on the ice of the ponds, near the ruins of the houses. But two hundred and fifty of our comrades had fallen, killed or wounded, during those twelve hours of furious fighting.

The German tanks left again, one hour later, for another sector that was threatened. Of the isbas of Gromovaya-Balka, nothing remained but cinders, their dying glow dwindling slowly in the glacial evening.

## Front of Ice

On the evening of 28 February 1943, the smoking remains of Gromovaya-Balka were in our hands. It was necessary, however, to face facts: the position was untenable. The village had been demolished. Above all, it was located at the bottom of a depression. From the slope to the east, the enemy could follow all our movements.

For ten days, we had gotten our bearings and had worked hard. We had held on to the village, in spite of four thousand Soviet soldiers and fourteen tanks, only because the honor of our people was at stake. All of us preferred death to giving ground.

A burning patriotism inspired our soldiers: they were representing their country; for it, half of our men had fallen, frozen in death, bathed in blood. Only national pride had enabled the miracle of three counterattacks and the reconquest.

It would have been useless to repeat a similar struggle the next day. Wisdom demanded that we abandon the basin and set up our defense on the western hillside, which overlooked Gromovaya-Balka. There we would no longer be easy targets for the Red gunners.

The commander of the 100th Division, General Sanne, ordered that our battalion take position on the ridge, under cover of night. Our advanced posts were maintained until the last minute. The Russians noticed nothing. At dawn, they crushed the ruins of Gromovaya-Balka under a hellish barrage, then attacked the empty space.

It was now our artillery's turn to make life impossible for them in the hollow of the village. They were no more able than we were to keep their forces there. Beaten, they drew back a few hundred meters, up the hill to the east.

From then on we glared at each other and machine-gunned each other from ridge to ridge. The village became a no-man's land where only a few blackened chimneys rose from the rubble of the isbas and the whiteness of winter.

Our new positions, improvised in the middle of the steppe, while the temperature stayed at 30 degrees below zero, were dug deep into the snow and ice.

Several heavy German tanks returned, snorting, firing. Squat, like medieval bastions, they laid claim to the crest, while in the meantime the German artillery batteries were emplaced in a valley to the west.

We had not the slightest hut at our disposal, not the weakest fire; nothing but white holes in the snow, where our two hundred survivors, lacking any winter equipment, had to face the Soviet forces.

Shells burst in all directions. An ammunition depot blew up. Our men's teeth chattered like castanets, so deeply had the cold gripped them. The faces of some of them were almost green. Since the previous night the ice had numbed these two hundred unprotected men. Another night followed, more bitter yet. Our situation seemed utterly desperate. It was scarcely conceivable that in the middle of the steppe, in such frigid weather, men exhausted by a month of combat still lived, motionless for dozens of hours, tormented, exhausted by the terrible cold.

Our battalion, formed up into a square, had sworn to hold out until the end. Only the dead were evacuated. The next day, at dawn, the Wallonian Legion was still at its post. Neither the Russians nor the ice could blunt its spirit.

* * * * *

To diminish our own suffering, we compared our troubles to those of the 150 wounded whom dozens of sleds had taken away over the steppe.

At Gromovaya-Balka it had been necessary to wait for nightfall to evacuate most of our comrades, because during the day many of our wounded had been hit for a second time by Soviet machine-gunners firing on medical convoys, black and clear in the bright snow.

Our sleds were just barely able to travel the seven kilometers from our positions to the village of Novo-Andrievska. They deposited their bloody loads there and returned quickly.

We had used, for the first transports, such rare covers as had escaped being burned in the isbas. Later, it was necessary to make do with dry fodder or with the thatch of the last houses in the town. Throughout the wearing night the hapless wounded shivered in the snow, protected only by ragged clothes, a little straw or a little hay. Their suffering was unspeakable.

At Novo-Andrievska, the doctors at the first aid post did not know where to lodge them. They lay about by the dozens on the bare ground of the huts. The village was only a relay station. It was necessary to evacuate the unfortunates across forty kilometers from there to Grichino. The storm had returned, stirring the white steppe to a fury of blinding snow.

The sleds took two or three days to reach Grichino and the field hospital.

The wounded, their wounds hastily dressed, their broken bones hastily splinted, dying from the cold, with grenade fragments and bullets still in their bodies, suffered a horrible martyrdom.

The pile-up of the wounded at Grichino was unimaginable. Eleven thousand were taken there in five weeks. Some of our gravely wounded men had to wait five days before someone removed their temporary dressings, which had become black and as hard as iron. They had difficulty explaining their needs, since most of them spoke no German. In their distress they could not receive a word of comfort from anyone. They reached the depths of physical and mental suffering.

Many never survived the field hospitals; they ended their suffering in the long military cemeteries where, below their steel helmets, were blazoned the black, yellow and red, the colors of the country for which they so valiantly struggled and suffered.

* * * * *

By the morning of 2 March 1942, the Wallonian Legion had been reduced to less than a third of its original strength. Out of 26 officers, there remained two, one of whom, suffering a nervous breakdown, was evacuated a short time later.

Some German troops were on route and were going to replace us. Our scouts dug them some underground shelters which would allow them to survive, with a little less discomfort, on that storm-swept ridge. Nevertheless, despite the construction of those refuges, the battalion which succeeded ours on the plateau lost more than thirty percent of its men to the freezing weather during the month of March alone.

We were relieved at noon.

Our boys, emaciated, unshaven, returned from their posts with proud looks on their faces. The heroism they had shown in combat was already a watchword all along the Donets front. The commander of the 100th Division had just awarded them 33 Iron Crosses. At that time this was, for one battalion, an extraordinary number. A still more striking honor came as we were especially cited in the Wehrmacht order of the day, in the communique from the High Command.

We settled into an area behind the front lines, at Blagodach.

The snowy fields had been cleared of the hundreds of bodies, blue-clad Cossacks, Mongols in white greatcoats, by which we had passed a month before, at the time of the offensive.

We found some houses, poor to be sure, miserable to be sure, but houses! We no longer had in front of us hordes of Asiatics with tiny flashing eyes, leaping like cats for savage hand-to-hand combat.

We looked at one another, we sought out one another. Our poor dead comrades, brothers who had shared our dreams, seemed to move about us, dominating our thoughts. Each of us had lost very dear friends. Our legion was like a band of brothers: we were united in all things.

Our hearts were tormented, and the savor of our glory was as a frozen, bitter fruit in our mouths.

# Chapter Three
# THE BATTLE OF KHARKOV

The battle of Gromovaya-Balka had marked the last great effort by the Soviets in the Donets during the winter of 1941-1942. Our legion, settled at Blagodach, was held in reserve, ready to be called upon at the first danger. But the front was no longer seriously endangered.

At night heavy machine-gun fire could still be heard. From the doorsteps of our huts we could watch the muzzles flash and the tracers crisscross above the steppe. The blow dealt the Reds on 28 February had been decisive, however: their offensive had been halted, then thrown back for good.

Blagodach was still buried under deep snowdrifts. Snowfall alternated with ice storms. The winter seemed to last forever. We spent six months in whiteness. We ended up being haunted by that whiteness; the white steppe, the white roofs, the white sky which slithered above our heads.

* * * * *

The village, racked by the fighting, was extremely poor. We slept on planks or straw, even on the earth floors of the cottages. The wan brats' squalling assailed our ears. These poor people lived only on potatoes which they ate uncooked, seasoned only with salt. All the cows had been killed. The villagers had tossed their dead horses, along with the bodies of five hundred Soviet soldiers, pell-mell into a large quarry, a grisly abattoir from which poked out horses' hooves and human heads.

We drew our water from the village well. One day our bucket fell in and sank to the bottom. We sent a man armed with a hook attached to a heavy rope to search the bottom of the well. The hook soon caught on what we all thought was the bucket. It seemed to have become awfully heavy, though, and it took the strong arms and backs of several men to haul it up again. At last our catch emerged: a Mongol, huge, hideous, half-rotted, his belt hooked to our rope. We'd been drinking him for weeks.

The isbas were nothing more than fleas' nests. In ours there was a supply of seed grain for sowing, which shook with continual rustlings, so abundant were the vermin there.

The majority of us suffered from "flea fever" or volhynian fever, a type of malaria, which put us in a severe state of listlessness. In the evenings we had fevers of 39 degrees centigrade. Come morning, the fever would decline to 35 or 35.5 degrees, at most. We barely picked at our food; we grew progressively weaker. The isbas, the steppe spun around us. We were incapable of working or even going out.

The crisis, even in its acute stage, lasted for three or four weeks, at the end of which we got to our feet again painfully, with heads hanging like those of poor, sad, old horses.

Recovery was rarely permanent. The flea fever recurred time after time, like malaria. Against that pandemic of the Eastern Front our doctors had no medicine, except for the ever-present aspirin, cure-all of every army in the world.

* * * * *

We tried to return to our normal habits of hygiene.

We confiscated, for an hour, the kneading trough from the house, a sort of shallow canoe, hewn with an axe from a block of wood. Melting a half-meter cube of snow in it, we sat down in that tiny, comic boat. At the first slightly too vigorous movement, we tipped over on our butts!

The Russians did not wash their bodies during the entire winter. They had picturesque ways of cleaning their faces. Filling up their mouths with water, they spat out the liquid, four or five times, into their hands, then rubbed them over their cheeks. In the same manner, they sprinkled, the faces of their whining brats.

The sessions for killing fleas were virtual ceremonies.

The neighbor woman would come by. Squatting down on the ground, she'd unbraid her hair on the knees of her crony, who then spent an hour or two removing hundreds of little beasts, using a large wooden comb. Then she would sit on the ground, while the other one, chattering away, took her turn at returning the favor.

During the summer those operations took place on the door step. It was awfully nice: they killed each other's fleas together, a very decent sort of communism.

As soon as our lightly wounded men recovered, we reorganized our companies, at half their former strength.

A corporal at the start of the counteroffensive, I had been named a noncommissioned officer in the middle of the battle of Gromovaya-Balka. I supervised the dismantling of the machine guns and the quality of the soup with as much diligence as if I were directing a gathering of 50,000 political followers. I loved the life of a soldier, simple as could be, free of worldly concerns, ambitions, and interests.

It had been months since I'd received the least bit of news of the scuffles of the Forum. The viperous swarm of office seekers, the temptations and dishonesties of the political arena sickened me. I preferred my filthy isba to the ministerial palaces, my worn trooper's jacket to the stifling comfort of middle class mediocrity. As I looked at the pure eyes of my soldiers, cleansed by sacrifice, I felt rising toward me the wholesome gift of their ideal. I gave them, from my side, all that burned in my heart.

* * * * *

We often received visits from our German comrades. We would even go to spend the evening in their shelters. For hours we would discuss the problems of the post-war period.

Besides the dead, what would there be?

The questions about frontiers, about material affairs didn't interest us very much. Living ceaselessly face to face with death, we came to understand to an intense degree the importance of spiritual forces. The front held only because at the front there were souls, souls which believed, which burned with ardor, which radiated strength. Our victories were won not only with weapons, but with virtues.

The problems of the post-war period would be identical. Economic victories would not be enough. Political reorganizations would not be enough. A great moral redemption would be necessary, which would cleanse away the blemishes of our time, which would restore our souls with the fresh air of passion and of unconditional service.

National revolution, yes. Social revolution, yes. European revolution, yes. But above all else a spiritual revolution a thousand times more necessary than external order, than external justice, than fraternity in words alone.

The world emerging from the killing and the hatred of the war would need, first, pure hearts, believing in their mission, dedicating themselves to it, pure hearts in whom the masses could believe and to whom they could devote themselves.

Our discussions blazed to life like fires. A paltry little gas lamp emphasized the lines in our faces. Those faces radiated. That winter we offered up our sufferings for the purification of our dreams. Never had we felt in our hearts so much strength, so much clarity, so much joy.

Once, we had been able to lead commonplace lives, soiled by petty abdications to daily necessity. The front had given us a taste for privation. We were purged of all hatred and of all desire. We had mortified our bodies, extinguished our ambition, purified and offered our sacrifice. Death itself no longer frightened us.

The snow remained for a long time.

On Holy Thursday it fell again, in enormous flakes, for several hours. Then the air grew milder. We looked out over the white steppe, where the black stalks of the sunflowers reached higher and higher. The hills had the gray gleam of the end of winter. The sun came out again.

The sparrows frolicked wildly in the straw. Each day the sun beat down on the plain. Melt water trickled off in rivulets. The peasants, using their axes, adzes, and picks, broke up the ice, thirty or forty centimeters deep, which surrounded the cottages. After several days of this, the town was transformed into an immense cesspool. The fields were like seas of sticky molasses. We could only go from one end of the village to the other on horseback, making a vast detour by way of the ridges.

Certain of the boldest among us had built surfboards; they went around Blagodach in swim suits, pulled by mules. From isba to isba we built footbridges, thrown across mud a half meter deep. The water, fed by a thousand streams, rushed down the slopes with the power of rivers, forty or fifty meters wide, forming rumbling cataracts. The first peasant cart that tried to cross them was swept away; the woman driving it was carried off, bobbing up and sinking down a hundred times in the current.

* * * * *

After two weeks of sunshine, we were able to return to the haystacks of the previous autumn, at the top of the ridge. There we lay down, cheered up, shirts removed, offering our bodies to the warm life-giving spring.

The place where the village's ponds had been had disappeared; large frozen carp floated by the hundreds near the gratings of the dikes.

One day I rode on horseback far to the west. The river curved. I noticed, in the distance, a small forest. It was beginning to green, a soft yellow green. I rose up on my stirrups, and breathed in the new springtime in great gulps. It felt so good!

The sun had conquered winter!

The roads dried out. The windmill turned before a completely blue sky.

May arrived. On the 10th, we received a secret order. We were changing sectors, moving out that very night. Great military events were imminent. Joyful, rambunctious, we left our isbas, singing of war, adventure, glory, and the warm spring which flowered in our hearts.

## A Cuckoo Cry

Never during the frightful winter of 1941-1942 had doubt afflicted the spirits of the German soldiers or the European volunteers on the Eastern Front. Their sufferings had been extraordinary, but they knew that the howling blasts of winter, the ice at forty-two degrees below zero, the lack of equipment had been the only causes of their misfortunes. Stalin had no hand in the matter. At present, the railway lines were beginning to function properly; the bridges were rebuilt; letters arrived speedily. Fur coats had even been distributed, voluptuous feminine furs or Bavarian herdsmen's old goatskins. We received them in the middle of the thaw. We had just enough time to amuse ourselves with them and then return them.

No serious news troubled the spring. America, which had officially entered the world war in December 1941, had experienced nothing but defeats during the winter. The English, up until then the undisputed world champions in evacuation by boat, had evacuated Hong Kong and Singapore after having bettered the speed records of cheetahs, panthers, and other cats in the jungles of Burma. The army on the Eastern Front firmly believed that the English and the Americans, countries deeply involved in Asia, no longer represented any danger for the Reich. While they continued to retreat to their last Pacific refuges, Germany could calmly give the *coup de grace* to the USSR.

It was true that Stalin had fought back, that he had regained some territory that winter. But of course the armies of the Reich had thrown caution to the winds the previous autumn. Sometimes the sectors they held had proved impossible to defend. There had been perilous moments, yet despite the irregular front, despite the cold, despite the snafus, our situation had been restored that same winter to one of impressive strength.

The Russians in 1941 had suffered enormous losses. Their winter offensive had failed, failed unquestionably.

This would be the final round. Or so we thought, absolutely certain that the struggle's outcome was a foregone conclusion.

* * * * *

Never had the German army been so powerful.

The Reich had made a prodigious effort to repair the damage of winter and to bring its units up to snuff. The regiments were once more at complete strength. The divisions had been reinforced, moreover, by reserve battalions comprising up to 1500 men each, replacements for the losses which would be incurred as the renewed offensive advanced across the steppe.

Each unit had been outfitted with new equipment, and bristled with weapons in perfect condition. It was a pleasure to see those divisions, made up of 15,000 to 17,000 magnificent, lively young men, as straight and strong as trees, led by officers and non-commissioned officers the like of which no army in the world has ever had.

The winter was forgotten. We spoke about it no longer except to laugh about it. The more one suffers at a given moment in life, the more one delights later on in recounting misfortunes overcome. Which man's nose had been frozen most solid, whose isba had been the filthiest, whose bread had been the moldiest, whose fleas had been the worst man-eaters: all that was grist for amusement. Once they got involved in that kind of conversation, the men were indefatigable.

A sensational turn of events suddenly took place, which allowed the German command once more to demonstrate its supreme mastery.

The higher ranking German officers possessed a coolness and placidity absolutely without parallel. The generals would sit down in front of their maps at headquarters like chess champions at their boards hunched over their pawns. They took their time, and made only moves carefully calculated in advance.

On the 10th and 11th of May, 1942, the German High Command had set in motion all of its forces in the Donets, in order to attack to the east. While all these troop movements were underway, the Soviet Marshal Timoshenko, with a formidable thrust, took the offensive at the northernmost point of our sector. He broke from cover below Kharkov, hurling several hundred thousand men toward Poltava and the Dnieper River.

Timoshenko's forces opened a deep breach. Stalin published resounding victory bulletins. Radio Moscow and the BBC announced the imminent arrival of the Russians at the Dnieper. Fleeing troops fell back as far as our lines, spreading sinister rumors.

The German High Command had been completely anticipated by the Soviets. It suffered the mishap without a wasted word, without a wince of pain. Most important, it deviated not at all from its own plan of attack. Preparations continued to be carried out according to plan. The High Command allowed the Russians to advance for five days, thereby creating an enormous bulge, the center of which was Poltava. During that time, each German battalion took position with the greatest calm. Not a single operation was advanced by so much as an hour.

* * * * *

Our legion had not yet been brought up to strength by new recruits. It had, however, been assigned a vast sector, just at a neck of the Donets front.

Our bunkers and trenches were in excellent shape. They wound along the crest of large bare hills whose cliffs plunged down to a river valley and a place named Yablenskaya. Yablenskaya commanded a pass, and the Reds had made of it a powerful barrier. Their artillery had the entire valley in range. The shells came pounding down on our positions like bowling balls toppling tenpins.

At night, volunteers from our legion would crawl, lithe as weasels, between the mines which covered our sector, in order to prowl around the Russian sector. Their missions consisted in hiding themselves in the midst of the enemy forces and spending a day on the lookout. They studied carefully the comings and goings of the Reds and the emplacements of their machine-gun nests and artillery.

At daybreak we'd observe the Soviet hills with our binoculars. From a hay stack there would extend a hand, which, just for a moment, shook a handkerchief. That was how our men camouflaged themselves. Our machine guns would sweep the surrounding area with fire, to cover our daredevils in case of a Soviet response.

Some squads risked these expeditions every night, two men at a time. On the following night, we would hear soft rustlings at the appointed rendezvous; then we'd crawl to the edge of the minefield to welcome our comrades back. They always returned safe and sound, furnished with detailed information and risible stories.

* * * * *

On the evening of 16 May orders for the attack arrived.

We did not know where the attack would lead us. As must be the case, the objectives are only made known day by day. In the army, it is unnecessary to rack your brains uselessly, nor to try to see farther than the immediate. For us the war, on 16 May 1942, was the Yablenskaya neck.

The offensive would began at 2:55 A.M. On our left wing, on the northeast side of the river, the German armor would attack en masse, roll past Yablenskaya, and then turn back toward the small valley.

We had to engage only part of our volunteers. Their job was to flush out the Russian defenders of Yablenskaya by challenging them from the front. But our attack would be only a feint. While the Soviet troops were being distracted by us, the tanks would carry out the principal assault against their northeast flank. The rest of our forces would temporarily hold their positions on the ridge, waiting to see what would happen.

* * * * *

The night of the 16-17 May flowed by, drop by drop, in extraordinary silence.

At 2:30 A.M. the very first rustlings of dawn grew audible.[1] Thousands of men, ready for the attack, held their breaths. Not a single rifle report broke the peace that accompanied the birth of the day.

Green and silver streaks spread slowly above the walls of the valley. Suddenly an unexpected song arose, in short, passionate, joyous bursts: "Cuckoo! Cuckoo!" A cuckoo sang! All for himself, above that valley where, at any moment, cannons would thunder and the awful face of Death loom forth!

"Cuckoo!"

Then the cry fell silent. The rumble of tank treads reverberated through the air. 17 May 1942. Five minutes before three in the morning. The Donets-Kharkov offensive had been unleashed.

## Yablenskaya

The beginning of an offensive suddenly drives thousands of men into a stupor, as if a hurricane were battering them.

On the morning of 17 May 1942, at 3:00 A.M., the Soviet troops of the Donets basin were obviously expecting nothing. They were all delighted about their Kharkov-Poltava offensive and couldn't imagine that the farther west their divisions raced, the faster they were hurrying to their destruction!

From the village of Yablenskaya, at the end of the valley, not a shot had been fired for quite some time. A night like any other was ending.

As soon as the noise of the German tanks spread, however, we saw a line of rounded backs moving about feverishly in the trenches of the small Soviet forts.

The tanks' mighty roar echoed off fields on the plateau. For about ten minutes, there was only that dramatic din of iron tank treads, as dawn broke, quite cool, orange and green in color. Then the artillery began to boom, hundreds of guns simultaneously.

From our posts on the hillside, we watched, amazed, as the shells hit home. The Soviet village was blown apart, turned inside out, blasted to smithereens, as if a giant had smashed it with a huge pickaxe.

Thereupon our men rushed forward into the little valley.

* * * * *

The slopes were bare and steep. At the bottom, the river flowed close to the enemy flank and skirted fields scattered with old abandoned haystacks. The avenue of attack narrowed, but then the fields widened out along the water, for 1500 meters, up to the first houses of Yablenskaya, perched on a spur of hill.

According to the plan, our volunteers were only to keep the enemys' hands full, to pin them down, while the tanks cleared the plateaus. But our boys were impetuous. Once thrown into the little valley, instead of stopping in time, taking cover in the ravines and harrassing the Russians from a distance, they continued to charge ahead, crossing about 1100 meters in a single bound.

We marveled at their courage, but, knowing the importance of the enemy position, we sensed an imminent catastrophe.

It was not slow in coming. The small plain across which our men sped was, in an instant, riddled with shells. The unfortunates scarcely slowed down in their charge. They had become entangled in lines of barbed wire, but they drove on toward Yablenskaya. We saw that, any second, a small number of them were going to reach the first houses.

Then the explosions around them blocked our view. Everywhere the ground exploded in large showers of dirt. Our men fell back in all directions. We thought they had been wiped out. Nearly all of them lay about motionless. Only a few wounded were crawling. We saw them, through our binoculars, curl themselves up behind a small fold in the terrain and try to unroll some bandages.

To go to their aid was impossible. The entrance to the pass was barred by a barrage of shells and grenades so intense that to advance that far would have been an unpardonable mistake.

* * * * *

Our soldiers were going to extricate themselves on their own, magnificently, without breaking and running. It took us quite a while before we discovered their stratagem.

Our binoculars went from one small haystack to the next, searching the small valley; it seemed to us that certain of those haystacks were no longer in the same place.We decided to focus on one haystack for several minutes. It was moving, beyond question: almost imperceptibly, but it was moving.

Some of our men, under the torrent of fire, had thrown themselves behind those piles of hay. They had crept under them; now, like tortoises, they were advancing toward the enemy in furtive movements.

It was a spectacle that was as funny as it was exciting. The Russians could not machine-gun the valley indefinitely. With each respite, the haystacks moved forward several meters. The movements were so cautious that we could only judge the result by establishing some points of reference.

Our soldier-tortoises must certainly have called softly to their comrades who, spread out in the middle of the rolling countryside, were pretending to be dead. Certain of them had, for an hour, remained as still as blocks of stone. But, when a haystack approached, a slight movement let the supposed corpse slip under the hay to join his comrades!

There were many haystacks; it was almost impossible for the Russians to get their bearings and discover which were those that hid the advance of our sly companions. At the end of two hours, the trick had succeeded completely. Most of our men had been able, under their novel camouflage, to reach the foot of the small ridges, a hundred meters from the enemy. Their machine guns began to blast the Red positions.

Throughout the morning, our men carried out out their mission beyond all expectations, ceaselessly raking the Russians with fire, forcing them to concentrate their forces at the neck, while along the hillside our tanks had moved forward several kilometers.

The German infantry followed the tanks. We saw them slip along the northeast embankment, with the admirable caution of German units, so different from the impetuousity of our Walloons, as spontaneous as young kids. After several hours, the thin green line of the Wehrmacht extended far into the area the Russians held. The Russians' situation at Yablenskaya seemed desperate.

* * * * *

They defended themselves with marvelous courage. Our machine guns battered their defenses. The German artillery poured hundreds of shells on them, with incredible precision, hitting the enemy bunkers dead center. We saw the shelters blow up and the isbas collapse. The Russians constantly came back, dug themselves into the ruins, reorganized their positions. A Soviet battery rushed forward from a village located three kilometers behind the lines. The German artillery found the range of their guns and caissons, which they pulverized on the road. In spite of that obstacle, Russian reinforcements came up constantly.

Then the German Stukas intervened.

During the winter battles, we had only rarely been supported by the Reich's air power. It appeared only in desperate situations, only a few planes at a time.

Now, in the sparkling sky, more than 60 Stukas wheeled above our heads! Sixty-four, to be exact, for our sector alone! It was grand. The whole sky sang with man-made power. The planes glided one behind the other, then swooped down like lead weights, sirens wailing. They pulled up at the last second, as a tremendous column of earth, men, and smashed roofs rose ten meters in the air. They came back, in impeccable order, turned magnificently, and once more began their dive.

With heroic tenacity, the Russians leaped from their ruins as soon as the Stukas had pulled away. Hunkering down, they curled up in new holes and resumed their fire.

* * * * *

Their incredible resistance ended at three o'clock that afternoon.

The tanks, followed by the infantry, came down the slopes behind the town of Yablenskaya. Our soldiers then leapt from their haystacks,loath to accord anyone else the honor of entering the burning town first. They threw themselves across the river and rushed the last Russian positions.

One of our companies, at the same time, surged down from our own positions and seized a village across from Yablenskaya, on the other side of the water.

The valley was open.

It was necessary to allow the conquered enemy no respite.

The fate of Yablenskaya must have spread terror in the Soviet rear echelons. The German command intended to profit from the situation at once. At eight o'clock in the evening, the second leap forward began.

Large, burning haystacks lit up the hills as we slipped through the Russian mine fields. Thousands of men advanced in this way, crawling along, since the bright flames drew sharp silhouettes. From time to time a soldier hit a mine and was thrown in the air, torn to pieces. In the valley artillery teams would be blown up, four or six horses at a time, along with their cannon. But it was necessary to advance to a new line of heights, eight kilometers farther east, before dawn.

By 4:00 A.M. we had reached our goal, where a dazzling surprise greeted us. The previous night the temperature had suddenly soared to over 40 degrees above zero centigrade; in one night, hundreds of cherry trees had burst into bloom in the valley. It was through a marvelous sea of white, fresh flowers that several thousand of us plunged toward the enemy.

## Fifty Degrees

The battle of Yablenskaya had been one component of the battle of Kharkov. All over the Donets pocket, the Soviet forces had been flushed out of hiding, overwhelmed, and pulverized, in exactly the same manner as in our sector. Everywhere the front, stabilized since the beginning of March, had been pierced by the tanks and Stukas. The fortifications of the Reds were, from then on, swamped under waves of attack. Where and how would the Soviets recoup their losses?

In fact, they were in full retreat throughout the entire Donets basin. On 18 May 1942, at the time of our morning thrust into the valley, we had only the rear guard and a few stragglers to confront. We followed hard on the heels of the enemy, dashing forward at full speed into the dusty steppe.

An annihilating sun had risen, sending the temperature soaring yet higher.

Marching briskly through a cloud of dust, three or four meters high, we passed hundreds of women and children in flight, peasant women in blue or red kerchiefs, bare-footed youngsters, cows dragging along their little calves so they wouldn't scamper away. They had piled up their meager possessions on their light carts, one or two baskets of wheat, a wooden kneading-trough, their scarlet quilts, the bucket from the well. We winked at the prettiest girls. The crowd deduced from this that we weren't cannibals, and it stopped. We sent it marching in the other direction again, toward the conquered villages, while the small calves snorted comically at the ends of their mother's tails.

We crossed twenty kilometers at full speed, covered with dust, licking lips that stood out, all red, on our black faces.

A cloud even higher than ours rose above the road. It was the cavalry, just as in the wars of the past! One of the Soviets' magnificent Cossack divisions was in full flight, and now the German cavalry streamed past us at a gallop, leading the chase.

We halted in villages redolent with the perfume of these softly rustling spring days. We took Communion under the cherry trees, as the sun's rays peeked playfully through a million fragile blossoms. The temperature rose to 55 degrees. That February we had experienced temperatures down to 42 below in the same region, a range of nearly 100 degrees centigrade! All in the same uniform . . .

The farmhouses gleamed beneath the budding leaves, resplendent with color: the grays and yellows of the thatch, the shutters in blue, green, or red, carved with doves and wildflowers. Pigs, pink and black, scampered through the yards. The women's eyes shone, glad to fear no more, glad to see so many young men.

After our arrival, we stripped down to our shorts and stretched out our pale bodies in the sun. The river was ice-cold, but we plunged in anyway, just for the thrill of it. We had conquered winter; now we surged with life! Backs offered to the radiant sun, drinking in its heat, we tanned ourselves and brimmed with a new vigor. Naked but for our shorts, we leaped on horses we had rounded up, exulting in our speed, our strength, and our youth, eyes blazing, masters of the steppe!

In the shadowy gorges of the little valleys, the snow was still piled in white clumps, but the sky was blue, the vanes of the windmills turned, the warblers chirped, we ate the petals of the cherry blossoms. The enemy was in flight.

We reached the forests.

Along the trails numerous corpses were rotting away. The battle had been fierce at the edge of these strongly defended forests. Pieces of Mongols and Tatars lay about, half decomposed, with yellowish larvae swarming from every orifice. As we rode forward, we stumbled on an abandoned Soviet camp.

The camp, carefully camouflaged under the trees, was remarkably laid out in passages lined with conical huts, like those of the Laplanders. The entrances to these simple lairs were tiny. Inside the Reds slept under piles of dead leaves. The winter must have been far more bearable there than in our battered isbas, their windows blown out by the bursting shells. Accommodations for the horses were ingeniously simple. It was nothing more nor less than the camp of a small Siberian tribe, men who knew much better than we did how to withstand the deadly winter.

The struggle in Russia was one between barbarians and civilized men. The barbarian would bed down anywhere, would eat anything. The civilized man was constrained by his habits, by his need for comfort, by his ignorance of nature. A pile of leaves is enough for a Tatar, a Samoyed, or a Mongol. But we others, we couldn't do without the toothbrushes which took two months to reach us!

The complicated trappings and the excess baggage of civilization would inevitably be beaten. And the man in the leaf piles, after having crossed thousands of kilometers having won the battles of the savage over the man of refinement, would end up marching, shaggy, overjoyed, under the glorious quadriga on Unter den Linden.[2]

* * * * *

We set up our small green tents in a section of the forest where there were not so many dead bodies.

The weather became chilly and rainy once again. We shivered under our soaked canvas.

Because of the war the forest had resumed the appearance of a jungle. Numerous horses, escaping the perils of combat, had reverted to their natural state. They lived a wild existence, far from men and isbas, in the dark shadows.

We lay in wait for them at the edge of the black ponds. Our men had changed into cowboys and brought off some very entertaining lasso tricks. They returned in triumph with prancing horses whose eyes flashed with pride and spirit.

Sometimes they caught a mare. From our tents, we would see a little trembling muzzle through the foliage. It would be a handsome colt, perhaps eight days old, who was looking for his mother, still unsteady on his long legs.

We adopted several of them. We never had to tie them up. They trotted and gamboled nicely along our line of march, their heads tossing, their eyes affectionate and unruly. When we stopped, they would stick their large necks under their mother's stomachs, drink for a long time, then look at us mischievously, licking their lips, as if to say: "That was awfully good!"

But the job of being cowboy was dangerous. Our forest stud farm still teemed with Soviet soldiers, hiding in the thickets. They had seen our riding school and stationed snipers near the ponds. Several men were killed or wounded, and we had to give up our new found vocation as tamers of wild horses.

* * * * *

It was our job to tame the Soviets.

One night the march began again, over chalky paths, white and damp. The vise was closing tighter. The Bolshevik divisions, cornered at Poltava, had fallen back to the east, struggling, battering in vain against the iron defensive walls of the Wehrmacht.

The German command feared a desperate thrust toward Izyum, on the Donets River, and had ordered us to take position athwart the projected line of Soviet attack. We were supplied with trucks so that we could move rapidly along the sector.

The Soviet troops were firmly surrounded, however. A few men tried to get through and were mowed down. Marshal Timoshenko's divisions, almost annihilated, fell back one after the other.

Across from us were two Cossack cavalry divisions. The Cossacks loved their mounts, high-strung little horses, ferret-eyed, half wild, with nostrils ever on the alert for the smells of the parched steppe. They hadn't wanted their mounts to fall as booty to the conqueror, so they drove them by the thousands into a small valley, where each man killed his companion of the road; in the end there were more than 12,000 bodies of horses piled up one next to the other.

The Cossacks came back alone.

The stench of 12,000 rotting carcasses soon became such that we had to shun that abattoir thereafter.

* * * * *

The battle was over.

The peasants returned to the fields, the beautiful, black, warm fields. They planted corn by hand, thrusting the seeds into the soil one by one. They sometimes stopped and launched into a chorus of passionate, quavering, sad songs.

New recruits had arrived from Belgium, hundreds of very young lads who regarded with curious and laughing eyes, these sunny villages, these vividly colored isbas, these robust, simple women and crying children.

All the squalor of Russia was painted over by spring.

We had combed the last Russian fugitives from the birch stands, when, one evening, in a torrential thunderstorm, we ascended the wooded bank of the Donets.

## The Banks of the Donets

Russian thunderstorms are apocalyptic.

The days of May and June are scorching. The entire country stifles in heat. But, after three days, the sky cracks, opens up and, in a quarter of an hour, transforms the fields and roads into ponds and black swamps.

A large offensive cannot be carried out at times like that. In July, in August, in September, the thunderstorms are less frequent, occurring every three weeks or so. At that time one can rush ahead, at the risk of stopping temporarily when the downpour comes.

The battle of Kharkov in May 1942 had been quick; the enemy had been thrown back to the valley of the Donets, from east of Kharkov to Izyum. On its new line it awaited the dry months.

We advanced to the river at the end of May. We spent half the night freeing ourselves from the mud on the road that led to the hills on the right bank. The unit strayed in the water-flooded woods. Not one ammunition cart could follow; the feet of the animals became mired in cement-like mud.

At about 1:00 A.M. we reached the top of the hills. From there we had to go back down to the steep banks of the Donets. To reach its positions, each company had to follow a little footpath in the forest which went up and down and back again, in a zig-zag pattern, for three kilometers. No one could see a thing; we were guided only by a telephone wire, a real Ariadne's thread which ran through the shadows and which each one held on to for dear life.

* * * * *

Our positions extended seven kilometers downstream from the town of Izyum, whose polished cupolas we saw glistening at the foot of the high, whitish cliffs.

The left wing of our sector was camouflaged by wooded, very steep hills, crossed by firebreaks fifty meters wide. To cross the open terrain, continually swept by Red fire, was almost impossible during the day.

Our foxholes ran down to the gray-green river, which flowed carelessly between banks of white sand. The woods, the steep bank and the path that led there were strewn with overturned carts, propaganda leaflets, and bags of mail.

The letters, folded into triangles, written clumsily in pencil, nearly all ended with pious advice and appeals for divine protection.

The soldiers' letters showed us—as did everything in European Russia—that, if the peasantry had suffered from communism, it had not in any way been influenced intellectually. Those simple and primitive farmers wrote exactly the same letters as in the time of the patriarchs and the czars, blessing their families, talking about their villages and their isbas. Not one letter-writer mentioned the name of Stalin.

These unfortunates, driven in herds by the *politruky,* * did not even know why they were fighting and asked only to return to their homes. It was only the relentless domination of the secret police in Moscow and the brutal terrorism which its secret agents exercised at the front that kept the muzhiks in place, drowned them in rivers of semi-savage Asiatics, drove several millions of them to their deaths, and regimented and politically poisoned the survivors.

Nevertheless, in 1942 the Russian peasants were still the peasants of 1912.

* * * * *

The sand on the bank was strewn with the bodies of men and horses which were rotting in the sun. The horses lay on their sides, ribcages protruding through rotting, grayish hides. Foul rodents swarmed in and out of dead soldiers' guts. The blackened bodies sometimes moved, as if they were still alive. At night all the vermin danced a macabre sarabande.

The Russians were lying in wait, a stone's throw from us, on the other side of the water. The left bank of the Donets was flat, but covered with a thick forest. Russian heads appeared and disappeared. The least carelessness, among them or among us, would cost a life. A burst of fire would flame through the green leaves; a man would fall, face down. They would half open his jacket, streaked with blood already drying: too late.

The river flowed majestically beneath the overhanging branches of the trees along the banks; the water shone, sparkled, a wonderful stream of clear and solemn life.

The forest hummed with voracious insects. Although we had received some small green mosquito nets which covered our faces, the bugs stung us in spite of everything, trembling with greed. Each morning we were disfigured by dozens of swellings.

Millions of pretty white flowers, wild strawberries, bloomed in the underbrush. Beyond the tall plants of the clearings slept innumerable little blue butterflies, very pale and soft in color. Spring thus lavished its beauty and its poetry, while at our feet the rapacious field mice rummaged about in the rotten entrails of the Soviet corpses.

We had some noisy neighbors: the Rumanians. Their officers came to join us sometimes, wearing caps that looked like tarts. Nearly all of them spoke a sing-song and lisping French.

Their soldiers produced an infernal din. There were more than 20,000 of them on our left wing. They fired their guns constantly. But we weren't under attack! We scorned their incessant, careless fire. It merely provoked the Russians, bringing needless reaction. In a single night, the Rumanians used up as many cartridges as all the rest of the sector did in two weeks. This was no longer war. It was a nocturnal disturbance of the peace.

The European legions ought to have been made up only of volunteers. Those who were, whether they were Norwegians, Swedes, Danes, Dutch, Swiss, Flemish, Walloons, French or Spaniards, fought magnificently, to the very last day. By contrast, involuntary participation brought disasters.

Thousands of Rumanian soldiers were subverted by communist propaganda. It could be seen clearly at the time of the tragedy of Stalingrad. It was against them and against the Italians—who had also come without enthusiasm—that Stalin very skillfully launched his attack in November 1942. He routed them as if he were bowling over toy soldiers.

The Rumanian soldiers had unquestionably performed many exploits since June 1941. They had liberated Bessarabia and conquered Odessa. They had fought gloriously in the Crimea and in the Donets. But they had a savage nature and massacred their prisoners, thus bringing about reprisals in which everyone suffered.

Their massacres were not only savage, they were stupid.

Many Russians asked only to surrender, disgusted as they were with communism, demoralized by a year of defeats. At night, from our little lookout posts, we would hear them moving aside the branches on the other side of the Donets. Holding our breaths, we would hear the splash of a body entering the water. As the man drew near, we murmured: *"Suda! Suda!"* ("Come! Come!"). Nearly naked, the Russian would emerge from the water. Then we'd take him away to warm himself up. A cigarette, and he regained the happy eyes of a good animal soothed. One hour later, he would tell us in detail everything that was taking place on the other side. He would leave with a supply train for the rear then, delighted at having seen the end of the war and of Bolshevism!

One night we fished out a young man who, in order to approach us more easily, had kept only his shorts. He held in his teeth one of the safe conduct passes which German planes dropped on the Red sector. Those little passes guaranteed the deserter's life, tempting the muzhiks and resulting in thousands of desertions.

The deserter that night had a lively face, with eyes that sparkled, but we couldn't succeed in making ourselves understood by him. Each of us had used the four words of Russian that he knew. Nothing worked. Finally, out of patience, one of our men spat out a resounding, "Merde!"

"Ah, well then, you are French, you people?" exclaimed the Russian, in a matchless Parisian accent.

He was in interpreter from the Intourist Agency! He had lived in Montmartre for several years. The expletive "Merde!" had suddenly brought him to the heights of lyricism! His delight was boundless. He had had it up to here with Soviet poverty. He told us a thousand priceless stories about our opponents. We gave him a shirt and a pair of hobnailed boots. Whistling to himself, he in turn left, carrying the cooks' empty kettles, in the direction of the general's command post.

* * * * *

Unfortunately, the Rumanians, in spite of our pleading, continued to massacre all the Russians who presented themselves at their posts. The poor devils who splashed about in the water, arms raised, were mowed down before they set foot on the bank; or, if they succeeded in getting through the bursts of gunfire, they were shot in the morning, amidst great gales of laughter. The Danubian assassins threw the bullet-riddled bodies back into the water, on which they floated mournfully down the Donets.

The Russians, squatting behind their branches, could see this macabre flotsam go by. After several days, they lost any taste for crossing the river. They became enraged, embittered, eager for revenge. We were going spend some busy weeks.

## Blood and Traps

The forest positions we occupied in June 1942 were relatively well camouflaged. There were ways of moving under the cover of the trees if you were careful. Nevertheless, the bullets whizzed by at random, crashing into an oak or drilling the back of an unfortunate soldier seated, for a moment, at the entrance to a shelter.

On the other hand, the closer our positions came to the town of Izyum, the barer was the terrain. Then the front spread out widely, for a kilometer, across marshes dried and cracking in the sun. Only a few clumps of filthy rushes populated these dismal low lands.

Our platoon of engineers set up in the center of this muddy lagoon, building positions in depth, from which our machine guns commanded the course of the Donets. These boys, covered with muck, dried by the heat, had become as black as moles. They were devoured by swarms of insects.

It was virtually impossible to approach their small forts during the day. I succeeded in doing it, one day at noon, only by running a mad race under the Russians' noses. I did it only to give confidence to our couriers. But the fire was so infernal that no one else dared trying it. We could only maintain liaison at night, after dark. Then several volunteers, loaded with sacks of bread, would venture out to the positions in the swamps. The positions were continually raked by bursts of fire, and constantly lit up by flares.

Some men crumpled to their knees. The dry bread was often soaked with the blood of a courier they carried back, sallow, his eyes haggard, clutching his stomach.

* * * * *

To the south of the belt formed by the marshes and the hazle trees there was some unused pasture land, then cultivated fields and a village.

At night our scouts would make their way from the edge of the hamlet to the river. They would withdraw just before dawn. It was then necessary, for fifteen hours, discreetly to play dead. To cross twenty meters, from one isba to another, was to throw away your life.

The scouts reached the town by crossing a long slope, extraordinarily bare.

Despite the fighting, the peasant women continued to work the soil. Between the Donets and the small market town, which is to say between the enemy and us, stretched two hundred meters of rich fields, bountifully fertile. The Ukrainians did not want to lose their harvest. We let them go to their lands and to their homes. The Reds tolerated, as we did, the humble labor of the village.

Between two lines of machine guns, fifty women busied themselves in the black fields. They were a distraction for the troops. A beautiful tall girl bending over and rising again is always a charming spectacle. We followed the movement of their hips, we heard their voices singing, inwardly rejoicing, but with our fingers on the trigger.

In the evenings, darkness fell at 9:00 P.M. It was necessary to protect oneself from the last rays which outlined the silhouettes on the hillside. At 10:00, our men would sneak out to the forward posts on the river bank. The trenches leading to the forward posts passed below some open sheds and zig-zagged through the rich fields. At the end, it was necessary to crawl for several dozen meters.

The Russians used various means to illuminate the area. They riddled the sky with rockets, a delightful fireworks display. They could not launch rockets every thirty seconds all along the sector, so they adopted a much simpler system. They fired incendiary bullets at two or three isbas until they burst into flames. Then the village burned until morning, like a mirror.

Those torches completely lit up the warm, clear nights. In order to move, we had to drag ourselves slowly along the fences, making long pauses while the bullets slapped the boards above our heads or threw clumps of dirt into our faces.

Our soldiers were posted near the Donets embankment, two or three men at a time, a hundred meters beyond the burning huts. They were at the mercy of surprise attacks and sometimes they were cut off. Then I would go from foxhole to foxhole to say hello. Slipping up to the edge of the water, I'd listen for a long time to the slightest sounds from the other bank. Often I heard Russians talking quietly, twenty meters away, unaware that someone, stretched out on the sand, lay in wait for them.

* * * * *

One evening a chaplain came at ten o'clock to say Mass at our command post.

That was fine. The telephone men, the cook, and the couriers were delighted. They were not the ones who had the most need of consolation, however. I suggested to the good father that he follow me to the forward posts.

He spent the night dragging himself on his stomach through the plowed fields. The bullets which snapped all around us affected him terribly. He tried to burrow into the ground. I had to come back to him.

"Chaplain, do you or do you not believe in heaven?"

"Yes . . ."

"Then, what worries you so much about going there?"

The fine man had to reaffirm his passion for celestial voyages and then set out once more, crawling right behind me.

Rockets danced above our heads. We had to hit the dirt. The bullets kicked up clumps of soil. We finally arrived at our lookouts' little foxholes.

I took over the machine gun from our comrades, who then went to confession and took communion behind me. I tried not to hear anything when their grave sins emerged. Then we departed for another trench, another foxhole, another filthy head, secretly transfigured by the little white Host which was elevated, for a moment, several dozen meters from the Bolsheviks.

The unfortunate chaplain could do no more, because of fatigue and emotion. We were nearly mowed down ten times. At 2:00 A.M. I led him back to the top of the slope. The weather was lovely and the day was already beginning to brighten. The priest cleaned himself off, and paid his thanks effusively to heaven: "Deo gratias! Deo gratias!" he repeated, tirelessly.

The saints who were on duty at night must have smiled sweetly from on high, at the lookout posts of heaven.

* * * * *

Twice, patrols of volunteers left our foxholes at night, crossed the Donets and, loaded with explosives, penetrated several kilometers behind the Russian bunkers to mine the railway which brought in their supplies.

We guessed that the Russians made identical excursions among us.

Our posts watched without respite. They were too far apart, so the enemy could slip between them. One night I received proof of that.

I had become the ordinance officer and had to maintain liaison between units. It was one in the morning. I was trying, with one of my men, to reach the southern extremity of our sector. We had to cross nearly two kilometers of clearings and bare hillocks separated by a little valley and a grove of trees. The Reds fired rocket after rocket. As one rocket finished burning, I told my companion: "Wait here. I'm going to run to the trees. If I make it, follow me at full speed."

Leaping out, I ran like the wind to the woods.

No sooner than I was at the wood when I cried out involuntarily. Then, throwing myself to the ground, I rolled 30 meters to the other side of the hillock. I had sensed a human presence at the very edge of the leafy blackness. Every fiber of my being told me, assured me that I had been within inches of the enemy.

I rejoined my comrade again after a long detour. Although I recounted the incident to the staff, they didn't believe me. I was certain, however; I'd sensed those spies with all my "electricity," more surely than if I had seen or touched them. Two days later, I was to be proved correct, in tragic fashion.

On that night, a patrol of four men from the 1st Company made an identical contact while coming from the other direction. Our men had unavoidably to pass by the grove. At the moment they reached it, a dozen Reds fired on them from ambush. One of our soldiers, whom the Russians had grabbed by the hair, succeeded in escaping, but he wrenched himself from the hands which held him with such force that he was horribly scalped. He ran like a madman, falling in front of one of our posts, where he lay motionless, his skull and face sticky with blood. The others, caught in the trap, fought in vain. The Reds dragged them to the Donets.

We heard their cries as they struggled and yelled in the water. But the Bolsheviks were three or four times more numerous and they wrestled our comrades to the far bank.

From the Soviet-held woods across the river, our unfortunate comrades still cried out. They must have been beaten terribly, but they continued to call for help.

Then the voices grew fainter, and at last died out.

A small tragedy, among the many others, from one night on the front. Soon the silent Donets, its gleaming waters troubled for only an instant, streamed silently past once more.

## Toward Asia

May 1942 had seen the battle of Donets-Kharkov unfold and witnessed the annihilation of the forces of Marshal Timoshenko.

In June 1942, the second great blow of the battering ram which was to break the Russian front in two, was struck; the German armies swooped down on the city of Voronezh, seized it, crossed the Don, and established a bridgehead on the left bank of the river.

Nearer to us, the Donets were likewise crossed and Kupyansk reached. Our front advanced to the other side of the water. Izyum was surrounded after a two days' march across the deep and burning sands. The bases for launching the great autumn offensive were ready.

The divisions which were to advance across the steppe were sent back to the rear areas to enjoy several days of rest (the only week of rest we were ever to experience on the eastern front). A brief march led us to our vacation village, some thirty kilometers to the northwest of Slavyansk.

* * * * *

Our relaxation was total. We quite properly had an official ceremony for the awarding of Iron Crosses to the heroes of the battles in the Donets.[3] General Rupp himself came to pin on the decorations. He commanded a celebrated division of rangers, the 97th, made up of Tirolians, among whom we were to spend some unforgettable months.

A marvelous reprovision was distributed to us, in great profusion. The musicians of the division diverted us with band concerts in the mornings, while each evening commodious buses took our men to the movies.

The village was wealthy, the peasants peaceful, the sky golden. The steppe was decked out in dazzling colors. As the women laid out the wheat in swaths, the air hummed with the laborious song of millions of bees. Above us, rapturous larks sang.

Keyed-up at the thought of the coming offensive, we breathed deeply of the steppe, like the mounts of the Cossacks. I myself had received a gigantic brown and white horse, almost unapproachable. Sure of the future, I called him Caucasus. He would accompany me there, that brave beast, and die there, riddled with twenty bullets, during the battle of Tjerjakov.

The news of the war was electrifying.

Marshal Rommel had swept 25,000 Englishmen into his net at the Libyan port of Tobruk. His tanks had cleared the shores of Libya, penetrating Egypt as far as El Alamein. We waited, crouched by our field radios, for the bulletin which would herald the fall of Alexandria.

Nearer to us, the German noose was tightening around Sevastopol. The last Soviet port in the Crimea saw its enormous fortifications annihilated, one by one, by the air power and the heavy artillery of the Reich.

Finally the city fell. The same evening, the sky flashed with hundreds of lights, while the whole region trembled with the roar of motors; a fabulous aerial flotilla, returning from Sevastopol, had landed in our sector.

Goering's Stukas were here. The offensive was imminent.

* * * * *

Secret orders informed our commander that the offensive would begin on 9 July.

We didn't have to wait that long because a surprise accelerated the operation. On the night of 6-7 July, German patrols in the Slavyansk sector, scouting out the Soviet lines, were astonished by the lack of activity which reigned there. They risked crawling farther forward. Silence was always very strange. One man spied out a bunker: it was empty. The entire line was empty! Stealing silently away, the Russians had vanished!

The Reds had to be pursued, caught, engaged, and defeated at all costs. Otherwise they could set a trap.

The order to go over to the attack was immediately communicated to all divisions. On the evening of 7 July 1942 the Wallonian Legion moved off with the entire army of the southeast front. It would stop again only at the threshold of Asia, before Mount Elbrus.

# Chapter Four
# TO THE CAUCASUS ON FOOT

The months of the summer offensive of 1942 were the most exciting months of the anti-Soviet war.

The South! Its dazzling fruits, its semi-tropical vegetation, its African sun, its great sparkling rivers!

Each one of us believed that victory lay at the end of that miraculous cavalcade. The Soviets had not even risen to the challenge. They were fleeing. At a mad pace, hundreds of thousands of men rushed off in pursuit of them.

By the morning of 8 July, our legion had passed Slavyansk and had reached, to the east of that city, a park where gigantic plane trees overshadowed the large ruined buildings, formerly sumptuous, of the old imperial palaces, in the salons of which the horses killed by the Bolsheviks lay about among heaps of dried horse manure.

The Donets had already been reached to the southeast of Slavyansk and the German engineers were busying themselves installing tow lines and ferries.

The next day we scaled the ridges on the right bank of the river, from which the Russians had been able to bar our passage. Their bunkers had been cut into the white chalk hills, the raw color of which dazzled the eyes. The positions were well constructed, commanding all the avenues of access, and were surrounded with dense networks of barbed wire.

The Reds had not even taken their equipment. They had not blown up a single shelter. They had decamped in total mystery.

At nightfall we descended to the bank of the Donets, but other units took priority in crossing.

* * * * *

We waited patiently for two days and two nights. The munitions convoys for the armored columns, sent as an advance guard, went first.

The ferries were formed by linking together a half-dozen rubber boats on which planks had been fitted. Cables ran from one bank to the other and were used to haul the barges.

It was amusing to watch. Panic-stricken horses and mules would often fall between the small boats. Then the towlines had to be cut, since the beasts, eyes rolling, would thrash wildly. Once freed, the animals would swim to the opposite bank, arriving before the boats, snorting, eyes flashing with triumph.

The sandy cliffs on the other side of the Donets made landing very difficult. Tractors were needed to pull the vehicles to the top of the ridge.

We pitched our little tents on the grass and philosophically waited our turn, while angling for fish with iridescent scales which rose unwisely to the surface.

At the end of two days, however, we became worried, because our division had had the chance to take the principal route, several kilometers above the Donets. Time passed. I went to prepare the quarters on the other bank, seven kilometers from the ferries. I was horrified. The trail had completely disappeared! Hundreds of tanks, trucks, and carts had churned up the burning sand, up to half a meter or a meter in depth. The tank on which I rode took several hours to advance: bogging down, then laboriously working free, just to cover a short distance. The sand was so fine that, even on foot, you sank to your knees in it.

We were dragging heavily loaded wagons and numerous small iron carts, with very low wheels attached to the sides, on which the heavy machine guns and the ammo boxes had been fitted.

I took care of the billeting, then waited at the edge of a village, at a fork in the road. I stayed on the lookout for exactly fifty-one hours, dead tired. I ended up believing that the battalion had lost its way or had taken another direction. But no; at the end of fifty-one hours, the first carts appeared. It had taken more than two days and two nights to push the vehicles through the sand, after carrying all the ammunition by hand, box by box, a kilometer.

We finally regained the main road, covering twenty kilometers in a fantastic cloud of dust, threading our way through thousands of trucks, gas tankers, sections of pontoon-bridges, and wagons of all kinds. When, worn out, sticky with sweat, we finally stopped, in the afternoon, we found out that we were three days behind.

At six o'clock in the evening, we started off again.

* * * * *

For two weeks we chased after the division.

We marched by night across an undulating steppe clothed with meter-high blue flowers, as white as camellias in the moonlight. Then we reached several small rivers flowing through blasted isbas. The Russians had blown up the bridges, so for several kilometers we had to follow the chalky river valleys, through the mud of which men and horses danced an exhausting waltz.

Then we plunged into the sands again. The main route was often blocked. We often had to make detours on paths that were scarcely marked out, intended only for the high-wheeled and very light carts of the Russian peasants.

We did not go into the isbas, unpleasant stuffy places buzzing with flies. We slept on the small terraces of hard-packed soil, curled up in blankets.

Soon we marched every night, taking a rest only in the middle of the day, since the sun then reached 55 degrees centigrade. We'd stretch out under a tree at the entrance to the farms, our heads in mosquito netting, our hands in our pockets, surrounded with cheeping baby chickens.

* * * * *

We passed long rows of worker housing, sinister blocks of apartment-barracks, and Party headquarters strewn with official papers and broken busts of the grandees of the regime.

According to their customary tactic, the Bolsheviks had demolished or put out of commission all industrial installations. And, what especially amazed us, those plunderers had destroyed everything some time before. The railway tracks had been cut every eight or ten meters. From all the evidence, the Soviets had undertaken this colossal sabotage well before the German thrust toward Voronezh.

The most spectacular destructions were the fires in the coal fields. Enormous deposits of coal and slag heaps thirty or forty meters high burned for days, a dark red, with deep blue and black reflections. Beneath the sun the fires generated a stunning heat.

It was impossible to stay away from them, since all of the area around the roads of sand had been mined by the enemy; numerous broken harnesses, and the monstrous carcasses of horses, gray-green, crawling with larvae, gave ample indication that the least carelessness would bring death. Our horses, in sand up to their hooves, floundered, struggled, snorted. Certain of them, whipped in vain, died standing upright, their coats smoking, eyes bulging from their heads.

It had been in vain for us to sweat blood and water, to sleep scarcely or not at all, to cross the steppe by moonlight, to pass like a whirlwind through the burning industrial basins, the chalky rivers and fords! We had covered hundreds of kilometers, left the Ukraine and entered the great bend of the Don, just across from Stalingrad. Our infantry division was always galloping faster then we were! We were now five days' march behind!

Two messages reached us simultaneously: first, the division was branching off to the southwest in order to participate in the final attack on Rostov; secondly, if we did not rejoin it in a very short time, it was going to ask the army corps to be relieved of our dead weight! We clung to that division because it was famous and because we wanted glory. We made some wild dashes and arrived once more at the Donets, an imposing Donets, just about to rejoin the Don, at Kamensk.

There still remained 70 kilometers to cover in order to reach the 97th Division. We covered it in a single day's march.

But Rostov had just fallen that very day. The 97th received the order to go back immediately up the course of the Don. We scarcely had time to shave. We were already leaving again, snatched up once more by the burning steppe.

## The Crossing of the Don

The triumphal march of the armies of the Reich toward Stalingrad and toward the Caucasus was at the cost of superhuman fatigue, but evoked an optimism as blazing as the firmament.

The lands between the Donets and the Don, between the Don and Kuban, unfurled such splendors that from dawn our spirits sang before the green and orange east. We would cross thirty or thirty-five kilometers on foot during the night. The marches were exhausting because we were moving forward in loose sand or on winding roads, two or three columns abreast, which constantly risked bumping up against one another. The advance was at the tempo of a bicycle race. The darkness couldn't prevent these thousands of men from converging at narrow bridges, thrown up in haste. We fell into holes. Our carts tipped over. Sometimes a truck or a tank would sweep up a horse which was crushed while neighing desperately.

But the dawn made up for everything else.

At about 1:30 in the morning, a few pale green and pale gold rays, as delicate as silk, appeared in the east. They rose in the sky, overran it, expanded, becoming fabulous sheets of green, orange, rose, vivid and marvelously delicate.

We witnessed the awakening of fantastic fields of sunflowers. These giant daisies, two meters high, had golden petals as long as the fingers of your hand and a brown center swollen with several thousand seeds. The same field would extend for kilometers; millions of heads rose toward the rising sun, turning at the same time it did, as if drawn upward by its strength. We felt our bodies seized by that elementary power which linked the soil, the sky, and the great efflorescence. The sky was nothing but a golden field. The earth was nothing but a golden field. Everything was life, strength, splendor, grandeur. With our collars open, breathing in those emanations, we hurled our youthful songs, bursting with dreams, toward the sun!

Sometimes the boundless sunflowers gave way to boundless thistles;

thistles to knock your eyes out, not at all our ridiculous little thistles which stain and sting, but thistles adorned like prickly pears, as tall as the ponies of the steppe, crowned, brimming with pink or violet flowers, the sweet and fragile plumes of which wound almost to the ground.

Crossing the sunflowers, the thistles, the corn, as straight and strong as lances, we arrived, at about 9:00 A.M., in a village that had glistened for a long time before our eyes and where our infantrymen scattered, overwhelmed by the sun.

The villages of the Don were wealthy. The isbas, more comfortable than those in the Donets, included up to three or four poorly furnished rooms, sometimes brightened up by a dresser, a sauce-boat, a kneading-trough or an old cupboard, magnificently carved.

Each farm had some hens, a few cattle, and a good ration of wheat, all reclaimed from the *kolkhoz,* whose despotic, ramshackle offices, surrounded by plows, haymakers, threshers, and sowing machines, dominated each small market town. The peasants had taken revenge on the regime, had emptied the cowbarns and the sheds; the piglets of the state-owned sows, set free, gamboled and frisked in all directions, delighted with this unforeseen holiday; everywhere geese honked and young turkeys gobbled.

The natives received us with obvious joy. Often we were the first troops to enter their hamlet. The good people immediately went to the outbuildings, removed their icons from their former hiding places, and hung them once more on their dried mud walls, tears streaming down their faces.

The greatest gift that one could confer on them was to give them a portrait of Hitler. Often they would hang it next to their icons. They would even put it between the photos of their boys, dressed in the uniform of the Soviet army, red stars on their caps!

Such photographic fraternization appeared perfectly natural to them. They loved their boys very much. They loved Hitler very much for having liberated their village. They combined the two.

Very strict orders had been given that the troops be friendly with the population. In 1941, the Germans had believed that they would find every Russian to be a Bolshevik. Experience had taught them that the muzhiks, if they had been plundered and held for ransom by the Soviets, had not been contaminated by them.

These were the most peaceful people in the world, friendly, very accommodating, asking only to work, to live as a family, to be of service. Germans in high places had finally made a distinction between the peasant masses of European Russia, so simple and naive, and the Bolshevik mafiosos and police of Moscow. The least abuse of them was stopped immediately; the old *pan** and the old *mamka** were friends of the troops.

It was pointless to ask the peasants for anything at all. They led us to the henhouses. They would offer us generous amounts of their chickens, their potatoes, and their fat geese. They had a thick honey, rich with the strong, wild perfumes of the giant flowers on the neighboring steppe. As avid for delicacies as gourmets, we whiled away hours in the cherry orchards, gorging on heart cherries, morellos, and white heart cherries which ran with crimson juice.

We slept for several hours; the sun restored our lost energy. The old *mamka* brought a large stoneware jug full of milk as fresh as spring water. Leading us to the threshold of her riches, a storehold, ten meters from the isba, she unlatched the trap door. Through the opening we went down a ladder into a magnificently cold cellar, a real well where everything perishable kept as well as in a refrigerator.

The stove was located near the door, so that the isba, with its small closed windows and its low roof, could stay cool. We ate outdoors under the shelter of the poplars or the acacia trees, encouraged by the peasant woman, who came back to us ten times, her arms loaded, and helped us truss up and brown the poultry.

Our soldiers, after the wearying night marches, recovered their strength with Breughel-like gusto. They were not for nothing the men of the land of kermesses. They were able to eat and drink prodigious amounts of food. I knew one who, when he arrived at the hamlet, regularly ate for breakfast a kilo of fried bacon. I saw two others gulp down a mere 21 chickens, from gizzard to tail feathers in three days. Many would devour a whole goose, just in case, at 9:00 in the morning. One of my young officers filled his belly one morning, before my very eyes, with thirty fried eggs.

They washed down these morning hunger chasers with a pitcher of milk, then slept, replete and unbuttoned, as in the old Flemish paintings.

At dusk, before we left, our hosts gave us several enormous pans of sauteed potatoes, bundles of large radishes, and baskets of vegetables.

The peasants accompanied us to the road out of the village, as impressed by our appetite as by our kindness.

During our entire offensive, we did not have a single untoward incident. We were received as part of the family. Not knowing how to say good-bye to us, those good people often blessed us. Protected by the blessings from their pure hearts, we set out again, happy, across the great fields of sunflowers.

* * * * *

Marching at top speed, we sometimes caught up with units of fleeing Reds. The battles were short.

The advance was carried out at such a pace that it was quite impossible to bury the remains of the enemy dead after each rout. The roads were littered with loathsome corpses. In the 50 °C heat the soldiers mowed down in front of us by the Stukas rotted and liquified in two or three days. Then the sun began to bake them. The dead horses gave off a dreadful smell. It was necessary to hold your nose for a hundred meters before you got to them. Each stomach was a monstrous balloon, often burst. Streams of greenish larvae swarmed in and out. The dead Bolsheviks shone blacker than Negroes as they putrefied.

Thousands, tens of thousands of Soviet soldiers surrendered. They could do no more. To tell the truth, we carried out the offensive much more with our feet than with our rifles. Many of our men, their feet sore, fell out. That hardly mattered. They would catch up to us later. The Soviet soldiers just let themselves be captured. They sat there by the thousands, sucking their bare and bloody toes.

Most of them were Asiatics. They had the good large heads of cannibals, delighted not to be eaten in their turn. They repeated tirelessly: "Stalin kaput! Stalin kaput!," stopping their monologue only to suck the swollen corns on their feet.

We hadn't the time either to guard or to escort such a caravan. Choosing the two most wide-awake fellows from the column, we gave them a rifle. Appointed to guard their comrades, they immediately threw out their chests. We pointed out to them the name of a town a hundred or two hundred kilometers to the west. Delighted, the simpletons set off, chattering.

The problem was solved. They were heading for Germany all by themselves!

We were about to cross the Don River. Some days before, we had tried to cross, but the access had been blocked, for a distance of two kilometers, by such a tangle of matériel and Soviet corpses battered by the Luftwaffe that the division couldn't get its vehicles and equipment across.

Approaching the legendary river at about two in the morning, we scaled a hill on the right bank, at the very moment when dawn was breaking over the vast gray-green stream.

Standing in my stirrups, I filled my eyes with an imposing view. The road was strewn with hundreds of Soviet tanks of American manufacture, overturned wagons, abandoned equipment. But I had eyes only for the Don, vast, tree-lined, glistening beneath the great green, pink, and silver curtains which billowed in the sky.

The Don, like all the great rivers of southern Russia, had a steep right bank, while the left bank was almost at water level. When the Reds were driven into a valley on the far side, it was impossible to resist whoever held the high ground on the right. The left bank of the Don was therefore at our mercy.

Russian planes dropped their bomb-loads into the red-soiled ravine by which we made our descent, but inflicted little damage. The burnished tendrils of the first vineyards shone amid the ruins of the isbas. Doffing his clothes, our commanding general became the first to swim the Don, a submachine gun on his back. We crossed over a hastily constructed pontoon bridge. Our hearts were soaring.

We were now approaching the land of the Kalmuks. A solitary camel came up to the road, droll, his nose huge and wet, his hide as shabby looking as the leather of an old armchair.

We adopted him. He smelled already of the Asia toward which we hurried.

## Kuban

The first week of August of 1942 saw the armies of the Reich fanning out from the Don toward the Caucasus. A dazzling sun beat down. The villages, several kilometers away, seemed one great smoking torch; you would have thought the whole region were ablaze. But the dark columns were only dust, stirred up by our advancing armor.

Our faces were gray-black masks, on which the whites of our eyes shone strangely, and which were crossed by our large pink lips. It was impossible to escape this "make-up": the dust rose several meters above our heads. Our motorcyclists looked like something out of a comedy film, their faces completely painted, as they roared out of clouds of dust bringing new maps. Our advance was so rapid that we needed new maps each day. Indeed, special trucks had been attached to our column to print maps as quickly as the offensive unrolled.

The smallest details were provided for with superb dispatch.

Each unit had its objectives, its villages to march through, its resting places to settle down in. Towns and hamlets fell by the thousands without the enemy being able to establish a single focus of resistance in our rear. We had only to pass through the towns, and whatever opposition remained was winkled out methodically, without a hitch or an oversight.

Our losses were insignificant. The thousands of Red soldiers whom we passed by were dead tired from having run for a thousand kilometers and from having swallowed so many kilos of dust. For a glass of water, they would willingly have turned over Stalin, Kalinin, Molotov and ten other lords of equally high lineage.

The most serious problem was, in fact, that of drinking water.

We would advance for ten or twenty kilometers without finding a liter of drinkable water. A few green pools stagnated in the sun. To lap up that foul mud, our men would throw themselves flat on their stomachs. We would lose our tempers and violently shove the drinkers aside The horses' long tongues hung down and quivered.

Our column alone consisted of more than 20,000 men. Every ten kilometers or so, the road passed through a village. There would be a well, or several wells, intended to supply water for the residents and the livestock of several dozen isbas. The vanguard of the column soon drank all the water. After a while the men had nothing more than mud to quarrel over. Behind them, thousands of infantrymen and hundreds of horses found that the wells had been drained to the last drop.

Here and there a mill drew up water in abundance. But everyone had to wait his turn for five hours, for eight hours, ten hours, his tongue swollen at the bottom of his throat. The animals consumed fabulous quantities of water. My horse Caucasus gulped down five large bucketfuls alone, or forty liters without a pause! The men filled themselves up like goatskin bottles, and sprinkled their necks, arms and backs, so scorched were they by the sun.

That did no good. The best thing was to drink very little and to be contented with here and there shaking a cherry tree.

The search for water took us more time than covering the kilometers did.

* * * * *

One night we arrived at the Manich, near the land of the Kalmuks, a river which forms a string of marvelous lakes, halfway between the Sea of Azov and the Caspian Sea.

Our line of march crossed a great dam built to hold back the waters of one of the lakes. The Reds had dynamited it, and water poured through a twenty-meter-wide breach across which the German engineers had built a wooden footbridge for the infantry and the horses. The heavy equipment had to go across by motor boat.

We spent several hours in front of the dike, waiting our turn. The lake was studded with a marvelous field of daisies sown by the moon on the little waves. A few Soviet planes tried to break our makeshift bridge, but their bombs served only to set fire to the nearby isbas. The burning huts lit red and orange torches in the night, which added their pathetic splendor to the poetry of the flowered lake and the starry sky.

Daybreak was at 2:00 A.M. The green sky was reflected by the countryside, flooded as far as the eye could see by the waters that had gushed forth from the dam. The waters bore the pale color of the dawn, a fresh aquamarine, laced with gleams of light gold, nearly translucent.

Who could have dwelt, in the presence of that enchantment, on the exhaustion of the night marches, on the mercilessly scorching days? The columns advanced, singing, in magnificent order. The officers marched at the front, on foot, to set a good example. Behind them, the stable-attendants led the horses. The mounts were used only for maintaining contact between units, often a very arduous ordeal. To reach a divisional command post, I once crossed a hundred kilometers in one stretch, at breakneck speed across the burning steppe. But the normal marches were made on foot, with officers and soldiers fraternally united in fatigue as in battle.

* * * * *

The mosquitos became more and more numerous. In the evening, they swirled in whirring clusters around the least candle light.

Other tiny beasts beset our soldiers: ferocious lice, which planted themselves in the region of the groin. They dug in in close ranks there, like stakes planted in the ground. One could see, just barely, the backs of those greedy suckers, the size of pinheads, all black.

The unfortunates who sustained that attack suffered torture. They had, in the bargain, to suffer the gibes of the entire column each time they ran out of patience and stopped at the side of the road to try to remove, out in the open, their indiscreet parasites!

On 7 August 1942, in the morning, we neared the Kuban. There still remained twenty kilometers to cross. We were going like the wind. At one in the afternoon, we caught sight of the cliffs above the right bank, which plunged perpendicularly to the flat steppes. The waters of the river, a magnificent green, gushed beside lush woods.

The Soviet artillery had tried to resist, but after a brief engagement it was forced to retreat.

We were in the heart of the Caucasus! The last great plain before the glaciers shone gleaming in the rays of a royal summer!

At three in the morning, we resumed our advance, marching back up the course of the Kuban in order to reach a ford downstream from Armavir. We advanced along ledges which fell straight down from a height of 200 meters to the green river. Thousands of us marched along the edge of those cliffs, jostled by hundreds and hundreds of large brown cows driven by Slovakian herdsmen with hard and sun-burned faces.

* * * * *

We had to mark time for thirty hours before crossing the pontoon footbridge which the engineers had built over the rushing river. The waters tossed, throwing green and white spray over the bridge.

There was a small market town on the other side of the water. There we discovered a pretty young girl of 17 who had taken refuge in a supply hole. She had wanted to guard the family isba. A bomb had fallen near her, horribly tearing away one breast. She lay there, feverish, her eyes blazing. Her slashed breast was already growing black. We did the impossible to care for her. Tears ran down her cheeks, red with fever. The poor little girl wanted to live. Looking at her injured chest, we knew however that she was going to die.

To die, when above the perfumed steppe there gleamed a sky divinely pure, without blemish, blue as far as the eye could see, crossed with ripples of silver and gold.

## Maikop

The Kuban River plain is the paradise of Russia. Agricultural holdings as big as 10,000 hectares produce, beneath the fires of the sun, immensities of corn. Millions of stalks, two meters high, thrust their marvelously ordered cobs into the burning air, wrapped in glossy husks, rustling as if an electric current were passing through them.

In the shadow of these forests of gilded stalks, we saw green watermelons ripening, watermelons as long as your arm. We cut them open with our knives. Rejoicing, we drank the fresh juice. The watermelons' skin was banded with green, red, and orange stripes, similar to the mottled dawn on the steppe. We marched on with our faces buried in enormous slices of those sublime fruits.

The sun burned in a sky clear to distraction. We gorged ourselves on its strength and its poetry. We were taking part in a wonderful exchange of strength, warmth and freshness, of colors springing from the soil and falling from the sky. Everything was new, primitive, pure, grand: the corn, standing like plumed spears; the melon beds tossed down by the gods like innumerable fountains; the bright, metallic clouds; golden earth, fiery sky, rainbow of gashed fruits!

* * * * *

The torrents also gave us inexpressible delights.

We reached the Laba River, which falls tumultuously from the slopes of the Elbrus. We could not yet discern the outline of the mountains, but they were sending us, as a first gift, large streams, green and ice-cold, which leaped over millions of red and reddish-brown pebbles.

What mattered the unending waits before crossing these rivers on our makeshift bridges! We threw ourselves into the turbulent waves, irresistibly strong. We were swept away between the great polished rocks, whipped by a current which splashed us with emerald spray. Our bodies loved the rough bite of those crystal clear waters. They hugged us, gave us life, purified our bodies, stirred our blood! Then we ran in the sun like wild horses!

Ah life! How magnificent! We hurled ourselves into its luminence, into its warmth, into its brilliance, into its spotless colors, as if we were leaping into the first days of the world, when base spirits and corrupt matter had not yet tarnished any element or any impulse!

* * * * *

The flight of the Soviet forces was such that we took hardly any prisoners. The steppe was empty, abandoned to the triumphant sun and to our victorious march.

One afternoon we reached the railway line from Maikop. Hundreds of Russian trains, abandoned, were lined up over a distance of twenty kilometers, car after car, along the two tracks. The Stukas had cut the line relentlessly, making it impossible for the trains trapped in that gigantic cul-de-sac to move forward or backward. Goods in incredible profusion were piled upon thousands of cars on which the Soviets had vainly tried to evacuate their goods. There were airplane engines, spare parts, unfinished tanks, machines, raw materials of all kinds. Lines of tank cars stretched out endlessly, scorched by fire or sticky from the hundreds of thousands of liters of gas spilled on the track.

But, on the whole, this fantastic plunder was nearly intact, except for the breaches made here and there by the Stukas. The Reds had not even taken the time to set fire to these enormous trains.

Each division, when it reached the railroad, immediately stuck on labels proclaiming its property rights to the spoils. The cars filled with alcohol were the object of very special attention.

We even found a stock of caviar jars. Sitting on the railway embankment, each of us spread a half kilo of those spendid eggs on our bread! Vodka was employed to ease our digestion; we had captured thirty thousand bottles of it, like mineral water in smart little bottles.

But there could be no question of lingering at these Capuan feasts.[1] Our orders were to reach the mountains as soon as possible. We were allowed only a few hours to sleep, right on the ground. We were awakened at 3:00 or 4:00 A.M. by the poultry of the neighborhood, greatly intrigued by all these events.

We reached the first hills, very steep, where, coming down the other side, the wagons plunged to the head of the line behind the horses.

We got under way in the cool of the day, at about one in the morning. At dawn, we thought we were dreaming. A slender dark blue thread, to the south, festooned the sky. It was the Caucasus!

The mountains were still fifty kilometers distant, but their summits stood out clearly against the sky. We were flooded with a joy which goaded us forward. There they were, the peaks which had lived in our imaginations for weeks!

We quickened our steps through the thick sands.

Columns of German tanks were heading back in our direction; they had completed their work, had tracked the enemy up to the forests. It was for us, the infantry, to complete the job. At nine o'clock in the morning, we arrived at long, straight streets: Maikop!

Our tanks had cleared the town without the Reds even being able to blow up the bridge which, in one magnificent leap, spanned a deep valley at the bottom of which roared a green river, the Belaya. A few houses were offhandedly perched at the top of the cliff. We promptly crossed over to the other side in order immediately to occupy a mountain which overlooked the region. From there, we could prevent an eventual reaction by the defeated enemy.

The slope was steep and heavily wooded. At last we saw trees again! Without any fighting we set up our machine guns on the ridges. To the south, there spread out before us a grand panorama of streams, small waterfalls, and plum-colored blue mountains. The Caucasus chain stretched out along the entire horizon.

A dense forest surrounded us. Numerous Soviet soldiers were still hidden there, watching for an opportunity to surrender.

The opportunity presented itself in a somewhat Rabelaisian fashion. One of our NCO's had crept off into the shadowy foliage in order to get away by himself, safe from prying eyes. With a piece of paper in his hands he set to work, at the same time admiring the foliage. He was not very dangerous, armed with only his quarter page of an old newspaper. This was the moment that the Russians had been waiting for. The leaves parted; our comrade saw a long line of Soviet soldiers approaching him, their hands up, sure of surrendering on the best terms. It only remained for our non-commissioned officer to hastily readjust a uniform whose prestige risked being seriously compromised!

Several minutes later he returned, snickering, followed by a veritable caravan of muzhiks, as solemn as popes in spite of the comical character of their surrender.

That was how we captured the last Russian forces in the oak grove at Maikop. It was not very poetic, to be sure, but the forest had been purged at the same time as our non-commissioned officer, a little embarrassed at first, but soon as proud as Artaban[2] about his adventure.

In the meantime, the bulk of the division had occupied Maikop. We all believed the war was over. Everything had been cleared, and we were about to cross the range of the Caucasus. The orders for the division had arrived. Objective: Adler, then Sukhumi, not far from the Turkish border.

We made some bets: Tiflis by Christmas; Babylon in the spring! On the banks of those sacred rivers, the Tigris and Euphrates, we would meet Marshal Rommel's Afrika Korps, advancing from the Suez Canal! The war would end in the cradle of civilization!

In order to celebrate 15 August (the Feast of the Ascension), the command had distributed to the troops a local drink like wine, in a ration of four liters per person. We swigged it, pouring it into our mouths quite confidently. It was alcohol from the fruit of the blackthorn tree, which had a terrible smell. Nevertheless the stuff promptly evoked an unparalleled enthusiasm. The party lasted until the wee hours of the morning.

Then, staggering a bit, the 97th Division and the Wallonian Legion moved off. 16 August 1942. The great mountains of the Caucasus looked down on us, blue-black at first, then white and pink, very high in the sky. Sukhumi, its coastline and its palm trees! Tiflis and its houses clinging to the cliffs of the Transcaucasus! The lunar lakes of Azerbaidzhan! The great declivity of the crystalline sand toward the Persian Gulf! Our eyes sparkled as we contemplated our mighty epic!

We arrived at a large green river which surged through the rubble of a dynamited bridge. A soldier advanced, straddling the jagged platform. A rifle shot rang out from a tree on the other side, the man fell into the river.

A second man tried. Then a third. They fell, hit in turn.

The mountains were still twenty kilometers away, but already the Caucasus was sending us a warning.

We had raced south for 1,150 kilometers. We believed that we had conquered everything. The three bodies bobbing in the torrents informed us suddenly that perhaps the war in the South, rather than ending, was just beginning.

## The Trap

The expectation of the High Command was that the troops taking part in the offensive on the Caucasus front would not encounter many obstacles. Each division had been assigned a fantastic area of operations. The 97th Division, to which we were tactically attached, would cross, with its two regiments of infantry and our legion, an area twice the size of Belgium! The mountains to be crossed rose to a height of 3,200 meters; the oak forests were nearly 200 kilometers deep.

One of the two regiments advanced immediately toward the west, in the direction of Tuapse. The other, the Otte regiment, to which we were attached, advanced through the forests in order to reach Adler on the Black Sea. The division commander very boldly advanced between those two thrusts, which diverged from one another more and more. He was covered only by a general staff company which had more specialists in pen-pushing and rubber-stamping than in machine guns and grenades.

Leap-frogging, the battalions relieved one another. Having been the advance guard at the time of the fall of Maikop, we were to form the rear guard during the first days of the advance into the mountains.

We skirmished with some Bolshevik soldiers who had returned to a market town. The peasants immediately rushed to call us, and the Reds were promptly disposed of.

On 18 August we attacked a village five hundred meters above us where the enemy forces, disregarded by the Otte regiment, had barricaded themselves. Two of our companies silently climbed up the height and engaged them in hand-to-hand combat. The Reds offered little resistance. They soon fled, leaving behind all their equipment .

Everything was going well.

By dint of incredible boldness the Otte regiment had in three days cleared a road of more than 150 kilometers through the jungle, the ravines, and the peaks. The news was excellent. The spearhead was no more than three kilometers from the road leading down to the Black Sea. Stupendous!

The fears of the first day had dissipated. Our turn to go to the front was coming. In one week, we would be at the threshold of Georgia!

That same evening everything changed.

Our regiment had penetrated very deeply into the mountains and was approaching its goal. To the rear, however, where the regiment was strung out along dozens of kilometers, the Soviets suddenly cut off the roads.

Lurking in the dark blackthorn trees, the Reds had let 2,000 men pass, and then closed the net. They had lain in wait in every ravine. Trying to retreat, the regiment fell into one snare after another. Now it risked disaster.

In the center, the general staff company which accompanied General Rupp and which advanced unescorted, several dozen kilometers away from the two infantry regiments, was cut off in turn. For several hours the general was surrounded in the village of Shirvanskaya. The old orderlies, the secretaries, the veterinarians, the supply sergeants were fighting as well as they could. But the approaches to the village were already in the hands of the Soviet troops.

The Reds also held the road which linked Shirvanskaya to the rear. There the Soviets had established a formidable position at the highest crossroads.

We received an urgent radio message ordering our legion to cover, that same night, twenty kilometers of mountains and then hurl itself at the enemy, flushing them from ambush and relieving the divisional command post at Shirvanskaya.

The night was as black as a shroud. There wasn't a star in the sky. After an hour of marching, it was impossible to continue. One of our men had badly injured his back, and several horses had fallen into precipices hundreds of meters deep.

* * * * *

At two in the morning we resumed the march. The dawn ambled up over the mountains behind large, threatening white clouds. We skirted very picturesque ravines, then entered forests of giant oaks. Some trees had recently been felled across the road. The enemy was on the prowl. We advanced, our fingers on our triggers.

The heat was stifling. A thunder storm rumbled in the sky. At about ten in the morning, on the bare side of the mountain opposite us, we caught sight of the white village of Prussskaya, our last resting place before contact with the enemy.

Then came the deluge, a thunderous torrent from the firmament which fell in sledgehammer blows. In an instant, we were as soaked as if we had fallen into a river. After we reached the first isbas, a clayey mud, fifteen centimeters deep, virtually barred any forward movement by our column.

We *had* to move forward, however. We slogged on ahead.

Two German officers rushed toward us, on foot. Their cars, together with several other vehicles, had blundered into the Russian positions before the thunderstorm. They had been able to escape only after a furious hand-to-hand struggle.

The rain stopped. The valleys steamed with mighty vapors swirling from the depths, slowly reaching crests where the sun, here and there, gilded the newly washed grass.

We did two more kilometers, our feet encased in large clumps of mud. Then we had to take cover. We had arrived before the mountain occupied by the Soviets. We watched the road rise, turn, and plunge into the forest. The entire summit was wooded. An oak grove descended to the south-east and then back up to the summit of an impressive mountain.

Our commander gave the combat orders to the three columns which were about to spring to the attack. We knew very little about the enemy, except that he disposed of two infantry battalions and a squadron of cavalry; that he had artillery, motorized transport, and some captured anti-tank guns. He remained absolutely silent. He doubtless thought that, ignorant of the site, we too were going to throw ourselves into his trap.

When the Reds saw our companies deploying, however, they grasped our intentions.

* * * * *

We were able to descend the slope without difficulty. Not a rifle shot broke the strange silence of the valley. Two cars burning at the top of the mountain were all that spoiled the scene.

We wanted to advance up to a thicket on a small knoll. There we would find temporary cover.

I crawled toward the knoll, moving forward through a tangle of brushwood, supporting myself on my left elbow, my revolver in my right hand. Twenty meters behind me, the men waited.

I reached the crest of the hillock; one jump away from me, a Russian officer was crawling forward flat on his stomach, exactly as I was doing! We fired simultaneously. His bullet whistled by my ear. Mine hit my luckless adversary right in the middle of the face. The battle for Prusskaya was on.

## Prusskaya

The crossroads that we had to attack, between Prusskaya and Shirvanskaya, on the afternoon of 19 August 1942, was approached by rolling vales with only a few trees. We rushed toward the bulk of the enemy, descending the slope by throwing ourselves to the ground every fifteen or twenty meters, at each fold in the terrain or every plum tree or two.

Before us, the slope rose again, nearly bare. When the Russians saw we were reaching the bottom of the valley, they had a diabolical inspiration. Setting fire to some German ammunition wagons they'd gotten hold of, they pushed them down toward us. These monsters rattled down the slope at a mad speed, while the burning ammunition exploded in all directions. Our noses glued to the ground, we were pinned down by a thousand blazing fragments.

The frontal attack promised to be lethal. Therefore, I took three volunteers, all of them expert in combat; while the companies advanced as well as they could, I threaded my way along the right flank, reaching some holly groves, then the forest, and succeeded in crawling between the first Russian posts. My three lads followed me at a distance of ten meters. I wanted to flank the enemy. I arrived right behind him: I could see the Soviet camp through the branches.

At that very moment, our men were scaling the slopes to attack the Reds. This was it! I leaped out behind the Bolsheviks, raking them with machine gun bursts and unleashing bloodcurdling shouts. My companions stormed right behind me into the middle of the camp with a similar uproar.

Panic reigned. The Reds, believing themselves cornered, ran about in circles, finally fleeing in utter confusion into the ravine to the southwest. They had gone completely mad. The four of us alone had chased them from their lair; all their trucks were ours, magnificent Ford trucks, drawn up in a square, keys still in the ignition! The cannons which had shelled us were also in our hands, as well as ten machine guns! Supplies, equipment, ammunition, helmets overflowing with fruit, nothing was lacking! Our cries and our bursts of fire, exploding suddenly behind them, had been enough to convince several hundred Reds of disaster and to drive them across the plateau!

We sped after them, howling all the louder and shooting off all our machine gun clips. Shortly afterwards, one of our companies, arriving on the double, met us at the crossroads.

* * * * *

We couldn't let the Soviet troops tumbling down through the forest get away. We were ordered to hunt them down and destroy them.

At first they did us some damage, killing one of our most brilliant comrades, a young doctor of philology, who took five bullets through his chest. But our elan was irresistible. Tossing grenades, we captured an anti-tank gun the Russians were trying to pull into the oak grove, along the muddy path. We reached the bottom of the valley, a veritable equatorial jungle. It was flooded by the waters of the morning thunderstorm and cut by steep ravines, ten or fifteen meters deep, as straight as trees.

We had to slide down on our heels. To go back up the other slope we hung on to stumps and roots. The thick vegetation gave off intoxicating aromas. Hundreds of bees, whose swarms had been put to flight in the course of the battle, buzzed around, mad with rage. I had exhausted all of my machine guns's ammuntion. For hand-to-hand fighting, I had only my revolver and twenty cartridges. We ran from tree to tree, overwhelming the enemy in the mud and the brambles. We chased the bulk of his forces back up the other side of the mountain, which was very steep, completely bare, and split by a wide muddy trail. The Reds rushed there in disorder.

In the meantime, the German artillery which supported us had reached the captured crossroads. It set up its guns just across from the Reds' road. The Russian cavalry, unable to fight in the underbrush and the thick woods, tried to save their animals, sliding, falling in the slippery mud. One couldn't have dreamed of a clearer target. The German shells tore into them, ripping the fleeing troops and the tumbling animals to shreds. The Bolsheviks were running away in all directions, relentlessly plastered by hundreds of shells.

Our rocket launchers chimed in. The Soviet column was practically wiped out. Many Russians however, whom we passed by, remained in the thickets and in the dark recesses of the little valleys.

We had raced too far, caught up in the frenzy of pursuit. Now, almost out of ammunition, the fugitives annihilated, we wanted to return to our unit.

But we found ourselves in the middle of a jungle. We had thrown ourselves at the enemy without paying much attention to the direction of the battle. Scarcely had we gone back a hundred meters when a burst of machine gun fire cut our path; the Bolsheviks were in the bushes! We ran into them repeatedly. They fired, thinking they were surrounded. Each time, we scattered into the thick groves of blackberry bushes, where we were hampered by the spongy ground.

My clothes were cut to shreds. Of my riding breeches, split from the top to the bottom of the crotch, there remained only two muddy skirts. This, however, was the only comic aspect of the situation. Dusk had fallen and we could no longer make out a thing. Crossing the ravines, which ran perpendicularly, was a terrifying operation. We could see the moment when we would be overtaken by night in the labyrinthine holly groves, surrounded by Russian ambushes.

We must have been about two kilometers from the rest of the battalion. I gathered together everyone with me and, at the risk of drawing all the enemies scattered through the woods, I gave out, in a thundering voice, great shouts through woods full of darkness and water. We listened anxiously. We heard voices answer, from a distance, almost inaudible. We advanced towards them.

The Russians, badly burned, mustn't have been in any better position that we were. They had also been cut off. From time to time we stopped to take a breather and to cry out again. We were answered more clearly. The direction was right. From ravine to ravine, from mire to mire, we got closer. Mixed voices hailed us. It was one of our patrols: we were saved.

We re-formed in the dark of night.

The enemy no longer offered the least resistance. Undoubtedly, the groups scattered in the forest, or in the mudholes of the little valley were fleeing toward the southwest, trying to rejoin their battalions, decimated by our attack. We advanced directly south, marching through muddy water. At one o'clock in the morning, our lead column entered Shirvanskaya without any difficulties.

On the next day we buried our dead. We heaped their grave mounds with golden sunflowers, flowers of greatness and glory.

The mud was so bad that no one was any longer able to move, unless by horse. For two days I rode nearly naked on my horse, while they tried to clean and sew up my clothes, torn to pieces during the hand-to-hand combat. Our soldiers stood guard without shoes, barefoot in twenty centimeters of water. Not one motorcyclist could move about in the region.

On the afternoon of 20 August the sun beat down mercilessly. At dusk it ignited great conflagrations of purple and gold. Good weather meant combat; new battles were at hand.

## Tyeryakov

Our march across the Caucasus resumed on 21 August 1942, early in the morning. Over a small bridge that had been hastily built by the engineers we crossed a leaping river, then we entered the forest. After several kilometers of climbing we saw a clearing and some isbas. A few Soviet soldiers fled without firing a rifle shot. The village was called Paparotni. Beautiful vines, apple orchards, and blackthorn groves spread out in the sun.

We had to advance a dozen kilometers to the village of Tyeryakov. At Paparotni, a radiotelegram reported the situation to our commander: "Tyeryakov strongly occupied by the enemy." Leaving our supply train and our heavy equipment in a clearing, we started cautiously through the giant oaks and the brushwood.

From the top of a ridge we could see, through a gap to our right, a long village held by the Russians. We followed a faint path, overgrown with grass and weeds. According to our maps Tyeryakov wasn't much farther. We left the trail and moved forward through the foliage, following our compass, for twenty minutes.

We then heard the a cock crow.

It was Tyeryakov.

* * * * *

A patrol was sent out to reconnoiter. Creeping under the trees and between the large brown crags, it neared the edge of the forest. Situated on a broad hillock, Tyeryakov shone over the mountain pass. The village was spacious, but entirely surrounded by corn which, two or three meters high, came up to the thatched roofs. A white school was perched on a mountain spur. Right below the village, at the edge of our forest, lay the *kolkhoz.*

The men of our patrol didn't miss a detail of the scene. Twenty meters in front of them, three Russians were moving back and forth around a field kitchen. They were laughing loudly, telling each other jokes, hardly suspecting what was awaiting them. Our men crawled up to the tree line, approached without being seen and, suddenly, thrust their revolvers under the noses of the cooks!

Not one of the three dared to utter a sound or make a move. Our patrol immediately pushed the cooks in front of them as far as the oak grove and from there led them to us without a single shot being fired.

One of the Russians had in his pocket the roster of the men to be fed that evening: 304 men. We could not have had better intelligence! We learned also that the enemy had artillery and anti-tank guns.

* * * * *

We had finished interrogating our three Stalinist Vatels when an outburst of gunfire erupted thirty meters from us.[3] The Russians had returned our courtesy.

Unquestionably, one of their men, passing by the roasting spits, had found the abandoned kitchen. The alert had been given. Some Reds had silently moved forward in search of us at the edge of the woods, in order to catch us napping. One of our non-commissioned officers noticed them just in time. Firing his machine gun, he was riddled with Soviet bullets. His lungs punctured, vomiting large amounts of blood, he nevertheless continued to fire. There had been a moment of panic among us. The heroism of that NCO allowed the men to regroup. The wounded man collapsed only after we leaped over him into a hand-to-hand struggle.

The two companies who had been charged with attacking the village were sent into combat without further delay. Since we'd been spotted it was better to get it over with immediately.

As aide-de-camp, it was my job to give encouragement in the places where the attack was heavy or where the men were wavering.

One part of our troops was to attack the village through the *kolkhoz*, while the other would take the long way around so as to overrun Tyeryakov from the heights. The men were in a tight spot. For many of the new recruits, this was their baptism of fire. We saw that they hesitated to move away from the rocks and the trees.

Six more determined soldiers, armed with submachine guns, had reached the corner of a shed in the *kolkhoz*. With a machine gun in my hands, I ran up close to them. In a few minutes, alternating our fire, we got a hundred meters inside of Tyeryakov itself. Our anti-tank gun, unfortunately, was firing short, and its shells were exploding above our heads.

The Reds had occupied an isba from which they held the street under fire. While my comrades fired their weapons at the hut, I leaped through the corn, reaching the west side of the isba. Jumping up to the side window of the isba, I broke it completely as I stuck my machine gun through it. My burst of fire into the middle of the room had an overwhelming effect. I rounded up the survivors, who surrendered. One woman who was fighting with the Reds was rolling on the ground, in the middle of an attack of hysteria.

Standing, firing my machine gun, I had stormed into the village in pursuit of the Soviet soldiers. Soon I had a veritable mob of prisoners around me. Not knowing what to do with them, I distributed to each of them a piece of a Brussels newspaper for which I had prosaically devised uses other than the nourishment of the mind. *"Dokument! Dokument!"* I yelled to each of my captives. Those heavy-jowled asses believed in the magic of the *Dokument.* With their hands raised, brandishing their papers, they all ran to the rear, where people were at first a little surprised to discover so many Mongolian readers of the Belgian press, but where they finally understood that they must have first been met by some ingenious and efficient Walloons.

In close combat, it's best to run in short, speedy bursts. I ran to the end of the village, firing into each window as I went. I stopped only beyond the town, while my six daredevils flushed out the Bolsheviks who had taken refuge in the isbas and the stables. Many others emerged from the fields and the corn of their own accord.

My machine gun was well positioned. At the end of the twenty minutes, an entire Walloon company was able to reach me. Our comrades attacking from the heights joined us in turn.

Not only were we able to gather up a long line of prisoners, but we captured the Russians' cannons and anti-tank weapons in perfect condition, supplied with abundant ammunition.

Wisecracking, we visited the *kolkhoz.* The mobile kitchens of the Soviets were still there, stocked with a magnificent soup, ready to eat, and an enormous vat of porridge. A cart had been left behind, filled with hundreds of large pancakes. We returned the cooks to their ovens and to their ladles. They were delighted to resume their jobs. Never had they made their soup in such lively circumstances! Bolsheviks at one moment, then prisoners being slapped around, then promoted to honorary Walloons! All in less than an hour! Their soup had not even had time to burn. Their little teeth shone with pleasure in their wide saffron-colored faces. How comic life was!

We were all overjoyed. The village had been conquered merrily, easily, colorfully, with a maximum of profit. We drank soup and porridge seasoned by our latest exploit. We ourselves were astonished that all had gone so quickly and so well.

Too quickly! And too well! Because the bullets began to whine again, a few at first, then hundreds.

We barely had time to hit the dirt, behind some tree trunks, among the overturned mess-kits. What was going on?

We looked at each other, bewildered.

Dusk was falling. Large black eagles circled, screaming ominously above the small valley. A harassing fire was now springing up all along the forest which plunged from the south to the cornfields of Tyeryakov.

## Bloody Gorge

For two hundred men to find themselves at nightfall at the bottom of a gorge, to sense themselves boxed in on all sides by the high Caucasian mountains, black and violet to the east, edged with reddish gold to the west, all equally inhuman and treacherous, being shot at by a thousand invisible enemies crouched in the thickly wooded country, all of that was hardly comforting to us on 21 August 1942, at eight o'clock in the evening.

Fortunately, as soon as we took Tyeryakov we had established a perimeter at the edge of the corn fields, all along the thicket. There our pickets valiantly absorbed the first blow.

We organized ourselves promptly for battle, but the enemy was there in force. We were machine-gunned by attackers who dominated the heights. In the twinkling of an eye we brought up our anti-tank guns and fired them point blank at the Russians fanning out en masse, fifty meters in front of us, at the edge of the woods. Our shells came crashing down on the tree line like bright red fireballs. The weapons we captured from the enemy joined in. That rain of iron blunted the Soviet attack. A savage battle, fought at close quarters, raged for the next five hours. Only one of our posts fell; there our comrades were massacred at their weapons. The rest held out.

Finally, at about midnight, the enemy fire tapered off, then stopped. We sent some patrols into the trees. Our men stepped over numerous bodies, but the Soviet forces had pulled back, had disappeared.

* * * * *

At 1:00 in the morning, another firefight broke out, this time to the north beyond the *kolkhoz,* in the forest under the cover of which we had approached Tyeryakov in the afternoon. There an extremely violent struggle was taking place in the vicinity of the crude forest road coming from Paparotni.

We experienced real mental torture. The rest of the legion, including all our equipment, had been ordered to join us. It was they who were fighting, without a doubt.

A couple of couriers reached us, wide-eyed. The column had suddenly been attacked from behind by hundreds of Russians attempting to cut the long line of transport. Both sides machine-gunned each other at point-blank range, but on the whole it seemed our people were holding.

We rushed everything we had in the direction of the brawl. At about 3:00

A.M. the battle ended, just as our men and our trucks arrived in a grand procession.

It was a question of who could recount the more extraordinary exploits. The wounded were the most voluble, tossing on their blood-red straw, adding a thousand more wry laughable details to the stories of the troops. No one understood what could have happened, where the Russians had come from, why they had thrown themselves so desperately against our convoy.

It took the interrogations of the prisoners to enlighten us. They had been part of a reinforced regiment which was in retreat. Tyeryakov had been pointed out to them as a friendly position. At dusk, with no special care, they had approached the village a half-hour after we had finished capturing it. They had tried for five hours to force their way through, all in vain. Their losses had been heavy. Their regimental command post had been hit, point blank, by one of our anti-tank shells. Finally, not able to get through, they had disengaged and tried to go around the village to the north. Their streak of bad luck continued: they blundered right in to the middle of our column of reinforcements and supplies

At first, they put it in great danger, but there also the tenaciousness of our men blocked their passage. Not knowing how large our force was, disoriented and exhausted, they fell back a second time in great disorder.

During the rest of the night, we heard a column jolting along far to the south. Those were the remnants of the Soviet regiment moving away with their carts over the forest paths.

At day break we went to repair and put back into action vehicles of which the animals had been killed. The scene bespoke the savage violence of the melee. Two Russian officers, killed on our horses and riddled with a dozen bullets, still held machine guns clasped in their yellowish hands.

We buried our dead near the school. The piled up earth was covered with the usual bright sunflowers. Not one shellburst troubled the peace of the valley.

It was Sunday. The mountain scenery was spectacular. We spent the day drinking in the sunlight and the color. An incredible sunset, with long gleams of red, gold, and violet beams crossed by pink clouds spread for a long time above the ridges while, at the bottom of the gorge, we were already sunk in the blue and velvety shadows of evening.

The night did not last long.

It was perhaps 3:30 A.M. No one had heard so much as a piece of dead wood break. However, gliding on their light sandals made of pig-skin, hundreds of Bolsheviks had arrived quite near the corn below the town. A terrible yelling wrenched us out of our half-sleep: "Ourra! Pobyeda!" ("Hurray! Victory!") cried the two Soviet battalions which threw themselves at our posts. Hundreds of snarling enemies ran through the corn and reached the isbas. A terrible fray, illuminated by the tracer rounds, locked our soldiers in mortal combat with the attackers. They exchanged bursts of machine gun fire in the stables, where the horses fell as if pole-axed.

Ah! What a terrible hour! When would the dawn break so we could regroup? Would we not be overwhelmed before then?

Firing away, we watched the damnable crests. They finally began to brighten and cast pale gleams into the little valley. The enemy was everywhere, yet no essential position had given way. Even at the edge of the forest our posts were resisting furiously.

The Red forces trying to throttle the German units engaged in the forests of the Caucasus were made up of shock battalions consisting of the most fanatical Bolsheviks, who had fallen back from the Donets to the Caucasus. They were reinforced by hundreds of cut-throats, common criminals freed from the penitentiaries. These were followed by a wave of half-savages hastily scraped together by the Soviet authorities in Azerbaidzhan and among the Kirghiz. The two battalions which attacked us that night ought to have pulverized us. They succeeded only in capturing a few isbas. From there they had to clamber up fifty meters if they wanted to reach the ledge on which we were perched. Our machine guns swept away each of their attacks.

A third Soviet battalion settled down about noon on the other slope, to the east, in the oak groves which completely dominated the village and our positions. That battalion had a very special armament: only mortars, no larger than a woman's umbrella. But a hundred such mortars were a catastrophe for the fighting men who found themselves at their mercy.

* * * * *

Throughout Monday the Russians multiplied their attacks.

We held out against them only with great difficulty. Dozens of men had to leave us to drag themselves to the first-aid post. We were surrounded by the bodies of our comrades, disfigured by the abominable explosive bullets of the Soviets, which tore off half the head, or blew it off entirely.

We were almost encircled. In the little valley there remained in our hands only the *kolkhoz* and a gorge to the north through which, at certain moments of lull in the battle, we could send our wounded to the rear.

The Reds had captured the lower part of the village. They occupied all the woods which ran down towards us from the south, the east and the west. To hem us in for good it remained only for them to seize the *kolkhoz* and the gorge to the north. At five o'clock in the afternoon, several hundred of them poured out of the forest and threw themselves at the *kolkhoz* offices located forty meters below our ledge.

We shot off our machine guns like madmen. But we were not able to prevent the mass of the Reds from bursting into the building. Night was falling. If the *kolkhoz* remained in enemy hands, the night would see the Soviet convicts and the hordes from Kirghiz complete our encirclement.

It was necessary to drive them out, at all costs, before darkness came. We hastily dragged two anti-tank weapons to the very edge of the parapet and, in spite of the hail of bullets and grenades from the Russians, we unleashed a hailstorm of fire, almost straight down, right onto the roofs of the *kolkhoz*. Ten, twenty, fifty shells flew, blasting in the roof, and throwing up enormous swirls of dust and flames.

The Reds saved themselves by leaping into the corn and fleeing towards the woods. The *kolkhoz* was once more in our hands. Our men settled down there again, in an extraordinary tangle of Bolshevik bodies, disemboweled horses, and fallen beams.

## One Hundred and Twenty-Six Hours

Our battle for Tyeryakov lasted for 126 hours, 126 hours during which hand-to-hand combat was almost ceaseless, except for the several hours when the night raised to the very top to the mountains an extraordinary orange moon. Its reddish gleams animated the night with fairy-like life. The clouds had the grace of flowers and the softness of silk draperies.

The lights floated between the summits and barely reached our slope, boxed in at the bottom of our narrow valley. We benefited from that short calm to hastily dig up the chalky soil. We laid there the stiff bodies of dozens of our comrades whose arms we had crossed, like the stone tomb figures in our old cathedrals. We were torn by grief as we threw the shovelfuls of dirt that covered first their legs, then their chests; at last the face had to disappear. We did it quickly, for each of the dead was a brother, a companion in our suffering, our glory, and our faith.

We used the rest of the night to cut down the corn between our posts and the woods. The heavy husks were a half meter taller than our heads and allowed the Reds to approach us without being seen and to surprise us at any moment. We crawled through the darkness, armed with pruning knives. In several nights we cleared the whole area, meter by meter.

It was a disagreeable job, because the Reds were also moving around. A few meetings took place, disturbing the entire surrounding area. From 4:00 A.M., however, it was necessary to go to ground in our little bunkers. The first green rifts in the night appeared between the notches in the mountains and began to caress the golden heads of the sunflowers strewn on the newly dug graves from the night before. At that hour there was generally a full brawl already in progress.

* * * * *

Our plight in Tyeryakov became ever more desperate. Our positions had contracted terribly, leaving us no place to fall back further. We had to prepare an attempt to break the stranglehold. We decided to strike a heavy blow to the southwest, below the village, where the enemy had shown himself most aggressive. The *kolkhoz* was still within reach of his attacks, and each night we risked being overwhelmed, then wiped out on our knoll.

To counterattack the Reds by plunging straight down on them was to resign ourselves to losing half of the battalion. The result would be minimal, as well: a hundred meters from the isbas, at the end of the cornfield, there was a river, beyond which the woods sloped up. We could never have crossed the water, nor could we have ever cleared that height by a frontal assault.

We made an appeal for volunteers to sew the skin of the fox to that of the lion. The commander of the legion and I had formulated a very bold solution: to slip through the little defile to the north, then advance far to the west, across the woods, behind the Reds, finally to catch them unawares and drive them against our lines in Tyeryakov.

The impossible strokes are those which always succeed, because no one thinks of protecting oneself against them. Some lads from the company of the Rexist Youth descended into the ravine, penetrating the Reds' sector under cover of the trees. Two hours passed during which we awaited their attack.

It didn't take place. At the beginning of the afternoon, our lads reappeared, exhausted. The terrain was very uneven; Soviet patrols infested the forest. Their officer thought that our plan was unrealizable. As was his right, he ordered the withdrawal of the expedition.

* * * * *

The operation, however, absolutely had to take place.

The enemy had more and more room to maneuver. If we did not strike a decisive blow, we would suffer one. We had to choose: to risk everything or to lose everything. I asked once more for volunteers; the expedition, at full strength, was about to set out once more. The officer, convinced of the necessity of the bold blow, took his men in hand again. In a subdued voice I lectured them at the bottom of the gorge.

The eyes of those boys flashed with magnificent sparks. Some of them had received the Iron Cross that very morning and were anxious to do honor to it. They set out again. We followed them through our binoculars for a fleeting moment.

Two hours passed once more. It was five o'clock in the afternoon. The Reds, eager to seize the *kolkhoz* a second time, leaped to the assault with the usual cries.

Another cry, shrill, the cry of weaker voices, answered them. The Reds had scarcely come into view when our young men, who, hidden behind them, had been waiting for just this moment, pounced! They leaped into the water and came on like lions!

The Bolsheviks believed themselves surrounded. Most of them, not knowing where to run, fled into our machine gun fire or hugged the ground beneath the thickets. Many of them surrendered, giants with slit eyes, like gorillas, whom our tender-skinned lads brought to heel with blows of their rifle butts.

Alas! Half of these child-gladiators had been struck down coming out of the thicket or crossing the water. Their thin bodies floated under the waterfalls. We had won, but the price of the victory had been the freshest and purest blood.

Each one of our young heroes was worth more than the rag-bag of shaggy prisoners, their flat yellow heads covered with bristles as hard as needles, who crouched trembling in the cellars of the school. This brutal contrast established exactly the implications of the duel: was it to be Europe, refined by twenty centuries of civilization, or the savage hordes of Asia, bestial and grimacing behind the red emblems of the Soviets? Our little volunteers had chosen. They had died as bravely as any *vieux grognards*[2] for the ideal which shone in their young eyes.

The Reds, bloodied by this set-to, withdrew back into the forest to the west and southwest. They risked no more hand-to-hand fighting in this sector, littered with the bodies of their compatriots.

Several disgusting pigs patrolled in front of the Soviet posts, eating without scruple the nauseating corpses which rotted rapidly in the sun. The Reds enviously watched these porcine flesh eaters as they wallowed, twenty meters away, in the greening intestines of their compatriots. Obviously they burned with desire to lure the disgusting beasts behind their lines. Finally they managed to seize one of them. We heard their shouts of joy. Thus was, at Tyeryakov, Soviet anthropophagy practiced through the intermediary of an animal.

* * * * *

We were able to obtain all the details we wanted on the situation of these delicate lovers of pig meat.

One of our medical orderlies, a certain Brohet, had been taken prisoner while trying to save a wounded man who had been hit at the edge of the water. The Reds conducted him from post to post.

Like a great number of soldiers he had learned the Russian language. He was amazingly resourceful. He chatted glibly with them until at last he was taken to the rear. He had had enough time to locate the enemy positions and judge their strength. Darkness fell during the march. The path followed a deep ravine. Our medical orderly leaped and rolled into the precipice. Let the Russians blaze away as they would, Brohet was in flight!

He lost his way ten times. At the first light of morning we saw a head emerge from a swamp fifty meters in front of us. It was our brave fellow.

He slithered along and got to us safely, as muddy and green as a hippopotamus of the Niger. From that moment on the Reds were completely countered in the west, pounded by our Pak all the way to their forest hideouts.

There remained the oak groves which loomed over us on the southeast and from which the Soviet mortar battalion menaced us formidably. From dawn to dusk we had to entrench ourselves in shelters cut in the chalky soil or under the isbas. Our commander, attempting a brief inspection, had narrowly escaped three shellbursts.

We had to clean up the heights and dislodge the devilish "potato launchers," as the troops called them, without fail. One of our companies deftly encircled the enemy and hammered the Russian battalion with all its might.

But we paid dearly for this counterattack. A shell had killed the national leader of the Rexist Youth, Provost John Hagemans, formerly a communist student at the University of Brussels who, converted to our ideal, had become the herald of the greatest of our ancient Low Countries and an epic guide and enchanter passionately loved by the new generation.

* * * * *

Tyeryakov had been only partially freed. Each day our sorties drove back the enemy, but our soldiers would scarcely return to the isbas before the shooting would resume a hundred meters behind them. They had barely enough time to dash for the bunkers. The adversary folded in on himself, then sprang back again like an accordian of death. Elite Soviet marksmen climbed in the trees like jaguars. Sometimes we would make one of them out, then take careful aim. The body would topple to the earth or dangle in the branches.

But most of these Bolshevik climbers were invisible. A dozen of them would interdict all movement. It was impossible to make ten meters in partially wooded terrain. Tyeryakov was surrounded by marksmen, sparing of their cartridges and astoundingly skillful.

All the same, their harassment could not alter the fact: Tyeryakov was saved. The Reds had not been able to retake the pass, which was indispensable to their counterattacks.

We had been the only ones to retain an advanced position in the Caucasian forests of the southwest. Everywhere else our forces had withdrawn. Tyeryakov remained, a battering ram against the Soviet sector. It was from there that we mounted the last offensive of the West Caucasus in October.

Our division slipped further to the south. After having been relieved by forces of the SS Viking Division, we took part in this movement. On a luminous afternoon at the end of August, we left the graves of our dead and set out cautiously, across the oak forests of the west, where the enemy still patrolled. Our group almost crossed the path of a long line of Soviet soldiers. They were seven or eight times more numerous than we. They passed over a crest several meters above our heads without guessing our presence among the bushes where we waited, fingers on our triggers.

After a two-hour march we came to a little village like a fleck of gold among the tall blue peaks. It was Kubano-Armyansky, a hamlet established in the Caucasus by a tribe of Armenian refugees in Tsarist days. Strange prune-colored youngsters with little owl-heads perched on wooden posts in front of the huts, as immobile as fetishes.

## Armenia

The month of September, 1942, was a month of rest for the divisions in the West Caucasus. The German assault of the second half of August had failed for want of enough troops to open the way and assure control of the zones conquered in the forests. The forces sent ahead would perhaps have sufficed if they could have, as in July, mounted an offensive in the open spaces. This easy course, however, was no longer open. The enemy had patiently waited until we had traversed almost twelve hundred kilometers and were entangled in the jungle. When we were well bogged down in the passes and the ravines, cut off from our rear by kilometers of shadowy forests, then the guerrilla unleased his attacks, violent, often invisible, always murderous.

In many places we had to retreat. Furthermore, we had to await the arrival of reinforcements. Without new divisions, any further advance would be impossible.

So we waited.

The Armenian village of Kubano-Armyansky had been conquered by one of our companies the very day that we had taken Tyeryakov by assault. The enemy hadn't responded, had drawn back beyond the open spaces. The front stabilized near the outskirts of the woods.

We had never seen a village like this one. No longer were the isbas built on the ground, as in the steppe. On the contrary, they were raised up on strong poles, for fear of wild beasts, which would leave the forest in winter and come to prowl and feed in the little valley. Atop these pilings the Armenians were safe. The stables perched four or five meters high. The people took more precautions for the livestock than for their women and children. With great effort they would hoist the cattle to these roosts, where they would pass the months of snow in peace, while packs of famished wolves howled below them.

* * * * *

The inhabitants had carefully preserved the customs of the tribes of Asia Minor. The women had the long eyes, coal-black and slanted like almonds, one sees on Cretan pottery. They lived among millions of flies, stirring for hours and hours with their toes a delicate, slender cask full of milk, which hung from the ceiling by a cord. After half a day's churning, they would draw off a semi-liquid butter. The milk was buffalo milk, from the slow consorts of the great black bulls whose dewlaps hung like boas, right to the ground.

The village grew the inevitable corn, the shiny kernels of which the peasant women dried on the ground before freeing them from their silky envelope.

The countryside was even more awe-inspiring than at Tyeryakov. When we returned from patrol at the end of the day, we had to stop twenty times, so gripping was the splendor of the sky and the peaks. The mountains rose in ranges, each one a different shade, flowing from gold and red into purple and violet. The great rock faces, lighted from behind, would already be dark, a soft black-like velvet. Kubano-Armyansky, in the trough of the valley, would be sunk in a deep blue twilight, the white scarves of a few evening fires still floating above the chimney tops.

We would go slowly down, never ceasing to watch, through the tree trunks, the stunning colors which festooned the rocks and the village drowning in the glowing blue shadow.

To reach the command post of the 97th Division we had to cross about fifteen kilometers along the summit of the mountains. I rode a little Russian horse which clung like a chamois to the narrowest ridges above abysses carved out by fantastic cliffs. At last an unbelievable panorama spread before us, a great lagoon framed by crags a thousand meters high. At the very bottom shone a square of yellow light. It was there the village lay.

It took an hour to reach it. The horse would dig his hooves in like claws among the crumbling rocks. Then we'd reach a pale green torrent, ice cold, tumultuous.

Soon liaison became impossible. The Reds, seeing our momentum blunted, passed from the defensive to the attack. They didn't rush us in entire battalions, as at Tyeryakov, but infiltrated in little groups, all across wild forests where age-old oaks, storm-blasted, tangled their blackened trunks, where a thousand gloomy thickets lent themselves to ambush.

Our patrols moved with difficulty through this dense, trackless jungle, whose secrets no maps disclosed.

Luckily, the populations of the clearings were ferociously anti-Bolshevik. Certain of our Armenian peasants went off about fifteen or twenty kilometers away from Kubano-Armyansky. Two days afterwards they reappeared, bringing us a long ling of Red Army soldiers.

The hatred which these peasants felt for the Soviet regime amazed us. Poor, even miserable, they ought to have been tempted by Bolshevism. Instead they had such a horror of it that they risked their lives every day to help us fight it. A grizzled old peasant, whom the Reds had condemned to many years of forced labor, bore witness to a particularly fanatical devotion. Shod in light pigskin sandals, stealing about everywhere, he led our daily patrols.

Several of our Armenian guides fell into the hands of the Bolsheviks and were massacred. The ardor of the village diminished not at all.

* * * * *

Nevertheless our situation grew ever more precarious. The enemy was nowhere, yet he was everywhere. We made reconnaissances which lasted entire days. Pushing deep into the enemy sector, we wouldn't see so much as a fleeting shadow. The next day, at the gates of our village, a hail of gunfire from a holly thicket would cut down several of our men.

In the end we were completely surrounded by these invisible enemies, who laired under the trees, wherever they could, like wild boars, and who lived on crab apples and pillage.

We could no longer communicate with the division except by radio. Our liaisons with the rear required carefully organized expeditions to which we had to commit half the battalion each time. We were about to learn to our cost the meaning of guerrilla warfare in the Asiatic manner.

## On Watch

The number of soldiers was of little importance in this war of booby-traps waged deep in the forests of the Caucasus. Three ambushers crouched among the bushy thorns at a propitious location could massacre a patrol in a few seconds. They would flee as soon as they struck, and the next day mount another ambush somewhere else.

We had to bring supplies from the base at Shirvanskaya, a dozen kilometers from our positions at Kubano-Armyansky. Twice a week, several carts, pulled by great oxen, would advance as far as the village of Paparotni, then cross the thick oak forest, a distance of five or six kilometers. The path was narrow and choked by weeds. Coming to a little steep-banked stream whose wooden bridge had been destroyed, the convoy would descend to the pebbly river bed. After following it for about a hundred meters, the supply train would re-enter the majestic oaks and the holly.

One day the Russians, who lay in ambush, let the oxen approach to within two meters of their bush. Their volley mowed down men and oxen. Only two of our soldiers were able to take cover in a thicket. The rest of the escort had been slaughtered before they could so much as move a muscle.

From then on, we had to send half our men, twice a week, to meet the convoy at Paparotni. The men would methodically comb the forest on both sides of the path.

We would wait anxiously. The convoy generally arrived toward six o'clock in the evening. Our eyes wouldn't leave the clearing which the forest path emerged from right at the top of the slope.

We'd hear the crackle of machine-gun fire and the blast of grenades resounding right to the end of the valley. Then we'd see a cart emerge, then others, trundling down the slope. Panting, our men would bring the wounded to the infirmary.

The next day we would have to patrol again toward Paparotni. To stop using the path would have been to capitulate. The men were disheartened by the ambushes, so I took command of the soldiers who maintained liaison. In order to avoid a general carnage, I would walk twenty meters ahead of them. We'd heave a great sigh of relief when we finally reached the apple and plum orchards of Paparotni, frontier of abundance and tranquility.

* * * * *

The Bolsheviks would come and lie in wait for hours, like felines on watch for their prey, only several dozen meters from our isbas. We couldn't rest except fully dressed, our machine guns beside us. Our smokers, no matter how desperate they became, would hesitate before worming their way to the fields of Armenian tobacco. One afternoon one of our cooks wanted to dig up a few potatoes from a sloping field which bordered the woods. The Reds were lying flat in a bramble thicket. They let him come very close. A burst of gunfire, and the cook fell, shot in the leg. The Bolsheviks leaped on him and dragged him into the foliage.

With two men, I dashed in pursuit. We could hear the cries of the unlucky wounded man as his executioners dragged him over pebbles and roots. The Reds had to let him go just as I was on the point of catching them. When I bent over our poor comrade, he looked at me with his kind eyes full of tears. Out of his mouth came a froth of bloody bubbles. The Soviet patrol, before abandoning him, had punctured his chest with some ten knife thrusts. He gasped, his wounds palpitating as if they were living things.

He struggled against death for half an hour. We had to cover his face with a mosquito net, the flies buzzed so around his blood-covered mouth. The net quivered one last time. "Mama! Mama!" he repeated with that child's voice which men have at the moment of dying.

We buried him near the others at the top of a slope. We had surrounded the little graveyard with solid wooden stakes to protect it from wild beasts in winter. But who were the more ferocious, the beasts of the woods, or the Bolsheviks who, disdaining fair combat, would go to ground like assassins, to waylay and knife their victims?

The preparations for the new German offensive were drawing to close. Each day, shortly before nightfall, the Soviet planes would come, three at a time, to survey the sector. They never stayed more than a few minutes. One or two machines, hit by the flak, would spiral down in flames, while parachutists danced above the forest.

One morning in early October dozens of German Stukas passed over our heads and dove straight down in front of Tyeryakov. They returned from hour to hour. The mountains rumbled. The autumn offensive had begun.

On 8 October, 1942, toward the day's end we too began to march. We looked down at the valley one last time, to where Kubano-Armyansky lay blue in the first shadows. Down there our dead rested behind the great black stakes around which, in the impending snows, would stalk the famished muzzles and the nervous paws of wolves. Here and there the green mountains unfurled red and brown flags, banners of autumn which shone in the golden fires of dusk.

Then night fell. We advanced silently until morning, beneath a canopy of majestic oaks, pierced by the silvery and dancing fires of millions of stars.

## Jungles and Mountains

The October 1942 offensive on the Caucasian front had been long awaited. It began in an atmosphere of malaise.

The previous August the German High Command had attacked the formidable massif on two flanks: in the southeast along the Terek River in the direction of the Baku oil fields; in the southwest, our sector, in the direction of Batumi and the Turkish frontier.

The battle of Terek had been very arduous, without yielding decisive results. The German armored divisions had been stopped near Grozny. In October they didn't advance much farther. Our drive toward Adler had also failed.

The October push no longer had the goal of reaching Georgia and the Transcaucasus. It took as its objective Tuapse on the Black Sea, and the control of the pipeline which ended at this port. The pipeline was no thicker than the body of a child. For this black tube we to battle for weeks and weeks.

The only oil fields we took before the Reds could burn them were the Maikop fields. These oil-bearing strata were in fact situated at Neftegorsk, between Maikop and Tuapse. The installations had been dynamited by the Reds. The oil continued to spread, prevading all the rivers with its thick flood, browning the bulrushes and the vegetation. With their genius for organization the Germans set about returning these fields to use. The oil was extraordinarily rich, and especially suitable for aviation fuel. When we arrived at Neftegorsk on the morning of 9 October, we were absolutely amazed to see what, in one and a half months, the German engineers had accomplished. Great buildings of brick, brand new, stood completely finished.

We had to finish our work by conquering the pipeline as far as Tuapse, so that it could pour millions of liters of this precious liquid into the Black Sea oil tankers. That was our business as soldiers. The autumn offensive would be as much an economic operation as a military one. This wouldn't be the first time, nor doubtless the last, that thousands of soldiers would fall for oil fields.

* * * * *

The highway and the railroad line from Maikop to Tuapse were strongly defended by the Reds, who knew as well as we did the importance of this ardently coveted pipeline. In August the tanks of the Reich had stormed the Soviet barriers without putting a dent in them. At the beginning of October, 1942, the German High Command threw its assault divisions, to which we were attached, into a very well-planned operation. Across wooded mountains rising to altitudes of a thousand meters or more, devoid of any path, tens of thousands of foot-soldiers coming from the east and south would hew themselves a passage with axes. Advancing stage by stage, they would flank the enemy lines joining to his rear, on the Tuapse road, at twenty, then at forty, then at fifty kilometers beyond Neftegorsk.

Our ranger divisions, specialists in mountain operations, led the way. We left the oil-bearing basin in a driving rain. After two days of marching through quagmires we confronted the great mountains, freshly gilded by the sun.

* * * * *

The woods, fantastically tangled, bristled with gigantic oaks which had never felt the ax and thousands of crab apple trees which exuded a wonderful, tart perfume.

We climbed to the summit, where the Reds had occupied a great camp still strewn with spoils. Through breaks in the clouds we saw a mighty panorama of oak forests, still green, dotted with the golden leaves of crab apple trees already vanquished by autumn.

We rushed down the slopes. The horses would slide on their hooves for ten or fifteen meters; we checked ourselves by grabbing at roots. We camped under the stars in a miniscule town, drolly named Travalera. More than a hundred soldiers had fallen in an attack on these few wretched straw huts.

This was the last hamlet. Afterwards the forest rose, dozens of kilometers deep, as wild as the Congolese jungle.

* * * * *

The army fought above all with the ax, the saw, and the pick. The spearhead would track the enemy, drive him away, kilometer by kilometer. Behind them, hundreds of engineers were opening a route chopped bit by bit through terrible obstacles, across the very mountains. It defied belief. This path was crowned with tens of thousands of logs, fastened to projections in the rock perched above vertiginous ravines and reinforced by walls of stakes. The most powerful tractors could use these trails perfectly well for many kilometers, enabling them to reach the summits. Every two or three meters the earthworks curved off to permit crossings.

As we advanced, passage for vehicles became more difficult and we stopped using them. We replaced the tractors with thousands of prisoners of war, transformed into porters. We might have believed ourselves in the equatorial brush. Each man carried on his shoulders a most cleverly contrived wooden container, to which would be fastened perhaps an ammo box, perhaps a canteen, possibly a bag of food. Everything, including drink, had to be back-packed. The lines of porters advanced, one after another, day and night.

Our division had brought along innumerable mules, magnificently packed. We Walloons had kept several horses, but there wasn't a single mountain pasture at these heights. We no longer possessed so much as an armful of fodder, nor a grain of oats. Unable to pasture their animals, the drivers fed them on birch branches. Ceaselessly their axes hammered the trunks, felling the beautiful trees by the hundreds, solely for their branches. The beasts browsed avidly on bundles of the green branches, but their flanks grew gaunter every day.

While the engineers carved this access route toward the Tuapse road, thousands of mountain troops and muleteers waited, camped in cabins built by the troops themselves.

Veritable forest cities sprang up. Every German has in his soul a moutain chalet. Some of these little buildings were masterpieces of grace, comfort, and solidity. Each one had a name. The most insignificant was entitled, with good humor, "House of German Art."

The autumn was beautiful. We would dine in front of our bosky huts among the rock plants. We had built tables out of white wood and installed rustic benches. Only the sun pierced the boughs. The enemy airplanes searched in vain for our campsites. In the evening we could see, far off in the valleys, the blazing railway stations of the Maikop-Tuapse line. Burning trains glowed fifteen kilometers away. Through our binoculars we could make out perfectly the blackened skeletons and the vivid red squares of the compartments. Our Stukas were making life untenable for the forces of the USSR.

* * * * *

At the far end of the forest, the forward troops and the engineers had finally reached a forest path which joined, three kilometers farther on, the famous Black Sea highway. The Reds defended it furiously. We took the highest rocks only after dramatic hand-to-hand fighting. Numerous bodies, half-charred by the fires among the trees, were strewn on the scorched earth.

Our whole division set off to deliver the finishing blow. We marched up the ingeniously constructed roadway. At each curve witty placards, painted with no small talent, would signal the dangers, for that matter quite evident without the signs! Refractory mules, loaded with ammo boxes or kitchen stewpots, would topple and fall with an infernal din, smashing themselves on rocks a hundred meters beneath our feet.

We reached the valley and a logging road which ran straight as a ruler between two rocky hills. The Reds had swept this path mercilessly for the past week. Every German patrol that had come near the Soviet positions had been annihilated.

The Stukas pounded the Russian bunkers ceaselessly. On one particular day they inflicted so much damage that we were able to seize the enemy trenches, which had become a frightful charnel house.

That evening another officer and I came across heaps of corpses accumulated during the last week. They were in a monstrous state of putrefaction. I was especially moved at seeing a line of Reds felled by a burst of machine-gun fire. They had collapsed one atop the other like a house of cards. Each still held his tommy-gun in his rotting fingers.

At 6:00 A.M. I began to photograph this macabre scene.

Just as I looked through the viewfinder, I thought I saw one of the corpses move slightly. Even though they were crawling with thousands of disgusting yellowish maggots, I wanted to put my mind at ease. The body which seemed to have quivered had his hood pulled over his head. I approached, revolver in hand, and suddenly yanked back the clothing. Two eyes, frightening in their fury, fixed on me like carbuncles. It was a Bolshevik leader. He had lain amid this rot since the evening before, letting the larvae cover him over. He had on his person a last will in which he had sworn that, as a Jew, he was resolved to do everything to avenge the Jews.

Men's fanaticism has no limits.

* * * * *

The Stukas had utterly annihilated the junction of the forest path with the highway from the sea. Hundreds of Soviet corpses filled the fox-holes. Some still grasped, in blackened fingers, bandages unrolled too late. An officer wounded in the legs had barely had the time to pull down his pants when he fell dead into a nest of machine guns, head first. His pale bottom, crawling with hundreds of sticky caterpillars, shone from the ground.

Three young Germans on patrol had managed, at the beginning of the operation—which is to say some ten days earlier—to worm their way down to the rocky stream bed between the Russian forts. Their bodies lay on the stones, their eyes wide open, their beards red and fine. Their dessicated ribs had already punctured their green jackets.

We reached the famous Tuapse highway. The village at the crossing was no longer anything but a series of fabulous craters. Beneath the railway line the little tunnels destined for the run-off of the mountain waters had been converted by the Reds into narrow hospital rooms. The wounded, abandoned for the last two days in these icy corridors, had all perished on their stretchers for lack of care.

A beautiful river spread out above a dam. I began to take a bath there, but quickly jumped back out: putrefied bodies, floating at waist height, were everywhere. You couldn't move an arm without bumping into one.

We passed the night bedded down on the ground amid the stink of these slimy charnel houses, which taught us, better than any sermon, the vanity of our mortal flesh.

## Storms and Ravines

The conquest during the month of October, 1942, of a large section of the route from Maikop to Tuapse had been an important victory. We had no more than a good twenty kilometers to cross to reach the great Black Sea oil port. We were approaching our goal.

We had only one night's rest. The next morning we again left the highway to begin a second flanking operation through the woods. We advanced several kilometers across the bottom of a valley, then re-entered the wild oak forest. It rained in torrents. The earth, sown with rotted corpses, had become horribly viscous. We possessed none of the magnificent equipment of the Alpine divisions, neither short jackets nor iron-shod shoes. Our long greatcoats dragged miserably in the mud. We skidded on the smooth earth. The advance meant, for us, in this chaotic and dripping jungle, nothing but constant suffering. Men tumbled into the ravines.

Reaching the top of a mountain, we saw the famous pipeline. It passed, half-way down the slope, from one hill to another, audaciously spanning the valley. On the opposite ridge the Russians had built fortifications. Their trench lines swept down from on high into the valley. While one group of our men advanced along a bend in the valley, I climbed, astride the fat black pipe, tommy-gun in my hands. In fits and starts I rode above the pass, while, fifty meters below me, precipices yawned one after another. I arrived safely on the far slope followed by a whole cavalry of volunteers gladdened by this unforeseen exercise on "horseback."

* * * * *

A little before evening we succeeded in climbing to the summit of the enemy mountains, which had just been overrun by the advance guard of the

German Alpine troops. The Reds had been massacred in place, killed in long rows, standing in their narrow trenches.

We had barely the time to set up our miniscule tents on the crest before the first great tempest of autumn broke loose.

Our tents were made of little triangular canvases, slit in the middle, which served individual troops as ponchos. To erect a tent, one had to combine four of these canvases, staking them over an area of about two by two meters. But four canvases meant four men, so we had to sleep four in a tent in a tiny space, as well as shelter a full kit there.

To complicate matters further, the tent had to be taken down during the day so that everyone could have his poncho back to cover himself.

We had neither straw nor dry leaves to stretch out on, nothing except the drenched soil. The storm howled the whole night. We were right at the summit of the mountain. The torrents of rain, hail, and snow could carry off our fragile habitations at any instant. The water streamed in, penetrating holes punctured at a dozen places in canvases that had seen a year and a half of service, drenching our faces. Men cried out against the tempest. Their tent-shelters bowled over, soaked to the skin, they struggled and swore.

* * * * *

A number of Soviet soldiers had been captured on the mountain toward the end of the afternoon. They had been sent to us during the night.

They formed a lamentable flock around our bivouac. They were for the most part puny urchins from Krasnodar, about sixteen years of age, dragooned to Tuapse where they had been quartered exactly four days, just the time it took to learn to use a tommy-gun. Their outsized infantry boots had tortured their feet. Most of them had thrown away their footgear and had gone on, barefoot, in the mud. Without so much as a hut to sleep in, they huddled in the storm, one against another, half-drowned and exhausted.

In broad daylight, with the stolid fatalism of the Slav, they began to pick over the bodies of compatriots who had been killed in the area. After an hour, the bodies were, every one of them, stark naked. The prisoners put on not only the greatcoats and jackets of the dead, but their socks and even their drawers. When the column of prisoners moved off toward the rear, they left us in the company of long lines of white corpses, glistening under the heavy rain.

* * * * *

The tempest lasted three days. Mingled snow and rain swept down in gusts. We tried to light fires under our little tents, but the wood was soaked. All we could achieve was an acrid smoke which tore at our eyes and throats.

All day, all night, without an instant's truce, the tempest raged, flattening tents, drenching uniforms. A few soldiers hadn't even any canvases, and several would have to squeeze together in one hole.

The first evening we had managed to hoist our last horses clear up onto the mountain tops. Lashed by the rain, they gazed at us despairingly. Drawing aside my awning on the final morning, I saw them collapsed on their forelegs, dead of exhaustion and suffering.

The Russian corpses grew ever more livid. Their bellies had begun to green with the tender green of young shoots. The continual presence of naked corpses all around us finally maddened us. With kicks we pushed them, one after another to splatter from the height of the parapets five hundred meters below in the mud and water of the ravines.

Our exhausting climb, the days and nights of suffering on these storm-swept crests, were of absolutely no avail. We received orders to withdraw to the Tuapse route and return to the southern forests by another path. Dazed with fatigue, we crossed the pipeline again and set up camp in a valley facing back the other way.

The highway from the sea was strewn with the blackened remains of Russian wagon-teams. Everywhere, dead horses had been flattened by hundreds of German tanks and cannons. Nothing remained of them but pools with floating skins. The artillery fired steadily; Soviet planes dived at us, dropping their bombs without skill. A powerful watercourse, called the Pshish, flowed on our left across great red and grey rocks. We crossed it in dinghies fastened to a line stretched across the river, which bore us, like acrobats, to the mouth of the Tuapse railroad tunnel.

The tunnel was about one kilometer long. The Reds had not only blown up the bridge spanning the river at the entrance to the tunnel; they had created, inside, a wreckage of monumental proportions. Entire trains had been crashed one on top of another. At least a hundred cars had been junked in this dark corridor.

The infantry succeeded in slithering into the wreckage with extreme caution. For a quarter of an hour, they had to advance in the most total darkness, keeping their right hands flat against the rock. Then they had to crawl under two telescoped railway cars to reach the other wall of the tunnel, beginning the same process in the blackness all over again, their left hands glued to the damp rock. The men would shout to let the others know where they were. After a half hour's march we could make out a pale glimmer. The Reds had dynamited the mouth of the tunnel, opening an immense crater which we scaled at the end of this Dantesque corridor.

The convoy climbed to the summit of the mountain, then descended by a path, hastily cut by the engineers, flanking the muddy forest. It took the animals an entire day to manage it, at any rate those which didn't die in the muck or fall into a ravine.

At the mouth of the tunnel we did another balancing act across the debris of a second bridge over the Pshish, and then set out along the railway line. We bedded down for the night in a wallow of fetid mud.

In the end, we counted the mud a blessing, for the enemy had opened fire. Shells fell endlessly, lodging harmlessly in the clay with a dull plop.

The next day we had to cross a valley. The great bridge of the Tuapse railroad dangled over the void. The Red artillery was methodically pounding the village that we had to cross to reach the southwestern oak forests. All around us isbas were being blown ten meters in the air. Any attempt to cross would have been folly.

We waited for nightfall, then, passing through swampy bottomlands thick with cadavers, crouched at the foot of an enormous mountain, as sticky with mud as everywhere else. A little before midnight, we began the climb, loaded with full kits and all our weapons, light and heavy.

The slope of the summit we had to climb was as steep as a ladder, rising to an altitude of nine hundred meters. The earth was as slippery as shoe polish. We skidded on our worn-out and un-nailed shoes. We had only a telephone wire which the guide unrolled to guide us through the darkness. At any moment we risked bumping into the Russians. Had the guide gone the least bit astray, the whole column would have foundered. Our young soldiers were half dead with exhaustion. The strongest among us had had to load themselves down with the arms of the weakest in order to relieve them. I carried one tommy gun around my neck, another on my shoulder. A nervous man's whispered oath could have doomed us all.

The last few hundred meters were unspeakably hard. Many collapsed, no longer able to climb. They would cling to tree trunks to keep from rolling into the abyss. The damp darkness was so thick that we could see neither stumps nor rocks, nor the bodies of fallen men.

It was four o'clock in the morning when we reached the crest of the mountain. We hurriedly set up machine-gun nests and put automatic riflemen on the largest crags. The first gleams of a flat and glaucous daylight broke the shadows. We watched, with consternation, the trees rustling in the wind above the gray ravines.

## The Indjuc

Days passed. The sun returned. Although the crests of the Caucasus were an uncomfortable roost for soldiers, nature still displayed herself with such majesty from the height of these mountains that she consoled us for our labors and our sufferings on the slopes. Russets, sumptuous reds, the colors descended for kilometers to the white waters leaping across the ravines between the green rocks. At five o'clock in the morning, dawn reached the top of the passes. For a long time the fog continued to clasp the sinuous valleys. Dense and milky, it spread from one to another, as clean as the water of a rosary of lakes. Over this white sheet the mountains rose like gold and rust-colored islands. For an hour we lived a fairy dream. From the depths of the lakes of fog, new islets would emerge, ever lower peaks rising forth in their turn, like legendary worlds engulfed long ago by deep waters.

* * * * *

With the daylight began the artillery duels. Germans and Russians bombarded each other with determination. Our mountain rose between the guns, our combat positions fastened like storks' nests to its summit.

During the night both we and the Soviet infantrymen made surreptitious forays. During the day both kept silent. Then the spoilsport artillerymen would again hammer at one another. The protracted wail of the shells, sometimes fired at a mad cadence, would deafen us for hours. The projectiles, wherever they came from, would graze our mountain, just over our heads. We would hear the shells whistle one behind the other in the treetops. Often pieces of branches would fall.

We were at the mercy of any lazy or haphazard shell. Our troubles began immediately: one of our posts was blown up. Another shell—120mm—particularly whimsical, fell eighty centimeters from me, tossing me through the air on a whirlwind of fire. When I regained consciousness, I found myself amid heaps of wreakage. Around me, everything had been slashed or razed for twenty meters. The right side of my steel helmet had been completely caved in and splintered, up to my ear. My canteen had blossomed like a flower. My machine gun, set down within arm's reach, had been blown to bits.

Everyone thought I'd been vaporized. I had, all in all, a shell splinter in my right forearm, a perforated eardrum, and a long rent in my stomach. This last wound would prove serious later on and mar for a long time my life in exile.

* * * * *

After several days the German troops prepared for the final assault. We stole further to the south, always along the crest of the same chain of mountains. Across from us the impressive mass of Mount Indjuc rose 1300 meters high, above a formidable oak forest as dense as a thicket, where nothing but a few gray rock faces could be distinguished here and there. From up here, the prisoners told us, the sea could be seen.

When the mountain was conquered we would have only to descend towards the palm trees and the blue shores of Tuapse.

About one thousand meters beneath our machine guns, between Mount Indjuc and our mountain, flowed the river Pshish. Our sector was cut in two by a ravine several hundred meters deep, accessible only with great difficulty. In the trough of this gorge a torrent streamed over gigantic rocks.

Our positions went up the other side without interruption, followed the crest for several kilometers, then plunged precipitously toward the main river. There we occupied an advanced post, right at the bottom of the valley, several meters from the roaring water.

According to the combat plan, the German Alpine rangers would carry the assault to Indjuc, starting from the southern extremity of the sector. To begin, they would take the first Soviet positions from the rear, below the rocks on the other side of the Pshish. As for us, perched in our eagles' eyries, we had only to reconnoiter the enemy and wait for new orders.

We didn't miss a detail of the last great battle of the Caucasus.

The Stukas opened the dance, just at daybreak. They would plunge precipitously toward the golden sea of the valley. Their skill was incredible. They never pulled back, in the very depths of the pass, until they were on the point of crashing into the trees.

We could only see a few Soviet soldiers fleeing and running toward some rocky crests. The Stukas saw no more than we did. The oak forest was like a roof. It was impossible to tell where the Reds' bunkers were. The Stukas sought more to frighten than to destroy.

Then the German Alpine troops charged into the thickets.

We could hear the firefight, and were able to follow closely the progress of our allies by the white flares which rose regularly above the trees. It was a moving sight. Their advance was rapid. The flares reached our height, then rose closer and closer to the summit of the passes. At the end of two hours, flares were bursting from the foliage to almost above Mt. Indjuc. We thought, all aquiver, of the first fighters who would reach the summit. We remembered the "Thalassa! Thalassa!" of the *Anabasis*. Like the ten thousand ancient heroes of the retreat narrated by Xenophon, our soldiers were about to shout, "The sea! The sea!"

Alas, they never shouted it. The progress of the flares stopped. The machine gun and tommy gun reports came further apart. The Stukas stopped diving between the two mountains. Even the artillery fell silent for long stretches.

The indecision lasted for a long time. Several green flares threw up their flowers and their spangles, now much lower. We heard a few more frenzied splutters, but it was the end. The ranger companies had not been able to conquer the enormous forest. Their attack unraveled as it went forward, swallowed up by the forest.

The assault had failed. In the evening, Mount Indjuc seemed to us more wild and proud then ever, in the violet fires of dusk. It had definitively barred the route to us.

Autumn blew on the mountains, disheveled them, littered the earth with millions of shriveled leaves, light and dry.

We watched the forest die.

Our little posts were balconies poised over the valley. The mountainside fell away beneath them, terribly steep for hundreds of meters. At night the Russians came on patrol on this sheer flank. We had hung steel wires there from which dangled hundreds of old tin cans. They rattled against one another on contact with prowlers. Our guns would crack. The next day we would see several brown heaps at the foot of the tin shop.

The German rangers whom we had relieved had dug themselves little individual shelters a meter under the earth in order to rest there by turns. We took our turn, along with the others. We would let ourselves down through the mouth of holes just the size of a body. At the bottom, you had to roll into a ball, then crawl into a pit no larger than a coffin.

There were too few holes. We had to wriggle into them and bed down by twos, crushed one against the other, noses scraping the ground. We had the horrible feeling of being buried alive, and had to master ourselves to remain thus, stretched out like dead men buried a bit too soon. Some preferred to roll themselves up in blankets under the trees, despite the bursting shells and the fog, so terribly did fear grasp them by the throat in those icy black tombs.

* * * * *

One night the weather changed. The wind shifted to the north. The tempest shook the tops of the great oaks, growing into a hurricane. It drowned our tomb-shelters, into which the water gushed along the branching roots, rising to the level of the holes.

We tried frantically to bail out the pits with our mess tins, but soon we had to declare ourselves beaten.

The mountainside, swept by the wind and rain, lost its foliage in a few days. The Pshish swelled, rolling into the valley in tumultuous torrents, carrying off the wooden bridges, cutting off behind us all possibility of resupply, of rations as well as munitions.

## The Last

The great autumn tempests, mastering the mountains of the Caucasus at once, put an end to any notion of an offensive.

We had to dig in in the mud wherever the fate of battle had deposited us. At the foot of our mountain the Russians floundered like us in shelters invaded by water. We could hear them yelling in the night.

The soldiers groped in the darkness, buckets in hand, trying vainly to empty their holes. Across both lines, it was an international swearing contest. The Germans shouted cries of "Sacrament!" The Russians spewed forth "Satana!" We let off steam with a lot of "For God's sake!"

The Bolsheviks were luckier than we, for the winter saved them. Thanks to it, the forces of the Reich were stopped with only a few kilometers of mountains and forests left to conquer between them and the Black Sea at Tuapse.

This halt, within ten kilometers of victory, was crushing.

There was nothing we could do about it, however, except stabilize the front on the bare crests where we had spent three months of fighting and effort.

* * * * *

The most urgent problem was shelter. All our old foxholes were overflowing with muddy water. We had neither axes nor saws, nor any of the supplies of the engineers. Patrols were sent to dig through the ruins of the nearest village in order to pull nails, to search for hatchets.

With our infantrymen's spades we had dug sites for huts a few meters below the ridge of the mountain, cutting ditches for water drainage. We managed to sink posts and to hang three rows of tree trunks over them, which we covered with another meter of earth. This makeshift roof could muffle the shock of a blast, but the rainwater kept infiltrating between the beams.

Inside these hermit's cabins we planted stakes a half meter high and spread bare branches on top of them to serve us as mattresses. All during the night the water would rise in the room. By morning it reached a height of twenty or thirty centimeters. We used it to drown our lice. We could find handfuls of them any time under our jackets and between our legs. Resignedly we threw them into the water which lapped against the boughs.

For the last two months we had not been changing our underwear. Vermin were eating us alive. One morning I undressed myself outdoors and killed more than seven hundred lice in a single session.

Our woolens were completely riddled with them. They were squashed together like kernels of corn, interlocked one with another. We succeeded in dislodging them only by changing our sweaters over a wood fire. Then we would see hundreds of enormous whitish lice climbing toward the upper part of the garment.

We would shake them out onto a sheet of red-hot metal. They would sputter and burst in all directions like fire-crackers. Finally the sheet would be shiny with their melted grease.

* * * * *

The Pshish in flood looked like a major river. It had in one night reached the foot of our mountain and converted the meadows into a muddy gulf, absolutely unfordable, in which floated the swollen corpses of Bolsheviks, washed along at random by the currents.

Our kitchens were cut off at the foot of the sheer banks. The water submerged them. The next day we could no longer see anything but the metal tubes of the chimneys and the heads of a few horses still struggling here and there. We saved them, but they died of their privations in the foothills.

Their nauseating carrion was soon the staple of our diet.

Nothing more came from our supply bases, since the engineers' bridges had been swept off like straws by the water, which attained a height of two or three meters. For a week we lived by chewing pieces of the muddy meat which we carved with our knives from the skinny haunches of the dead mares. We hacked out this unspeakable meat as best we could and swallowed it raw without salt.

We had saved several bowlfuls of flour, and succeeded in kneading a few pancakes with rainwater.

The tiniest fire would put the whole sector in danger, however. The crest had been denuded of almost all foliage. The Russians were on the lookout for us. A thin thread of smoke, wafting above the mountain, would instantly get us thirty or forty grenades. Besides, the smoke made life unbearable in our rude huts. Our eyes would water with huge tears, and we had to extinguish the fire instantly.

Drenched, gnawed by hunger, lying in disgusting watery dens, we were soon prey to all sorts of diseases. An epidemic of jaundice had invaded our sector. Every morning lines of soldiers would leave their holes, feverish and dazed, faces yellow. As soon as a temporary bridge could be built we evacuated them in frightening numbers. More than twelve thousand sick left the Caucasus in a few weeks.

With jaundice, pneumonia, and ten other diseases lying in wait for every one of us, our manpower melted away. We rapidly lost half our men.

* * * * *

Nevertheless we had to soldier on and wear the yoke of suffering right to the end. We spent interminable hours keeping watch on the enemy, mowing down with machine guns and tommy guns any Russian who sneaked near or between our posts, spaced fifty or a hundred meters apart.

Every night our patrols would go down toward the Russian foxholes, an exhausting task. Our soldiers, nevertheless, took these impossible missions in their stride.

One such patrol, surprised at daybreak by the Soviets, and swept by their fire, returned without its leader, whose name was Dubois. He had fallen near the Pshish. They believed him dead.

That night, among the sheer rocks which separated us from the enemy, we heard calls for help, shouted in French. Two volunteers went down into the ravines and brought back Dubois's "dead" body.

To tell the truth, he was almost dead. His shoulder smashed by a bullet, he had come to long after the battle. It would have been impossible to climb back up the mountainside in broad daylight. Besides, he didn't want to miss the chance to carry out in an exceptional manner, the orders he had received to locate the Soviet positions. He crossed the river, slipped between two bunkers, and spent several hours studying the layout of the whole enemy sector.

He did it all too well. Discovering the telephone line of the Russian command post, he managed, with great difficulty, for he could no longer use one hand, to cut the cable with his knife.

The Russians, puzzled, came out to reconnoiter. Dubois, tracked by them, had to dive into the river again, this time under frenzied firing. He was hit several times. An explosive bullet smashed a hole in his leg the size of a grapefruit. He dragged himself into the brush, somehow or other made a tourniquet, and, when night came, crawled up toward our rocks perched nine hundred meters above him. He dragged himself halfway, with the energy of a man who is gambling for his life.

He was brought in almost exsanguinated. The medics would have to take him back down the other side of the mountain again through mud and darkness.

Before being chloroformed by the surgeon, he asked for a pencil and paper. In front of the German colonel who commanded the sector, he sketched, for twenty minutes, a map of the Soviet position, gulping a little cognac every time he felt faint. After he'd laid everything out clearly, then and only then did he lie down.

He was a junior officer like the others, one of many. But our boys had faith. They knew wherefore they offered their lives.

* * * * *

The ideal alone could still sustain our comrades, even in the skeletal state to which they were reduced.

On our icy peak we lived in an atmosphere of madness. Several hundred Russian corpses rotted and grimaced several meters from us.

One night in October, the Russians had tried to re-take the crest. At eleven o'clock in the evening they had climbed to the very top of the mountain. They thought no one had heard them, but every machinegunner was at his weapon. When the Bolsheviks were a few meters from our guns, a raking fire roared out. The Soviet battalion was cut to pieces.

The Reds had been surprised with their fingers clawing at the roots of the trees, at the very end of their ascent. They died clinging to the soil. Some rolled among the rocks. Others had been able to get several meters farther along and died on the plateau. But the most horrible corpses were those grimacing under our very noses, still clutching the trunks of the oaks.

It was impossible to reach these corpses without being swept by the Soviet machine guns and mortars, which, from the other side, watched for the tiniest movement on our bare peak.

For several weeks we had to witness the slow decomposition of the corpses stacked up under our very eyes. Finally the heads came loose, fell off, one after another, and toppled in among the rocks. Nothing was left above the shoulders except the off-white neck vertebrae, spookily superposed like African necklaces.

* * * * *

At three-thirty in the afternoon shadows already clung to the mountain. By four o'clock it was completely dark. We had to burrow into black dugouts full of water, stretching out on slats made of branches, tormented by the innumerable vermin. By eleven at night, we could stand it no longer. Shivering, we would wait out the hours for the first pale gleam to pierce the sodden dawn.

The enemy grew more and more surly. The Americans had just landed in Morocco and Algeria. The Bolsheviks hadn't believed in the Yankees until this surprise. The fall of North Africa changed everything.

Before, numerous prisoners would come and surrender. Often, for that matter, just as they got to us, the poor devils would be blown up on our mines in the night. The panicky survivors would race back to their positions where they immediately got themselves shot. From the day after the landing at Rabat and Algiers, the Russians came no more. They had regained their confidence.

We had to be on the lookout constantly. Our soldiers relieved one another every two hours. These reliefs were ghastly. We kept tumbling into our former shelters, now overflowing with water. Men would disappear into them completely. We would pull them out drenched right to the bone. Some would burst into tears like children.

We were horrified by the dreadful Russian corpses liquefying between our posts even more than by the holes full of water. Feeling our way in the dark, we would skid on these putrid sacks, sinking an entire foot into an oozing belly. Then we would be gripped by despair, at a loss to cleanse ourselves of this frightful human corruption which clung to our skin and sickened us to the point of vomiting.

We were at the end. The end!

The end of our physical strength.

The end of our spiritual resources.

We struggled on only because our honor as soldiers was on the line. Volunteers, we wanted to remain so until the bitter end, until the last beat of our exhausted hearts.

We no longer hoped for anything.

One morning, reading the orders, we stared with vacant eyes at a paragraph which named the hour and conditions for our relief.

It took us a long time to understand. Nevertheless, it was really true. The Wallonian Legion was to return to Belgium. It would receive three weeks home leave, and there be reinforced by several thousand Belgian volunteers.

We went back down the long muddy mountainside we had climbed so painfully one night in October. What had become of our wretched companions who, that night, had toiled and suffered while hauling themselves silently to the summit of the mountain? Of our legion, decimated by the first winter in the Donets, completely rebuilt in June, 1942, before the great southern offensive, there still remained, in all, exactly, one hundred eighty-seven men when we came again to the little wooden bridge over the Pshish.

We made our way slowly back towards the crest where we had suffered so much. Far above us floated the golden banner of the few trees that the oncoming winter couldn't conquer. Like them, our ideal, proud and tormented, still fluttered grimly against the hostile sky.

# Chapter Five
# DUG IN ON THE DNIEPER

One evening in December, 1942, our train, packed with soldiers on leave, passed the river Kuban. At that time, German engineers were busy building an enormous steel bridge across the green waters, a bridge with two lanes, the ultimate.

Yet the front was showing sinister cracks to the north and northwest of Stalingrad.

The Germans, methodical as always, impervious to the slightest doubt, continued to bring massive girders to the work-site, which would replace the wooden bridges thrown up in haste at the time of the preceding August's victories.

With equal serenity they had amassed, at Maikop and at Krasnodar, stocks of fur-lined boots, padded garments, pairs of skis, cigarettes and chocolates. One month later these stores would be scattered over the roofs with the help of plenty of dynamite.

The Germans listened only to the German radio. We, more indiscreet, had learned that the Russians were hastening up from the east and planned to cut off communications to the Caucasus at Rostov. We knew they were coming.

The region remained perfectly calm. A few sentinels watched the roads along the pale green ice-bound lagoons. We heard nothing. We saw nothing. Only a few crows animated the cloudy sky.

* * * * *

One morning we arrived at the bridges of Rostov, protected against the ice floes by huge cutwaters.

Since the union of the Ukraine with Europe all this hinterland had become a fabulous construction yard. Where one year earlier we had found nothing but railroad lines, corroded thanks to the Soviet habit of letting everything go, and buildings blackened by systematic Soviet arson, we now saw modern railway stations with fifteen or twenty lines, dotted with huge new buildings of concrete and brick.

We gazed wide-eyed at this incredible transformation through the half-opened door of our car. Hundreds of billboards bearing the names of the principal German firms were posted proudly on the factories and hangars, honors list of the conquerers in this industrial war.

We, the soldiers, had conquered a waste land which the Soviets had totally annihilated or wrecked piece by piece before retreating toward the east. German industry had needed only fourteen months to rebuild, create, establish order, to transform everything from the ground up.

On the Dnieper it was the same as in the Donets basin. A two-story bridge, one story for the trains, another for motor vehicles, had been built in a few months across this mighty river, more than a kilometer wide. The city sparkled with lights as far as the eye could see: at night the lights of mighty factories could be seen everywhere. Immense and black, the river flowed toward the sea, sprinkled with innumerable reflections which shifted in the current like will-o'-the-wisps.

Beneath the snow stretched the Ukraine, its vast horizons dotted with ice and with coppery groves, embroidered with the blue and green shutters of white isbas. Everywhere new stations, warehouses, huge sugar refineries had been built. We unloaded hundreds of agricultural machines, green and red, as smart as Nuremberg toys. In one year Germany had created in Russia the richest colony in the world.

Magnificent work!

But also magnificent illusion, for the Reich squandered prematurely on this work of European peace the strength which, according to the jungle law of hatred and self-interest, should have been turned exclusively towards warlike works of carnage, of killing, of extermination.

* * * * *

In 1943 the war dragged on. More than ever brave spirits were called for. In 1941 we had left on the Eastern crusade because our consciences demanded it. As the cause remained the same in 1943, so the sacrifice had to remain the same. Whatever may have been the risks and torments of the struggle, the pain of separation, the lack of understanding with which we often felt ourselves surrounded, we had to hold firm in the service of our duty.

Life is worthwhile only to the extent it is illuminated by generous giving.

Everyone wanted to experience the epic. At the end of January 1943, our legion reassembled for a second departure at the Sports Palace in Brussels. Tens of thousands of Belgians were there to cheer our soldiers. Then the train took us toward Russia.

Nevertheless we weren't immediately going to join the anti-Soviet front. We still lacked some of our combat groups, who, during the intervening months, had reinforced the German troops falling back from the Caucasus.

From Maikop they had retreated as far as the Kuban delta, the Isthmus of Perekop, and finally the Crimea. By way of Simferopol and Kherson, on the Dnieper, they joined us at the Polish frontier after a lengthy round trip of nearly four months.

Our hard battles of 1941 and 1942, far from intimidating the youth of our country, had drawn them to the call en masse. Almost two thousand Belgian volunteers were in training. Our first task was to form a cohesive unit. Most of the recruits were mine-workers. Some had come out of distaste for their labor in the coal mines. Many had been attracted by our ideal of social justice and dreamed of fairness and decency. A number of officers and soldiers of the old Belgian army who had been prisoners in the Reich camps had asked to enlist. They came to us, several hundred of them, in the glorious old uniforms in which they tried to check the German advance in May 1940.

Thus the two armies joined together fraternally, the one which had heroically defended the integrity of our country in 1940, and the one which, overcoming past resentments, had striven, since August 1941, to help save the essential: Europe and our fatherlands all across Europe.

* * * * *

The working-class constituted three-fourths of the strength of our legion, but the legion also included numerous young people from the aristocracy and the Belgian bourgeois class, gold medallists from Jesuit colleges, sons of well-known diplomats, jurists, civil servants, businessmen.

An identical purpose united us all: to represent our people brilliantly among the twenty nations who had joined the struggle; to fulfill, without servility, our duty as Europeans, by fighting against the mortal enemy of Europe; to obtain for our mother country a strong voice in the continental community which would be born out of the war; and finally, to gird the shock troops whose might would guarantee social justice upon our permanent return to our country after the hostilities.

For this ideal we offered our lives.

This offering was not mere rhetoric. Of the six thousand Belgian volunteers who joined the Wallonian Legion between autumn of 1941 and spring of 1945, two thousand five hundred died as heroes. Eighty-three percent of our soldiers received one or more wounds in the course of this mighty epic. Of the first eight hundred volunteers, three alone of those who had taken part in all the battles reached the end of the war alive: a simple soldier, a junior officer who became a captain, wounded three times, and the author of these lines, himself wounded on five occasions.

## The Return to the Dnieper

By November 1943 our legion, now, as the Assault Brigade "Wallonia," a powerful unit of the Waffen SS, disposed of 2,000 combat-ready men and 354 trucks and armored vehicles.

Our convoys followed the rivers, the avenues of willows, the yellowing poplars, then crossed the leafless woods of Silesia. In 1943 this industrial basin was still intact; the coal mines and the synthetic oil refineries were working at full capacity. The villages in the small valleys were neat and peaceful.

But already the rumblings of distant thunder, harbinger of great storms, could be heard growling in Southern Europe. The Anglo-American troops had crossed the Mediterranean in the month of August 1943, a crossing definitely helped by the double dealing and the defection of Italy, but also by first-class ships and planes. Sicily had been taken by storm. The continent itself, Calabria on one hand, Naples on the other, found itself invaded. The Allies couldn't have been pushed back, nor even contained, no more at the Straits of Messina than at Syracuse or under the palms of Tunisia.

A massive landing, backed by several thousand airplanes, had been quickly and totally successful. That was clear. Could this formula, repeated on the shores of the Atlantic, fail when it had been shown to be irresistible in the Mediterranean?

* * * * *

A second test of strength had taken place on the Ukrainian front, towards which our three hundred trucks rolled.

Until the summer of 1943 we had all believed in the possibility of a German resurgence in the East. Stalingrad had been indisputably a painful blow. But the counterattack would surely come, as in the spring of 1942.

The counterattack came. Germany hurled all available forces in the direction of Voronezh on the Don. The assault failed after tragic battles in which several thousand tanks had been destroyed. The Soviets, pressing their advantage, had driven the German troops as far as Kharkov, then had conquered the city.

Its fall was infinitely more serious than that of Stalingrad, although less spectacular. We could no longer chalk it up to accident. What country hasn't had an accident in wartime? It was too systematic. We hadn't been able to drive the Soviet steam-roller back, nor even to block it. From Kharkov, the forces of the USSR had driven even to the Dnieper, crossed it, advancing beyond Kiev and Dniepropetrovsk.

But in any case, our own group, anti-Bolshevik volunteers, was committed. We had resolved to fight to the very last second against the Soviets. We knew that each blow struck would one day have its effect.

Moreover, in war, as long as everything is not lost, nothing is lost. Germany still had a very large margin of security, from Minsk to Bordeaux, from Athens to Narvik. She still disposed of immense material resources, and her ingenious inventors might suddenly provide brilliant and terrifying surprises against an adversary too sure of himself. Numerous convoys of splendid shock troops were joining up with us, notably the famous Adolf Hitler and Death's Head divisions. "In one month we'll retake Kiev!" these elite soldiers shouted to us as they passed.

* * * * *

Our trains skirted the south of Poland, under a clear sky of pale blue and rose. It was Sunday. The women in dark-colored dresses, coiffed in green bonnets, left their little mud-walled isbas, walking down dirt paths to reach the painted wooden churches.

We breathed the icy soil's aroma.

The next day at dawn we made a short stop at Lemberg, where we received an enormous amount of winter gear: clothing lined completely with down, padded boots, white greatcoats, fur-lined hoods.

Under the weight of these clothes we felt huge and clumsy, not knowing any longer how to tote all our equipment. We remembered the terrible winter of 1941 on the Donets, with our threadbare jackets cut right through by the howling north wind. This time the commander had taken every precaution. It was almost too much of a good thing, and wiser heads among us were asking themselves how they could keep such a phenomenal amount of luggage when the day came that they would have to move without trucks.

But in general our soldiers took a childish pleasure in their padded clothing. Each baggage car soon contained a full platoon of Santa Clauses.

* * * *

We set out again across Galicia, drenched by the autumn rains. Then the long trains turned toward the south. Blue mountains shone far to the west. A great muddy river, bordered by thousands of dry bulrushes, slipped beneath the cars. Crossing the Dniester, we entered into Bessarabia.

From then on the lines of communication were so encumbered that it took us fifteen or twenty days to make our way, by the direct route, from Lemberg to the front. Masses of soldiers on leave who were not overly enthusiastic to return to battle looked for ways to avoid duty. Dazzling sleeping coaches and restaurant cars still glided with clockwork regularity in the direction of Odessa. From the platforms of the stations where we twiddled our thumbs during a forty or fifty hour waits, we would suddenly see long luxurious cars, with their orange lamps, parade by.

But the general traffic became more and more paralyzed. The barmen went through, as always, without a hitch, but the army didn't move at all any more except by dribs and drabs. Our trains were shunted across Rumania on a one-track line.

* * * * *

We had been led to believe that we were going to the Crimea.

The Crimean Peninsula had just been cut off from the mainland by the Soviet offensive, but German reinforcements had been sent to Odessa by sea. Thus we saw without astonishment one morning the red ramparts of the old fortress of Tiraspol, high on the right bank of the Dniester.

From the other side of the river we recognized the uniform isbas, the wells with long, black, wood handles, the millions of sunflower stalks, gray and beheaded, stricken by the nascent winter. We would be at Odessa by evening!

But the train stopped in a gloomy station, then clearly switched over towards the east. The trip to the Crimea was over. For two days we ascended interminably. Northeast, northeast, northeast. The huge Ukrainian stations passed in succession, covered with snow. Happy-looking women, strong and buxom in their padded clothing, chewed and spat sunflower seeds as they worked as stevedores on the loading docks.

We were approaching closer and closer to the Dnieper, far to the north of Dniepropetrovsk. We could hear the artillery already.

The last evening we noticed sheaves of brilliant flares to our right, then equally brilliant ones to our left. The train advanced for several hours, cutting these weird fireworks in half. We were getting deeper and deeper into a bottleneck. Airplanes came down to strafe the road. Before us we saw buildings in flames. It was Korsun.

We detrained there in the middle of the night.

## The Olshanka

We were to take up our positions about thirty kilometers to the east of Korsun.

It took our three hundred fifty-four motor vehicles three days to complete this stage of the journey, which normally would have taken two hours.

An enormous river of mud, the awful Russian mud, as thick as melted rubber, mired all the roads. It was up to forty or fifty centimeters deep across the bottom lands in the hamlets.

Our new drivers had to make their way through this viscous muck, chopping down cherry orchards to improvise new passages. Just before a forest of firs we came to some large marshes. There we had to use a track made of thousands of logs, riveted together. We danced across them as though we were at the fair.

The track which crossed the pine forest was itself shored with thousands of tree trunks, no longer because of the mud, but because of the fine sand, into which our cars would sink up to their engines.

The Bolsheviks knew the difficulties of this passage. Consequently the forest was infested by prowling partisans who skillfully set mines at night. In the morning two or three cars would be blown up. It was our daily toll fee.

Every five hundred meters, enormous wooden redoubts had been built, like African forts. Surveillance teams lived there, sheltered by impressive stockades.

* * * * *

To the east of this pine forest opened out the Dnieper plain.

The staff of the renowned SS Viking Division was installed in Belozerye, a large village stretching out over a radius of several kilometers. We would be with them until the summer of 1944.

Marvelously armed, completely motorized, comprising thousands of extraordinary young men, barrel-chested and as strong as lumberjacks, the Viking had been given the mission of defending the Dnieper, already flanked on the northeast and to the south by Stalin's divisions.

Soviet troops had parachuted onto the right bank of the river, in the region of Belozerye, at the moment when the retreating German divisions were ebbing back toward the left bank and were awaiting en masse their turn to cross the few bridges which were passable.

The enemy parachutists had been promptly pursued. Many had perished during quick skirmishes; the survivors had let themselves be swallowed up in the great forest of Cherkassy. There they had linked up with the numerous partisans.

* * * * *

The zone which had been assigned to us, at the south of the Viking's sector, was bordered by the western edge of the forest. The paratroops and Ukrainian partisans had flourished for several weeks in this wooded enclave on the right bank of the Dnieper. They ended up establishing liaison with the main Soviet army, which had crossed the river downstream.

The forest was hemmed at the west by a river, the Olshanka, fifteen to twenty meters wide. Flowing from the south, the stream came to a village called Staroselye, veered for a short time towards the northwest, then returned along the woods and descended eastward. It passed a village fetchingly named Baibusy, perched on a hill on the left bank. On the other side of the river, hard against the very edge of the forest and occupied by the enemy, was a hamlet, Sakrevka.

The Olshanka twisted and turned between the cliffs. After five or six kilometers it reached a fourth village, Moshny. There the Olshanka finally left the forest completely. It had grown wider, and here a long wooden bridge crossed it. Every isba had wicker fish traps, hoop nets, seines, square nets, in bizarre shapes. An admirable church with an oriental dome embellished the entire horizon.

From Moshny the Olshanka flowed towards the east for several kilometers more. At the far end of a reedy steppe, a last town, with the cavernous name of Losovok, spread out under the dappled November sky. High white dunes overlooked the river as it flowed into the muddy Dnieper, between the islands of golden sands and the black firs.

Thus our warlike landscape and villages.

* * * * *

We were to occupy first the localities of Moshny and Baibusy.

The larger part of our brigade went down to Moshny, its fishermen and its blackened bridge.

As commander of the third company I had to defend Baibusy. The company was made up in great part of future heads of our Youth Movement, who had been carefully screened and had completed a long course of training in leadership. These boys of sixteen and seventeen years old were of a crystalline purity and idealism.

I arrived with them at Baibusy. Two long lines of isbas marked the crest. At the foot of these thatched cottages, the terrain sloped gently toward the Olshanka for a kilometer. The forest, mysterious, watched us.

The Russians had fortified themselves at the entrance to the woods, or so it would seem, since they didn't make their existence known. We set up our grenade throwers, our artillery, our anti-aircraft guns, and our Paks*. Our infantry took up position.

The village was calm. The woods were calm. Not one back was seen crawling among the grey sunflower stalks. I established my command post at the first isba on the southwest.

At eight o'clock a burst of gunfire, a single one, ripped through the darkness.

Five minutes later my command post, riddled with incendiary bullets, exploded in flames at the top of the hill, a golden torch with millions of sparkling spangles.

The whole crest was illuminated.

Nonetheless, we heard nothing more after the blast, although several brown forms must have crept by as they stole slyly back to the rushes on the river bank. Down there in the thicket, shining eyes watched the fire.

The battle between us and the forest had begun.

## The Silent Forest

We settled in at our new sector of the Ukrainian front on 21 November 1943. Several days later, in order to test my recruits and to feel out the terrain, I crossed over to the Soviet bank at the first glimmerings of dawn.

The wooden Baibusy-Sakrevka bridge was still standing, a narrow span that the Russians could have blown up just as well as we, but each of us was saving against sudden reversal.

We turned off toward the south. A dozen men strong, we slithered across a field of sunflower stalks and reached the river Olshanka. The water was icy and it came up to our waists. I placed a machine-gunner on the other bank to cover our passage. Then we crawled for a long time through a bog before we reached the forest.

The tall firs were silent; the golden sand was unmarred. In a clearing we found a flock and two shepards. That was all.

Just to return the Bolsheviks' compliments of the first evening, we set fire, on the way back, to three haystacks which bordered the enemy sector.

We returned empty-handed. The forest kept its secret.

When our trenches and barbettes were firmly in place on the eastern and southeastern outskirts of the village of Baibusy, the general commanding the army corps gave, as might have been expected, the order to change all the positions and to move them forward, right up to the bank of the Olshanka.

The troops now had to bivouac in the open country. What's more, winter was coming on. Above Baibusy we would take shelter by turns in the isbas, miserable shacks built on the bare earth, their mud walls oozing water. At least we had a roof and two small windows. Below, it was the barren plain, the mud, or the wet sand of the open river banks.

We spaced out our firing points over seven kilometers, along the cliffs or near the little bridge of Sakrevka. Two hundred meters from the Olshanka there was a knoll surmounted by a birch grove. We made it the pivot of our defense. Our anti-aircraft guns were hauled there during the night. A network of trenches fronted by barbed wire ran above the contravallations.

At the end of two weeks our brigade had to expand operations toward the south, to the village of Staroselye. The new sector, dropping down in a steep slope onto a village called Irdyn, was in the hands of the Soviets. Between this town and our bunkers lay a vast spread of mud. Entangled in this morass were straggly hazels, brambles, and bulrushes.

It had snowed. Rabbits would run wiggling their bobtails, poking lines of blue and green holes into the crunchy steppe. Rosy evenings fell upon the forest.

Our boys had a hard life. Often when patrols ventured into the bog, the icy crust would break. We had lots of frostbitten feet.

These inconveniences didn't keep our morale from being as warlike as possible. For each patrol of six men, eighty swashbuckling soldiers would bluster and shove in hopes of being chosen.

At the other end of the sector, our comrades at Moshny had dug in along the River Olshanka.

A track skirted the steep river bank. In the enemy zone, below the mauve and purple forest, the ruins of a monastery could be seen, and the yellowed foliage of the old enclosure. Our men dug and shored up the trenches while the guards scanned the right bank, striped with corn stalks.

The Soviets came in the evening to feel out the terrain haphazardly.

Our soldiers, too, stole into the darkness across the other side of the water.

The fields, sticky with black mud or covered by the first snows were thick with mines. We would wait for noises in the night. A flash, a boom, cries, and those who escaped would bring back the wounded, warm with blood.

One of them, a small mine-worker from Charleroi, seventeen years old, as slender as a girl, had had both feet and a hand torn to shreds in the course of one of these raids.

He held on for a month on his cot in the field hospital at Korsun. Every day be grew frailer, but he smiled at every visit. He found happiness in his Iron Cross. He died holding its scarlet ribbon in his hands as if he had been stroking a bird of paradise.

* * * * *

The forest was as mysterious as ever.

Nevertheless, every night men would slip through our posts, as cautious as leopards. We would hear soft hooting in the darkness. From far off, another hoot would reply. We understood the signs, we felt the presences. Sometimes our sentinels would shoot. But in the morning we would discover no trace of blood or of footprints.

We could increase our patrols all we liked. I went out myself and spent hours during the nights, crouched with one of my men near the water. We didn't catch a thing. It was enough to drive us to despair, for every morning, five, ten, or fifteen kilometers behind us, our trucks would blow up on new mines.

The village came alive at dark. Signals were exchanged; partisans were harbored. The Reds glided in the shadows in their pigskin sandals. They knew every inch of the terrain. They were uncatchable.

At the end of a month, neither we nor the Viking Division had taken a single prisoner.

## Blood in the Thickets

We had to know, at any cost, what was going on in that purple and white forest.

The peasants would whisper. We ended up learning from them that about ten thousand men were hiding out in this wooded massif of Cherkassy.

But where?

They were receiving equipment. We saw, thanks to our forward observation posts, the Bolsheviks construct numerous bunkers and bring up anti-tank guns, which they moved frequently.

But we saw only the first hundred meters. What lay beyond, under the immensity of pines and dark oaks stretching clear to the Dnieper on the east and to Cherkassy on the southwest?

Every isba was a mystery.

Our villagers were friendly, as were almost all the country-folk of the Ukraine. They cursed the Communism which had subjugated them, ruined them, and sealed their churches. But they had sometimes been tactlessly treated by the German administrators. A certain number of families had, since then, a father or son in the lairs of the neighboring woods.

I carefully made sure that my village of Baibusy would be a happy village in spite of the war. The Walloon is amiable by nature. He would quickly make himself one of the household, do favors, win them over with small presents.

I had re-established worship. A marvelous priest, returned from the woods where he had been hiding for twenty-three years, officiated on Sundays, from dawn until midday, dressed in purple and gold. The entire village attended the ceremonies, prostrating themselves a hundred times, kissing the earth a hundred times, intoning for hours melancholy and passionate chorales which would break your heart. Dozens of icons shone by candlelight in their copper and silver shrines. The yellow-bearded priest would baptise the week's babies. He made them kiss the icons interminably, one by one. Then he paraded each one of the newborns across the chapel, howling their heads off. He held them up at arm's length towards the congregation, so that the whole village could see and contemplate the arrival of new parishioners. He would finally return them, dead tired, to their flat-cheeked mothers, modest, yet glowing, dressed, like all the women of Baibusy, in long monastic capes, brown, decorated with a few ruffles above the waist, woven in the village.

No matter what the combats of the night, I regularly attended the Orthodox worship on Sunday mornings, among elderly peasants with bushy beards, beside honest mamkas and louse-ridden brats. After hours and hours of prayers by the priest, our chaplain would chant the Catholic Mass. Not a single member of the Ukrainian congregation would leave. These people were starved for religious life, and they would kneel, deeply moved, during our Communion.

While helping the elderly gentleman of my isba, who had lost his right leg in the last war, I returned to my command post covered with vermin, but moved by the admirable simplicity of manners and the faith of these peasants.

Nevertheless, from the same little houses, every night, the hootings of owls would go forth, directed at the partisans.

We couldn't be angry with our villagers for having paternal hearts, but we watched them vigilantly.

Their naive goodness quite naturally overcame all our western complexities. They loved their compatriots who were shooting at us from the neighboring outskirts of the forest. But they also bore witness to us personally, who lived in their town and under their roofs, of an equal affection, simple, strong, and sincere.

In the evenings, when I put on my white coat and crossed my cartridge clips in the Cossack manner, the old mamka would kneel before the icons. At dawn, when I returned from combat, the old folks were waiting for me. I would put down my arms, steaming with the cold. The old mama would cross herself, cry, touch my garments. I wasn't dead! Poor people, gentle and good, who had to pray at the same time for us, taken in as sons of the house, and for their own children hiding out across the way.

* * * * *

We received the order to go deep into the woods. We absolutely had to hunt out the enemy and take some prisoners.

Twice a platoon of my company crossed the River Olshanka in the darkness. I sent fifty skirmishers. They reached the wooded hills beyond Sakrevka at daybreak.

The forest was nothing but a series of crests where it was impossible to take up combat positions. Nowhere would our soldiers have been able to make themselves masters of the terrain. New crests, covered with bushes, kept looming up, from which the enemy could annihilate a company in a few minutes. The men advanced two kilometers into the forest. They discovered trails, wagon ruts and footprints. But no pistol shot resounded. The enemy was staying away, playing dead, or had gone to ground. Our expeditions discovered, in all, two cowards who fled immediately, after having shed their shabby coats to run faster.

These were the only spoils of war which my company brought back.

The 1st Company received orders in its turn to probe the terrain. At four o'clock in the morning fifteen volunteers, led by a young officer with a temperament like burning coals, entered silently into the icy water of the Olshanka and disappeared across the darkness.

They reached the old cloister. At that point, the first Soviet watch posts had been passed, but no warning hoots had troubled the demise of the night.

Glimmerings of light touched the tops of the branches. A dove-colored dawn was rising above the Dnieper. The lieutenant and his fifteen patrollers kept advancing.

They heard the cattle lowing, saw tracks. Crawling from thicket to thicket, they reached the top of a crest. Just a few meters away, two Soviet soldiers stood guard! The sought-after prisoners were at their mercy!

In the twinkling of an eye, they threw themselves upon the two sentinels, brought them down, and gagged them. Everything happened without a cry. Our men went thirty meters out of their way in order to regain the bottom of the little valley on the west and then return.

There were several icy ponds. One of the two captives suddenly tripped his guard and bolted. The fatal gunshot which dropped him gave the alert. In a few seconds an unbelievable army fell upon them, an army such as our men had never even imagined.

When capturing the two sentinels our comrades had reached, without knowing it, the entrance to a large encampment of partisans, sheltered behind the hill. Hundreds of civilian fighters rushed up and surrounded them.

And who were these fighters? Not only men, bronzed by life in the woods, but howling bands of disheveled women and packs of grimy boys of thirteen or fourteen years old, armed with seventy-two round submachine guns.

Our patrollers immediately formed a circle. But more than four hundred Soviet partisans were blazing away at them.

Our young lieutenant was among the first struck down, a bullet in his head. The others had to get out of the trap at all costs, without further delay. It was vain to try to go back. Retreat had been cut off. A submachine gun spat its ribbon of fire from behind every tree.

The only possibility of escape was to make a dash straight through the Soviet camp, then try to escape later with a circular movement. Through the cows, the sheep, the fires, the huts, our soldiers dodged frantically, spreading mad panic among the hordes of ragged old women.

Only two of our comrades escaped the massacre. They wandered for a long time in the forest. During the night one of our forward posts picked them up, half dead.

* * * * *

The most powerful divisions of the Reich had, at the beginning of December, 1943, begun a great counteroffensive to reconquer Kiev. At first they were successful, breaking through the front at Zhitomir and penetrating eighty kilometers beyond the Soviet bridgehead.

Once again they were stopped by the mud and pushed back, with huge losses.

Instead of reverting to the status quo, the situation had greatly worsened. This time it was we who were directly menaced in the north and northwest. Elsewhere, in the south and southeast, the divisions of the Russian general Koniev were hammering hard, expanding their thrust well beyond the Dnieper in the direction of Kirovograd and Uman. We would see the great red fires which marked the progress of the enemy against an opaline horizon.

The general staff of the army corps was absolutely determined to learn the intentions of the Soviets in the center of the sector.

The north front was cracking; the south front was cracking. Opposite, in the east, in the accursed forest of Cherkassy, what was being prepared?

Orders came through to undertake an operation on a larger scale, to take place at daybreak on the third of December. The plan was extremely audacious. Three hundred of our men would cross secretly, during the night, the three kilometers of deep marsh which separated the forest of Cherkassy from the southwest of Staroselye.

The column would infiltrate between the Soviet guard posts, then enter the forest behind the enemy positions. Then it would advance laterally for several kilometers from the southeast to the north as far as the heights near Irdyn.

At H-hour, three hundred men would rush to the assault, falling on the Soviets from behind and annihilating them.

I was to command the operation. On the evening of the 22nd I left my will on the little white wooden table of my isba and set off on this new escapade.

## Irdyn

We were supposed to be at Staroselye at midnight. It was snowing.

Our trucks took four hours to cross, on a log road, the fifteen kilometers which would bring us across the pine woods of the southwest to the staging area. We had to make this detour behind the front so that the enemy would not be able to discover our plans.

From Staroselye we descended towards the marshes. We had to approach them from south of the positions to be destroyed, so that the Reds of Irdyn, too, would suspect nothing.

The 2nd and 3rd Companies of infantry of the Wallonian Brigade worked in tandem. German engineer detachments, well-supplied with mines and flame throwers, accompanied us. Their mission would be to destroy every fortified building in Irdyn in the wake of our assault. Our infantry companies, once successfully behind the enemy lines, would deploy themselves in the woods to the east of Irdyn, across the entire width of the town; then, thrusting behind the Russians, they would take possession of the area and hold the terrain as long as necessary for the work of annihilation. When this probable jumping-off place for a Soviet attack against the center of our line was completely annihilated by mines and by fire, we would have to regain our own lines as best we could across the bogs.

We climbed a steep path in total silence. The march of the column packed down the snow. From time to time a man would tumble from the heights of the path, losing his machine gun and his helmet and falling to the bottom of the ravine.

The column came to a halt near the swamps. It was almost four o'clock. The full moon had just been swallowed up by a propitious fog.

The black marshes spread mysteriously, more than three kilometers deep, full of pitfalls, full of traps.

A scout went on ahead. The night before he had attempted the crossing alone and knew, more or less, the way. I set off behind him, followed by three hundred men in single file, silent, fearful of the least noise.

Almost everywhere the snow had melted into water and slime.

My soldiers, swathed in their voluminous winter gear, were suffocating. Their faces were sticky with sweat under their thick fur hoods. Sometimes we had to cross a stream over a log bridge. Their legs would tremble. In the profound darkness, soldiers would slip and fall waist-deep into the water.

It was then that the dismal wail of a siren resounded from the southeast. I thought everything was lost. Everyone threw himself down into the mud, but the siren kept on wailing.

Nothing happened. We never found out anything at all about this incident. Perhaps there was an alarm elsewhere. The wailing dragged on for twenty minutes.

We resumed our march.

We could make out the indistinct mass of some large bushes in the darkness. There lay the bank. But the enemy posts had to be there as well.

We walked with extreme caution, so as to give not the least sign of our presence. What a tragedy if suddenly Soviet shots rang out among exhausted troops who had only watery marshes to retreat to.

I reached a little thicket. A man joined me, then another. Our three hundred smugglers passed, as furtive as bats. The forest enveloped us. In a ghostly silence the troops rested for a few minutes, hidden in the snow.

We had taken the right approach. The Soviet posts to our left and right must have been far enough away, or else the Russians sentinels had slept too soundly, confident that no enemy troops would ever cross three kilometers of unknown quicksands in force.

Here we were, a party of several hundred men, behind the Soviet combat line. It remained for us to continue cautiously along for four kilometers, to where we would be due east of the Russian base at Irdyn.

In total silence we made a nocturnal march, deep in the enemy sector, along a logging road through the Cherkassy forest. Scouts and engineers equipped with mine detectors advanced fifty meters in front of our column.

Fingers on our triggers, we followed them along the shoulders of the road, ready to fall back into the woods in case of an attack.

But it was better not even to think about an attack in such a situation, in the very heart of the Soviet sector, without a single possibility of help or escape. Had the enemy guessed that three hundred men were strolling behind their lines at five o'clock in the morning, they would have sprung the trap on us. Sooner or later we would have been wiped out no matter what our resistance.

* * * * *

The sky was lightening faintly.

We were nearing our goal. I sent the infantry, guided by compass, to the edge of the woods near Irdyn. The 2nd Company had the order to assume position for an attack from the southeast. It moved out quickly. The 3rd Company would attack driving from east to west. Under cover of the trees, it had to recircle the entire outskirts of the town, interminable, like most Russian villages.

The snow fell heavily among the densely packed young fir trees. I spread my men out, for I knew nothing of the location of the enemy's lookout posts. At any second the fray might erupt. I wanted to delay it until the very last moment. If not, how would we ever get east of Irdyn? We absolutely had to succeed in getting there without raising the alarm.

We crawled for a long time in the snow, a hundred meters from the edge of the pine woods. We could see the roofs of Irdyn below us, a few wisps of smoke, some fences.

We had been advancing for twenty minutes when I noticed two Soviet soldiers. They must have heard something. They were wearing their thick, brown, coarsely padded chapskas. They looked in our direction, worried.

My men were shrouded in snow. Raising myself slightly, I surveyed the terrain. Other Russians loomed, twenty, then thirty, as silent as we, tommy guns in their hands.

We began crawling again. The Reds advanced in a line parallel with ours, clearly comprehending nothing of what was going on in the woods, since the German front was in the other direction, to the west, not to the east. As far as they were concerned, the direction in which we were to be found was behind them. Why, then, did the dead wood crack? Why did the fir branches tremble?

Flanked on our left by this strange escort, we were able to cross another fifty or so meters. The target was tempting: a few bursts and thirty Reds would have been cut down. I made desperate motions for my men to restrain their impatience. We weren't there to kill thirty men, but to take Irdyn. The only thing which counted for the moment was to get as far as possible to the east.

On our left the center of the town came into view.

Suddenly the blow came. There were two Soviet bunkers twenty meters in front of us, right in the forest. They opened fire. Howling, we threw ourselves against them at close quarters. The Russians, hirsute giants, defended themselves bitterly. I had my tommy-gun broken in two right in my hands. I seized a wounded man's submachine gun and jumped right into the middle of the Soviet fortifications. Our men mowed the Reds down. Those among them who survived our assault fell back toward the village. We leaped after them.

* * * * *

After taking the bunkers we had to confront the entire Soviet garrison, temporarily confounded, but still powerful. To the south I could hear the noise of the fight begun by the 2nd Company. From bunker to bunker a terrible combat raged. Dozens of houses were in flames, proof that the engineers were at work. While waiting for the 2nd Company to join us, we had to hold firm, to conquer.

The Reds struck back at us with their machine guns, their mortars, and their artillery. Shells and grenades rained down all around us, starring the white snow with gray scars.

I was wounded in the right hand. Men were falling everywhere. The terrain was absolutely bare, right up to the outskirts of the houses. A few of us just made it to the first isba when we had to roll like barrels back down the snowy slope, machine guns pinned to our bodies. The soil was spangled with small cherry-red flowers sown in the snow with the blood of the wounded.

Our tanks, on the opposite slope, had seen our flares. They moved in to support our advance. Their shells opened breaches for us, and we occupied the crest of the town, from where our machine guns hammered the enemy. Just a few scuffles more, savage but decisive, and the Soviets were driven from the whole sector, pushed back toward the woods in the northeast.

The 2nd Company had demonstrated its prowess, and its most audacious combatants joined us with loud enthusiasm. Irdyn was taken. More than eighty Soviet corpses, fallen in the hand-to-hand fighting, were littered about, legs apart, hands sticky with blood. Numerous wounded men were crawling in the snow. One Russian, a single one, had surrendered intact.

The German engineers proceeded slowly and methodically, as always. Luckily the village was empty of civilians. The fortified bunkers, blasted by mines, flew into the air, then fell back down as flat as boards. The entire *kolkhoz* waved the great gold and red flags of conflagration against the crystalline sky of dawn. One more hour and the Reds' entire installation would be annihilated.

We soon saw that this hour would be an hour of hell.

The noise of combat had promptly alerted the whole forest. Soviet reinforcements arrived from all sides. The enemy, thrown back into the steep woods, poured fire on the village. Picked Russian snipers had scaled the trees. We had formed a line just at the edge of the woods, but we were enduring a withering fire.

The German engineers hurried: they still had to carry their task through to the end. The enemy swirled around us, hemmed us in. What would we do when it was time for our column to retreat, to re-enter the sticky mire of the marshes and cross those three kilometers out in the open?

I ordered three quarters of the troop to begin retreating. Meanwhile we would carry out counterattack after counterattack.

At the end of an hour, the greater part of the column was out of firing range of the Soviet machine guns. We could see men struggling like flies in the glue of the marshes. They, in any case, were saved.

The engineers finished their titanic work completely. They drew back in turn. Nothing was left for us but to get away.

It would not be easy.

* * * * *

It took us three hours to cross the three kilometers of muddy bottomland.

I had set up positions with several machine guns outside the village along a rail track used before the war to transport peat from the marshes. From this rampart we did as much shooting as we could to keep the enemy pinned down outside the woods.

The greater part of my rearguard platoon had entered the marshes, carrying the last of the wounded. Some among them knew that they were done for. A young Parisian metallurgist (we had about a hundred French volunteers in our brigade) had had an arm torn off and his belly opened. Mangled as he was, he insisted that we prop him up against a haystack. "I want to die standing up watching my buddies fight," he said simply.

Most of the wounded could no longer walk. One of my "Youth" had had both lungs punctured. Lying, torso naked, against the snow with two little pink holes quivering in his sallow skin, his face was absolutely green. We felt we must save these poor boys at any price. The strongest among us carried them on our backs, but the mud kept giving way underfoot. When we crossed deep streams, the wounded men would fall, disappearing into the icy water, from which we pulled them out only with great difficulty.

We took turns covering this last retreat in two small teams. As we fired, the other team would take position a hundred meters behind us. When they were ready to open fire we would run round the flanks to take position a hundred meters further on.

One of my last companions had been horribly wounded in the belly. Each of us carried him in turn as best we could. Our backs were completely drenched with his blood. We were able to drag him along with us until the end of the fight, but he died two days later, in pain, but free.

At noon we finally reached Staroselye's hill at the end of the marshes, without having abandoned a single wounded man and without losing our Soviet prisoner, so important to the High Command.

We rejoined our Panzers along steep paths, carrying our bleeding companions on litters of branches.

Our success had been complete. Irdyn was annihilated. But our faces were strained; our thoughts were elsewhere. We climbed up into our trucks, surprised and dispirited at so much room.

## Festivities

For Christmas of 1943 each hut had set up a Christmas tree, whitened with cotton wool taken from the medics.

At the front I had never seen Christmas be anything but sad. Men would drink, sing, joke. For an hour everything was fine. Then each would recall Christmas at home: the blushing cheeks, the dazzled children, the tender wife, the sweet songs. Eyes would gaze into the distance with a far-away look, seeing hamlets and rooms once filled with joy. A soldier would leave, and we would find him crying all alone beneath the moon.

That evening there were fifteen suicides in the division, hearts broken from the strain of so many months of separation and suffering.

I had wanted to visit all our volunteers' bunkers. Amid the snow and the darkness, I made some ten kilometers, entering each smoky shelter. Some squads, the young especially, were putting a good face on things and whooping it up, but I found a great many more grave faces than smiling ones. One soldier who could contain himself no longer had thrown himself to the earth and lay sobbing against the ground calling for his parents.

At exactly midnight, at the moment when those who were still brazening it out had just started to intone "O Holy Night," the sky burst into flames: it wasn't the Herald Angels, nor the trumpets of Bethlehem. It was an attack! The Reds, thinking that by this time our men would be under the table, had opened fire with all their artillery and were hastening to the combat.

In fact this was a relief. We leaped up. And in the snow illuminated by shells, by tracer bullets, by the flash of cannon fire, by the red, green, and white flares of the signalers, we spent our Christmas Eve preventing a raging enemy from crossing the Olshanka River.

At dawn the firing let up. Our chaplain gave Communion to the troops, who went up from their positions, squad by squad, to the Orthodox chapel where our Walloon priest dressed in *Feldgrau* joined in a truly Christian fashion with the old Russian village priest in his purple miter.

There sad and bitter hearts were soothed. Their parents, wives, and beloved children had heard the same Mass back home and received the same Eucharist. The soldiers went back down with simple souls, pure as the great white steppe which glistened in the Christmas afternoon.

Around the little isba which I used as an observation and command post, the grenades and shells had gashed or blown up all the buildings. My little house, with its three bare cherry trees and its iced-up well, was somehow still standing after the blitz. The old peasant woman would look with horror at the jagged holes in the walls, and then quickly retire into the blackness of her shanty, crossing herself several times.

The two neighbor women had been torn to shreds on Christmas Day, just as they were drinking their borscht. The shell had come straight in through a little window.

At the front death is everywhere. One has only to lose one's head for an instant, or step backwards, to be struck down.

In combat, a frightened man is a dead man. Courage makes a man powerful, rather than vulnerable. Death can be intimidated, but it must be looked right in the face.

* * * * *

New Year's, 1944, arrived.

We wanted it to be the third or fourth of January, for the year to finally be underway, for the days to become just ordinary days again, when you don't think, or think as little as possible.

But we had to anticipate a new strike from the rascals across the way. Wouldn't they be likely to replay the sudden thrust of Christmas Eve at the stroke of midnight?

We received orders to anticipate the enemy. It was we who would attack this New Year's eve.

Two platoons of my company entered the darkness of the snowy plain, crossed the water, and spread out into the tangled bushes.

My third platoon had crossed the Olshanka one kilometer to our right. Its mission was purely provocative, to go behind the brambles several hundred meters to the south of the village of Sakrevka and open heavy fire so that the enemy would hasten en masse in that direction. Then my two other platoons would storm the redoubts facing our positions at Baibusy.

Our soldiers charged. They threw the enemy into total confusion.

We returned at dawn. I carried on my back a young volunteer who, first to charge a Soviet bunker, had run right into a submachine gun blast.

Although both his knees were crushed, he didn't so much as moan. His hair, fine as a child's, was stuck in little curls to his moist brow. Poor youngster, to suffer atrocious mutilation and martyrdom at the very hour when all over the world millions of human beings were finishing a night of carousing.

First of January, five o'clock in the morning. A soft red sun was rising above the white and rust-colored forest. The steppe was no longer blue. In the valley, the weapons had grown still. Everywhere in the world at this moment, people were dancing; people were drinking; women were laughing; and the faces of drunken men bore the stigmata of all the vices which burdened them. And in the day slowly rising over the white steppe, a broken youngster was going to die because he had believed in something great, because an ideal pure and strong had brought him to the sacrifice.

That morning near my isba I sadly laid upon the diamond-like snow this child with his frozen curls. His eyes had ceased to look upon a world whose baseness he had been able to measure and for whose salvation he had died.

## Sakrevka

1944 began badly.

The Soviet troops were thrusting powerfully to the northeast as well as to the southeast of our sector. Their advance was impressive and undeniable.

Nonetheless, not a trace of anxiety appeared in the orders which we received. We were deemed installed at the confluence of the Olshanka and the Dnieper until the end of the world.

Some actresses from Berlin had even arrived a few kilometers behind our lines. The motorcycle dispatch riders, who had no more than splashed these war-like lovelies as they passed, described their charms with feverish eloquence.

Nevertheless, every day the huge jaws of the Soviet pincer were drawing closer and closer behind us.

But it wasn't up to us to worry about such contingencies. For a soldier the war is his sector. The rest is the business of generals and journalists.

* * * * *

The Assault Brigade "Wallonia" received orders to proceed, just before the dawn of 4 January, to an operation which would include our tanks. Our goal was the village of Sakrevka, which we had already overrun during the night of 1 January. This time we were supposed to blow up fortifications constructed deep in the forest beyond the hamlet.

Above all, they told us, bring back some prisoners.

In 1941 and 1942 we didn't know where to put them all. Now, however, the Soviet soldiers were fighting to the death or slipping between our fingers like grass snakes. General Gille, commandant of the Viking, wanted at least five prisoners so that verification of our intelligence would be possible.

The 1st Company would cross the Olshanka at three o'clock in the morning and hide in the enemy-held forest northeast of Sakrevka to prevent Soviet reinforcements from arriving during the battle. My company would cross the river on inflatable boats at 2:00 A.M. and slip up to the western entrance to Sakrevka to await the hour of assault. The 2nd Company would attack from the south, coming from Staroselye by the forest route.

During the night the engineers would discreetly detect any mines in this road. At 5:00 A.M. the tanks would start, carrying the mass of our men on their armor. They would speed toward Sakrevka. The infantry would then attack, deployed between the Panzers.

It was a chancy operation.

Our tanks could hit mines and blow up en route, and at the front weapons are of primary importance.

* * * * *

My company was concealed not far from the Olshanka at about three hundred meters to the north of the enemy's lookouts. Our long white greatcoats blended perfectly with the snow. I moved right down to the waterline in the dense darkness and stayed there for more than an hour, my ear glued to the ground. Not a step sounded on the frozen earth. No splash disturbed the water's flow.

The engineers had finished inflating our dinghies. They launched them quietly onto the black water.

We had to stretch a cable, for the current was strong. One hundred men passed, boat by boat, to the right bank.

We still had to cross about a thousand meters before reaching the forest. From my little command post, just in front of Sakrevka, I listened to the whistling of the wind, every nerve straining. The wind was blowing on the steppe, but it brought no other noise, neither the wailing of a vampire (either real or false) nor the click of a trigger.

My men had reached the wooded hills.

Time passed. Soon we heard the far-off rumble of our tanks entering the forest by the southern route. Already our engineers had penetrated the Soviet lines, finding the mines and discreetly unearthing them. The forest teemed with mute presences. My stomach knotted as I thought of these courageous boys who, without dramatics, were advancing in the icy night, or working or waiting or crawling in the snow to transmit orders.

It was almost 5:00 A.M. The tank treads made a rumble and a clatter of steel. The Reds occupying the outskirts of the forest to the south hadn't even had time to wake up properly. Our soldiers, leaping from the panzers, rushed into the shelters, grenades in hands.

Dazed, the Russians had hastily seized their submachine guns, but the surprise was complete. Everyone was overcome: killed, wounded, or taken prisoner. Without stopping, our tanks continued their advance, sowing terror across the forest.

I began firing attack flares as soon as the 2nd Company's flares had sent their dazzling arcs into the sky. One party of my men rushed across Sakrevka from the northeast and the east, behind the enemy, to meet our tanks coming from the south. The others flushed and routed the men operating the anti-tank weapons on the wooded crests.

The hand-to-hand fighting, in which the Walloons were without peer, decided the business. The Soviet officer who commanded the artillery batteries blew himself up with a grenade when he saw that his guns were lost.

Dozens of individual combats took place at the foot of the forest. Men were running each other through in the isbas, in the ravines, around the haystacks. One of our communications squads was cornered at the eastern extremity of the battlefield. In a few seconds the five specialists, burdened by their reels and telephones, were overwhelmed and dragged into the woods, never to be seen again.

One of our tanks had been hit, but we were able to repair it without too much difficulty. We made an impressive haul: everything which was to be found in Sakrevka.

We brought back more than thirty Soviet prisoners, in tatters as always, but as strong as beasts and, for that matter, living like them, bedding in any lair, wrapped in grimy rags.

These crude soldiers would live on what they found in the isbas or in the winter fields or what they could take off corpses: moldy heads of sunflowers, muddy ears of corn, stale bread.

They had the brute endurance of cavemen, but they possessed, besides their brute strength, ultra-modern submachine guns which took clips of seventy rounds. In the sticky knapsacks fastened to their backs by a coarse cord they kept the wherewithal to fight for a week, two weeks, hidden in the brambles at a forest crossing or at the entry to a village.

These shaggy giants, these lop-eared Mongols with melon-shaped heads, scrubby black hair, and cheeks as flat as slices of pork rind, these feline Asiatics with bright, beady eyes, unwashed, ragged, indefatigable, looked like prehistoric monsters alongside our young soldiers with their slender bodies, their greyhound waists, and their fine skin.

We herded back this rabble as if we had seized wild boars in their wallows. Their coarse, savage faces laughed because we hadn't killed them and because we gave them cigarettes.

But if we had taken thirty savages, there were still ten thousand across the way. There were hundreds of thousands to the east, to the northeast, and to the southeast.

These shaggy masses were advancing.

Already we could feel the pressure of the horde.

## First Cracks

The Soviet armies pouring down from the north and the Soviet armies unleashed in the southeast were coming closer and closer together. In the west, eighty kilometers to our rear, an opening of not more than a hundred and fifty kilometers remained between the two Soviet wings closing the gap.

By 7 and 8 January, 1944, we could well believe that everything was lost on the Dnieper. Thrusting from the northeast, the Red panzers had dashed across the rear lines of the German front, spiking through a hundred kilometers in two stages.

The Soviets' methods were simple. They stuffed some of their tanks full of submachine guns and clips. Then they invaded the towns pell-mell with five, six, or ten tanks at once and immediately assembled the civilian population. Every available ragamuffin, every barefoot boy received an automatic weapon. An hour later, without any other combat training, two hundred, three hundred bashibazouks* in rags would accompany the tanks of the USSR.

The Soviet army replenished itself thus without difficulty and without instruction as its thrusts progressed. These reserves of human "materiel" were in practice inexhaustible.

Fortunately the Red thrust of 7 and 8 January, 1944, had been only a lucky but isolated strike, magnificently audacious. Unaided, a few dozen Soviet tanks had forced a passage and without stopping had carried their extraordinary saraband a hundred kilometers deep behind the front.

The German tanks, hastily redeployed, ended up boxing them in. The Russian tank crewman ran out of gas. Then they tried to hide their panzers in the copses and thickets, but they were all spotted within two or three days and destroyed one after another.

* * * * *

But the alert had been sharp. If the Soviets had sent a stronger force, the strike would have definitely succeeded.

To tell the truth our position at point on the Dnieper was untenable. We occupied the tip of a long lance. The Viking Division and the Assault Brigade "Wallonia" were the only southeast forces still positioned on the great Ukrainian river. Sooner or later we were going to be cut off.

On our arrival in November, 1943, it was already evident that we were doomed. At the beginning of January, 1944, the truth of this was more overwhelming still. Only the elimination of our salient and a rigorous realignment of the front could, if it were done quickly, save us from certain encirclement.

We thought that the higher-ups had understood our situation, for we received orders to disengage, to pull back and reposition ourselves on a second line drawn twenty kilometers further to the southwest.

This wasn't brilliant, but it was doubtless a first step.

The retreat was supposed to take place at midnight. We had already reconnoitered the new positions. Everything was ready.

At eleven o'clock in the evening a counter-order from the division canceled all the arrangements. Hitler himself had vehemently insisted that we stay on the Dnieper. To abandon the Dnieper would be to accept a moral defeat. It would also mean losing the last position on the river which might one day serve as a point of departure for a German offensive towards Kharkov and the Donets. In any case, the countermand was official.

The soldiers, conservative by nature, and who, for that matter, understood little of the situation, got back down from the trucks and philosophically took up their positions once again on the confluence of the Olshanka and the Dnieper. But we who heard the Soviet communiques on the radio every day and who were marking out on the map the two-pronged advance of the enemy to the north and southeast, we knew that we were in extreme danger.

* * * * *

Formidable blows were rocking the whole sector. The Viking Division had had to withdraw half its strength from the Dnieper to send them west of the city of Cherkassy.

In this second sector, the forest of Teclino formed a formidable triangle which jutted out like a wedge. It had fallen entirely into Soviet hands, and all counterattacks had been in vain.

General Gille decided to send the Walloons to attack this wooded massif.

On the evening of 13 January 1944, we left the bank of the Olshanka in the greatest secrecy. One night's journey in our heavy trucks took us through snow and ice to a few kilometers west of the blue forest of Teclino.

## Teclino

The assault of Teclino was to take place the very next day, 15 January 1944.

The officers went to reconnoiter the staging positions before nightfall. For several kilometers we followed the highway leading to Cherkassy. We turned off to the left onto a rutted path leading to an aspen grove. From there we could see the whole region.

Huge snow fields swept up toward the forest of Teclino. This one, narrow enough in the beginning, broadened more and more toward the east.

Each company commander received his mission and compared his maps and the terrain. Dusk fell. The woods were nothing but a huge purple tapestry. Deeply worried, we watched these spotless fields, these blue ravines, through which our men would climb at night to the forest where the enemy lurked, massively fortified, according to German survivors of fruitless counterattacks.

The division's artillery regiment was to support us. It had been positioned at full strength behind the western crests.

Several days earlier I had become aide-de-camp to the commander of our brigade. At three o'clock in the morning he and I met with General Gille.

We installed ourselves in a little command post connected by telephone to each of our companies.

Since one o'clock in the morning they had been stealing into the ravines and mounting cat-footed to occupy their positions for the assault. Light white sleds like Finnish sleighs were silently bringing the ammunition reserves across the thick snow. Every quarter hour at the other end of the wire the almost inaudible voices of the company commanders would report on their progress.

* * * * *

At four o'clock in the morning the artillery barrage crashed onto the outskirts of the forest.

The guns of the Viking Division were old. They had done one and a half years of campaign in Russia without an overhaul. We had to perform incredibly complicated calculations to regulate our fire, yet the fire was magnificently accurate. Four thousand shells swept down onto the enemy, pulverized his trenches one by one, cut the oaks to shreds with incredible force.

Our soldiers, bowed under this prodigious roof of shell fire, their ears ringing, their eyes wide, rushed to the assault at the precise instant when the artillery lengthened its range.

My old company, the 3rd Company, threw itself into the hand-to-hand fighting with such impetuosity that it promptly lost contact with the rest of the brigade. After an epic climb it seized two terribly steep hills as bare as cliffs, from the heights of which the Russians doggedly continued to fight in the overrun trenches despite the bombardment.

Some young women soldiers were particularly ferocious, howling, mad with fury.

Our soldiers weren't used to killing women. And these were pretty. One especially with a prettily freckled face fought like a tiger. Her small white breast had popped out of her khaki tunic in the fury of battle. She died thus. The freckles shone on her face like winter heather, and her breast, small and frozen, glowed softly. After the battle we covered her with snow so that the weight of Death would be light on her remains.

Leaping beyond these positions, so bitterly defended, the 3rd Company straightaway began an assault on the other bunkers of the forest. These were scattered over a breadth of four kilometers. At the end of one kilometer our decimated company was holding the terrain with difficulty, waiting in vain for the rest of the brigade to align itself on its right wing.

The other companies had had a hard time of it.

They had been able to penetrate five hundred kilometers into the hilly forest only with great difficulty. The combat was stubborn. The Viking Division's artillery supported the troops' efforts, flattening the Reds dug in beneath the trees at the top of a series of crests.

It was then that the counterbatteries of the Soviets intervened. They had, to the east of the forest, some "Stalin's organs": astonishing paired rocket launchers with thirty-six tubes which could riddle a whole sector in an instant under a frightening barrage of explosives. In one hour we had 125 killed and wounded.

From the command post we saw our little sleds come down the snowy hill, each one carrying a wounded man. The field ambulance was full. Dozens of wretches, stretched out on the snow shivering and half-naked, their blood caked by the cold, agonizingly waited their turn while the medics went back and forth unendingly with their reddened sleds to the bloody forest.

* * * * *

Then the Soviets counterattacked, repulsing our brigade. Only the 3rd Company remained, holding its ridges, cut off from everybody from then on.

We ran, the commander and I, to try to check the retreat. But the Soviet push was phenomenally violent. We could foresee the moment when, apart from the 3rd Company, lost in the depths of the woods, the entire brigade would be chased from its outposts in the forest and pushed back into the bare fields, where the rout would become a massacre.

At five o'clock in the evening the situation stabilized, but was still tragic nonetheless. The forest had not been taken. The brigade held only two hundred meters at the fringe of the woods. The 3rd Company was lost. We didn't know exactly where it was. It could be wiped out at any time.

We held had an impromptu council of war in an isba at the bottom of the valley. Everyone nodded his head dolefully. General Gille, as was his habit, waited ten minutes without saying anything. He had prominent cheekbones, clenched jaws, and hard eyes when he lifted his face and stood up.

"The attack will continue," he said simply. He looked us straight in the eye, without a smile.

"And you will take the forest," he added.

* * * * *

A glacial night fell.

It was twenty degrees below zero.

The men, at the edge of the oak forest, had nowhere to lie down and couldn't build a fire. They were freezing to death in spite of their winter equipment. They would huddle in a heap in the snow while the sentinels kept watch in front of them.

The engineers unrolled their barbed wire and fastened it from tree to tree, then mined the terrain except for narrow passages, almost imperceptibly marked, through which our reconnaisance patrols could slip.

We tried to establish contact with the 3rd Company. A platoon composed exclusively of volunteers started into the woods towards the northeast.

But our information was inaccurate. In fact, the 3rd Company had not advanced as far as we thought. Our platoon went too far to the east and ran into powerful Soviet positions. There was a monster melee in the night. Our platoon leader, a colossus as wide as a house, the life of the party of his company, threw himself with all his weight right into the middle of an enemy bunker. They brought him back, his guts ripped open by submachine-gun fire. At the first-aid post he panted like a locomotive. They cared for him without much hope, but he recovered nonetheless. Eight months later he returned to our garrison at Breslau, as massive as before, his breast decorated with the Iron Cross First Class.

But the frightful wounds in his lower belly, although scarred over, had permanently impaired his health. At the end of a few weeks he realized that he could never again live like the others. So he took a one-kilogram mine from the armory, went to the bank of the Oder, and blew himself up.

On the riverbank we found a lung and several vertebrae. That was all. On his little table at the barracks he had left these words: "I don't want to be half a man. Farewell my friends! Vive la Legion!"

* * * * *

The night attack of this Spartan's platoon yielded no results. Our 3rd Company could not be found. The next morning I tried to look for our young comrades alone.

The armor of our brigade was hidden on the northern edge of the forest. I lay down flat on my stomach on the armor of one of the *Sturmgeschuetzen** and followed the steppe two kilometers east of our staging attack the previous evening. It was there, headquarters thought, that the lost company must be.

They were wrong. It was only halfway to this point. I entered the oak forest a kilometer too far. Stunned but powerless to do anything, our lost soldiers saw the Panzer emerge far in front of them and put me down right in the middle of the Soviet sector.

The fiery welcome I received near the first trees quickly convinced me there were few friends to be discovered here. The tank driver brought me back with great difficulty amid twenty showers of earth and snow thrown up by shell bursts.

But that afternoon the engineers who were stringing their reels of barbed-wire between the oaks as far as possible towards the northeast stumbled onto several boys of the 3rd Company who were holding the southeastern end of their sector. The poor lads were blue with cold. They were encamped amid some twenty Russian corpses. We quickly linked up with them, consolidating our liaison with hundreds of mines. By nightfall, finally, we had a continuous front.

But what a night!

The 3rd Company was holding the crests it had taken. In the subsoil below them they found a sort of tombs, dug before the frost, into which two or three men at most might slip. These mole-holes, real Soviet specialties, were as high as a coffin. The Soviets would spread dry leaves in them and, once inside the den, would close the opening with an old piece of canvas or horsehair cloth. In these burrows where no one could enter except by crawling, Mongols, Tartars, and Siberians clung together one against another, making one another comfortable, like the beasts, by means of their animal warmth alone.

Our young people had taken the place of the muzhiks, whose bodies, shriveled and hard as stone, were scattered about outside. On these two sheer crests alone our volunteers had captured seven Soviet cannons. The German artillery had aided them powerfully. The terrain was completely cut up, every tree mowed down or split, slashed a hundred times. Clusters of bodies were all tangled together, dead hands still clutching bandages, round and hairy faces from Kirghizistan, their beards red with frozen blood, girls in khaki, fallen on their backs, their hair in the snow.

For our child-soldiers this macabre cohabitation in the freezing night was ghastly. Like the famous Walloon "Greenhorns" of the Empress Maria-Theresa, they had among them all barely ten or twelve wisps of blond down on their chins.[1] Although their eyes were dark with exhaustion, they mounted guard bravely among the stiff corpses they bumped in the night at each change of guard.

* * * * *

The other companies were camped on ground like concrete. We managed to build makeshift bunkers there at night only by dragging piles of tree trunks across the snow and arranging them as best we could. We huddled together, feeling the cold slice through us right to the marrow.

On 17 January 1944 General Gille came to ascertain the state of the sector.

A tank followed his reconnaissance vehicle. It was full of chocolate, cigarettes, and cognac. The soldiers understood perfectly what this distribution meant: we were going to attack again.

It was hardly credible.

The men's faces were sallow and green as leeks, just like the faces of the dead Soviets toppled everywhere in the snow.

Night, which would cover our preparations, came sharp and crystalline.

## Seven Hundred Bunkers

To send our entire brigade into the attack on the forest of Teclino, as on the first day, would have been to send it to certain death.

We could no longer count on the effect of surprise. The Soviets were holding all the high ground in the heart of the forest. Only the sort of audacious strike at which our soldiers exceled might render a new attack possible.

It was agreed that at midnight five groups of Walloons, armed with machine guns, would slip through the narrow passages in our mine fields. They would infiltrate deeply into the enemy positions. They had orders to penetrate at least eight hundred meters. If one of these squads should attract the attention of the Soviets, one man was to sacrifice himself and pretend to flee, so that the enemy would think they had to do only with an isolated scout.

The goal was not to reconnoiter the terrain, but to hide and remain there. Under cover of darkness our groups would crouch among or behind the enemy positions at points which gave the most command of the terrain. From there, at dawn, at the moment when our brigade began the assault, they would unleash the full force of their guns in a devastating fire onto the Bolsheviks, who would be dazed to find themselves attacked in so many places inside their lines and even in their counter-dikes.

The five groups all comprised highly motivated volunteers. Two Walloons would stay among the enemy to man each machine gun. A third would try to regain our lines to inform us of the outcome of this extraordinary mission and give us precise reference points.

* * * * *

High overhead, crystalline stars trembled here and there, and the ermined halo of the moon's red disk shimmered between the mighty crowns of the great oaks. But under the domes of the branches the darkness was thick, pierced only by the blue glimmer of a few lunar flowers strewn where a fallen tree had torn the black lace of the sky.

For hours we had been watching the shadows.

The Soviets, too, were probing all around. Three times Red soldiers were blown up on one of our mines in a great red flashes. Our lookouts received a shock each time, for the explosions took place within a few meters of our log posts. "Another one!" they would mutter, rubbing their frozen noses with snow. Then silence would reign once again in the gloomy forest.

Finally it was midnight. Our boys, carrying their machine guns, advanced to the secret corridors which our engineers had left free of mines.

Two hours, three hours of waiting, and the anxiety diminished.

The cold was horrible; we were cold if we walked, we were cold if we didn't walk. The woods continued to be shaken from time to time by the fiery spray as a muzhik touched the trip wire of one of our mines with his padded foot.

Each of our lookouts scanned the forest until his eyes almost popped out of his head. If the raids had succeeded, our messengers should soon arrive in front of our mined barbed-wire. They too were being stalked by death, just like the Russians.

A mine blew up. "Help! Help!" cried a voice. It was the first of our comrades, who had touched an enemy mine.

He dragged himself through the blackness. We could hear him crawling toward us, his breath labored. A second explosion shook us, more terrible even than the first. The poor wretch had triggered one of our own mines this time.

We had to go and pick him up, a bundle of mangled flesh lying there amid his scattered intestines. He still had the strength to tell us that the others had succeeded and that all would go well.

For the sake of the other messengers who had to chance this trip across the maze of Soviet mines, we began calling out from time to time. Four times we heard a whisper. "Don't move, someone is coming!" we would murmur, and a brave comrade would slip through the narrow mine-free passage to guide the messenger and bring him to the command post.

At four o'clock complete success was confirmed. The five groups had posted themselves at least a thousand meters in front of our avenues of attack. One of them was installed thirteen hundred meters ahead, behind the second enemy line.

It was wonderful.

* * * * *

At five o'clock, when the woods were beginning to purple with the first light of day, each of our companies crossed the mine-free passage of its sector, marked by two little white ribbons.

We now had only to charge the enemy.

It was a well-prepared operation. The field telephone advanced alongside the company commanders, so that each one of these knew the general state of progress minute by minute. On the right wing the hilltops were promptly taken. The groups of machine-gunners, astutely placed, had evidently worked miracles from the beginning of the fray. Heaps of Soviet dead were piling up on the edge of the hills.

The center had paralleled the movement across easier terrain. As for the left wing, supported by the tanks which advanced along the length of the woods and furiously battered the north of the oak forest, its advance was very rapid.

By special invitation I had once more taken command of the 3rd Company for several hours. I preceded the main body of my cadets by about thirty meters in order to avoid any unnecessary casualties. The ground was covered by half a meter of snow. The enemy, sure of his trap, was waiting.

There was a huge explosion. The first three boys who followed twenty-meters behind me, practically in the tracks of my boots, had just been blown up on a mine field. I had got through without touching a single wire among a hundred and fifty explosives strung together in every direction. The others had been less lucky, alas! Their legs were horribly slashed. Within five minutes their bloody feet were totally frozen, irremediably frozen, ivory-colored and as hard as stone.

The Russian winter was pitiless. A serious wound to any limb meant a dead limb. Sleds took away the mutilated men while our advance continued.

The enemy was strongly barricaded. The fight lasted a long time. We fought until evening. The next day, very early, we occupied the forest totally.

Before our assault the German artillery had pulverized the enemy positions one last time. We had to step over a hardened body every meter, and scattered on the earth near it, a brown kepi, a submachine gun, and some stale bread. But prior to the final hand-to-hand fighting, the Reds had treated their prisoners horribly. One young SS man had been crucified alive. Another was lying there, his belly and legs brown with congealed blood: the monsters had cut off his sexual organs and stuffed them into his mouth.

In spite of the victory, this vision of savagery terrified us.

* * * * *

In four days of battle we had captured seven hundred bunkers.

Latvians in long white jackets came to relieve us.

Two hundred meters below our trenches, the valley shone. The great forest at our back was free. Once again it had taken on its peaceful colors: white, blue, lilac. The corpses had become as stiff as tree branches. They were no longer as frightening as on the first day.

Our companies disengaged one by one. The big trucks of the brigade were waiting for us below the valley. We left by a snowy path which followed along the heights, turning back often to look at the triangle of the forest of Teclino in the distance.

An ever-smaller triangle. But already the future was elsewhere.

## The Closed Trap

Ten days had yet to pass before the great drama.

We had again taken up our positions along the Olshanka.

Descending from the north, the Soviet armies had spread irresistibly across the whole breadth of the Ukraine. They were even nearing Vinnitsa, two hundred kilometers to our rear, and the last great river the Germans still held before the Romanian frontier, the Bug.

The northern armies were no longer seeking to throttle us in a restricted encirclement, as at the beginning of January. From now on a gigantic operation was in progress.

The Soviet armies of the southeast had swept into Kirovograd from their side. If they succeeded in linking up with the armies of the southwest a phenomenal *Kessel** would enclose us all.

To try to ward off this menace, almost all of the Viking Division was posted to the southeastern sector, on our right wing, whereas before it had been on our left wing, to the northeast, along the Dnieper for eighty kilometers and then coming back up the Olshanka River as far as our positions at the village of Moshny.

We had to extend ourselves from Moshny clear to Losovok, then to the Dnieper itself, thus supporting the burden of some hundred kilometers of front all by ourselves.

If our complement of artillery, anti-tank weapons, anti-aircraft weapons, and engineers was still almost intact, our infantry companies had been greatly weakened by two months of raids and battles and had at their disposal less than a thousand or so front line troops. Thus in reality we would have to face the very worst threats with our men spaced out on the average at the rate of twenty per kilometer.

We spaced out our strongpoints more and more, so that every night they risked being choked off or overrun.

To the northeast of the big bridge at Moshny stretched an irregular wilderness: rust-colored scrub, reeds, sand, bogs. After having crossed kilometers of somber moors, we reached our positions at Losovok.

There we had no more than a handful of soldiers, one company in all, Captain Derickx's Second Company, which had been transferred from Staroselye. It had to cover the entire east of the sector, in other words the steppe, the town of Losovok, several kilometers of bases on the dunes, and to complete the picture, a section of the right bank of the Dnieper.

We were happy to be there and to fly proudly the colors of our country. But these pretty sentiments aside, our men felt uneasy on the bank of this great muddy river, before these magnificent islands, amidst a countryside riddled with pitiless enemies.

The division headquarters had moved thirty kilometers to the south. We had installed the command post of our brigade at Belozerye, which had become a central point for us from then on. There, where yesterday the commander of the Viking Division had concentrated his telephone installations, his radio vans, his innumerable vehicles, his *Abteilungen** of all kinds, his *Feldgendarmes** in every corner, our modest signals platoon rattled around as in a ghost town.

On Friday, 28 January 1944, I was ordered to the division staff office at Gorodishche. The countryside, planted with thousands of fruit trees, had much charm. On the snowy hills the black or reddish sails of tall windmills stood out romantically.

General Gille had his headquarters near the green and white Orthodox church in a modern building that the Soviet aircraft came to machine-gun every quarter hour.

The superior officers kept making jokes, but the repartee had a false ring. I was shown confidentially the text of the radio telegram that the Division had just sent to Himmler: "In three hours, the encirclement of the Viking will have been achieved."

Nevertheless, no one wanted to believe that this was be definitive. Someone would surely do something to come to our rescue. General Gille just stared silently. The Soviet airplanes reappeared incessantly, bombarding the whole quarter furiously. In the midst of all this the *Feldgendarmes* were ransacking the isbas and pulling out clusters of malingerers. The atmosphere was bizarre. Despite their assurances, the officers were visibly worried, and the soldiers were dead tired.

I returned to Belozerye, sniffing the dry air, admiring the brilliant blue of the marvelously clear sky, moved in spite of all our troubles.

Back at the command post two hours later, a telephone call from the division informed us in one fateful sentence, "The Soviet forces have made their junction in the southeast."

Eleven German divisions, more or less complete, were surrounded. Exactly one year after the tragedy on the Volga, a second Stalingrad was beginning.

# Chapter Six
# SURROUNDED AT CHERKASSY

The knot completing the encirclement of the eleven German divisions in the Cherkassy zone was tied on 28 January 1944, eighty kilometers to the rear of our lines.

But the enemy had arrived within fifteen kilometers of Korsun, to the west of our command post of Belozerye. We could hear the tanks roaring.

Day and night, we lived in our boots and clothes and kept submachine guns and grenades within reach at all times. The engineers were busy with countless demolitions. The nights were filled with sinister noises.

Three days passed.

We were beginning to get used to the *Kessel.* Survivors of a hundred traps, on the Donets, on the Don, and in the Caucasus, we felt this was scarcely our first crisis. We all wanted to think this encirclement would be just one more adventure. The high command wouldn't abandon us here. The counterattack would break the Soviet ring for certain.

A radio-telegram from the celebrated General Hube had in theory settled the business. This telegram was nice and short: "I'm coming."

The general came.

An enormous column of German tanks was coming up from the south. It had unceremoniously taken a bite out of the Soviet corridor established in our rear. Avidly, we followed the progress of our liberators on the map. Dozens of villages were falling. The communique announced the destruction of one hundred ten Russian tanks. At the end of two days, nothing was left but to break through a line of enemy trenches nine kilometers across.

Those who returned from that sector told us with shining eyes that contact with our rescuers had already been established by way of the little radio sets in the battalion command post. Another blow of the German battering ram, and the breakthrough and our extrication would be accomplished.

The blow of the battering ram did indeed take place. It was the Soviets who delivered it. They had promptly brought up new armored forces. The three hundred German tanks which had managed to come so close to us had had to stop, then give ground, then retreat. Soon the Reds had a security zone fifty kilometers wide in our rear. Emboldened by their success, the Soviet divisions rushed from the southeast and the south toward the interior of our *Kessel,* this time pushing the mass of the surrounded troops back toward the north and east, removing them farther and farther from the German front from which might eventually come their salvation. Another catastrophe was looming.

Since the beginning of the encirclement, a spring-like warmth had followed the freeze. It was like early May. During the winter of 1941-42, during the counteroffensive of the Donets, we had seen how two days of sudden thaw had turned the paths into a muddy sea. But the cold had returned immediately and put things right again.

Therefore we watched the snow melt with curiosity at first. Fast-moving black clouds sailed through the sky. Lashed by a sharp little rain, we skidded on an almost impassable shining wet ice. Then the fields became brown and yellow again. The forest, thoroughly laved, spread its purple spoils on the hills. The clearings cut black screens. The roads softened under the weight of incessant traffic, then liquefied. The greyish water rose halfway up the doors.

We were still laughing. It was funny. Every one of us was plastered from head to toe.

At the end of four or five days the frost hadn't returned. Every shelter and trench was flooded under its melt water. The soldiers, armed with pitchers and mess tins, tried to bail out these bathtubs.

The fields were so viscous that they became totally impassable. The roads sank more and more. Many crossroads became totally unusable, the water-level reaching a meter high. The slopes were frightful skating rinks, as sticky as resin. The tractors worked night and day to get stuck vehicles going again.

Now there were fifteen thousand motorized vehicles inside the *Kessel,* fifteen thousand vehicles which were beginning to form a circle, squeezed closer and closer together by the thrusts of a primitive enemy, indifferent to the elements, an enemy whose soldiers just loved to crawl in the mire of the interminable marshes.

* * * * *

The Soviets had seized several important depots concentrated fifty or sixty kilometers to the south of the Cherkassy sector at the point where the Red armies had met. Considerable quantities of gasoline and munitions had been lost on the first day.

Thanks to some big Junkers airplanes the German command had immediately sent help to the besieged divisions.

Korsun had a landing strip. The Ju's ran the airlift with sublime precision. Each day about seventy machines would arrive loaded with munitions, gas, and food. As soon as they unloaded they would be filled with the gravely wounded. We were thus able to evacuate all the hospitals in the *Kessel* in the nick of time.

But the Soviet fighters were watching. They would patrol the drizzling sky, circling like hawks above the field. Every day twelve or fifteen of our Ju's, shot down after a few minutes of flight, would fall down in flames amid the screams of the wounded, who were being grilled alive.

It was a frightful spectacle.

The airlift continued, methodically, heroically, without an instant's lapse until the time when, there too, the monstrous mire made any work impossible.

At the end of a week of thaw and flood, the landing field was completely submerged. The engineers tried by every means to drain the mud and consolidate the plain. It was useless. The last airplanes capsized in mire a meter deep. Thereafter until the end, not a single airplane managed to take off or even to land in the *Kessel.*

We were left to our own resources.

* * * * *

Posted at the easternmost point, the Assault Brigade "Wallonia" escaped the worst of the enemy's clawing during the first few days.

As expected, the enemy concentrated its thrust south and west of the *Kessel.* The two Soviet spearheads, daringly linked, absorbed the blows of the German forces trying to break out. The Soviets threw all their tanks and the mass of their infantry and cavalry divisions into this corridor.

At the Olshanka and the Dnieper, the Red offensive was as yet only by radio. A powerful transmitter, installed just opposite our lines, peddled propaganda every day in a honeyed French. A speaker with a Parisian accent charitably informed us of our situation. Then he tried to seduce us, vaunting the marvels of friend Stalin's regime and inviting us to come over to General De Gaulle. He would allow us to approach the Russian lines holding a white handkerchief in our hands, like sentimental aunties.

This sugar-coated Soviet propaganda was lacking neither in imagination nor in ruse. Two of our soldiers captured at Losovok had been taken to the command post of a division general. He invited them to his table, served them a royal dinner, toasted them with excellent champagne, and stuffed their pockets with chocolate. Then the bespangled hypocrite had them taken in his car near the lines. The guards let the two guests go off in our direction, as one opens the cage door to canaries or nightingales.

The adventure was a huge success with the troops. Everyone licked his chops to think of the champagne and chocolate of those two lucky devils. But the philanthropic and Walloon-loving general got nothing out of it. No one took the hook, which was a little bit too visible under the lure.

As the enemy hammered the rear front of the *Kessel* the Viking Division had to pull back the units it was still keeping on the bank of the Dnieper and send them to the southeast. After a few days our left flank was almost completely unprotected. No one was left to defend the eighty kilometers along the Dnieper to the northeast of our positions but a detachment of about two hundred Germans of the Viking, mounted on little armored cars which ceaselessly ploughed back and forth on the mucky trails.

The Reds sent patrols beyond the river and found the gap. Now nothing was left except our weak positions at the confluence of the Dnieper and the Olshanka. All the Soviets had to do now to annihilate the last obstacle still remaining at the east of the *Kessel* was to force their way through or attack from the rear.

We were particularly worried about the great wooden bridge built over the Olshanka at the west end of Moshny.

Beyond the river we occupied two strong points defended by about ten men armed with two machine guns. If the Reds attacked in force during the night they would crush this unlucky post and succeed in taking the bridge intact.

Warned of the danger, the staff office of the Viking Division turned a deaf ear. We could not, we were told, either yield one inch of ground or give the enemy the impression that we were losing confidence in the outcome of the combat.

The general was far away, whereas we, on the other hand, beheld the imminent catastrophe right before our eyes. The German liaison officer effected the blowing up of the bridge with all possible discretion. By a telephone call at 6:00 A.M. he notified the general that a Soviet shell had just fallen right in the middle of our explosives, completely destroying the bridge. We were, he added, ever so sorry.

So was the general.

But the question of the bridge was thus resolved.

* * * * *

We lost our last scruples that very night.

At Moshny we had a platoon of about fifty Russian auxiliaries at our disposition, former prisoners who had enlisted voluntarily in the ranks of the German army.

Until then they had been very devoted and very disciplined. But sending them back to fight in their own country had been an error. Their ancestry overcame their new allegiance. At the end of three months their race, their precious race, reasserted its claim.

They used to hold long confabulations with the natives, of which our officers didn't understand a word. Finally the partisans got in touch with them. The night of 1-2 February 1944, these Russians, who worked the heavy mortars behind the lines, slipped on cat's feet toward the Olshanka.

A brave young Walloon who was standing guard in the darkness was killed silently by a knife thrust in the back. The fleeing column stepped over his warm corpse, descended the ditch, and crossed the water.

From then on we had some fifty deserters across from us who had lived at Moshny for three months, who knew exactly the placement of our positions, of our artillery, and of the command, telephone, and radio posts. Fifty guides were at the disposition of the Soviet command.

* * * * *

Sure of themselves, the Reds launched their assault at 8:00 A.M., beyond Moshny, between Losovok and the Dnieper at the very eastern extremity of our sector.

The few dozen Walloons who were scattered in these sandy moors were swamped by grenades and overrun in one hour's time. On the same morning we learned from the brigade command post that Losovok was under attack and had fallen.

The 2nd Company, driven from the last houses, had to recross a watercourse to the south of the village and had even been pushed back a kilometer beyond that. They had managed somehow or other to cling to an embankment right on the steppe.

The defense of the Dnieper bank was at an impasse. Losovok, atop of a sandy slope, seemed definitively lost. We asked Division to bring the survivors of Losovok back to Moshny, where the greatest danger imperiled our meager strength.

But the orders were pitiless. Not only was the 2nd Company not to withdraw to the south, but it was to make an immediate counterattack and retake Losovok regardless of obstacles.

Far away at the end of the telephone wire an almost inaudible voice told us where the 2nd Company had withdrawn to. I knew the Losovok sector very well, and succeeded in being put in charge of the counterattack. I received two Panzers and ordered a load of husky fellows to climb aboard.

Through great rivers of mud, along routes flooded with water spreading to a breadth of a hundred meters, we pushed eastwards. Overturned automobiles and the hooves of dead horses were everywhere, half sunk in the slime near the trails.

## Losovok

Beyond the reddish heather of the steppe rose the smoke from the battle for Losovok. We passed Moshny. The company command post was so buried in mud that the messengers could no longer reach it except by crossing on foot a makeshift bridge of some twenty isba doors.

After three kilometers of jolting over mire and bush our tanks reached the embankment where the survivors of Losovok were holding out. The enemy was pounding the marshes and the swollen river.

We took up positions for the assault. Division had promised us artillery support. After the shelling of Losovok we would advance, reinforced by our two Panzers.

It was three o'clock in the afternoon. After much palaver on the field telephone the artillery announced that in twenty minutes it would open fire. Crouched in the mire, we surveyed the plain to be crossed, across which a few horses galloped in panic.

Far to the east the signal flares lit the sky, showing us that our troops still resisted on the Dnieper, although the Soviet troops had advanced several kilometers past them.

Bullets whistled by endlessly. The enemy had taken roost at the south of the village, twenty meters above a stream. It wouldn't be easy to get back up there.

* * * * *

A first German shell fell. Then, long afterwards, another.

Eighteen fell.

That was all.

We insisted. In vain. It was impossible to help us more than that. Munitions in the *Kessel* were frightfully low.

We would just have to make do with this pitiful hors d'oeuvre. Surging down the slope, we sprinted across thickets and fields, cut by a swift torrent three or four meters wide.

Shells rained down. No one hesitated before throwing himself into the icy water. From copse to copse, we approached the river below Losovok.

Our two Panzers, riddled by machine gun fire, fired incendiary bullets into the Soviet-occupied isbas. The houses ignited one after another, bursting into flames. The Reds fled from hedge to hedge.

In the heat of battle a handful of Walloons rushed with incredible pluck toward the wooden bridge which joined the plain to the sunken path to the village. They crossed it and took cover below the cliff. One, armed with a machine gun, climbed to the top of the crest, and the others, covered by him, crawled through the sand like serpents. Twenty, then thirty Walloons made it to the summit.

The Panzers which seconded the infantry should also have started across the bridge. But a placard read, "Three Tons." The first German tank preferred to cross the river, some twenty meters wide. The riverbed was sandy. A chain broke. The tank was stuck in the water.

The second tank didn't want to attack alone. It fired several more shells into the houses, then went to work to dig out the panzer mired in the sand.

Now we couldn't count on anything but our infantry. House by house, we retook the village in hand-to-hand fighting.

* * * * *

At six o'clock in the evening a dazzling, pearly twilight blended with the orange lights of burning isbas. It was our last look at Losovok, at the white and gold dunes beyond the Olshanka's union with the Dnieper amidst large yellow and green islands.

We would not see another red and purple dawn rise on the sand cliffs where for weeks had flown, modest yet proud, the flag of our country. We would not again stand pensive on the shore of the huge and shining legendary river flowing down toward Dniepropetrovsk, toward the brown rocks, the delta, and the sea. The field telephone had just rung, thin and febrile. The division was calling us, dictating new orders: "General retreat from the sector!"

On the left wing, the movement was already completed. The last two hundred German motorized riflemen protecting our flank on the Dnieper had been withdrawn. We were to evacuate Losovok by nightfall, rejoin the two Walloon companies at Moshny, and withdraw with them in the morning toward new, more southerly positions.

Our assault had been worthless, except perhaps as a proof of courage and discipline. But we were the last, the very last, of the armies of the east to fight on the bank of the Dnieper. Our hearts pounding, we savored the aroma of the river. We watched the grey glimmerings, threaded with silver, of the powerful waters in the twilight. Sadly, we lowered our little flag.

Across the quicksands, the bogs, the muddy trails, we streamed back with our wounded. We turned to look back toward the east a hundred times. There our hearts had lived. At last Losovok aflame was no more than a red ember in the depth of the night.

Dnieper! Dnieper! Dnieper!

* * * * *

The closer we drew to Moshny, the more amazed we were by the violence of the sounds of battle.

We had left one melee only to find another.

The enemy had just attacked Moshny. The fifty Russian and Asiatic auxiliaries who had betrayed us the previous evening were at the head of the Soviet troops and had guided them through the darkness to the vital points of our sector.

When we reached the village hundreds of men were battling with a terrible fury around our pieces of artillery, which were shooting point-blank at the assailants. On every street, in the courtyard of every isba hand-to-hand fighting raged amidst the quagmires and the clammy slopes, in the blinding light of millions of sparks from the blazing hovels.

We had more than fifty trucks at Moshny, numerous pieces of artillery, anti-tank weapons, anti-aircraft guns, tractors, field kitchens, communications equipment, and the offices of several companies. Everywhere men were killing one another frenziedly. Drivers, cooks, paymasters, telephone operators, everyone was defending his weapon, his equipment, his skin.

The orders of the Viking Division staff office were categorical. We were not to leave Moshny until the end of the night in order to cover the general retreat which now stretched across twenty kilometers.

The tragedy was that the Soviets had attacked in force a few hours before the withdrawal was to take place. Therefore we absolutely had to oppose them at any price, hanging on in Moshny until morning.

The night was nothing but an interminable free-for-all, savage, howling, amid the blackness and the raw red of the fires. The long village was evacuated quarter by quarter, hour by hour, only when all the equipment had been hauled to the southern route.

Our telephone communications weren't interrupted for a single minute. We knew with absolute precision how our equipment was being withdrawn. The soldiers fought from isba to isba, their fury mirrored in their eyes, beset by waves of Mongols who leaped from bushes, hedges, sheds, and even from the filth of the dunghills.

The killing lasted ten hours. At dawn, covered by one last platoon, the haggard defenders of Losovok and Moshny, their uniforms glued to their skin, found themselves once more on the southern route, marching on each side of the column of trucks, which kept skidding in a half meter of slime.

The men shielding them were to hold the houses in southwest Moshny the whole morning. These orders were followed heroically. Only after noon did the Reds finally take the village. They took only two Walloons alive, both telephone operators who stood fast, obeying orders to report enemy progress to our command right to the end.

They were still calling us when the Reds passed in front of their window.

But by this time, thanks to the fanatical resistance at Moshny, the Wallonian Brigade had already been able to regroup at Belozerye, ready for the next mission.

Six kilometers of tar-like mud separated us from an enemy uncertain of our intentions.

## Steps

It was Thursday, 3 February 1944.

Orders to evacuate Losovok and the last sector of the right bank to the east of the *Kessel* hadn't been given until the general situation had considerably worsened.

The battering-ram thrusts of the enemy in the south had pushed the surrounded troops more and more to the north. Now the Soviet corridor was eighty kilometers wide. Every day the Reich's divisions lost another five or ten kilometers. Another week and the Soviets would be right behind us.

The High Command had withdrawn all the German forces from the Dnieper-Olshanka region. From then on we were the only ones protecting this zone and were at the mercy of a drive which in twenty-four hours could sweep us away like a straw and skewer the pocket.

Momentous decisions had been made. The southern and southeastern sectors would be progressively abandoned. The troops of the eastern sector would then withdraw gradually from east to north. Next, fighting every inch of the way, they would fall back towards the western end of the *Kessel,* where eleven divisions would gather.

German tanks would come up from southwestern Ukraine, outside the *Kessel,* to meet us. Our eleven divisions would rush toward them, risking everything.

There was no longer any other way out. Either this desperate attempt would break the encirclement or we would all die.

* * * * *

On the 3rd of February, 1944, however, we still had not massed for the final assault. Numerous secondary operations had to be carried out to evacuate the equipment and depots.

It was folly, in any case. Although every man was needed to fight, three quarters of the encircled forces were diverted from combat to save all this hardware. All became targets.

Already the road from Gorodishche to Korsun, our last chance to break out, was jammed by an incredible column. Thousands of trucks, spread over twenty kilometers, followed three front vehicles and skated in the black frogholes of the road, which had become a prodigious cloaca. The most powerful artillery tractors struggled painfully to open a passage. This enormous mass of vehicles was an incomparable target for planes. The Soviet machines, like strident swarms of wasps, would circle over the *Kessel* and dive down in squadrons every ten minutes onto the bogged-down columns.

Everywhere trucks were burning.

The mud, churned a thousand times, became so sticky and so bulky that it was soon absolutely impossible to cross.

We had to resort to desperate measures. To venture across the firmer ground of the fields would mean foundering within one or two hundred meters. The road? It was no longer thinkable. A thousand trucks at least were bogged down there for all time, and would have to be set on fire lest the enemy retrieve them. The only thing left was the railroad line from

Gorodishche to Korsun. That was the way we decided to send the endless motorized convoys.

We could guess where the traffic was ten kilometers away by watching the Soviet fighters dive. Huge flashes marked this makeshift route. We had to keep pushing broken-down trucks and flaming cars down the embankment.

In order to protect this unprecedented transfer of more than ten thousand vehicles on the bumpy ties of a pitiful railroad line, our troops had to hold the Soviet thrust for several days more.

* * * * *

From high in the sky the Stalinist pilots would contemplate at their leisure our attempts to withdraw the surrounded troops. Everything told them where we would gather: like hundreds of torches, burning trucks lit the way to Korsun.

To the south the Soviet assailants were striking the retreating troops hard and fast. From the northeast, open since the retreat of the Viking's last tanks, the troops of the USSR were now rushing in. From the north, too, the divisions of the Wehrmacht began to retreat faster and faster.

As for us, we would first have to fight at Belozerye to block the Soviet troops coming up from the Dnieper and from Moshny. From Belozerye we would have to reach, at the last minute, a line of defense we had constructed some fifteen kilometers further south at the beginning of January.

This line ran from the southwest to the northwest, from the village of Staroselye to the village of Derenkovez.

A third operation would regroup us all on this northwestern line, at Derenkovez itself: in concert with other Wehrmacht and Waffen SS units we would serve as the final shield.

Thus protected, fifty to sixty thousand men, withdrawing from all sectors, would reunite around Korsun for the decisive assault toward the west.

* * * * *

The first stop for us was therefore Belozerye. The withdrawal plan instructed us to resist east of this village for whatever time it would take for all the artillery and equipment to reach the line of Staroselye-Derenkovez without disaster.

The removal of our guns and heavy vehicles was being prepared along the Olshanka from Baibusy to Staroselye. The departure would take place under cover of darkness.

We were able to keep sending reconnaissance groups as far as Moshny. South of Moshny itself we still had a few machine guns hidden in the fir groves. Every Soviet patrol which ventured in our direction was received with heavy fire.

The night passed. The artillery men worked themselves to exhaustion in the quagmires to extract their weapons. At dawn only the infantry and the mortars were still in position at the edge of the water. The last vehicles left Baibusy shortly after daybreak.

One team had had a trace broken. The drivers returned to the village to repair it.

A deathly silence reigned everywhere. Dead peasants were sprawled across the muddy street, faces to the ground, still wearing on their right arms the white armbands marked *Deutsche Wehrmacht* in black letters. Our soldiers had been gone from Baibusy for barely ten minutes, and already the partisans had slaughtered all the Ukrainians who had served in the German auxiliary formations.

The village was quiet. Not a single curious face peeped out. But the corpses, lying in the mud, were eloquent.

* * * * *

The 3rd Company infantry, still holding the Olshanka passage east of Baibusy, were to withdraw the following night, worming their way along the river to the village of Staroselye.

As for the 2nd Company, after its odyssey at Losovok it had started withdrawal maneuvers on a broad front, heading first towards the northwest. It was supposed to check enemy pressure against Derenkovez until our right wing had finished its two-step maneuver.

I received orders to effect a liaison with this isolated unit. A muddy desert about ten kilometers across separated it from Belozerye. I had at my disposal only an old Volkswagen which toiled laboriously through the sand and mud. A single soldier accompanied me. We found our comrades at the edge of a dark pine forest, a tiny island of resistance lost in an entire country. We went through another lifeless village. A Soviet patrol was leaving the other end just as we entered. In princely fashion, it had left the peasants a box of matches bearing the hammer and sickle in exchange for their poultry.

The families were hiding in the rear of their isbas. The entire region was infested with enemy advance units.

We expected to fall into an ambush at any moment. The Volkswagen kept coughing, smoking, stalling, visibly disgusted with it all.

Belozerye at dusk was no longer recognizable.

My little tan rattletrap was taken for the first Soviet automobile by the population. From behind the hedges, a few fearful heads appeared. An incredible silence reigned.

We jolted from pothole to pothole through the watery streets to rejoin the last platoon awaiting the hour of evacuation. Guns, trucks, equipment, everything had gone.

Our rear guard was not to leave Belozerye until night, after giving the appearance of resolute resistance right up to the end. The village was square, and we could be overrun from any direction. We still numbered about forty soldiers in all.

The telephone unit had been withdrawn. Evening fell, veiled in mist.

Finally the men left their dank toad-holes and climbed aboard the last two trucks. Not a cry. Not a pistol shot. Not a silhouette. Only a few peasants opened their doors a crack to see us leave.

* * * * *

The positions that we were to occupy ran along a distance of about thirty kilometers from Staroselye to Derenkovez.

One part of the brigade was to go directly to Derenkovez. That night it came upon some groups of partisans who had sneaked from copse to copse and had already cut off all escape to the west. Our soldiers had to wage a gun battle at point-blank range right in the forest. Two of our weapons were lost in the scuffle.

The southern road to Staroselye was even more dangerous. If our last combat units, covering our left along the Olshanka, had shown a moment's weakness, our only line of retreat would have been irremediably cut off.

We had crossed scarcely two kilometers when we came upon vehicles stuck in the mud. The columns we had covered, and which had been withdrawing for many hours, had got bogged down. Trucks were stalled in the road. Hundreds of men stormed about, sunk in the filthy muck up to mid-thigh. Tractors were breaking down trying to pull out the heavy vehicles. The Reds might fall upon us at any moment.

After hours of herculean labor the equipment was put back into working order and we reached the forest, then the vast marshlands which came before Staroselye.

It was one o'clock in the morning.

The road ended in a gigantic puddle. The trucks could only cross it by racing through at top speed.

The left bank of the Olshanka at Staroselye was dominated by a high ridge rising vertically from the Derenkovez canal. All the isbas on this hill were on fire. Hundreds of women pulling children along or carrying pigs in their arms stood out tragically, black against the brilliant background of the fires. They kept calling out in shrill voices, crying, pleading, stamping their feet in an atmosphere of madness.

The fire flowed like a fabulous red and yellow mane. It made the viscid slope, which not a single truck managed to climb, glow like marble. With great labor, enormous artillery tractors hauled the automobiles and the trucks up the hill through the slime.

All night the shrill cries of the women echoed the howling of the beasts and the frantic swearing of the drivers, scarlet in the light of the fires.

When day came vehicles were still being towed.

But to the northeast of the bottomlands, brown points were advancing. We could make out lines of men, horses, and gear.

The Reds were coming.

## Staroselye

The line of retreat from Staroselye to Derenkovez had been dug by thousands of Ukrainians at the beginning of January. At dawn on 5 February 1944, the Assault Brigade "Wallonia" occupied it.

The layout of the line had been well chosen. It extended from southeast to northwest atop high crests which overlooked the valley, the bogs, and the canal from Derenkovez to the Olshanka. Far away we could make out the forests by which we had returned from Belozerye.

The trench, dotted with numerous firing emplacements, extended in a zigzag for thirty kilometers. Unluckily it didn't have any fascines and had been dug too deep. It was so deep that, once inside this clayey serpent, we could no longer see a thing.

If the whole line of combat had been strongly held, this inconvenience would have been reduced. But we had only three hundred infantry men to defend thirty kilometers.

The 2nd Company was to have taken position fifteen kilometers north of Derenkovez. Another of our companies occupied a line facing the east which departed Staroselye at a right angle, straight toward the south.

We were left with three hundred infantrymen to hold the principal line. Thus we only had, on the average, a group of ten men to defend each kilometer of front.

The rest of the brigade, the drivers of our three hundred trucks, the artillery men, the anti-tank men, the anti-aircraft men, and the communications troops had fallen back behind the line of combat or were defending with light weapons the points of the trench which were particularly menaced.

* * * * *

We were extremely pessimistic.

It had been impossible to install a complete telephone network along so vast a line. It took dozens of kilometers of wire just to connect the company posts to the brigade command.

This trench, so vulnerable, was the only rampart in the northeast which could shelter the general withdrawal towards Korsun. If our barrier crumbled, it would be every man for himself in the heart of the *Kessel.*

Our men were dispersed in tiny groups, each isolated from the others. They were exhausted by the recent battles, by the nights of huddling together, by the icy mists, by the torturous slogging in pitch-like mud. They had no shelter. Filthy, their faces drawn and worried, they watched the plain where the Soviet advance guard was bustling about.

Our artillery had become useless: from Saturday afternoon on, the marshes were dotted with a thousand swarming enemies whom neither mud nor shells could stop.

* * * * *

The next day they penetrated our line before dawn.

The Reds had scaled the counterscarp during the night. They had had the good fortune to jump into an empty trench between two different posts. These were cut off, strangled. The Reds reached a mill dominating the hill in a few minutes. From there they plunged down toward the Olshanka, attacking a party of our men from behind. At seven o'clock in the morning the left bank of the river, in the village of Staroselye, was in the hands of the Bolsheviks.

The enemy now dominated the region from the hills to the west. By eight o'clock in the morning they were already spreading out several kilometers to the south.

Our command could just match this thrust. The commander immediately decided to go on ahead. I leaped into a Volkswagen with him and, driving through a stampede of horse drivers and trucks fleeing in panic, we reached the right bank of the Olshanka at Staroselye.

A heroic group of about thirty men was still resisting on the knolls of the left bank. I got into an armored command vehicle, crossed the water, climbed the slope, and joined our comrades. We immediately engaged in hand-to-hand combat, advancing upwards from isba to isba, rolling pell-mell in the mud with the Asiatics.

After an hour of battle we had liberated the village and reached the western end of town. Unluckily we were dominated by the bold mass of the crest and the picturesque mill, its wide black sails at rest. The Reds had installed machine-gun nests there, and their snipers were tracking our every move.

Kneeling in the corner of the last isba, I shot down every head which showed itself. But my position was too visible. A bullet had wounded me in the finger. Another creased by thigh. Within two minutes, a sixteen-year-old volunteer who had started to shoot beside me took a bullet right in the mouth. The poor youngster stood up for an instant, horrified, understanding nothing of what had happened to him. He opened his mouth wide, full of blood, no longer able to speak but wanting to explain all the same. He fell back down, writhed about in the mud, and hiccuped for a few seconds before dying.

Behind us the corpses of our companions, killed during the Soviet attack at dawn, had been completely despoiled during the half hour that the enemy controlled the west of Sakrevka. The bodies were completely nude, yellowed and reddened by the oily mud.

From the corner of our isba we saw the plain fill up with Soviet reinforcements in the north and northeast. Across the marshes lines of floundering men dragged anti-tank weapons. The hillside and the mill above us seemed impregnable.

The commander was sending us all the men he could gather in the area. But what could we do other than to prevent the Reds from retaking back the town? To venture beyond our isba, to attack a hill as smooth as shoe polish and without cover, would mean sinking up to our knees and invite a general massacre.

Nevertheless, we had to take back the mill and the summit. If not, the following night the enemy would mass all his forces there.

We had to re-establish the line without delay or else face a definitive break in the front, with all the consequences that disaster would bring.

* * * * *

I had asked for Panzers. Behind them and under the protection of their harassing fire we might just reach the mill and the crest.

But nothing happened.

We had to act, confuse the enemy.

A few volunteers slipped into the big trench and followed it back up toward the Reds. They were led by Lieutenant Thyssen, a strapping young man two meters tall with a jaw like Fernandel and the mischievous eyes of an overgrown kid. He tossed back all the grenades that the Reds threw at him with ease. A bullet went through his left arm. He carried on, unflappable and laughing heartily, freeing a hundred meters of terrain.

Finally, at 1400 hours, the German tanks arrived. There were only two of them, but their noisy advance was enough to throw the Reds into a panic. Many took to their heels. We could see them hastily taking down their machine guns, encrusted with the oozing cement of the parapets.

The tanks rumbled. Our little column rushed to follow them.

On the plain the Soviets were rolling in like a flood tide, pulling along their light artillery. They spotted our two Panzers moving along the bare hillside. Immediately, an avalanche of shells rained down from their anti-tank weapons, boxing in our tanks, cutting off the top of the rampart, killing our men.

The mill was our first objective.

My driver, Leopold Van Daele, a hero of the 1914–1918 war, rushed into the open terrain even ahead of the tanks. He was Flemish; a windmill was a familiar sight in his homeland. He was the first to reach one of the black sails and mow down three Stalinists with his submachine gun. But a Mongol hiding close to a buttress at the bottom of the trench took aim at him, his gun raised. The bullet slammed into him under the jaw and came back out at the top of his skull. Incredibly, he still found the strength to reach into his pocket and, like the confirmed Christian he was, grab his chaplet. Then he fell dead, his blue eyes wide open, fixed on the large and powerful mill, so like the old mills on the ramparts of Bruges in the country of Flanders.

* * * * *

By four o'clock in the afternoon we had retaken the whole hill.

The trench was littered with crude cartridge pouches that had been thrown away by the fleeing enemy. They were, as always, stuffed with cartridges, with stale and moldy bread, and sunflower seeds.

We had taken quite a haul of machine guns, but our victory left us skeptical. What did we have more than yesterday? Nothing. In fact, we had lost a number of our comrades. Killing the Soviets didn't do any good. They multiplied like wood lice, kept on coming back endlessly, ten times, twenty times as numerous as we.

These kilometers of trenches were a laughable protection, defended here and there by a few handfuls of Walloons who were hopelessly isolated amid the drizzle and the returning darkness. To the left and right of every post stretched a kilometer's gap.

The trench, trampled in both directions during the battle, had become disgustingly mucky. The position was quite clearly untenable. The drama would unfold very soon. There was no doubt whatsoever about that. The night was full of incessant and furtive sounds. The whole hillside was alive with invisible presences. Hundreds of Soviets were crawling, reaching the trench, and spreading out along it.

At dawn the tragedy of the previous evening began again. At seven o'clock in the morning, for the second time, the Soviet assault overwhelmed and drove out our comrades.

We knew that from then on, hill, trench, and mill were lost forever.

Our panzers had been recalled to the south. They wouldn't be back again.

Now what? There was no possible question of an early withdrawal.

Thousands of trucks, thousands of men were hastening toward Korsun. The flank which had protected them was now open.

## Skiti

The whole day of Monday, 7 February 1944, was spent trying to plug the breach that the Russians had made in the Staroselye-Derenkovez line.

At Staroselye itself out troops had regrouped on the right bank of the Olshanka river. The positions were good, strongly trenched and stockaded, protected by multiple barbed wires and by mines planted on the banks.

At the other extremity of the line, at Derenkovez, the 1st Company had endured numerous assaults, but it had valiantly held off the enemy.

On a right angle fifteen kilometers to the north of Derenkovez, the 2nd Company was continuing its interminable maneuver of withdrawal from the east to the north, then from the north to the west. They were fighting difficult rear-guard battles very honorably, losing very few men, and adhering scrupulously to the established schedule.

The devil was the yawning gap to the west of Staroselye.

The remains of our 4th Company, overrun at dawn, had fallen back in the direction of Derenkovez. They had been joined by other forces. Helped by elements of the 1st Company they had been counterattacking during the whole day.

But the Soviets were in force. They surged through the breach at Staroselye and into the forest, which descended toward the south.

Our companies at Derenkovez and our troops at Staroselye were given the mission of sticking to the flanks of this forest to keep the enemy from coming out. We sent patrols to skirmish in every direction and return.

Moreover, our artillery had conserved its firepower and was now fighting without respite. On the bare crest, the only passageway for Soviet reinforcements, it unleashed tremendous firepower: we no longer had any illusions of retrieving our heavy weapons from the mire when the next withdrawal came.

Wrecked automobiles and trucks were everywhere in the muck. The most powerful of our tractors, a monster with caterpillar treads sent from Derenkowez to Staroselye to help with the new withdrawal, had spent an entire day and night to cross less than thirty kilometers.

The railroad line, last road to Korsun, was marked by countless fires. Thousands of trucks jolted along in fits and starts under a rain of shells.

We formed the rear guard to the northeast. The slower the retreat of this enormous convoy, the longer we would have to fight.

The German High Command kept the situation in hand with incomparable *sang-froid.* Despite the frightful situation of the fifty to sixty thousand survivors in the *Kessel,* we couldn't detect the least trace of agitation or hurry in the orders. The maneuvers were accomplished methodically and calmly. Nowhere did the enemy manage to seize the initiative.

In this terrible trap, the troops and equipment withdrew precisely according to the instructions they received. The rear guards and the flank guards would fight to the very minute as scheduled, holding the ground until the precise instant of redeployment.

The breaches were immediately closed, regardless of the price.

Everyone knew that it was best to hold to the plan laid out by the General Staff, since any premature withdrawal would infallibly draw counterattacks that would be pursued until the abandoned terrain was retaken.

The orders were hard. But this was not the time for softness. Every soldier knew he had to choose: either orderly regrouping with the possibility of a final breakthrough, thanks to a methodical withdrawal, or annihilation amid the tumult of a general rout.

We reached the morning of Tuesday, 8 February 1944.

Staroselye was still holding.

So was Derenkovez.

The danger from the opened breach had been more or less neutralized by our shock patrols hanging on to the western, southern, and southeastern edges of the forest invaded by the Soviets.

But the enemy was no longer satisfied with this assault. He kept attacking furiously all around the *Kessel.* Wave after wave lashed the south, where the German Army was in the midst of its most important withdrawal. The whole Soviet empire had been falling on us from the east since 2 February.

Our sector comprised more than just the thirty kilometer trench from Derenkovez to Staroselye and the advanced positions of the 2nd Company in the northern sector. We also defended a supplementary line more than a league long which left from Staroselye at right angles toward the large village of Skiti in the south.

The enemy's breach threatened us in front, as well as on our right and left flanks. Staroselye was at the end of a long corridor. The enemy forces on our eastern flank had only to join the Soviet forces who had just outflanked us in the west, and our soldiers would be trapped and destroyed.

The Walloons covering our right flank had as neighbors the young recruits of the Viking, who had arrived at the front in civilian garb one month earlier, and who had barely received the rudiments of military instruction amid the bustle of January. These unfortunate boys were worn out with fatigue and emotion.

The enemy attacked them the morning of 8 February 1944, dislodged them, seized their posts one by one, and completely routed the survivors. We saw them drifting back with the current behind our bridgehead. This flotsam had nothing left to give. Some of them were crying like children.

During this rout the Soviets had poured through the breach. They had taken our southeast positions, located every hundred meters under the oaks. Our men had to abandon the woods and even the little village of Skiti on the plateau. They came down into the valley, closely followed by the adversary.

The enemy forces from the two breaches had almost joined. Only our little command post, where we hastily regrouped the fleeing men, remained like a tiny islet between the two Soviet battering rams.

We had to recover quickly and take the pressure off our position immediately. One hour's hesitation, and any breakout would be impossible.

The enemy had already occupied Skiti. Our anti-tank weapons climbed up the hill. The commander rushed forward, followed by our boys, dead tired but yelling just the same.

At five o'clock in the evening we retook the village. Fighting tooth and nail, we pushed the Soviets back into the woods. Once again the situation had been temporarily saved.

Orders came to our brigade command post to start the new withdrawal the next day.

We had only to hold firm for a few more hours, one evening, one night, and we would have saved not only our honor, but also the mass of friendly troops who were withdrawing slowly toward the west under cover of our rear guard.

* * * * *

Unfortunately the Communists, who could see through our plan, had decided to make an all-out attempt to destroy our positions.

To be effective the Soviet reduction of the Cherkassy *Kessel* had to be made sector by sector.

That was what the enemy had attempted at Moshny and was attempting at the southeast of Staroselye.

But it was in vain: all around the *Kessel* a hundred attacks failed.

Skiti was ours at five o'clock in the evening. The commander returned to the command post. In a simple trench of fine sand, one on top of another, we laid out the blood-spattered dead of the anguishing afternoon.

That evening, while we were setting up our next morning's plan for the brigade's withdrawal toward Derenkovez, a sentinel saw some men through the drizzle, covering the descent of our soldiers who had been routed, once again, on our eastern flank.

The enemy had broken cover a second time, had dislodged our boys and retaken Skiti.

Heading for the poplar groves in the valley and the east-west junction, the enemy would isolate Staroselye and finally choke off our sector.

Everything had to be done all over again without delay, with men who had been beaten twice in one day, who were worn out and decimated.

Division ordered me to push the enemy back. We had to reoccupy the hill protecting the line of retreat and not let go until six o'clock in the morning, when our forces at Staroselye would have been able to get out of the bottleneck.

Darkness had come.

The hill was covered with firs growing very close together. Some Reds were already stealthily starting the descent. We climbed slowly towards the plateau, for our weapons were heavy and we had to advance as far as possible without noise or fighting.

We were forty in all.

We crawled for the last hundred meters, then we sprung.

Our storming the enemy-held ridge provoked momentary confusion. We were able to use our machine-guns to the maximum and drive the enemy back to Skiti, while two of our anti-tank guns, hoisted to the summit in spite of the sand and the mud, supported our assault.

Faced with this reaction, the Reds chose to slip further south. This was even worse for us.

This time the operation which had failed abreast of us would be replayed in our rear.

At one o'clock in the morning, two kilometers behind our brigade command post, Soviets and Germans were battling a few hundred meters from the road, our only road.

Little groups of SS from the Viking, hugging the ground like cammock plants, checked the countless Soviet thrusts all by themselves. We heard the fracas from dozens of fire fights scattered over several kilometers from the east to the south.

The enemy was in front of us, at our right, at our left, behind our lines. The line that we had to follow at dawn was lit by a line of flaming isbas. Everywhere men were shouting.

Our lives, the lives of a thousand men, depended on those shouts.

Fortunately at five o'clock the sector was still shouting.

We burned the automobiles, unable to take on thirty kilometers of syrupy muck. The greater part of our troops slipped along the Olshanka River toward a wooden bridge which our men crossed at the exact place where a handful of the Viking's SS were still holding back the enemy.

A few of our machine-gunners were supposed to resist until the total evacuation of our companies.

They performed miracles for three hours.

Then with the suppleness of snakes they made their way through the fir stands of the south among the Soviets who had poured in from every direction.

Not a single one of our men was taken prisoner. Not one of our machine guns was left behind. In the midst of a diabolical hail of bullets, they crossed, last of all, belly to the ground, the wooden bridge of the Olshanka. It went up behind us like a geyser.

In epic mud, our men, our horses, our trucks scaled the opposite bank, as sticky as resin. We were separated from the enemy only by the swollen waters of the river, which carried a thousand floating remains, blasted into the valley by explosions.

## Thirty Kilometers

The general maneuver of retreat of 9 February 1944 was vast. The surrounded divisions left the south, the southeast, the east, and three-quarters of the northeast and the north Cherkassy pocket.

This pocket had the shape of Africa at the end of January. On 9 February 1944, "Africa" had shrunk to "Guinea," keeping only a loop as high as Lake Chad. This loop was the village of Derenkovez.

The capital of our Russian Guinea was Korsun, point of general assembly of the troops surrounded since the 28 January.

Right to the southwest of Korsun, coming from the outside of the *Kessel,* several hundred Tigers and Panthers, the most powerful German tanks in the armored divisions of southern Russia, were advancing furiously towards us in spite of bitter resistance.

The fifty to sixty thousand men of the *Kessel* withdrew methodically toward Korsun and saved a maximum of equipment.

Tens of thousands of men were taking their places for the decisive assault. They would move toward the Panzers coming up from the south. The rear guard forces would contain the pressure of the Soviet mass from the north and east or coming up from the southeast and south.

The most forward point of resistance north of Korsun would be Derenkovez, at the left end of our former line.

All our forces, stretched over thirty kilometers from Derenkovez to Staroselye and to the south of Staroselye, had received orders to withdraw to Derenkovez during the day of 9 February. Toward this locality our 2nd Company was to fall back also, from the north. Since the evacuation of Losovok this company had been moving in an arc from the east to the northwest.

Without anyone's support, our brigade would occupy the key position of Derenkovez.

The Wehrmacht units were deployed on the western flank of the Derenkovez-Korsun line. It was their task to resist the enemy thurst to the utmost. The eastern flank would be protected by the Nordland Regiment of the Viking Division.

Between these two lateral fronts a country road bordered by a river ran from Derenkovez to Korsun. The security zone of this road was about twenty kilometers wide from east to west.

Inarguably the most exposed position would be ours at the northern extremity of the corridor. We had to close off the road. Otherwise the enemy, surging up from the northeast and the north, would certainly try to reach Korsun with the design of finishing off the encircled troops once and for all.

* * * * *

The 2nd Company accomplished the last stage of its retreat to Derenkovez without incident.

By contrast, our departure at the other end of the line, taken *in extremis* while the enemy swarms harried us from a thousand directions, was going to be an operation full of drama.

The German units withdrawing from the southeast were flooding back toward the west at the same time as we, the Reds right on their heels.

The Olshanka River, swollen by the thaw, its bridge blown up, gave us a few minutes respite.

According to the High Command's plans, we were supposed to reach Derenkovez by following almost parallel to our old Staroselye-Derenkovez line. But this had been penetrated and overrun two days before. The forest where the enemy lurked hung like a goiter toward the south. The Soviets had been there in force since 9 February and had installed their anti-tank weapons.

The normal line of retreat used the southern end of this forest. The German trucks which went ahead of our brigade had just run into a hundred Soviet wasp's nests there.

One of our staff officers, a manufacturer from Ghent, a serious-minded and civilized man, straight as a sword and loyal as a knight, Captain Anthonissen, had been sent on a liaison mission to Derenkovez. He advanced at the head of the column. When it fell into an ambush he immediately regrouped the infantry which accompanied the first German trucks.

Unluckily he was dealing with exhausted *Volksdeutsche** recruits of the Viking, in retreat since the Skiti battle. These wrecks seemed to advance toward the enemy, then at the first shots broke into a rout.

Captain Anthonissen knew the traditions of the Wallonian Legion.

The others were fleeing in every direction but he stayed.

He fought with his submachine gun right to the end.

A counterattack organized by the Viking cleared out the road one hour later. A body lay near a thicket thirty meters to the east of the road. "It was a very tall man bearing the Belgian colors on his left sleeve," a German officer told us that evening.

Why were we fighting, why had Captain Anthonissen fought, if not to merit every day the honor of representing on the European front a country small but vibrant with glory—the proud *Leo belgicus* of our forefathers?[1]

* * * * *

At the tail of the column, the only line of retreat was an earthen path cut in a clay as viscous as fuel oil. The terrain became very steep and we could drag the trucks only with tractors. In the valleys the vehicles would slide and skid.

We had to cross flooded streams, still partly covered with ice. The wheels would skid on it, hacking out deeper and deeper gashes. Every crossing of these diabolical watercourses would cost us one or two vehicles.

We arrived on a plateau facing the forest just as the Viking Division was starting its counterattack. Our columns had to use a cart track which turned back to the south. At the end a few kilometers we veered eastward again. Once part of the immense automobile-snake there was no getting out. The path was narrow and bordered by a deep ravine. One clumsy turn of the wheel and the vehicle would tumble into the abyss.

At the base of the mountain a village was stagnating in the marshes near a glimmering pond. The path followed the water. It soon turned into a thick carbon black paste almost half a meter deep, absolutely impassable. We had to resort to extreme measures. We threw all the hay and straw stacks into the sinkhole, then added the thatch from the isbas and on top of that the doors, the shutters, the partitions, and even the tables, whose legs we cut off.

The entire village went into it.

The enemy was two kilometers away. It was no time to be soft-hearted.

And on these pitiful ruins, among the stunned peasants, a hundred trucks were able to haul themselves out, go back up toward high ground, and finally reach the crossroads of the Derenkovez road.

* * * * *

At five o'clock in the evening we were certain that we had saved almost all our men and, best of all, a good part of our transport.

We dared not wait any longer. The planes were machine-gunning the isbas at the crossroads. We had a store of flares there. The Soviet fighters hit it. Hundreds of red, green, white, and violet sprays streaked about in a frenzy, fell at our feet, and maddened our last horses.

To reach Derenkovez we had to approach the western border of the enemy-occupied forest. Our column skirted it at a distance of two kilometers.

The advance was nerve-wrackingly slow. Everywhere, all the time, half a meter of sticky mud. German trucks going to Derenkovez to get to Korsun and trucks of the Wallonian Brigade were mixed up in a long narrow line. Every minute or so a bogged-down vehicle would block everything.

We had to uproot and cut down the little fruit trees of the neighboring countryside in order to help firm up the road. A number of cars had been abandoned and overturned, their motors burned out. We went on foot for the most part, our muscles strained by the clumps of mud clinging to our feet.

Night was coming. Our nervousness grew.

We were being shot at from the edge of the woods. The Soviet airplanes were harassing us almost without respite.

Suddenly a huge red ball burst out of the forest, then another. "Panzers! Panzers!" yelled the foreign drivers as they threw themselves beneath their machines and set them on fire before fleeing.

No, it was the Soviet anti-tank weapons which were firing on our column.

This was no big crisis. We had seen it all before. But some of the burning trucks instantly forbade all movement. There were stocks of thousands of shells and grenades in the convoy.

The explosions began. Everyone had to throw himself flat in the muddy fields. I managed to jump onto a horse tried to regroup some of the men and try to save a few more vehicles.

But it was too late. The whole road was on fire. More than a hundred trucks were burning against the gray-violet sky, a long red and pink ribbon perforated with black spurts.

All our records were destroyed, all our papers, all our equipment. Only our glorious flags escaped. Those the company commanders had carried draped around their bodies under their jackets since the first day of the retreat.

* * * * *

That night several hundred men, their legs shaky with fatigue, harassed by Soviet fire, entered the sunken road of Derenkovez.

Mud, like a river of lava, flowed down in enormous ribbons to the little valley, cut off by the lake.

The bridge had been destroyed. The pond ice had melted. We had to cross this shadowy stretch in water up to our waists.

East of Derenkovez the enemy had been very aggressive for two days: harassing the 2nd Company in the north, it burst into the refuge as we arrived there. In the southeast it bombarded us with anti-tank shellbursts.

A torrential rain had begun to fall. During a night streaked with bursts from Soviet machine guns, we streamed in, half-blinded, falling in the mire, hampered by our weapons, drained of strength and almost of hope.

## The Bridgehead

The Assault Brigade "Wallonia" had achieved the *tour de force* of regrouping itself in its entirety at the bridgehead of Derenkovez.

Our situation would almost immediately become hellish.

We were positioned in a horseshoe around the village, facing north, northeast, and east.

From within the Korsun horseshoe the Korsun road started off behind us towards the south. The security zone of this highway was diminishing from hour to hour. Soviet tanks were harassing the positions of the Wehrmacht at the west of the corridor. Soviet snipers had sneaked in everywhere. Since Thursday morning the Reds had been able to machine-gun the convoy hurrying from Derenkovez to Korsun.

The twenty kilometers of relative security had become, in less than a day, one to two kilometers.

The southeastern and eastern flanks were in theory largely protected. The SS Nordland Regiment was to contain the enemy in this direction, about ten kilometers from the valley. Thanks to this cover, our bridgehead at the northern end of the corridor would be able to hold out as long as necessary. The general regrouping at Korsun could then be made smoothly.

Unfortunately the Nordland Regiment, since Thursday, had been badly knocked about. An enemy tidal wave had thrown it back to the last hill covering our road between Derenkovez and Korsun, some seven kilometers behind us.

We nearly lost everything then. The corridor was no longer more than a few hundred meters wide in all. Bullets were crossing it in both directions.

At this news General Gille became terribly angry. The Nordland's commander received a hurricane of imprecations over the field telephone and was ordered to take back the lost ground instantly.

But in the meantime the victorious Soviet troops were rushing towards Derenkovez in order to attack us from behind. At the beginning of the afternoon they appeared at the southeast near the most elevated isbas.

Derenkovez was an extended town, its houses set very far apart. From a strategic point of view, the Reds had just reached the most important location. That evening their equipment would be set up and we would be caught in a the crossfire of Soviet grenades and artillery.

We still had a few troops.

Every stroke of bad luck brings its own consolation. The hundreds of truckless drivers and weaponless artillerymen constituted growing reserves as the mire swallowed up our materiel. We immediately turned them into infantrymen who very usefully reinforced our decimated companies.

An artillery officer, Lieutenant Graff, was sent to retake the Derenkovez slope at the head of about fifty of his former men.

Pride entered into it. The artillerymen, whom the front line soldiers often teased, wanted to give them an eyeful. They gave the Reds such a beating that they withdrew two kilometers to the southeast. They took numerous prisoners, and as a finishing touch, took a mill and an agricultural complex by storming a knoll.

The men of the Nordland were somewhat embarrassed when, laboriously, in the course of their counterattack, they reached the sector they had lost several hours before. A handful of muddy and gleeful Belgians were already plucking chickens, cutting bacon, slicing pickles, preparing, their grenades on their belts, a discreetly heroic kermess.

* * * * *

They held this position unshakably. Our artillerymen were proud. And the produce was good.

But everywhere else danger was drawing its noose tighter again, bloodily. The east of Derenkovez was savagely harassed. Hordes of Mongols were surging in from all sides and throwing themselves in howling bands onto our little posts. We were pushed back right outside town.

In the evening the situation was this: the bridgehead at Derenkovez was practically choked off. Behind us at the mid-route between Derenkovez and Korsun, the corridor had only a tiny zone of protection left at the village of

Arbusino. It could be cut off at any moment, in which case, surrounded at Derenkovez, our fate would be sealed.

Moreover the enemy would then be able to break through from Arbusino to Korsun, where fifty thousand men, ensnared in the mire along with their equipment, were just beginning to regroup, expecting help from the southwest.

Now this help was looking more and more problematical. The column of German tanks which was supposed to liberate us was still forty kilometers away from Korsun. It, too, was sinking in seas of mud. Things looked grim everywhere. The news was all disastrous.

The encircled troops were at the end of their strength.

There were almost no more munitions or food.

The men were half dead from fatigue.

How much longer could we check the thrust of an enemy who knew we were on our knees? Would the tanks from the west muster enough strength to break through the encirclement and through the incredible mud?

At the most optimistic, we had no more than a few days before we would succumb.

That night a secret communication from the staff office of the division to our brigade commander left no more hope. "We have only four or five chances in a hundred of escaping total annihilation."

In the little command post, drenched with torrential rain, we looked at one another, our blood run cold.

We saw the faces of our children, far away, as in a mirage.

The hour was not far off when all would be lost.

* * * * *

The night of Thursday, 10 February to Friday, 11 February passed in confused and multiple battles.

We could no longer see a meter ahead. The air was nothing but solid water. The ground was a river in which we sank to our knees.

Like toads the Soviets were swarming everywhere across the black mud.

Bullets kept coming every minute or two from the same spot. It took us a quarter of an hour to find the place where the marksman must have been hiding. Nothing was left there but a pool like all the others. He had slipped silently away and posted himself in another watery, shadowy hole. We had scarcely moved off when bullets began whistling past again, sharp, brutal, nerve-wracking.

All around us the projectiles would criss-cross and explode into the walls, the doors, and the roofs.

Our men, who had not slept for a week, clothes glued to their bodies, felt that they would go crazy.

Division telephoned the command post every half hour. "You must hold!

You must hold!" If we lost a house we had to retake it immediately, in the dark.

The Reds were slipping in among us. We kept catching them in darkness. We would take them to the command post, shaggy swamp monsters, disgusting with mud, their cheeks flat and red, laughing in their yellow teeth.

They all said that they were ten times stronger then we. Then they would gobble up anything, would fall asleep anywhere like animals, snoring and mumbling, in a nauseating odor of grease and damp cloth.

## Five to Midnight

On Friday morning Derenkovez was still holding out.

The eastern and western flanks of the Korsun road had held, although almost everywhere the Soviet riflemen had sneaked in among the brambles and thickets alongside the road.

The Soviets knew far better than we how well they had us hemmed in. For several days their airplanes had been dropping us leaflets in which they described to us, fully documented, our desperate situation. They gave the list of the surrounded units and especially mentioned the so-called "Walloniian Motorized Brigade."

They were becoming more and more innovative in the art of propaganda. Regularly a white flag would wave. A Soviet soldier would advance, bringing an envelope addressed personally to the General of the Division or of the Army Corps. It would be a hand-written letter from a German general taken prisoner who had gone over to the enemy. This agent would insistently propose, in the name of his Soviet masters, the honorable surrender of the *Kessel*.

Every day photos were sent by the same postal service, photos of prisoners taken the preceding day, seated at a table with the general in question, perfectly alive and well cared for.

At eleven o'clock on Friday, 11 February 1944, after the habitual white flag had been raised, two very correct Soviet officers appeared bearing a message from the Soviet High Command for the commander in chief of the encircled forces.

The message was an ultimatum.

The two enemy officers passed behind our positions and were received with courtesy. The Soviet ultimatum was clear and plain: Either you will surrender and be treated as courageous soldiers or the attack will be unleased at 1300 hours, and you will be exterminated."

The ultimatum was rejected instantly and categorically. We escorted the two Soviet officers back across the muck to their own lines, riding on a vibrating tractor.

The Soviets did not delay their retort.

Immediately after noon, all around the terribly contracted *Kessel,* the Red Army broke cover.

It attacked our bridgehead and the Derenkovez-Korsun road with rage. The outcome was precarious.

The German forces had started reassembling at Korsun two days earlier. We knew that the final combat was going to begin, that tens of thousands of men were taking position and would throw themselves into the assault with the energy of despair. A radiotelegram from the German High Command had entreated us to combine our forces. They were going to send, in a last effort, all the panzers they had left.

We would have to risk everything.

The Soviets believed us irretrievably lost.

For the last two weeks, their attacks hadn't succeeded. They wanted to hurry and hasten the kill. Their ultimatum having been rejected without discussion, their attack broke from all sectors.

* * * * *

That evening the Korsun corridor became narrower and narrower. But at Derenkovez our brigade hadn't lost an inch of garden or a meter of hedge.

Our soldiers were sunk like posts in the ground. From then on they were unmoved by anything. Panzers could have fallen from the sky and they would have shown no surprise.

We had received new orders. The gravity of the situation was such that the breakthrough would be moved up. The next day, Saturday, 12 February 1944, the encircled army would make its last attempt, and would thrust through the enemy toward the southwest. At four o'clock in the morning we would evacuate Derenkovez and join the assault wave in the south end of the *Kessel.* The Nordland Regiment would establish the rearguard from Arbusino, covering Korsun.

But it was only seven o'clock in the evening.

It was an endless wait!

Almost all the lines were frayed and broken.

Could we manage to hold out for nine more hours, as ordered? Wouldn't our whole bridgehead suddenly crack and fall back in a terrible annihilation?

Bullets were clattering on the corrugated metal, dripping under the downpour. Never on earth had it rained with such violence.

Everywhere screams split the air.

At one o'clock in the morning our forward posts on the east withdrew. Already the Soviets, like reptiles of mud and night, were slithering into the isbas. No longer firing, not breathing a word, our men went down toward the rambling pond, several hundred meters wide, which they crossed in water up to their waists, their weapons held out at arm's length.

In the darkness we scanned the black water from which they emerged shiny as seals.

In the northwest and the west the firing intensified. Bullets went shrieking by, then died out or flattened themselves against obstacles.

But suddenly we were stunned by the droning noise of a dull rumble: tanks!

The Soviet tanks had just arrived on the northwest, several hundred meters away from us, moving toward the paved road where our last trucks were lined up in the shadows. These alone could save us at the last minute.

It was the sound of death, this great rolling of treads. Not five minutes would pass before the catastrophe would be upon us.

I leaped toward an anti-tank weapon left near the road. Helped by a soldier, I turned it around. Other soldiers ran up at my shout, and aimed another weapon. We unleashed a hell's fire of plunging shells, forcing the enemy tanks to a halt.

It was one-thirty in the morning.

Behind the tanks, the Russian footsoldiers had crept to within several dozen meters of us. They fired blindly at the black road.

We had to keep moving the trucks ceaselessly back and forth, waiting for hundreds of our comrades to climb out of the pond.

As they reached the road they threw themselves onto the vehicles. But at each loading some fell back onto the ground, mortally wounded.

At 4:00 A.M. the men of the last rearguard platoon joined us. We hastily loaded our two anti-tank weapons onto the last trucks.

Our bridgehead of Derenkovez had held out to the end without a hitch and right on schedule.

Arbusino was on fire. The Nordland Regiment had retaken cover behind the inferno. Farther on a few airplanes lay sadly, their noses in the mud.

At dawn we arrived at Korsun. Our brigade made it a point of honor to get down from the trucks, to re-form, and to enter the city in strict order, heads high, singing as if on parade.

## Departure from Korsun

Korsun was an admirable city.

It was brightened on the southeast by a very deep lake, several kilometers long. This lake, bordered by green, blue, white, and red isbas, framed by hills with coppery shrubs, and hemmed by a sandy road, ended in a gigantic dam. The water plunged onto enormous red and green rocks, then veered away roaring from the two sides of a glossy island, which bore on its summit an old white abbey with elegant oriental festoons.

Fifty meters above the leaping water, the Wagnerian roar of the fall rose to a dark and imposing cliff. It was there that all the dead of the Viking Division and the Assault Brigade "Wallonia" were buried.

After each battle we had brought them to this powerful and distant promontory, high place of death and glory.

From there they would see us leave along the great lake, toward sacrifice or deliverance.

* * * * *

The *Kessel* kept shrinking: a few kilometers of front to the north of Korsun, a few kilometers to the southwest: a double curtain of flank-guard protection.

That was all.

In the beginning the *Kessel* was as big as Belgium. Now it was smaller than a French department.

The enemy struck harder than ever. It was indispensable, as the withdrawal progressed, to take, in the southwest, the kilometers abandoned to the east and north. We had withdrawn from Derenkovez. Seven kilometers were therefore lost. The German assault waves would have to conquer seven others in the southwest before evening; otherwise the fifty thousand men of the *Kessel* would smother to death for lack of room to move.

Now at eleven o'clock in the morning, while the commander and I were receiving orders at Division, we saw General Gille turn red while on his telephone. He had received catastrophic news. Arbusino, which was supposed to serve as a barrier until the next day, had just fallen into the hands of the Soviets.

They were advancing at top speed against Korsun itself.

The General grabbed his thick baton, jumped into a Volkswagen, and hurried in the direction of Arbusino.

It was difficult to resist the anger of General Gille. The village was retaken and the barrier re-established.

Just in time!

* * * * *

Our divisions' attack in the southwest had been underway for several hours. It hadn't succeeded as well as the German commander desired. The Reds were fighting bitterly. A village had been taken six kilometers from Korsun. We observed several advances on the flanks.

But the enemy was pressing us very closely. Now we needed quick and total success. We had one or two days at the most.

The troops were being asked to make a superhuman effort.

Both officers and soldiers hadn't any rest for ten days. We were sustained by the ferocious energy that only the immediate proximity of death gives.

Since Moshny I hadn't slept an hour for a week. I fought off sleep only by swallowing Pervitine pills, a drug furnished to pilots to keep them awake during long flights.

It was in fact impossible to find a minute's respite. The telephones at the command post rang fifty or sixty times a night, whenever the enemy was breaking through our positions. I would have to rush to the critical point, take all the men I could find, and throw myself body and soul into the counterattack with them.

There was nothing left of us but a bundle of nerves.

How much longer could our nerves hold out?

Our ammunition had been used up entirely in the fierce combats of the past two weeks. For a week not an airplane had been able to land. It was only by parachute drops that the encircled army could still receive the wherewithal to fight.

We had scarcely arrived at Korsun when we heard the purring of airplanes in the lowering and rainy sky. A cloud of white parachutes fell through the drizzle.

We thought at first that it was a Soviet landing, the last phase of the struggle.

Then, instead of bodies hanging under the silken domes, we saw thick silver cigars. Every one of them contained twenty-five kilos of cartridges or little boxes of a bitter chocolate concentrate which helped fight off sleep.

Thanks to these aerial gifts, each unit could again receive a sensible ration of ammo.

The bakers of Korsun kneaded a last ovenful of ration loaves. This, along with the the parachuted chocolate, was the only food that was distributed to the troops on 13 February 1944.

As he took his bread, each soldier knew that it was the last bread he would receive before either conquering or dying.

* * * * *

Our departure toward the battle in the southwest was fixed for 2300 hours.

We still entertained certain illusions, for the German commander was deliberately giving false information, that is to say optimistic information. It was better, certainly, not to tell everything. If we had known the truth we would have given up trying.

To listen to the superior officers, the next day, Sunday, would see the end of our misfortune. There were only a few more kilometers to cross.

We believed it because man willingly believes the things which correspond to his desires.

Since morning the rain had stopped beating down onto the *Kessel.* The moon rose up in the evening. We saw there a portent. Korsun glowed softly.

The silvery gleams in the sky were delicate. The air was sharp. With the help of a few Pervitine pills, we were about to reach, in the end, victory.

We had lost a lot of trucks.

Our dead were also many; there was plenty of room on the trucks which remained. In the middle of the night our column reached the lake, white and blue under the moon.

The army crossed it on a wooden bridge nearly a kilometer long, built audaciously on top of the dam by the engineers. The bridge wasn't wide enough to permit traffic in both directions. The convoys therefore had to be interrupted hourly. In spite of the thousands of vehicles from the *Kessel* which took their turn on the bridge, the passage, incredibly, was accomplished without accidents.

The enemy was very close; the men were nervous; but nothing ruffled the iron discipline of the *Feldgendarmes*.

In spite of our fatigue we couldn't help admiring this efficient machine, this command in total control of itself, this withdrawal as regular as the timing of a race: the commissariat, the distribution of munitions and gas, the flow of traffic, the telephone, the radio, everything worked perfectly during these haunting weeks. Not so much as a grain of sand fouled the gears in spite of the concentration of disparate troops, harassed day and night, despite the loss of considerable materiel, sunk in the muddy thaw.

Nevertheless that night everything depended on a few dozen cubic meters of planks. If a pilot had had the guts to crash his plane into the dam on the lake, the wooden bridge would have crumbled. Not another German truck would have left Korsun.

But no enemy aviator tried this sensational coup, or else no Soviet general thought of it.

At two o'clock in the morning we were on the other side of the dam, traveling along the soft gleaming lake. We were underway to the assault line on the southwest.

* * * * *

We managed to advance a few kilometers. The cold was biting. The mud was freezing up, which made movement even more difficult. Hundreds of trucks broke down in this putty, blocking the way.

Everywhere we tried to pull out vehicles stuck in the hardening mud or push them onto the shoulders. But there were too many. For kilometers, the most unlikely vehicles were stopped three or four abreast: great red trucks of the *Feldpost,** staff cars, self-propelled guns, tanks, hundreds of carts drawn by ponies or by oxen. Motorcyclists were revving their engines in vain.

Finally we had to abandon our trucks and go forward on foot in this imbroglio, wishing our drivers lots of luck and the help of violent and propitious winds.

At dawn we reached the first village taken from the Soviets the day before.

We were dismayed to hear the news.

It had been impossible to open a deep breach in the enemy front. In the village of Sanderovka, after four kilometers of progress, the German troops had met incredible resistance. Only half the villages had been occupied.

The last three tanks of our brigade had been sent on an assault a little before our arrival and had been destroyed. The commander of our tanks, a very young captain as handsome as a god, with bright blue mischievous eyes, wearing magnificently a high white Cossack *shapska* topped with the death's head of the SS, had been blown up in his tank, which took a direct hit in the munitions reserve. He had been tossed ten meters into the air and fallen back, stone dead, his face absolutely intact.

The attack was about to begin again.

As for the German panzers which were supposed to come from the outside to meet us, we were still waiting for them. The information about them was extremely vague.

* * * * *

We were scarcely making any progress at all toward the southwest.

But we were fast retreating in the north. Not only Arbusino—lost in the morning, retaken at noon—had been lost again definitively in the evening, that is, twelve hours too soon, but the Soviets, refusing to let up on the retreating troops, had entered Korsun.

We had left it at eleven o'clock in the evening. The Soviets stormed it at dawn.

We had to move on to Novo-Buda, which on the map protected Sanderovka from the east, the town for which we had fought so hard.

Novo-Buda: strange name.

The village dominated a long steep ridge.

We set off in Indian file.

All the remaining German artillery was pounding Soviet-occupied Sanderovka.

We veered to the left. German soldiers lay here and there, freshly killed.

The muck was disgusting. Soviet planes came down on us, hedgehopping. We would throw ourselves to the ground, almost completely sinking into the mud, until the squadron disappeared. These dives were repeated ten times. It took three hours to cross four kilometers of muddy fields.

Finally we entered Novo-Buda. The village was as quiet as a cemetery. Two Wehrmacht regiments had just expelled the Reds in a masterful surprise attack. The enemy had abandoned some powerful guns and about twenty Ford trucks, but this unexpected victory didn't deceive anyone.

Fifteen Soviet tanks were coming up from the southeast. We could see them perfectly as they advanced up the road.

They stopped eight hundred meters away.

## Novo-Buda

We were to relieve the two German regiments which had taken Novo-Buda the next day, 14 February 1944, before daybreak. Commander Lippert and I went to confer with the colonel in charge of the sector.

Passing through Novo-Buda plunged us into bitter reflection. The dirt roads of the village—two sunken paths, parallel and deeply embanked—were utterly inundated. The water reached a depth of one and a half meters or more. We had to keep to the banks, slippery as paste, to cross the village.

At the German colonel's, the atmosphere was lugubrious. The village had fallen without a shot. The two regiments had approached stealthily just before dawn and thrown the Soviets, taken from the rear, into panic. The enemy had fled leaving even their anti-tank guns.

The Soviets had quickly regained their composure, however.

Their counterattack had established a wide arc from the northeast to the south of Novo-Buda.

Novo-Buda had been conquered for a few hours in order to protect the column exiting the *Kessel,* which was to seize Sanderovka and sweep toward the southwest. But Sanderovka hadn't been completely taken yet. Beyond Sanderovka, we had to expect stubborn resistance now that the enemy had been able to brake the German assault for two days and a night. Novo-Buda, position for a single day, had thus become crucial. If Novo-Buda fell, the enemy would have only to advance four kilometers west to cut off the road behind Sanderovka. Final disaster would be at hand.

The German colonel feared for the worst. Our sector was down to only five Panzers and our last anti-tank guns. These were almost out of ammunition, and we would scarcely be able to move them, so prodigious was the muck.

The three thousand men of the two regiments from Das Reich, who would leave at the end of the night, were to be replaced by a thousand Walloon soldiers, and a nondescript army of cooks, accountants, drivers, mechanics, quartermasters, and telephonists, flanked by the legal officer, the dentist, the pharmacist, and the postman, all transformed into reinforcements for our nine skeletal companies.

* * * * *

The German staff officers were waiting, elbows on the table, heads in their hands. No one breathed a word.

They were asking themselves whether they would have the luck to get through the night without another counterattack. We, on the other hand, asked ourselves whether we would have the ill luck to see the attack unleashed after the Germans had left.

Night fell. Our companies arrived in the mist, exhausted, having left laggards behind everywhere in the mud of the fields.

The men went into whatever isba they found in Novo-Buda. Most of them collapsed in corners, almost dead. The toughest pulled off their jackets and their trousers, streaming with filthy water, in front of the orange corn stalk fires.

At two o'clock in the morning knocking and shouting resounded from door to door. Unhappy messengers were slogging through the mud to muster the brigade.

We put our clothes back on. They were as hard as sheet iron. Everyone cleaned his gun or submachine gun as well as he could. Hundreds of men filed out of the isbas into the cold night, promptly and unavoidably tumbled into the water of the sunken path, and advanced stumbling and swearing.

It took nearly two hours to assemble the companies. Poor boys, dripping with mud, exhausted, having eaten nothing, drunk nothing other than the filthy water of the road. We had to guide them to the holes from out of which tottered the foot soldiers of the Reich Division. "Come on, old man, get into position, above all don't fall asleep, keep your eyes open, they're out there!"

Yes, they were out there, not only European Russians, but Mongols, Tatars, Kalmuks, Kirghiz, having lived for weeks like wild animals in the mud. They had slept in thickets and eaten food scrounged from the last year's corn and sunflower fields.

They were out there, sure of their submachine gun cartridge clips with seventy bullets, sure of their grenade throwers, sure of their "Stalin's organs," whose rocket volleys filled the night with horror.

They were out there.

And their fifteen tanks were out there. We waited, apprehensive in the darkness, for the sound of their treads.

* * * * *

The German senior officers, seated before us, waited for five o'clock. They had shown us the situation on the map.

A gap of several kilometers extended to the northeast. It had been impossible to establish a liaison in that direction. On the east and southeast the positions were spread thinly on the edge of the village to which the enemy had fallen back the day before.

Clearly we lacked a continuous front. We still had our five old tanks. We had to make the best of them.

It was almost five o'clock.

Suddenly the German colonel ordered us to be silent. A protracted rumble of tank treads rose in the dwindling night.

The colonel got up, gathered his maps, and made a sign to his staff. His troops, relieved by ours, had already left the town. By staying with us in the heat of the fray he would have risked being cut off far from his soldiers. An instant later he disappeared.

Commander Lippert, his eyes staring, listened. The noise of the tanks stopped. It was silent again. The enemy tanks had moved, that was all.

Two hours went by without anything happening.

Our flankers, rubbing their tired eyes, still watched the hill behind which the Soviet tanks sheltered. Katyusha rockets pounded the town on and off. Our command post was in the thick of it.

It had to end badly.

At seven o'clock the great flat rumbling of tanks filled Novo-Buda a second time. The five German Panzers backed down to change position. Men were running through the mud, seeing nothing, hearing nothing.

Three tank shells fired point-blank tore through our little isba. Everything came tumbling down on our heads; we were half-buried in the wreckage.

I had been hit by a huge piece of rubble right in the belly. I pulled myself up with great difficulty, all yellow with dirt from the mud-wall. On both sides of the flattened house soldiers rushed by pursued by Soviet tanks.

One of them had already passed us.

## Two Hundred Dead

The Soviets surged into Novo-Buda.

Grabbing two submachine guns, the commander and I rushed to join fifty of our men.

The two parallel roads between which we found ourselves were filled with the din of the tanks.

The fifteen enemy tanks had obliterated our riflemen's foxholes. The men had been crushed in the mud under the treads or massacred by mobs of screaming Asiatics following the Red tanks.

The five German Panzers had withdrawn to the end of the village. One of them, returning, found itself nose to nose with a Soviet tank. They destroyed one another in a few seconds.

Another Soviet tank thrust upon us with such rapidity that we hadn't the time to see anything. Thrown into the air, our ears ringing, we fell helter-skelter, dead or wounded.

Our German liaison officer was planted upright like a picket in the thick mud, his head submerged, his feet in the air. The tanks continued to thunder along the two roads, and to flatten our wretched infantrymen, whom they pursued from every direction.

I had managed to dive into a ditch. A long jagged splinter, very hot, protruded from my jacket. I could tell that I was wounded in the side and in the arm, but my legs were still good.

Men were running in panic to the western slopes of the village in the belief that all was lost. The tractor of one of our Paks plunged down into their midst. A shell from a Soviet tank knocked it for a loop.

I caught the men at mid-slope. I had one of our officers mount a runaway horse to race further ahead and rally all who had fled.

Our tanks and our anti-tank guns had withdrawn to the south of the village. But they were still fighting. It was there a stand would have to be made.

* * * * *

All along the red fences men were returning to the houses, under intensive fire from the "Stalin's organs." The effect of these grenade explosions was extraordinary. Every one of the thirty-six bursts threw up a spray shaped like an apple tree. Gray orchards, phantom orchards which scattered bloody fruits of torn human flesh.

In one isba we had a few panzerfausts,* individual anti-tank weapons just introduced to the Eastern front. At that time we had to wait for the tank to come within ten or fifteen meters before shooting a large metallic egg screwed onto the end of a hollow pipe. A flame four or five meters long would burst out the other end of the weapon, braced on the shoulder, at the moment of firing. Any man behind the shooter would be instantly carbonized. It was thus impossible to use the panzerfaust from a trench lest the fire bounce back and burn the shooter. The best thing was to kneel behind a haystack, a tree, or a window, then pull the trigger at the last minute.

It was very risky. Even if the tank blew up, the flame of the panzerfaust would instantly mark you to the other tanks. The riposte would not be long in coming.

But our soldiers relished dangerous games, exploits which asked little constancy and lots of audacity. Volunteers sneaked among the isbas, panzerfausts in their hands, behind the bundles of branches and the little walls. The Soviet tanks were promptly boxed in. The German tanks and our anti-tank guns gave everything they had. At the end of an hour the whole south of the village was ours once more, and five Soviet tanks were in flames. A blazing column of red and black rose ten meters above the slopes.

The Soviets held the east and the southeast of Novo-Buda. The nine tanks which they had left were camouflaged, guarding against any counterattack.

Our losses had been fearful. In two hours of fighting we had lost around two hundred men.

Groups of soldiers gone astray in the muddy fields the evening before toiled painfully toward our heights. I had been undressed and tended to behind a bush on the ridge. Two ribs had been broken by the shrapnel, which had also struck me in the right arm.

That wasn't too important, for my role was above all that of motivator.

The legs, the voice, the fire were intact. That was enough. I could still rally men, instruct officers.

Yet everyone had met the haggard parade of wounded and heard the stretcher-bearers' tales, always lavish with horrifying details.

The "Stalin's organs" rained an infernal fire. At each wave of rockets the ravine filled with big gray "apple trees" out of which would explode cries of suffering, cries for help, and death rattles.

Exhausted by a half month of horror, our soldiers' spirits were far heavier than their bodies. This town, where so many corpses lay in the mud, terrified them, but one had only to say a few words to chase away their anguish and lift their spirits. Then they would smile mud-covered smiles, and, readjusting their gear, they would rejoin their comrades in danger.

* * * * *

The weather had changed greatly. The rain had stopped falling since the full moon at Korsun. The cold, timid at first, had become quite biting. The wind whistled sharp as needles.

During two weeks of exhausting marches across phenomenal mud wallows, the men, streaming with sweat, had abandoned the greater part of their winter equipment. Sheepskins, padded tunics, napped trousers, all had been thrown away piece by piece, march by march. Most of the soldiers no long had even a coat.

In the great free-for-all of the morning no one had felt the freeze. But now it whipped their faces, gnawed their bodies under the lightweight uniforms caked with mud.

The enemy air force took immediate advantage of the clear sky. The planes descended in clamorous waves, skimming our bare hill. Each time, we had to cling to the ground, still soft while bullets fell all around us, breaking stones and twigs.

In the town, attacks and counterattacks followed one another without cease. We had hardly any more ammunition. The machine guns had an average of fifty cartridges per weapon remaining, enough to fire a burst of a few seconds.

* * * * *

Several resolute squads then tried to better our position by daring hand-to-hand forays.

Our commander, Lieutenant Colonel Lucien Lippert, who alone of all our staff officers was still unharmed, led the assault himself.

A young Belgian officer who graduated from the Military Academy in Brussels at the head of his class, he had come to the anti-Communist crusade as a true Christian knight. He had an admirably pure face, a clear complexion, and serious blue eyes. Lieutenant Colonel at twenty-nine, he lived only for his faith.

On that day Lucien Lippert, a natural hero, displayed a heroism such as to make one shiver. He was nonetheless a very calm young man who never spoke or acted out of measure.

Now he felt that it was all or nothing.

With a handful of Walloons he crossed the center of Novo-Buda and retook a group of isbas which plunged toward the southeast. The enemy would hide, then reappear in ten places, in any corner of a hovel, behind any tree or any knoll. Snipers mowed down our soldiers.

They had to cross several more meters to reach a house. Lucien Lippert rushed forward and made it to the door.

At that second he gave a terrifying scream, heard everywhere, the superhuman scream of a man whose life is suddenly torn from him. His chest ravaged by the enormous hole of an explosive bullet, Lucien Lippert fell to his knees like a stone.

He placed his hand across his forehead. He still had the extraordinary lucidity to pick up his kepi from the ground and put it back onto his head so as to die fittingly.

* * * * *

The isba near which he had succumbed was defended furiously until our tearful soldiers had finished burying him inside. The enemy retook the area, but the Wallonian Legion didn't want to leave its dead commander in the hands of the Communists. During the night Lieutenant Thyssen, his arm shot through by a bullet on February 6th and streaming with pus, crawled along with the volunteers, rushed the enemy, recaptured the isba, dug up the corpse, and brought it back, through machine-gun fire, to our positions.

We laid him out between some boards. We decided to make the breakthrough carrying his corpse with us. If we didn't make it, faithful to his memory, we would die on his coffin.

## Sanderovka

The noose kept tightening around the *Kessel.*

On Tuesday morning, 15 February 1944, the situation had not improved.

Sanderovka had been taken after three days and two nights of frightful hand-to-hand combat but that changed little.

The burning necessity was to break through the Soviet lines. The German Panzers were coming to our rescue from the southwest and we had to reach them.

Our divisions hadn't advanced more than three kilometers south of Sanderovka. In contrast, the enemy had taken Korsun. 12 February we had lost three times more ground in the north of the *Kessel* than the Soviets had in the south.

We were reduced to an area no greater than sixty square kilometers, into which a human tidal wave flowed. For every man who was fighting, seven or eight men were waiting, crammed into this last valley. There were the drivers of thousands of trucks, sunk into the mud during the withdrawal. There were the personnel of the auxiliary services: administration, supply, hospitals, motor pools, the *Feldpost.*

The village of Sanderovka was the capital of this army, hunted for the last eighteen days. This microscopic capital, pounded by sixty hours of fighting, had been reduced to crumbling isbas and broken windows. The isbas were the headquarters of the Viking Division, of each of its regiments, and of our brigade. Our H.Q., without fire or windowpanes, consisted of two small rooms without floors. About eighty people were packed into it, a few survivors of the staff office, the messengers, the dying, and numerous Germans separated from their units.

My wound burned. I had a fever of 40° centigrade. Stretched out in a corner, covered with a sheepskin, I had to direct the Wallonian Brigade, whose command I had been given the evening before. There was no longer an adjutant or an aide-de-camp. At every hour of the day and night catastrophic news would arrive along with NCOs at their limit, staggering men falling like lead weights or crying like children.

The orders were implacable. Our brigade was to hang onto Novo-Buda as a flank guard as long as the penetration in the southwest had not yet reached its final phase.

The companies, ten times repulsed and ten times returned to the counterattack, were occupying positions improvised according to the luck of battle. We had platoons engaged far to the east. Half the messengers who carried orders to them were picked off by Mongols in ambush. The officers kept sending me panicky notes announcing that everything was all over. Everyone would see ten tanks where there were two. I had to get angry, and send back formal orders and stinging comments.

The Viking's commander was in the next isba. He kept receiving a continual stream of pessimistic messages from units fighting near ours. Evidently, as is the custom in the army, everyone blamed his neighbor for the reverses of his own sector.

I was summoned by General Gille. With steely eyes, his teeth clenched, he gave me orders hard as iron. "Forbidden to retreat! The officers are responsible for the troops, you are responsible for the officers!"

The man was right to issue curt commands. Only an iron will could save us now.

It was no lark.

My orders to the officers were firm. Poor boys, all so devoted and so courageous, their skin sallow, gray, their hair unkempt, their eyes hollow, their nerves raw, they had to keep sending hundreds of men back into combat. They really had come to the limit of human endurance.

I had been able to obtain another fifty thousand cartridges. The brave Ju's still kept on delivering us ammunition, but the boundaries of the *Kessel* were so tenuous that a special way of parachuting had been initiated. At a given hour, while the airplanes circled above us, flares would rise from the four sides of the *Kessel.* They marked the limits of our miniscule territory exactly. The big silver cigars full of cartridges would be dropped. We would be saved for several hours more.

The worst hardship was the lack of food. There was not another forkful of meat or a thin slice of bread. There was nothing. The division had exhausted its last supplies at Korsun. The shivering sleepless men had not been fed for three days. The youngest would faint, their faces on their submachine guns.

* * * * *

Waiting in Novo-Buda, we had thought the thrust would take place on Monday.

It still hadn't happened on Tuesday.

When would it happen?

Would we starve to death if the bullets spared us?

I borrowed the horses which had hauled carts of wounded men to Sanderovka. I asked my most resourceful Walloons to ride them: "Get going! Look everywhere! Go to the farthest isbas! Sneak right under the Soviets' noses if you have to! But bring back something to make bread with! And do it quickly!"

I found some bakers among the troops. Our isba had a half-destroyed oven, which they put it back into shape. Several hours later our horsemen returned with bags of flour thrown across their saddles.

Did we still need leaven? No one had a gram. Our foragers went off again, looked everywhere, and finally found a little bag of sugar. With bread and sugar we could bake something. The fire flared up at once.

By the end of the afternoon. I sent some round loaves, flat as plates, and with a bizarre taste, to the positions. Everyone got a quarter of one.

Some other soldiers brought me a few stray cows. They were immediately butchered, and cut up into a hundred crude pieces with makeshift cleavers. It was impossible to find pans. We made huge fires from planking outside. The wounded and the handicapped each received a pike or a bayonet. It was their job to roast the meat. We had neither salt nor spices. But twice a day each man received his chunk of beef, more or less cooked, which he tore with his teeth like a tiger.

I even tried to give the brigade soup.

A stove was found two kilometers north of Sanderovka, sunken in the mud amidst hundreds of bogged trucks. Our cooks pulled it out with immense effort and made a sensational stew with whatever they found.

Finding two barrels to transport this choice gruel, we loaded them on a dump-truck. It took eight hours to cross the three kilometers of mud, now becoming very sticky in the cold. When the vehicle reached Novo-Buda at the end of the night, the casks, jostled about in all directions, were three-quarters empty. The rest had become filthy and frozen.

After that we stuck to bread and sugar and braised beef.

* * * * *

Wherever we took position we were met by enemy fire. Sanderovka was riddled day and night by the constant fire of the "Stalin's organs." Everywhere we had to step over dead horses, broken carts, and dead bodies that we could no longer bury.

We had converted the *kolkhoz* into a field hospital, open on all sides, but where our bleeding soldiers had at least a roof.

We had run out of medicine. There wasn't a single bandage in the whole *Kessel.* To bind our men's wounds the medics had to turn the peasant women upside down and yank off their long drawers, gifts of the Don Juans of the German Army.

They would shriek and run away with their hands pressed to their skirts.

Thus two or three horribly wounded men would receive a pitiful bandage.

The grotesque was blending with the tragic and the horrible.

* * * * *

Rocket volleys from the "Stalin's organs" began to pound the *kolkhoz.* The roof collaped. Dozens of wounded men died in bloody bundles. Others, gone mad, let out horrified screams. We had to evacuate. Our wounded would have to remain outdoors.

More than twelve hundred wounded men from the other units had already been stretched out under the stars for several days and nights on hundreds of village carts, sleeping on straw, drenched to the bone by the preceding week's rains, now shivering with cold.

Since Tuesday the temperature had stayed at twenty degrees below zero. Hundreds of wounded men, faces nothing but a frightful purplish pulp, amputees with one leg or arm, dying men with convulsive eyes, were exposed to atrocious conditions.

## Twenty-Three Hundred Hours

That night snow fell interminably on Sanderovka, reaching a depth of a quarter of a meter. The twenty or thirty thousand men who were waiting in our village for a military solution to the drama hadn't a single place to lie down. One might have thought oneself at the Beresina River, with the Napoleon's retreating army.

Everywhere, in spite of the danger, the men gathered around fires started in the snow. It was impossible to sleep. To lie down in the open air would mean an icy death.

Isbas were burning in vast conflagrations. In the valley hundreds of little brush fires flickered, around which crouching shadows, soldiers with reddened eyes, with ten-day beards, were holding out their sallow fingers over the flames.

They were waiting, but nothing was happening. Morning found them silent, not even searching for food. Their eyes looked toward the southwest. No one even bothered to listen to rumors.

The "Stalin's organs" would brutally break our wait. Everyone would throw himself in the snow, then rise painfully.

Wounded men cried out. The doctors cared for them only as a matter of conscience.

* * * * *

The twelve hundred wounded were still lying stretched out on their carts. Many of them had quit asking for anything, stopped wanting to know anything. They were huddled up in thin blankets, exerting all their energy in not dying.

Hundreds of teams were mixed up among them, their skeletal horses gnawing the planks of the carts in front of them. Here and there a wounded man would cry out or give a long drawn-out shudder. Men gone mad would rise to their feet, bleeding, their hair full of snow.

It was useless to try to feed all these wretches. They kept their heads buried under their covers. From time to time the drivers would brush away the snow that had accumulated on the inert bodies with their hands.

Many had been lying on these carts for ten days. They felt themselves rotting away. We couldn't numb the pain of their wounds, even the most horrible, with a single shot. We had nothing left. Nothing. We just had to wait, to wait for death or a miracle. The row of ivory cadavers next to the carts was growing longer.

Nothing astonished us or moved us. We had seen too much. The worst horrors left us numb.

* * * * *

Above Novo-Buda the enemy was still attacking.

The tanks, all muddy, were outlined against the white sky.

The men held on because they couldn't do anything else. On this bald mountain retreat would inevitably mean being cut down by the Soviet machine guns.

Our companies were sectioned over several kilometers, five men here, twenty men there.

No telephone. No radio.

We had to wait for darkness to drag the wounded and the dozens of boys with frozen wax-like feet across the snow. Their shoes, torn, soles sprung by the marshes and the mud, gave no protection any more, and with the water oozing in everywhere, they had by now become blocks of ice.

We took these wretches down as far as the valley. At daybreak we laid them out on carts in place of the stiff corpses, which we put down beside the wheels or on the snow banks.

Their beards frozen as hard as darts, shivering or indignant, they watched us with glassy eyes. What could we do? What could we say? Our deliverance was yet to come.

They knew it as well as we did, and in the end they would curl up again in silence.

* * * * *

Wednesday afternoon it became obvious that the tanks coming toward us from the southwest either wouldn't reach us or would find us dead. For the last two days they had made no progress at all.

Why? We didn't know.

We were supposed to have made the breakthrough across the Soviet lines on Saturday, 12 February.

Then Sunday.

Then Monday.

Five days had elapsed.

By now everyone could see that our efforts were either insufficient or in vain. The electrifying telegrams had been nothing but fictions. The tanks hadn't come.

The surrounded troops had held out as long as there was hope. Now everything was falling to pieces. We were down to our last cartridges. Since Sunday the quartermasters hadn't any food. The wounded were dying by the hundreds from exposure and loss of blood. We were suffocating under the enemy pressure.

In the north the Communist forces coming from Korsun had overrun our outposts. On 16 February they were three kilometers from Sanderovka.

At Novo-Buda our resistance was in its death throes. Huddled in the narrow valley, the German divisions were subjected to increasingly terrifying avalanches of shells and grenades.

Optimistic rumors were still making the rounds of the troops, tossed to them out of charity so that they would continue to hope.

But our leaders were dispirited before the specter of disaster.

We had to have a solution, an immediate solution.

* * * * *

I was summoned by General Gille. All the superior officers of the Sanderovka sector were there.

There was no lengthy discussion. "Only a desperate effort can still save us. It's no good waiting. Tomorrow morning at five o'clock the fifty thousand men in the *Kessel* must charge toward the southwest. We must either break through or die. We have no other choice. This evening at 2300 hours the movement of troops will begin."

The two generals of the army corps and General Gille had taken great care not to describe the situation too realistically. To hear them tell it, all we had to do was cross a zone of five and a half kilometers to reach the liberating army. This, they said, had advanced since the day before, and tomorrow would advance again toward us. Our fifty thousand men all charging at once would be able to overrun the enemy.

Everyone's nerves, whether leader or soldier, had been strained to the limit. Now hope rose in us in burning waves. We went back to give the orders and pass the sacred fire of inspiration to the troops.

* * * * *

The orders of the Assault Brigade "Wallonia" wouldn't be easy to carry out. We had to remain as rear guards atop Novo-Buda until the very end.

At eleven o'clock in the evening I sent all the walking wounded on their way toward the southwest. At one o'clock in the morning the Walloon infantry forces began to disengage from the east and west. We would have to hold firmly to the positions of Novo-Buda until four o'clock in the morning.

By this time the tens of thousands of men massed in the valley should be three kilometers to the southwest of Sanderovka. Then and only then could our rearguard withdraw, taking care to mislead the enemy with heavy fire right at the last minute.

The Wallonian Brigade would re-form while on the march and pass to the head of the column, at that time integrating itself with the advance guard of the troops for the breakthrough.

* * * * *

We had come to the point where anything was better than stagnation. The troops knew that they would be done for if they stood about any longer. They couldn't go on with their stomachs knotted with hunger, their bodies shaky with fatigue, and their minds tortured by worry.

The announcement that the following dawn we would break through galvanized the whole army. The weakest felt a spurt of new life. Exhausted, almost in tears, we were all sick with exultation.

Our eyes empty, our bodies limp, we kept repeating over and over to ourselves, "Tomorrow we'll be free! Free! Free!"

## The Last Night

One way or another the Cherkassy *Kessel* was coming to an end.

As soon as darkness hid the valley the German columns began their march toward the southwest. They had to pass through the village of Sanderovka, then cross a bridge. Beyond the bridge the open steppe extended as far as two villages situated a good three kilometers apart in the south and west.

These two towns had just been taken in a pitched battle. At five o'clock in the morning our divisions would launch their attack from there.

Our train was to assemble at the west of these two towns before daybreak. These vehicles were a source of hourly torment. From the first day of the *Kessel,* we should have lightened the army of the dead weight of these fifteen thousand trucks. Then the fifty to sixty thousand encircled men, able to move freely and organized in solid infantry columns, would have been able to break the enemy stranglehold easily enough.

But at first we had wanted to hold the terrain. Later the High Command had treated the saving of this fabulous caravansary as an affair of state.

General Gille had received a sharp dressing down for proposing that we burn them. We had spent three weeks towing these thousands of magnificent vehicles—radio cars, medical cars, command cars, enormous and impractical trucks loaded with millions of kilos of heterogeneous objects, bits of old paper, all sorts of trunks, reserves of survival rations, personal effects, dishes, armchairs, mattresses, even stocks of accordians, mouth organs, hygienic instruments, and parlor games.

From Petsamo to the Black Sea the German Army suffocated under the weight of overabundant equipment and baggage, a weight which grew greater every year.

We should have blown three quarters of it into the air and fought like the Asiatics, slept like the Asiatics, eaten like the Asiatics, advanced like the Asiatics, as roughly as they, as simply as they, without comfort and without useless burdens.

We dragged the handicap of civilization with us across impossible terrain. The horde on our tail had the mobility and the toughness of barbarians. The brute conquered the truck because the brute could go where the truck could not.

The German defeat in the snows and muck of Russia in 1943 and 1944 was in large part the defeat of a well-supplied army entangled in its impedimenta.

It was useless to discuss these problems in the midst of the *Kessel* with a command that was already tearing out its hair. The orders were to save the equipment. We lost precious days, therefore, in dragging thousands of doomed trucks through horrible mud wallows, nevertheless to end up sinking in the boggy trails or being demolished in a barrage of shells from the Soviet tanks and light artillery.

On the evening of 16 February 1944 we still had about twenty Panzers, something more than a thousand motorized vehicles (out of fifteen thousand), and hundreds of light carts requisitioned in the villages, on which lay about twelve hundred wounded.

These wounded men were sacred. The troops made a box around this sorrowful column and protected it during the drive toward the southwest. We had to try everything to save these wretches, whose suffering had surpassed anything that a man's mind could imagine. If tomorrow evening these men were across the infernal barrier, what overwhelming joy in our hearts! What relief to lay them in ambulances, to see these poor torn and frozen bodies finally receive care, to see these hearts that beat painfully under covers heavy with snow once again find the peaceful rhythm of men who can suffer with hope.

* * * * *

By nine o'clock in the evening the bottleneck in Sanderovka was unimaginable. At that time I was to regulate the withdrawal of my brigade at Novo-Buda methodically, platoon by platoon, sector by sector. One mishap at our rearguard positions and the whole maneuver of Sanderovka would have foundered.

Both boots set in the snow, racked by a fever of 40 °C which I couldn't shake off, I dispatched messengers, received reports, and attended to every detail.

All the hills were illuminated by the combat.

At eleven o'clock in the evening I tried to cross Sanderovka to help move the wounded of my brigade and to verify the positions that had been ordered for our soldiers' reassembly at daybreak. After fifty meters I had to abandon our last all-terrain vehicle. A phenomenal column obstructed the sunken road and the village. Trucks, telegas,* droshkies* were vainly trying to advance, four or five vehicles abreast.

I hurried to the carts of Walloon wounded and urged those of our comrades who could still use their legs to summon their last energy and take their chances on foot, whatever their wounds and their suffering. Gathering about fifty, I slipped between the baggage train and the trucks with them.

We were about to watch a horrible spectacle. The enemy, driving from the north, had been able to move his tanks and artillery up close to Sanderovka. Since ten o'clock in the evening the Soviet batteries had poured a rolling fire into the center of the town. Some isbas had gone up in flames, completely lighting the movement in progress.

From this time on the Soviet gunners had a field day. Their shells were falling implacably, with mathematical precision, onto the enormous column. The "Stalin's organs" were inundating this flood of every sort of vehicle with rockets. Gasoline trucks were blazing. All along the narrow road cars were burning. We had to keep constantly throwing ourselves into the snow, so violent was the fire from the "Stalin's organs."

Among the dozens of burning vehicles, horses struck down in the snow sounded their death rattles amid fearful convulsions. Near them clusters of soldiers hit by the machine gun fire were coughing, flat on their bellies, or lying on their backs. The flames made their faces particularly haunting, red with blood, a shining coppery red that filled one with horror. Some still tried to crawl. The others, disabled, writhed in pain, mouths gaping horribly.

The column was nothing but a frightful butchery, illuminated by fires which glowed red against a landscape of thick snow.

The trucks burning between the palisaded banks made progress almost impossible. Harassed by machine-gun fire, the infantry men could hardly move among those enormous torches, those bodies of dying men, those disembowelled horses whose intestines slithered about on the ice like great brown and green serpents.

The drivers gunned their motors in vain. A few big trucks advanced in spite of everything, crushing the horses struggling or dying among the flames. This savage expenditure of energy was nevertheless useless. The bottleneck grew ever more monstrous, aggravated by the noise of the motors, the explosions, the furious cries and implorings.

We finally saw the cause of this fantastic congestion. The entire army of Sanderovka had to cross a wooden bridge in order to leave the valley. An enormous German Panzer had fallen through right on the bridge, smashing it and completely cutting off the movement of traffic toward the southwest. When we saw that monster overturned amidst the rubbish of the planks we thought that this time everything was lost.

The river banks were steep and absolutely impassable. The bridge had been dynamited by the Communists at the time of their expulsion two days earlier. The Germans had reconstructed it hastily. The light tanks had been able to get out of Sanderovka. A heavy tank had then passed without difficulty. The second heavy tank had smashed everything in.

Two days of work by the engineers had been brought to nothing in one minute by this forty-ton mass of iron now planted like a stake in the middle of the bridge.

It was as bright as day. The wounded and the infantry wriggled by as best they could past the fatal Panzer. From atop the ravine we could see all Sanderovka, red and gold amid the shining snow. Screams rose up, uncountable. Out of the horror of the screams and the flickering flames rose a burning welter of madness.

When our wounded were across the bridge I turned them over to one of our doctors, with orders to stick with the troops three kilometers ahead of us, who formed the spearhead. They set out across the steppe, where the shadows weren't broken by the flames of the burning trucks.

At the end of two hours of unspeakable effort in this atmosphere of disaster, the German engineers managed to tip the tank into the precipice and to throw some massive beams across the gaping hole. The traffic started again under an increasingly terrible bombardment.

We were advancing over the dead and dying. But we were advancing. The men would have trampled over anyone in order to advance: they wanted to live.

* * * * *

To the northwest, on the icy hill of Novo-Buda, our Walloons, faithful to the orders they had been given, were still fearlessly resisting and returning the attack. They saw the burning of the blocked and broken columns in Sanderowka. To their ears came the fearful clamor of the thousands of men struggling amid the shellbursts and the flames.

From one o'clock until five in the morning our platoons disengaged one by one. They slipped silently away over the snow and the hard ground. They reached a small valley in the southeast and regrouped with still three kilometers to cross to reach Sanderovka. No need to look for the trail. Flaming orange torches danced above the brilliantly lighted village.

Our men passed as best they could between the burning trucks, the dead horses, and the contorted cadavers, bursting or burning away.

Throughout night the Walloons went down thus through the hurricane, in small fast-moving groups.

* * * * *

Unshakeable, our rear guard stayed at its post in Novo-Buda. It machine-gunned the enemy without respite, pinning him to the ridge. At five o'clock in the morning, carrying out the last phase of the plan, they adroitly slipped out of sight and forged ahead to rejoin the last line of SS, installed at the northern exit of Sanderovka. Then, following the last vehicles, they crossed the now notorious bridge to the south.

A column of trucks and carts two kilometers long and fifty meters wide had pushed up very close to the line of attack. I had climbed onto a load of munitions from which, as they passed, I hailed and regrouped my Walloons. They were still alert in spite of everything.

There was a fantastic jumble of units and transport. The sky was just beginning to lighten above this inextricable mass of tanks, automobiles, horse-drawn vehicles, combined battalions, Ukrainian civilians, and Soviet prisoners.

Suddenly a shell fell right in the middle of the throng. Then ten shells. Then a hundred shells.

The tanks and the enemy guns had reached the hillsides of Sanderovka across from us.

The last twenty German Panzers burst out of the column and rushed toward a gully, flattening everything in their path like straw. Truck drivers and cart drivers raced headlong in every direction. Horses fled, crazed. Others, their hooves crushed by the tanks, whinnied wildly. Thousands of explosions stirred gray and black whirlwinds, riddling the snow with rose-colored sparks.

## Through It All

The orders instructed the Assault Brigade "Wallonia" to spearhead the dawn attack that would decide our safety or our extermination. Amid the incredible confusion unleashed by the Soviet tanks bursting in among the last thousand German vehicles we thrust swiftly toward the southwest.

Behind us the noise was deafening. Sanderovka hadn't held out more than an hour. The Reds had already overrun the village. Their tanks were driving forward in our direction for the final strike.

The German panzers had been sent to the counterattack as a sacrifice unit, one against ten, just like the cavalry of Marshal Ney east of the Beresina a century earlier.[2]

I saw them just before they threw themselves against the enemy. The faces of those young tankers were admirable. Clothed in short black jackets with silver trim, their heads and shoulders protruding from the turrets, they knew that they were going to die.

Several proudly wore the tricolor ribbon and the large black and silver Knight's Cross on their necks, a glittering target for the enemy.

Not one of those marvelous warriors seemed nervous or even moved.

They ploughed up the snow with their treads as they departed through the tangle of the retreating army. Not one returned. Not one Panzer. Not one man. Orders were orders. The sacrifice was total.

To gain one hour, an hour that might yet save tens of thousands of soldiers of the Reich and of Europe, the German tank crews died to the very last man south of Sanderovka on the morning of 7 February 1944.

Shielded by those heroes, the army rushed toward the southwest.

Snow was falling in huge flakes. The thick snow completely blurred the sky down to eye level. In clear weather the enemy aircraft would have annihilated us all. Hidden by this veil of thick flakes we ran, panting.

The corridor was extremely narrow. The lead troops, who had opened the way before us, had made a passage only a few hundred meters wide.

The terrain was hilly. We dashed from one hill to another. The bottom of each ravine was a frightful crush of wrecked vehicles and dozens of dead soldiers sprawled across the red snow.

The enemy's guns hammered these passages savagely. We kept falling over wounded and bloody men. We had to take shelter alongside the dead. Carts tipped over. Horses flailed their hooves in the air until the machine-gun bullets spilled their hot intestines in the soiled snow.

We would scarcely have crossed a ravine before marksmen posted on both flanks would fire upon us. Men would cry out and fall to their knees in the snow, holding their guts. The snow quickly dusted the dying. Five minutes later we could still see their cheeks, their nose, and a few locks of hair. Ten minutes later there would be nothing but white heaps upon which other fleeing men would be mowed down.

The wounded of the *Kessel,* in their hundreds of carts, were being frightfully jarred in this frantic race. Horses bounded into frozen potholes. Carts would overturn, throwing the wounded pell-mell onto the ground.

Nevertheless, on the whole, the column remained fairly orderly.

It was then that a wave of Soviet tanks passed the last vehicles and swallowed up more than half of the transport. The drivers were thrown out of their seats.

We didn't have a single tank left. We rushed futilely to meet these enemy tanks and try to ward off the catastrophe. Nothing stopped them.

The Soviet tanks advanced through the carts with a horrible savagery, crushing them one by one like matchboxes under our very eyes, horses as well as wounded and dying men.

We pushed the walking wounded as quickly as we could. Somehow or other we covered the flight of the carts which had escaped the tanks.

But everywhere men were falling over head first or sinking to their knees, their lungs or their bellies punctured by the bullets which whistled in a mad pizzicato from both sides of the corridor.

* * * * *

We had a moment's respite while the Soviet tanks, bottlenecked in the pass, tried to untangle themselves from the tangle of the hundreds of broken carts under their treads. We skirted a wood, a beautiful russet and violet wood, and reached a little valley.

We were scarcely starting up the slope when, turning back, we saw hundreds of cavalry racing down a hill to the southeast. We thought at first that it was German uhlans.* Looking through my binoculars, I could clearly make out the uniform of the cavalry. They were Cossacks. I recognized their nervous little brown horses. They were rushing up behind us, swarming in every direction.

We were stupefied. The Soviet infantry was machine-gunning us. The Soviet tanks were following us. And now the Cossacks were storming in for the kill.

When? When would the German Panzers coming to meet us from the southwest show themselves?

We had already gone at least ten kilometers and seen nothing. We would have to go forward still faster.

Like many of the wounded, I couldn't take any more. The fever was sapping my strength. But the race had to be run at all costs. With my Walloons I hurried to the head of the column to urge our comrades on.

The hillside was steep. At our left an enormous crevasse opened, four meters wide, fifteen meters deep. We got almost to the top of the hill.

Then we saw three tanks drive toward us at high speed. We had a second of unspeakable joy. "It's them! Finally! The German Panzers are here!" But a volley of shells swooped down on us and mowed down our ranks. They were Soviet tanks.

The enemy tanks were on our heels. The foot soldiers were killing us on the flanks. Their Cossacks were driving into our ranks. And now instead of salvation, other Soviet tanks were surging up in front of us. We couldn't wait any longer. Caught napping on this naked slope, we were going to be swept away in a few seconds.

I looked at the ravine and cried out to my companions, "Do as I do!" Then I let myself fall from fifteen meters high.

There was a meter of very compressed snow at the bottom of the crevasse. I buried myself in it like a torpedo. All my comrades tumbled in one after the other.

* * * * *

In a flash hundreds of soldiers were massed in the bottom of this fault. At any minute we expected to see the Mongols appear atop the declivity and throw grenades down on us. Our lot was desperate.

Perversely, contrarily, some still wanted to try to advance. They followed the bottom of the crevasse to its southern extremity, then climbed to the surface. They immediately toppled back in horrible hot lumps, mangled by the tank fire. Their corpses formed a mound about two meters high onto which the snow again began to fall.

I had regrouped the Walloons in my vicinity and prepared them for disaster. We were huddled against one another so as not to freeze. Everyone had thrown away his papers, rings, even wedding rings. I consoled my companions as well as I could.

What hope did we have left of coming out alive or free from this narrow defile, with the enemy tanks barring the south? To turn back would be to face the first Soviet tanks, infantry, and cavalry which were rushing down from the north and sweeping away the last resistance.

It was then that the unbelievable happened. In our crevasse two exhausted German soldiers came forward, each holding a panzerfaust. They were so drained by fatigue that they seemed to understand nothing, and carried their panzerfausts mechanically, the way they carried their heads on their shoulders.

Two panzerfausts!

We pounced. A German volunteer and a Walloon volunteer seized these anti-tank weapons and climbed up to the ridge. They had time to aim without being seen. Two fantastic explosions echoed. The two nearest enemy tanks, hit almost point-blank, blew up.

A young German officer who had climbed onto the other bank saw the explosion. He gamboled about like a high school boy, shouting cries of triumph. I saw him suddenly explode, atomized. He had received a shell from the third tank full in the body.

Several horrible seconds passed. Then countless little bits of flesh no bigger than ears fell slowly back down into the snow all around us. Plink . . . plonk . . . It was all that was left of the joyous lieutenant who had been celebrating our momentary victory an instant earlier.

We couldn't lose a second. I grabbed my submachine gun and climbed onto the enormous heap of dead soldiers at the end of the ravine. I had six clips of thirty-two rounds on my belt, six more in my snow boots, and three hundred reserve cartridges in my pack. While hundreds of German and Walloon soldiers were leaving the crevasse, I could drive back the Cossacks already on the plateau with my fire.

At the shouts, the last carts of wounded men started out from the bottom of the slope. There was one more Soviet tank, forty meters away. It would ravage us terribly. But there was no other solution. We would have to charge straight ahead and salvage what we could. To remain in the crevasse was certain disaster. To thrust forward gave us a chance of avoiding death.

I knew the map of the whole country by heart. I had studied it for weeks and would have been able to reach the Romanian frontier, three hundred kilometers from Cherkassy, without help from anyone.

Having made up my mind not to fall into the hands of the Soviets alive, I had taken my precautions. I was carrying the wherewithal to fight in the forests for months if necessary.

Leaving the crevasse, I marked a large woods at the other end of the plateau, whose existence and location I had learned from the map. There, sheltered from the enemy tanks, we would at least be able to catch our breath.

Our soldiers ran toward it from every direction. We had to cross about eight hundred meters of flat terrain before reaching it. The remaining carts had managed to catch up with us. With them we darted forward.

The Soviet tank, too, had darted forward, surrounded by a bloodcurdling swarm of Cossacks. We had to fire our submachine guns, all the while cutting our way through the enemy, knocked down a dozen times by the shells exploding all around us.

Gasping, our lungs bursting, we couldn't go on. Right under my horrified eyes the Soviet tank drove down upon the carts of wounded, dumped them over and flattened them. Horrifying screams resounded, the cries of the dying and the indescribable shrieks of crushed horses, feverishly shaking their hooves.

We collapsed at the edge of the forest half dead. Behind us, the gray snow was littered with corpses. The tank, a horde of Cossacks charging all around it, was finishing its mad joust.

## Lysyanka

It was impossible for the tanks and the numerous cavalry following us to penetrate the dense thickets of the forest. A little path descended to a clearing where a fine old staff colonel riding an exhausted horse was vainly trying to make himself heard.

Several thousand men had collapsed in the snow. The area under the trees was being steadily machine-gunned. We couldn't abandon these thousands of soldiers to their fate after the great dangers they had already escaped.

I identified myself to the old colonel and asked him politely if I might direct the combat in the forest. He seemed delighted with my suggestion, got down from his mount, and sat down in the snow.

I found a young German officer who knew French. I had him translate the short talk that I gave to the troops one sentence at a time. "I know exactly where we are. We have only three kilometers left to go before reaching the southern columns. To rush toward them now is to get ourselves massacred. I will take the responsibility of leading everyone to them during the night. We will succeed. But while waiting for darkness we must form a square around the edge of the forest and not let the Soviet infantry invade it."

I asked for volunteers. I wanted nobody else. Somewhat dazed, the Germans advanced in a body.

I formed combat groups of ten men with a Walloon in each to serve me as a messenger. I requisitioned the weapons, munitions, and panzerfausts of all those who were no longer capable of fighting, and I quickly posted the Germans and Walloons on the rim of the forest.

The Soviets that we had pushed back to the southeast of the woods were firing fiercely. Our men received orders to stay strictly on the defensive since it wasn't in that direction that we would have to disengage in the evening.

The map showed that a town called Lysyanka was to be found three kilometers to the southwest. I was absolutely convinced that this town was in the hands of German forces coming to meet us. It wasn't possible that this large village, which was twenty kilometers beyond the starting point of that morning's assault, could still be occupied by the Soviets. Certainly the liberating tanks must have advanced that far.

I had seen on the map that a river passed through the town. It would therefore be enough to get to the first houses. We would then find or improvise a makeshift bridge.

Our forest went down toward Lysyanka. We would use it as long as possible in our night march.

Already the couriers were leaving to stealthily reconnoiter the terrain.

* * * * *

We ran the most immediate peril to the west of the forest. From the edge we saw a daunting column of Soviet tanks on the hill facing us three hundred meters away, the same column which had dispatched the three tanks that had very nearly annihilated us an hour earlier.

These tanks were posted along the route which led to Lysyanka. They were watching the entire region from the ridge. They kept the western sector, where another wave of encircled troops was advancing, under fire, and also controlled the little valley which separated them from the forest.

This absolutely bare valley was a continual temptation. It led to Lysyanka. One last bound and we would be free.

The Red tanks were surrounded by numerous infantry. Anyone who tried to charge through this naked valley would be crushed. It was written in the terrain.

I paid a visit to each of my posts to calm my men's impatience. Unfortunately I could restrain only my own men.

On our right flank, just at the northwest corner of the forest, a wave of several hundred German soldiers who had crossed the plateau after us suddenly appeared. They had stolen along the woods instead of entering them. A grand and terrifying shout resounded, gripping us right to the marrow. "Hurrah, Germania!" They rushed forward at breakneck speed.

We watched the carnage from the sidelines. Not one man, not a single one, got through. The enemy's tanks poured a withering fire into them. The wretches fell in clusters on the snow. It was a massacre.

Then the Soviet infantry pounced onto the piles of dead and wounded for the final pillage.

We were huddled in our machine-gun nests under the trees a hundred meters from the slaughter and didn't miss a detail of the horrible scene. Armed with knives, the Communist looters vied with one another to cut off the fingers of the dead and dying. It was too much trouble to take off their rings, so they cut off the fingers and stuffed them into their pockets in bloody handfuls to move faster.

Horrified, we had to watch these scenes of atrocity in silence. I had given strict orders not to shoot. It wouldn't have saved a single one of the dying men who lay in the valley, but on the contrary would have provoked a general attack against the forest from the horde of cutthroats. I wanted to save the three thousand men for whom I had taken the responsibility. I wouldn't succeed in this by throwing them blindly to a vain butchery without either artillery or tanks, but rather by having the strength to wait calmly for night, which would darken the valley and neutralize the hunters in the Soviet tanks.

* * * * *

In the morning the fifty thousand men of the *Kessel* had charged straight ahead, and all the units had been quickly mixed up.

As for us, we had managed to shelter several thousand men from the enemy tank thrusts, thanks to the tight screen of the forest trees.

This had not been so for the great mass of the German troops attacking to the right and left of us. Amid the noise of the battle we guessed that a major wave of Germans was descending to the west of the route occupied by the Soviet tanks, which had turned their turrets in the direction of the thrust and unleashed an incessant fire. Another even larger German wave had broken to the right in the southeast of our forest, trying to reach Lysyanka by the steppe.

Adding to all our difficulties was the crossing of the river. I had painstakingly studied the configuration of this obstacle on the topographic map and had decided to avoid it and descend by night directly to the town of Lysyanka, built on both sides of the water. Thus I would spare my troops having to cross this deep and swift watercourse in the open country in weather fifteen or twenty degrees below zero.

In the confusion we had been lucky enough to take to this providential forest in time to slip close to the large village in the darkness. I would wait as long as necessary, but I would profit from our privileged situation to the maximum when the time was ripe.

Unfortunately, the others, meaning tens of thousands of soldiers, had to face the west and southeast.

The southeast wing had been commanded by an army corps general who had been killed at the head of his men. General Gille immediately replaced him.

Toward one o'clock in the afternoon this wave, with the Soviet tanks on its heels, broke against the river. The three weeks of thaw had greatly swollen its waters. It was now two meters deep and eight wide. Its waters were strewn with huge sharp-edged blocks of ice from the cold of the last days, borne along by the rapid current.

In less than half an hour twenty thousand men found themselves cornered on the riverbank. The artillery teams who had escaped destruction were the first to rush into the waves and ice jams. The bank was steep. The horses turned back and were drowned.

Then some of the men tried to swim across, but they had barely emerged on the other side of the river when they turned into blocks of ice, their clothes frozen right to their bodies.

Some fell dead of heart failure.

Most of the soldiers preferred to strip. But when they tried to throw their belongings across the water, often the uniforms would fall into the current. Soon hundreds of soldiers, stark naked and red as lobsters, crowded on the other bank.

Inevitably, the enemy tanks fired into the human mass jammed at the edge of the watercourse, throwing themselves into the bloody game of massacre.

Many soldiers didn't know how to swim. Panicky at the approach of the Soviet tanks, which were shelling them as they descended the slope, they threw themselves pell-mell into the glacial waves. Many escaped death by hanging onto trees hastily felled across the water, but hundreds drowned.

The bank was littered with boots, packs, weapons, belts, and hundreds of cameras. The wounded lay everywhere, incapable of crossing the river. But the greater part of the army crossed all the same.

Under the tank fire thousands and thousands of soldiers, half-clothed or stark naked, streaming with icy water, were running through the snow toward the distant isbas of Lysyanka.

Three hundred meters away from us on the road, the tanks still kept their turrets aimed toward the northwest, second avenue of break-out from the *Kessel.*

There too the flight was massive. It partially absorbed the activity of the Soviet tanks and infantry for several hours. This diversion saved us.

Night fell on the debacle. Snow was falling in huge slow flakes. In the distance, at the very end of the steppe, we could hear the agonizing appeals of the wounded men, whose desperate cries tore out our hearts. "Comrades, comrades, comrades!" The appeals were unanswered. Poor companions of the morning, whom the snow and the night were covering up and who were still struggling, their hands full of blood, against a horrible death in the infinite steppe.

While waiting for total darkness the non-commissioned officers had regrouped the three thousand survivors scattered in our woods.

Every kind of unit and specialty was intermingled.

We had even pushed about thirty Soviet prisoners along with us right to the end of the *Kessel.* Numb to everything, they had raced through the shells and the Cossacks without trying to flee or giving us the least trouble.

We were also sheltering a number of civilians in the woods, notably some winded young women. These beautiful Ukrainians with pale blue eyes and hair the color of the harvest didn't want to fall back under Soviet domination. They preferred to break through the tempest of the fighting rather than return to slavery.

A number of female fugitives had been struck down by the machine-gun fire. One of them, a marvelous big radiant girl with a cheerful blue and white scarf, was running among us as supple as a doe as we mounted the last hillside. I saw her knocked down like a bowling pin, her head carried right off by a tank shell. Some were hugging little blond infants to their breasts, absolutely terrified by the horrors and the noise.

Without any food or drink, we had lived on handfuls of snow since morning, but that had made us thirstier than ever. The wounded that we had been able to save were shivering with fever. We huddled as close together as we could in the machine-gun nests in order to warm ourselves up a bit.

Above all we were waiting with a gnawing anxiety for this tragic day to end. Only then, when the tanks on the hill would be unable to track our movements, could our column leave its refuge.

* * * * *

At 1730 hours we moved out in strict order.

The doleful cries of the hundreds of dying men scattered on the steppe were still rising in the distance. From the whole plateau, sealed off by the Soviet tanks, and from the bottom of the valleys which we had crossed only that morning, rose up unendingly the poignant supplications brought to us by the snowy night with tragic clarity: "Comrades, comrades, comrades!"

What horrible death agonies down there! The hundreds of black spots had been inexorably whitened by the endlessly falling snow. Hundreds of bodies were suffering, hundreds of souls shivering in this invasion of ice, in total desolation. "Comrades, comrades!" took up the far away voices. Prayers, cries of pain, last spurts of hope fell back without an echo in the unfeeling steppe.

Closing our hearts to these frightful moans, we advanced toward deliverance, following a little road at the edge of the forest. The night became clearer. The column fell silent in the overpowering stillness. From this mass of three thousand men not even a hushed voice arose. We didn't hear so much as a whisper.

* * * * *

Other haunting cries hailed us in the fading twilight. They came from our right. There, the deadly valley which separated us from the Soviet tanks extended into enormous marshlands. During the breakout that morning, a number of German carts had charged through everything, at full gallop, toward these marshes. They ended up sinking in deep mud-wallows as thick as glue.

The horses sank completely into the mire. In the pale moonlight we could see only the heads and necks of the wretched beasts. They were still whinnying, their macabre neighing alternating with the drivers' maddened shouts as they too sank into the muck. They clung to the tops of the wheels, already almost entirely swallowed up.

With a fury born of the instinct of self-preservation, we cursed them for yelling so loudly as to attract the Soviets' attention. They should have perished in silence, the poor wretches.

We had to let these unlucky men sink to a slow death in the nocturnal mud just as we had let the heart-rending voices of the wounded on the steppe to fade away behind us, cut off from us by the enemy, each and every one dying in a loneliness more cruel than the steel that had wounded them, the mud that was swallowing them, or the snow which was pitilessly blanketing them.

* * * * *

Two kilometers farther on, guided by our scouts, we used a trail, marked with stakes, which crossed the marshes in a long, circuitous route. Even there we walked knee-deep in mud.

Not a Russian had seen us.

We climbed a snowy slope. On the other side an arm of water shone in the moonlight. We crossed it one by one on a huge, slippery beam. After another fifty meters, we had a heart-stopping shock. Three steel-helmeted shadows surged up in front of us. We fell into one another's arms, laughing, crying, dancing for joy, as all our worry and pain fell from our shoulders.

It was the first German post in the south. We were no longer hunted prey. We were no longer living under a stay of execution. The *Kessel* was now nothing more than a horrible dream.

Saved! Yes, saved! We were saved!

## The Bottleneck

After leaving the German forward post at Lysyanka we came to a sunken road. The snow swirled about us, flailed us, cutting visibility down to one meter. We settled down as well as we could in the neighboring isbas. We were still very close to the Soviets, but where could we go in the middle of the night, blinded by this whistling tempest?

Fifty of us entered a hovel and bedded down there. Every so often someone would jump up yelling, babbling nonsense, pummeling the air. In the months that followed, I myself would have horrible nightmares every night, crying out, striking the wall, the furniture, everything near me with my fists in the darkness. During the three weeks of encirclement I had personally engaged in seventeen hand-to-hand combats. For a long time, in my tormented nights, I would see again the grimacing faces of Tatars, of Kirghizes, of Samoyeds, of strangler Mongols against whom I had fought for my life almost every day.

Even now I am seized with a sort of dizziness when I think of those days of horror, the mocking grins, the leaping bodies, and the rat-a-tat-tat of my hot submachine gun.

* * * * *

At five o'clock in the morning I got everybody up. Struggling through the deep snow, we headed down the road. In the middle of Lysyanka we came to the river. Swollen by the snowfalls, it stretched very wide between its icy banks.

The Reds had destroyed the bridge, so thousands of men were waiting their turn to cross over a rickety line of planks thrown across a row of big gas barrels, which served as pillars.

The orders were to leave Lysyanka immediately, then to march as fast as we could as long as we could.

We formed an immense ribbon in the snow.

About eight thousand men had fallen in the course of the breakthrough, but more than forty thousand men had saved their lives. Only shock units like the SS Viking Division and the SS Assault Brigade "Wallonia" had suffered heavy losses. We arrived at the Dnieper in November, 1943, with a force of about two thousand men. We had exactly six hundred thirty-two left after the exit from the *Kessel* on 18 February 1944.

Of course, we had been able to evacuate our wounded of December and January during the first days of the encirclement, by airplane. Nevertheless we had to figure we'd lost half our comrades. This percentage was the highest among all the units which participated in the epic of Cherkassy.

* * * * *

After the fall of Korsun the Soviets were sure they had us. Their communiques had already announced the victory, which seemed to them to be in the bag. By means of an incredible thrust, which had brought to grips as many men as at Waterloo, our desperate effort had opened the breach to freedom.

The enemy, cheated, tried to vent its disappointment by subjecting our route to a furious bombardment. The Soviet artillery, their weapons lined up along both sides of our avenue of retreat, hammered the narrow corridor with an almost comic fury.

We advanced with difficulty in the thick snow. But everyone hastened his steps, no matter how exhausted, for the shells were falling every half minute or so, piercing the snow, throwing up geysers of earth.

The enemy infantry pursued us as well. The German Panzers of the flank guard, protecting our withdrawal, constantly scoured the terrain. We would watch the tanks rush to an embankment or a haystack forty or fifty meters from the road. The Red soldiers would rise with their hands raised. A tank would herd them to our column. They swarmed everywhere in the snow, like rats, ready for any mischief.

Batons in hand, the German generals marched on foot among the men, feeding like them on the air of the steppe. We had many kilometers to go before seeing the first supply depots. The command had hastily sent mobile kitchens to meet us, but they were almost inaccessible. We were more than forty thousand, all equally hungary and thirsty. A thousand or two thousand men would besiege one unlucky cook, who risked being tumbled to the bottom of his pot at any minute by the surging crowd.

It was useless to waste time lining up. We could barely fill a few flasks at the water fountain. The water was refreshingly icy; for the feverish wounded it was, at least temporarily, miraculous.

But this cold water was impossible to keep. Within five minutes the neck of the flask would be choked with ice; the water would ring like a crystal bell inside it.

As we advanced we saw what the progress of the Panzers coming from the south to meet us had entailed. The steppe was nothing but a cemetery for tanks. Eight hundred Soviet and three hundred German tanks had been destroyed during the three weeks' battle to free us, which almost had failed. Some "Stalin's organs," abandoned in the snow, still brandished their double rows of tubes, the color of dead leaves.

During the thaw many German tanks had bogged down in the spongy earth, sinking into it over their treads. The frost had come again, hardening and petrifying the mud, locking the Panzers into a formidable icy carapace.

Once out of the *Kessel,* it was clear that the corridor opened in our direction wouldn't last much longer. We had to free the ice-bound tanks promptly if we didn't want to abandon them to the Soviets. The tankers cut snow and ground that was harder than pig iron with axes. They lit great fires all around the immobilized tanks, pouring gasoline onto the ground, trying everything to thaw the mud and free the jammed treads, but their efforts seemed in vain.

We felt ourselves well protected by the dozens of Tigers and Panthers, the most powerful German tanks, equipped with armor of an elemental strength. Endlessly they went off to belabor the enemy who was both pressing our flanks and hot on our heels.

The escape hatch was barely ajar. We had to hurry.

The forty thousand men would have done better to stop in the night. We wandered for a long time. A storm had arisen. Gales of snow riddled us with millions of biting little crystals. We were still moving forward, not knowing whether we would fall on the left or the right.

The second day we still had twenty kilometers to cross. The storm had ceased. Although the snow was deep, the sun turned it pink and shining. The corridor was widening. The artillery had fallen silent. We could see beautiful windmills, blue, lilac, and pale green, which unfurled wide black sails against the white fields.

We reached a large village. There the corridor came to an end. German order immediately reasserted itself. Dozens of big fellows from the rear, well-fed, their cheeks as appetizing as beefsteaks, held big placards on which were inscribed the names of each of the units. It was necessary to re-form the platoons and the companies. The lifers were already bellowing out orders. If the *Stabsfeldwebeln** were blustering, it meant the adventure was truly over.

* * * * *

Somehow or other I reassembled my Walloons, who, less disciplined than their Prussian comrades, were enjoying their freedom a little while longer.

There was a stir. An Army Corps general came toward me. Shaggy and caked with frozen mud, I stood to attention.

"Come," he said to me. "The Fuehrer has telephoned three times. He is waiting for you. We've been looking for you everywhere for two days."

He led me away.

At the first light of day a Fieseler Storch appeared in the sky, a tiny little reconnaissance plane, a pretty mica cage from which one could study every detail of the ground.

The airplane slid in on its skis. My comrades pushed me into the cockpit just as I was, bundled in my big felt boots and my sheepskin.

## With Hitler

The little Fieseler Storch which had lifted me from the steppe now flew over the rear of the front. The interminable ribbons of the retreating army were outlined in black against the whiteness of the landscape. Lines of trucks and companies of soldiers as tiny as flies were beating back against the curent.

The villages swarmed with troops. It was an admirable scene, with the snow shining off into infinity, marked with the russet clusters of the orchards, the yellow edges of the thatched roofs, the long fences of black wood, the round humps of the wells and, atop the hills, the great mills turning in the blue and silver sky.

At Uman I took a place in one of the Fuehrer's special planes in company with General Liebe of the Army Corps and General Gille, glorious commander of the SS Viking.

The trimotor flew over the steppe for half an hour and then rose very high, swallowed up completely by the clouds. The Ukraine faded away underneath the machine. It was over. Never again would I see the white or golden steppe, nor the long villages smothered by the snows of winter or buzzing with the songs of the mosquitoes in the summer, nor the white-washed isbas with their green and brown shutters decorated with doves, nor the sumptuous amaranth sunsets, nor the big girls with high cheekbones, flowers of Asia among the millions of gilded sunflowers.

We passed into the opaline cotton-wool of the sky above the Pripet marshes.

The sky lightened a little bit. Through the holes in the clouds we could sometimes make out fir forests, poplar groves, a village with red roofs. Europe was below.

Finally we saw the blue lakes, flowered with whitening islets like moons in the water. We were nearing Lithuania, just north of the main headquarters of Hitler's Army.

* * * * *

I was expected first at Himmler's. In the automobile which drove me from the airport I could feel hundreds of lice devouring my body. My uniform was filthy.

They had guessed at headquarters, occupied only by neatly dressed people, that the wild men of the front like me might want to freshen up upon their arrival. So I entered the bath, where I simmered for an hour like a tough old piece of meat.

Himmler had made me a present of a beautiful green shirt. That spared me from having to pick up the old one which, tossed into a corner of the bathroom, was surrounded by a tribe of brave Ukrainian lice, flabbergasted to find themselves suddenly in so impressive an atmosphere. It seems they were talked about for a very long time among the entourage of the Reichsfuehrer SS.

A junior officer mended the collar of my jacket, torn in hand-to-hand combat in the *Kessel.* I kept on my field uniform, which they scraped, scrubbed, and brushed. Wearing my big felted boots, I sat down that evening beside Himmler in the big green car which he drove himself for the forty kilometers from his camp to the Fuehrer's command post.

Hitler's general headquarters, in the easternmost corner of Prussia, was one great construction yard at the beginning of 1944. We arrived there at midnight. Floodlights illuminated hundreds of men at work under the firs. They were constructing fantastic concrete shelters. A veritable subterranean Babylon was arising in the seclusion of this great fir forest.

The Fuehrer himself lived in a modest wooden barracks. We entered by a square vestibule. On the right was the cloakroom. At the end on the left a wide door separated us from Hitler's office. We waited for a little while. Himmler happily trotted out the few French words he knew.

The double doors opened. I hadn't time to look at or to think of anything. The Fuehrer came toward me, took my right hand in both his hands and grasped it affectionately. Magnesium lights lit the room: movie cameras were filming the meeting.

I myself saw nothing but Hitler's eyes. I felt nothing but his two hands pressing mine. I heard only his voice, a bit rough, welcoming me, repeating to me, "I've been very worried about you . . ."

We sat down in wooden armchairs facing a massive fireplace. I looked at the Fuehrer with amazement. There was still the same strange fire in his eyes, direct, bewitching. The preoccupations of four years of war had given the man an impressive majesty. His hair had whitened. His back was bent from studying the maps interminably and from bearing the weight of a world.

The Fuehrer of before the war had disappeared, the fiery Fuehrer with the chestnut hair, the trim body, the back as straight as an Alpen pine. He held a pair of tortoise-shell glasses in his hand.

Everything about him radiated thoughtfulness and concern.

But his energy was still lightning quick. He told me of his will to overcome, whatever the trials, then had me recount every scene of our tragedy, detail by detail.

He gathered his thoughts for five minutes, not saying a word. Only his jaws moved slightly, as if he were grinding down an obstacle in the silence. Everyone was quiet.

Then the Fuehrer ceased his meditation and returned to his questions.

* * * * *

He led us to the maps of the front in order to understand the odyssey of Cherkassy with complete precision. He had us recount the movements of the encircled troops, day by day, following every march on the map. The immense room was filled only with his voice, calmly inquiring, and our voices answering with poorly suppressed emotion.

Every detail of his study revealed a life of simplicity and order: the long tables of white wood, the bare walls, like those of a monk's refectory, the lamps with green-painted metallic shades, suspended over the maps by chromium lazy tongs.

The Fuehrer worked for entire nights in profound contemplation. He would pace the barracks, meditating, preparing his orders. The only things moving near him were the fire in the wide hearth, inspired by Germanic prehistory, and a beautiful big roan dog which slept in a box at the end of the table. The noble beast silently accompanied his master, who paced slowly, bent and grayed, ripening his worries and his dreams in the night.

Hitler bestowed on me the ribbon of the Knight's Cross. I had fought like a true soldier. The Fuehrer recognized that. I was proud, but what exalted me above all on this night of great emotion was the prestige that my soldiers had gained in the eyes of Hitler. He told me that all my officers of the *Kessel* were promoted one grade and that he was awarding a hundred and fifty Iron Crosses to my comrades.

We had left for the anti-Bolshevik crusade so that the name of our mother country, besmirched in May, 1940, would resound, glorious and honored, once more. Soldiers of Europe, we wanted our ancient country to rise again as brilliant as before in the new Europe which was being so painfully born.

We were the men of the country of Charlemagne, of the dukes of Burgundy, and of Charles the Fifth. After twenty centuries of soul-stiring radiance this country could not be allowed to sink into mediocrity or oblivion.

We had rushed to embrace suffering, so that grandeur and right would spring to life anew out of our sacrifice.

In this barracks, before this genius at the height of his power, I told myself that the next day the entire world would know what the Belgians had done at Cherkassy. It would know the glittering hommage that the Reich, nation of soldiers, had rendered them.

I felt myself broken, devoured by those terrible weeks. But my soul was singing! Glory there was, glory for our heroic legion, glory for our mother country, on its way to resurrection.

* * * * *

At dawn one of Hitler's planes took me to Berlin where I spoke to an assembly of European journalists. They in turn would report the exploits of the Assault Brigade "Wallonia" to the readers of a hundred dailies. Then I went to Paris where I talked before ten thousand people at Chaillot Palace. The French dailies brimmed with the tale of our odyssey. *L'Oeuvre* printed these simple words in its three column headline: "Leon Degrelle has done Belgium proud." It was true for Belgium. It wasn't true for me, for victory had been paid for with the suffering of all my soldiers and with the sacrifice of all our dead. In the storm-tossed sky of 1944, however, the name of our people shone once again.

## Brussels

During the night of 20-21 February, I obtained a promise from the Fuehrer that the Assault Brigade "Wallonia" should receive twenty-one days of leave. I telegraphed the orders from the GHQ. I knew my boys were en route, and I didn't worry about them too much.

This leave was a godsend. For hardly had our survivors boarded a train of soldiers on leave when the whole Ukrainian front split open like an old oak struck by lightning.

It came as no surprise to me. I had seen how difficult it was for the powerful force of German tanks on the southern front to clear a path to us, without even reaching us. We had had to smash our way through the enemy in order to cross the last twenty kilometers, before which the tanks of the Reich had been powerless.

The liberated troops of the *Kessel* had scarcely reached the billets where they were to be relieved when the Soviet wave broke, submerging the whole Ukraine, overflowed in every direction, and reached the Dniester at the Romanian frontier in a few days. It was a tidal wave.

The entire Ukraine,the beautiful Ukraine with its immense golden fields, its blue and white villages set in the middle of the harvests like baskets of flowers, the Ukraine overflowing with corn and wheat, endowed with hundreds of new factories in the last two years, that Ukraine was drowned under the snarling wave of Mongols and Kalmuks with damp moustaches and steel teeth, carrying heavy submachine guns with flat rotary magazines, dumbfounded to have raced from the Volga to Galicia and Bessarabia in a year and a half. Their pockets were full of gold rings, they ate well, and they had killed lots of "Fritz." They were happy men.

* * * * *

After many difficulties I found my men at the frontier of old Poland, at Wlodawa. The Reds were already across from us, streaming from the Pripet marshes in a veritable amphibian invasion.

We made a stop at the Bavarian camp of Wildflecken, from which we had departed on 11 November 1943. We returned a mutilated brigade, but once again a legion of new Walloon volunteers to take the place of the wounded and the dead awaited the conquerors of Cherkassy. In two weeks the new Assault Brigade "Wallonia" would be even stronger than the old one and would comprise three thousand men, enthusiastic as the veterans, already hardened by combat exercies, burning to set off and fight it out.

Before searching out other battlefields, we had still to march into our homeland, where the glory won by the Walloon volunteers at Cherkassy had stirred national pride intensely. We weren't loved, certainly, by the Anglophiles and the Communists, but our denigrators themselves couldn't deny that our soldiers had been faithful to military honor and to our people's traditions of courage.

On 2 April 1944, late in the morning, we arrived at the Dutch-Belgian frontier. Our march across the country began there.

Our armored column was seventeen kilometers long. From atop their powerful machines our young soldiers smiled down on our pretty villages with their blue roofs. It was for these pleasant towns, this ancient land, that they had crossed the steppes, endured such suffering, and challenged destiny.

The Brigade made its joyous entry into the industrial city of Charleroi at noon and renewed its oath of fidelity to the national socialist ideal there on the Grand-Place. Then the hundreds of tanks rolled rapidly across Wallonian Brabant, the great lion of Waterloo watching us pass from the top of his knoll.

We thought of all the heroes who had fought battles in these rich fields in days gone by, like those we had just fought in the Russian mud. That mud was far away, however. Our tanks were laden with flowers. Crowns of oak branches two meters high decorated the armor. Trains of welcoming young girls with vibrant eyes waited for us at the boundary of Brussels.

The center of the capital was a sea of faces and flags. The Panzers could hardly pass among the tens of thousands of people who had hurried to see and madly cheer our soldiers. The crowd tossed like the sea, shouting and throwing thousands of roses, the first, the sweetest, and the most tender roses, heralding the bright days of spring.

My tank stopped in front of the columns of the Bourse. I lifted all my excited children into the tank. I felt their little hot hands in mine. I watched this wonderful celebration, the communion of my soldiers and this people so sensitive to glory. New tanks rumbled without cease onto the flower-covered roadway. The Anglo-American tanks would enter Brussels by exactly the same route five months later.

# Chapter Seven
# THE EPIC OF ESTONIA

In May 1944, our Legion had gone to Poland for reorganization at the immense camp of Debika, between Cracow and Lemberg. More than eight hundred Belgian workers from the factories of the Reich had voluntarily enlisted in our brigade during the summer after my harangues.[1]

The first contingent, three hundred of these compatriots, had just arrived at the camp in July 1944 when the new Soviet offensive was unleashed.

They swept through Minsk. In two weeks a mighty tidal wave inundated the German front, breaking through everywhere and spreading out for three hundred kilometers. That very month the Soviet armies reached the frontiers of Lithuania and Prussia and seized half of Poland, reaching the suburbs of Warsaw. The route to Berlin was open.

The Viking Division, with its new tanks not even broken in, was dispatched to Warsaw, now torn by the uprising of the Polish Home Army.

A second and terrible blow from the Soviet battering ram struck the front. This time it shook the Estonian sector of the eastern front, below the Gulf of Finland. The outlying position of Narva was held by a picked corps of the SS, the Third Panzer Division, made up of Germanic volunteers from many countries, Flanders, Holland, Denmark, Sweden, Norway, Estonia, Latvia. All had fought valiantly, but they had suffered great losses.

There too the holes most urgently needed to be plugged up.

* * * * *

But plugged up with what?

Certain offices in Berlin bridled the ass by the tail and sent off unheard-of telegrams to the men waiting in the wings. The camp of Debika in particular received orders to embark our three hundred new Walloon volunteers who had just arrived, and send them to the Estonian front that very day.

A hundred among them had been enlisted in the regiment for only four days. The other two-thirds had been quartered for only two weeks and hardly knew how to use a gun. None had ever fired a machine gun.

At this time I had been recalled to Belgium, where my brother had just been savagely assassinated by terrorists. When a message informed me of these crazy instructions, our three hundred boys were already rolling toward the Baltic Sea, accompanied by about a hundred veterans who should have been their instructors at Debika. Everyone had been loaded up pell-mell. They had been given machine guns at the last minute with orders to learn en route in the train how to use these complicated weapons.

At first I didn't want to believe they had left. I telephoned Berlin. The news was confirmed. Other units were in exactly the same situation. The Flemish volunteers had been sent off exactly the same way as the Walloons.

I was floored. These three hundred new soldiers were going to take me for a nincompoop. They had come to our legion with confidence in me and, barely arrived, expecting in good faith to receive serious military training, they were rushed into a lunatic venture.

What added to my worry was the fact that after Cherkassy Hitler had forbidden my return to the front. What could I do to save my new soldiers or at least to share their fate with honor? I telegraphed Himmler's staff office, protesting vehemently against this departure, requesting the countermanding of this order or, if not, the authorization to rejoin my men.

No reply.

I was getting itchy feet. After three days of waiting I sent a new telegram: "With or without authorization I will leave tomorrow for the Estonian Front."

Berlin sent me a curt reply: "This is a court-martial offense."

I riposted, "It is also a court-martial offense to send four-days-old recruits to combat."

That night the final communication came from Berlin: "Do as you wish."

* * * * *

At dawn my car was ready. That evening I reached Berlin, which I carefully skirted for fear of receiving a personal countermand. I rolled on to Danzig. When I arrived there I learned that my soldiers had crossed into Lithuanian territory just before the railroad line of Riga was cut by the Soviet advance guards. It was no longer possible to reach Estonia by way of the Baltic countries.

There was no airplane available either.

Finally I discovered a wallowing old tub leaving for Finland at a dock. On its return it was supposed to go up to Reval. I parked my old Citroen on the bridge after much debate.

At noon our ship weighed anchor and left the imposing harbor, while above the narrow channel a Soviet squadron appeared in the blue and gold sky.

## Before Narva

Our ship, an old banana boat from Guinea, set off slowly toward the northeast, sticking to the Prussian coast. It was one of the last boats returning to Finland, which a few days later would capitulate.

There were a thousand men aboard from the most diverse branches of the service.

We scrutinized the calm sea, the color of a pigeon's breast. Sometimes, instead of a mermaid, a periscope would suddenly appear, then a submarine dripping like the back of a whale. It was a friendly submersible which was standing guard.

Submarines are like men, however. There are more bad than good ones. More than one troop transport had been sunk in the Baltic. We were loaded with life belts and slept all over the place, like big penguins, very close to the hatches on the bridge.

We travelled the length of Lithuania and Latvia. The last night, our coaster received the order to break its journey and put in at Reval, where hundreds of wounded needed to be embarked without delay.

At five o'clock in the morning we entered a calm steel-blue inlet opposite the capital of Estonia, the famous Reval[2] of the Teutonic Knights. Perched on a hillside, the glorious city was outlined by pointed steeples and dominated by its powerful ramparts.

Each ancient city of the Baltic countries bore the mark of the past. Each had its majestic castle from which Germanic civilization and order had radiated during the centuries. Each had its white churches with blue steeples rising like arrows, its great stone houses of commerce with the patina of a hundred winters, lovingly sculpted, grave and beautiful like their sister cities of Luebeck, Bremen, or Bruges, last flowers of the garland of riches and art of the Hansa.[3]

The dock of Reval lay in a fairy-tale valley which curved for a league around, strewn with enormous reddish stones. In the distance in the golden fields were outlined the mossy ruins of a gothic barn such as are still to be seen on the coastline of Flanders.

A general told me where my soldiers ought to be, somewhere before Narva. One hour afterwards I went back across the country along the Gulf of Finland by a sandy and rutted road in the direction of Leningrad.

The countryside was poor—moorlands and hazel copses, pine copses, aspen groves, reedy marshes, and wildflowers like pink birds. From time to time I could see the blue and shining sea. The houses were roofed with little wooden shingles. The inhabitants were few but the girls were magnificent, big strong-legged girls in fresh dresses of thin muslin or organdy.

After hours of dust I saw a barricade of about forty big oil drums. They guarded a huge factory where the German engineers were breaking up schist and extracting prodigious quantities of mineral oil. Just as we had fought for airplane fuel in the Caucasus, here we were fighting for oil for the submarines.

The front was near. The villages that I passed had been reduced to cinders. The trees along the route had been split, torn to pieces, or burned. The air had a grey color. Violent cannonading could be heard.

In the end I found my soldiers. They were quartered ten kilometers from the lines. The officer who had brought them knew that the Walloons had never been in combat without my being with them. Sure of himself, he had told the commander of the Army Corps that I would arrive at any moment, that the men weren't ready, and that he declined all responsibility while waiting for my arrival. The commander of the Corps was an excellent man, General Steiner. We had known one another in the Caucasus. He decided to wait.

I arrived at his command post at dusk. Wearing a white tie like Pierre Laval, very modish, still natty and perfumed, he hugged me effusively. That night when I returned to my men I had won them three weeks' respite and the pick of the instructors.

We camped at the top of a sand cliff from which the grandiose panorama of the Gulf of Finland could be seen. A hundred meters directly below our feet a strange ribbon of black trees clinging to the very edge of the shore stretched all along the water.

In the hot August night we went down to a shining creek. Vigorous and naked, we threw ourselves into the water, swimming endlessly in the singing sea.

## The Gulf of Finland

The Estonian front was a gamble. The Reds were at the doors of Warsaw, and several tens of thousands of volunteers from all the Germanic countries still clung to the ravaged woods near Leningrad.

Narva marked the boundry of old Europe with the East. The two worlds rose up on either side of the little river which cut the town in half. On the western bank was the old crenellated castle of the Teutonic Knights. Immediately opposite on the other side of the water the Russian city raised the tiers of her Orthodox churches' green onion domes.

The Third Germanic Corps, in which Germans were only a minority, stood guard over this gate. It had very nearly broken in July, 1944. Hundreds of Soviet tanks had been destroyed in the course of furious battles. The legions of European volunteers had been bled white. One of the two Dutch regiments had saved only twenty men in all, out of three thousand. The others, surrounded for several days, had been massacred where they stood.

The Soviet offensive had failed. The Third Corps had yielded only about fifteen kilometers in all.

But new blood was needed. Ours was there, entirely fresh, for the forthcoming battles.

* * * * *

Cannon fire thundered ceaselessly. During the night it seemed to come strangely closer. Often Soviet ships would appear, turning their sterns toward Finland. Our guns would open fire, forcing the crusiers to retreat.

The coastal batteries were marvelously well-camouflaged. They were widely spread out. The troops and the officers nested in perfect shelters dug out above the sea. Fifty or eighty meters below these eagles' aeries the waves dashed themselves on the sand and splashed against the trees. The sea shone as far as the eye could see. In the distance, when the sun was brightest, the line of a white island could be distinguished, as slender as a gull's wing.

The twilights were an incredible glow of burning orange and huge masses of pink and gold clouds.

These iridescent evenings which died in a tumult of reds and purples, these nights spangled with stars which called to one another, the cool solitude of the crystalline dawns were doubtless given to us soldiers, dutiful witnesses of beauty, to rekindle our spirits before the howling days when bodies would be torn apart and souls would gasp on the threshold of great departures.

* * * * *

In mid-August the Reds started a wide movement to crush Estonia definitively. Having failed to break the front between Narva and the southern point of Lake Peipus, they unleashed a huge offensive at the southern extremity of the lake, starting from the frontier town of Pskov.

Obviously their goal was to storm the Estonian city of Dorpat, then from there Reval, taking the whole sector of the Gulf of Finland from the rear.

Each day the Reich's aircraft followed the massive movement of the Soviet force from Narva. The Third Corps received the order to copy the movement and cling to the enemy. It was to send a powerful *Kampfgruppe* (battle group) to the south immediately, which would position itself athwart the Red armies, which, advancing by forced marches toward the northeast, were meeting almost no resistance.

General Steiner drew up his accounts. He had to use everything available, us as well as others. He decided to leave our least-trained recruits under instruction for a few days. But the three hundred men who were virtually ready were entered on the strength charts.

During the night of 15-16 August I received our marching orders. At five o'clock in the morning the trucks took us away. Singing the ancient songs of our country we rolled toward the little red dot on the map which in German was called Dorpat and in Estonian, Tartu.

Tartu! The ancient capital of learning in the Baltic countries. Tartu, whose famous library, whose nicely painted houses, whose art centers, printers, and ancient University we would see go up in flames that very month, gigantic black torches floating for a week between the smoking earth and the unfeeling sky.

## Face to Face

Lake Peipus, on both ends of which the life of Estonia hung in the balance, had long separated this country from the territory of the USSR. The lake was connected to the town of Narva on the Gulf of Finland by the Narva River. It formed a true inland sea, crossed by boats whose rust-colored hulls could be seen bobbing in the golden waters of August, 1944.

Lake Peipus could be reached from the north by going through forests of fragrant firs, dappled with rosy glimmers, and bursting with wild blueberries. The lake was bordered with a dry pebbly beach where spindly plants grew. A few large villages nestled in the hollows of shining bays under the turquoise sky, but their houses had been demolished by aircraft. Nothing was left but a few smashed dinghies and ruins, among which the German posts were set up.

The lake constituted in fact the longest part of the Estonian front. The Reds were on the other side of the water. One night's rowing would have been enough to reach them. The defense of our bank was nugatory. Rough log bunkers could be seen here and there, and a bit of trench in the sand, but troops were almost non-existent. When we were at the extreme southern end of the lake our left flank would be at the mercy of a Soviet landing.

According to the orders of the High Command the principal line of the *Kampfgruppe* was supposed to extend from Lake Wirz, almost in the middle of Estonia, to the southwest of Lake Peipus. The River Embach, which connected the two lakes, would be the natural line of combat if the enemy succeeded in approaching the Dorpat region.

I went to the town hall of the old university city for news. A debate was going on among some of the superior officers. The situation was extremely confused. The head of the *Kampfgruppe,* General Wagner of the Waffen SS, arrived. The man was a giant, holder of the Knight's Cross, as usual, with a well-established reputation as a fighter as clear-headed as he was daring, as robust as a *Landsknecht,* * a true Renaissance condottiere, merry, strong, gregarious, tireless, in brief, the man that was needed for the hard fight that was coming.

The column of the *Kampfgruppe* Wagner was spaced out over thirty kilometers, a column of armored reconnaissance cars, Panzers, and mechanized shock troops. The general in fact brought few people, but all were first-class fighters.

At Dorpat he would have to combine in haste with haggard and disparate reinforcements—a ragbag of dispersed German units and Estonian guards in civilian clothes, armbands on their sleeves, arriving in disorder, poorly armed, their wives alongside them, sweating with fatigue and fear on the dusty roads.

General Wagner prudently decided to halt his column north of Dorpat to study the terrain and the list of effectives first.

* * * * *

Our trucks stopped at a village called Maria-Magdalena.

At dawn a messenger awoke me. We were to move out immediately.

A paved road started out from Dorpat toward the southeast in the direction of Pskov. Another went toward the southwest in the direction of Riga. I sent up six advance posts twenty-five kilometers from Dorpat and the River Embach in the triangle formed by these two roads.

Never had we received a mission so complicated. I asked who would be between my posts and the enemy mass on the march. The response was disconcerting. Theoretically two friendly divisions were in contact. In practice no one knew anything about them. They had probably disintegrated somewhere over there in the west toward Riga. "At any rate," they added, "Don't count on them, and be ready."

Be ready to close off a sector forty kilometers wide as the crow flies with six handfuls of men!

All the rest of the front had had to be improvised in like manner. The Wagner *Kampfgruppe* sent patrols of armored reconnaissance cars to meet the enemy. They were wearing themselves out ploughing back and forth, day and night, over the many roads on which the advance guards of the Soviets were moving.

Instead of slipping between the two principal roads the enemy attacked straight ahead, never straying far from Lake Peipus and the Pskov-Dorpat highway. Searching for the weakest point, he found it east of this route and on Monday, 19 August 1944, made a thrust eight kilometers deep and ten wide, within rifle range of our left wing.

Trucks roared up at the same time as a motorcycle messenger brought me the order to attack. At five o'clock in the evening I was to charge from west to east across the breach opened by the Soviets with all the men I had.

German troops coming from east to west would meet us at the half-way point. We were to make the junction at the village of Patska, high on top of a bald hill. Four Panzers would reinforce us.

It was a fine idea for combat. The enemy was massed in the breach. If our counterattack succeeded, his offensive would be broken up for several days.

Now we needed to gain some time. The German engineers and thousands of civilians were hastily building a fortified line in a half-moon about eight kilometers south of Dorpat. The Command wanted to form a bridgehead there which would bar access to the town. It would be protected on the east and west by the River Embach, a deep natural barrier.

Yet these defenses weren't finished. Reinforcements were on the way, but they wouldn't be in position for several days. The morning's thrust had brought the enemy to within a few kilometers of the works. Tomorrow or the day after the Reds would reach them, unless a violent counterattack broke their impetus.

* * * * *

At four o'clock in the afternoon the trucks dropped my men off six kilometers from Patska.

I had some marvelous young officers, just out of the military school at Bad Toelz, in Bavaria. They were anxious to prove themselves.

Our Panzers were waiting, hidden in an apple orchard.

I set the plan of attack. At exactly five o'clock, accompanied by the four tanks, we would charge.

The companies were to take position immediately, without letting themselves be seen. The enemy was one kilometer away. I set a starting point for the assault for each company commander.

Our soldiers stole crawling through the ripe wheat, drying in the burning afternoon.

## The Mill of Patska

The minutes just before a hand-to-hand battle always weigh heavily. How many of the boys who are waiting will shortly be lying on their backs on the ground, eyes staring blankly? How many others will be dragging their bleeding bodies along trying to escape the machine-gun fire?

We could hear the noise of the enemy advance. The Reds must already be able to see the towers of Dorpat. The village of Patska, atop the slope, seemed to be strongly occupied.

I slipped behind a holly thicket from which I followed the passage of the Soviet forces with my binoculars. Strung out over a distance of five kilometers, major Red contingents, supported by artillery, were occupying both sides of the road we were to take.

The plain was totally bare, but the hills occupied by the enemy to the right and left were wooded. My soldiers were hidden on the sides of the road and in the wheat, as still and silent as dead wood.

At five o'clock I advanced with the tanks. Our men took position and leaped out. At the sound of the Panzers advancing on the plain there was a stir among the enemy troops. Red soldiers ran to the trenches, to the artillery and the mortars. A giant of a Russian officer took his stand out in the open on the ridge, giving his orders, braving us all.

The first shells from our tanks made a direct hit on the mill. The Russian officer didn't turn a hair. All the houses in the area blew up one after another. The giant remained calm. When the smoke cleared we could see him, still standing there like a block of wood.

Our companies climbed the slope. A deluge of metal rained down on our tanks. The Soviet machine guns raked the slope. A Panzer took a direct hit but went on anyway.

Our soldiers ran like the wind up nine hundred meters of gentle slope. The mill was bitterly defended. Two of our officers reached it, charging through everything. Both fell right at the entrance to the building, one killed outright, the other gravely wounded. But the company rushed over their bodies; the Russian giant fell in his turn; the mill was ours.

The other company, which was climbing the right flank, charged into the enemy positions with equal impetuosity and at the same price. The commander of this company was wounded three times. No longer able to move, he hung onto an anti-tank gun captured from the Reds and turned it against them in a final effort. He fired for twenty minutes longer before dying on the pile of cartridge cases.

In fifty minutes our thrust had penetrated five kilometers. Patska was taken and cleared. We captured the Soviet artillery.

* * * * *

Unfortunately we received no news of the supporting attack which was supposed to meet us from the east and join us at the mill.

We couldn't let the enemy recover. I led my men beyond Patska, entering the five-kilometer zone which had been left for our partners to attack. The Patska operation was no good unless we could cut off the enemy spearhead completely. If not, it was we who risked being cut off. We crossed seven of the ten kilometers in this way. Our losses were cruel. Of my four new officers from Bad Toelz, three were killed and the fourth gravely wounded. In the Waffen SS the average life of an officer at the front was three months.

My aide-de-camp had been evacuated, his left arm shot through. A hundred of my soldiers had been killed or wounded.

What had happened to the troops who were supposed to come from the east to meet us at the time of our charge?

We were fighting furiously on both flanks, the enemy trying unceasingly to throttle us. If we kept on trying to make headway we were eventually going to fall into a trap. The fact that the wave from the east hadn't come worried me terribly. At eight o'clock in the evening we were still alone. Summoned elsewhere, our tanks had to leave us.

At nine o'clock I was informed of the complete failure of the supporting attack. We were ordered to hold on west of the village of Patska. From there we could at least bar passage to new Soviet reinforcements. Nevertheless, the spearhead of the Russian offensive hadn't been cut off.

As soon as evening came, this force fell back to pound us.

Our flanks were guarded only by machine guns. We didn't have so much as a piece of light artillery. Our tanks hadn't returned.

The enemy brought up "Stalin's organs," which battered us throughout the night under thirty-six rockets' double rain of fire.

Dawn came. We were freezing in grass wet with dew. I placed a row of machine guns at the edge of a birch grove dominating the Soviet route of penetration toward Dorpat. The "Stalin's organs" were hacking up the little wood, meter by meter. But, gone to ground in narrow holes, we didn't yield the terrain. The enemy still couldn't go through Patska. We kept continually cleaning the bare road with our fire.

The messengers brought me some odd news. The Reds were already several kilometers behind us to the west. They were completely outflanking us, swarming out of the edge of the woods everywhere. Several Red soldiers had been killed right on the road three kilometers behind us.

General Wagner sent us enthusiastic congratulations, announcing that we would be cited in his communique to the Main Headquarters. But we had to keep on fighting while the command put the finishing touches to its blockade south of Dorpat.

We were distracted from our worries by hundreds of silver foxes running between our legs. There was a farm of about two thousand of these graceful animals to the right of us. The proprietors had opened all the doors of the cages before they fled. Wondrously supple, the foxes dashed between the explosions, brushing the ground with their long shining tails.

To the west, the enemy had expanded his assault. That afternoon the Pskov road fell. Farther west of the highway, at the very center of the Wagner sector, the attackers succeeded in driving a wedge through to a village called Kambja.

In the evening a motorcyclist burst through the enemy-infested forest and brought us orders to capture Kambja and its vicinity immediately, where the danger of a Red breakthrough was becoming more and more evident.

We slipped silently from copse to copse. At two o'clock in the morning, after a circuit of twenty kilometers, we found ourselves nose to nose with the other wave of Reds, already masters of the village of Kambja and obviously determined to press forward to join their victorious forces in the east and southeast.

## Kambja

On the morning of 21 August 1944, the situation at the Estonian front was as follows:

The advanced defense of Dorpat, between Lake Peipus and the Pskov road, had been gutted. The Soviets were even landing in force on the west bank of the lake. The central position had been violently hit by the Soviet waves which had seized Kambja. The western wing of the front, from Kambja to the Riga-Dorpat route and from this route to Lake Wirz, was still peaceful.

Briefly, when General Wagner looked at the enemy he saw his left wing crushed and his center gravely threatened. Only his right wing still enjoyed a last respite, since it was farthest from the starting point of the Soviet offensive.

A country road linked Kambja to the Pskov highway about fifteen kilometers south of Dorpat. But the fork itself was threatened by the Soviet forces coming from of the southeast.

I had—first mission—to hold the enemy at Kambja with five hundred infantry men, one mortar platoon, and several pieces of German artillery. I was—second mission—to assure the protection of the crossroads of the Pskov-Dorpat and the Kambja-Dorpat roads. The conquering enemy had come to within a kilometer of this intersection, which was completely flat and in the open. The enemy artillery, mortars, and "Stalin's organs" occupied the woods to our left. I had only three anti-tank guns with which to bar the passage.

I installed my command post in a small farm beside the crossroads. There we were hourly sprayed with machine-gun fire and strafed by Soviet planes. During the night we expected the Bolshevik tanks to enter the courtyard any minute. Booted, grenades and submachine gun within reach, we slept a maximum of ten minutes at a time.

Three or four times a day or night I sped from the intersection of our positions at Kambja, four kilometers to the southwest. The Reds were swarming everywhere. My little Volkswagen raced frantically along through bullets that whined like mosquitoes.

If I was at Kambja, I trembled for my anti-tank guns at the intersection. If I was at the crossroads I feared a catastrophe at Kambja and watched the road with terror, always expecting to see the debris of my unit flock in with a frenzied mob of Kirghizes and Kalmuks hot on their heels.

* * * * *

Behind us the spectacle was heart-rending. The whole of Estonia was fleeing panic-stricken before the Reds. Not a soul stayed in his hut. These people had known the Soviets, not those of 1918, but the so-called civilized, improved and democratized Soviets of 1940. They retained a terrible fear of them. This general panic taught us more than all the political speeches.

It wasn't only the bourgeois who were bolting, but tens of thousands of workers, handymen, small farmers, and sawyers fleeing the pine groves. The women would exhaust themselves on the roads, dragging along a pig and two or three sheep. The poor beasts' feet would be bleeding. One girl was pushing a pig in front of her like a wheelbarrow, holding it by its rear feet. The animals were all jumbled together, howling. Many died.

It was extremely hot. The old women were dead tired. Suddenly the Soviet fighter planes arrived, pounced on the columns of civilians, and machine-gunned them savagely amidst the horrified cries of the women and children and the sharp neighing of the horses, their bellies shot full of holes, which had fallen among the broken wheels of the hay wagons.

Burst comforters, food, all the meager possessions of fifty families lay scattered about on the sun-baked road. The wretches mopped at their sweat. Women, convulsively hugging their babies, were running toward the distant steeples on their cut feet. Old men, gathering copper pans and dragging cows that were at the end of their strength, were shaking their heads. Where were they going? Where would they meet? Or, rather, where would they die? For the same fleeing throngs were spreading from one end of the country to the other. The same fighter planes ravaged them.

After I had made my report at General Wagner's in a suburb of Dorpat, to get back to my command post I had to drive back through these corteges of anguish, the sight of which broke my heart.

Everything in front of me was in flames: the big square farmhouses with hundreds of black and white cows, the rich villages, the beautiful white castles near the blue lakes, the fine fir-shingled barn roofs, and even the cemetery gardens tiered on the hillsides, dignified by cypress groves and furnished with rustic benches from which the living had so often peaceably watched the fields while thinking of their dead.

A country was dying. The marvelous August nights were besmirched with the great red torches of villages on fire. Cows, pigs, chickens, and geese: all were abandoned on the farms and in the pastures. Not a living soul stirred. Everyone preferred the exodus and machine-gun fire to Soviet enslavement.

* * * * *

I received a third mission—to blow up the railroad from Pskov to Dorpat.

It was yet another skill for me to learn. An intrepid young German officer and a handful of resolute engineers had been sent to help me with the job. They mined the line every ten meters, and waited for orders then to blow up two hundred or five hundred meters of line.

I wasn't to sacrifice the rail except as a last resort. The Command at Dorpat was still hoping to begin a counteroffensive one day. So I was to wait until the last second. But I mustn't let it slip by, either, lest the Reds seize the rail intact.

The explosions coming one after another were eerie, especially at night. In a few days I blew up enough bridges, lines, stations, grade crossings, guard rails, and cuttings to be deafened for the rest of my life.

But we had to gain time. Always this same little sentence coming over the telephone wire—gain time. Gain time by sacrificing wealth beyond counting, and alas, countles human lives.

Ten kilometers behind us the population of Dorpat had finished digging its great defense belt. It was just about ready. But I was ill at ease when I crossed to see the hordes of defenders that were being pushed into these long black trenches. Battalions of rural guards, policemen, and the most unlikely civilians, militarized by means of a vague yellow arm badge and an old French rifle from the time of Napoleon III.

We were enduring the pressure of enormous Soviet forces. When would serious military forces, real divisions, arrive to resist them?

* * * * *

The Soviet tanks feared the Paks, which fired with great accuracy. The crossroads held out well.

I was staying more at Kambja, for our men were hard pressed there. We held the ridges above the northern road out of the village, where we endured the crushing fire of the "Stalin's organs."

But our men were fighters who wouldn't let themselves be bested. They had positioned their machine guns well. Our mortars, perfectly camouflaged in the shocks of wheat, did thorough work.

Morale was very high. I decorated our most valorous wounded right on the ground where they fell. Being hit by explosive bullets which blasted frightful holes in them still didn't prevent them from joking and drawing on the cigarettes which their buddies put between their lips, outlined in red blood.

These boys were unbeatable. Wherever they were placed, the Soviets stopped. I was deeply moved before their simple and smiling bravery, for if their remarks were funny, it was out of modesty, to make fun of themselves at the very moment they were rising to pure heroism. The Communists had to be stopped. They stopped them. They didn't let them by on 21 August. They didn't let them by on 22 August either. When our soldiers were relieved on 22 August at noon, the Reds hadn't been able to gain ten meters of ground north of Kambja. They had even had to abandon the village, which our mortars and the German artillery at my disposition were cutting to pieces.

* * * * *

The hundred and fifty recruits that we had left under instruction near Toila arrived at our supply base. I received orders to reinforce what was left of my troops with them. We met at Maria-Magdalena.

Theoretically it would take a week to rebuild the force and integrate the new men into the unit.

We had scarcely left the central sector, however, before the westernmost part of the German right wing was attacked. The Soviets reached and cut off the highway from Riga to Dorpat. Our anti-tank platoon didn't even have the time to disengage toward Maria-Magdalena. Already I was being ordered to hurry to the critical location. That very evening our guns went into battle at the entry to a town which had a strange name, Noo.

After supper I went to General Wagner's command post. His eyes were horribly bloodshot. He was constantly sending his light tanks to the secondary roads overrun by the Soviet onslaught. He had no more suitable infantry worth mentioning, but he was flooded with thousands of Estonians of every stamp, who were being sent to him by the truckload, bewildered, decked out in plumed or wide-crowned hats, armed with hunting rifles and pop-guns, all crazy to get away.

"Grosse Scheisse! Grosse Scheisse!" the General yelled tirelessly.

"Grosse Scheisse!" his chief of staff punctuated.

"Grosse Scheisse!" repeated the equally affirmative aide who brought us bread and butter.

I had the very strong impression that my companies weren't going to grow moldy at Maria-Magdalena.

I wanted to leave that very night for the Riga road in order to visit the crews of my anti-tank guns at Noo. But following my citation in the communique, General Wagner had just received a very stern telegram from Himmler making him responsible for my life. He used it as an excuse to formally forbid my proposed nocturnal raid.

I pretended to obey. But what went for the night didn't necessarily go for the day. Politics had taught me the art of hairsplitting, and it wasn't for nothing that I was nephew and great nephew of six Jesuit fathers.

I returned quietly to Maria-Magdalena. At five o'clock in the morning I finished dictating orders for the immediate reorganization of the battalion. At six o'clock, freshly shaved, I drove through Dorpat again toward the south.

To do it right I should have gone to General Wagner's to find out whether the situation had changed during the course of the night. But in that case I was sure to be the object of a new interdict, so, not risking a visit, I drove my little Volkswagen blindly onto the Riga road.

But something new *had* happened. At dawn the Reds had seized Noo. They were even well beyond.

I was on a collision course with them without knowing it.

## Lemnasti

I will remember the morning of 23 August 1944 until I die.

As soon as I left Dorpat I was struck by the number of trucks which I saw speeding toward the town. Soldiers were hanging on to them every which way.

Then I came across some isolated men running frantically. Bullets whistled by. One of them burst almost at shoulder height right into the windshield.

I jumped down from my Volkswagen and set myself across the road, submachine gun in my hands. I was wearing the Ritterkreuz ribbon around my neck. That always made some slight impression. With the help of the threat from the machine gun, the first truck stopped.

The driver, his eyes popping out of his head, screamed at me, "The Russians are there! The Russians are there!"

"Where's there?" I replied.

"Five hundred meters away! They're all over the place!"

Five hundred meters away. In a flash I saw the disaster. Not only had the Reds taken Noo, fifteen kilometers southwest of Dorpat, but they were coming full gallop right into Dorpat. The defense line had been conquered and already overrun. How? I didn't know, and I didn't have the time to find out.

I saw only one thing. It was that Dorpat was filled with hundreds of retreating trucks, and nothing had been evacuated for the good reason that during the night there hadn't been any fighting yet even ten kilometers from the suburbs. In half an hour the muzhiks would enter Dorpat, seize everything, make a surprise crossing of the Embach, and succeed in flanking the entire disordered sector.

I made all the soldiers get down from the first truck and then from two trucks which followed. Luckily there was a German junior officer who understood French marvelously. I had him translate my orders. "We are going to counterattack immediately. There will be Iron Crosses this very evening for those who are bravest. The Reds don't expect us to react so soon. It's the best time to jump them. You'll see. Everything depends on our daring. Forward, comrades!"

Bringing back by the scruff of the neck some sixty soldiers who five minutes earlier had been in rout, I rushed toward the Reds advancing on the road banks.

According to my old habit, I carried twelve cartridge clips, six at the waist, six in my boots, about four hundred cartridges. Enough to fire a few nice bursts. After fifteen minutes the Soviet troops, who had been strong only because they hadn't met any obstacles, cleared off in front of us, cut to pieces. We reached the belt of fortifications where that morning the thousands of civilians with arm badges and feathers had abandoned the fight in less than a second. Fiercely we dislodged the Reds in the trenches, reoccupying the whole western sector of the Dorpat bridgehead in the course of our charge.

But what a situation! Here I was in the half-kilometer of trench that was supposed to have held back an enemy attacking by the Riga road, leading an improvised defense by accident, commanding disparate groups of Germans and Estonians brought together by the shifting currents of panic.

I immediately catechized several of the more resourceful men and sent them to pursue the Reds through the neighboring pastures and copses.

I found a beautiful big Russian cannon, perfectly placed five meters to the right of the route by the German builders of the fall-back positions. It ruthlessly dominated the access to the road. Unfortunately—nothing is ever perfect on this earth—it didn't have a single shell. It was comforting to look at, but that was all.

Some distance away I noticed two cannon scurrying away across the fields. I rushed my Volkswagen toward them with the order to come back at once. They hastened back. They too were making off because everyone else was. I put them in battery; they still had twenty-five rounds. It was wonderful.

What was less wonderful was what had happened. That night the Reds had infiltrated between Noo and Dorpat. Then, falling back from the north, they had taken Noo from the rear and encircled it, sowing a terrifying disorder among the parked convoys. The drivers were sleeping peacefully, thinking themselves protected by the first line. The surprise was catastrophic.

The men came fleeing to us across the marshes and the fir woods, escaping from Noo itself. No doubt was possible. The gate was open.

It was very hard to know exactly the extent of the disaster. The line that we had just recaptured plunged into a little valley with a glistening stream at the bottom. No one had thought to blow up the bridge at the time of the Soviet breakthrough. Now it was too late. The few little farms, the hedges, and the copses all around us were occupied by the enemy. To retake this valley in hand-to-hand fighting with my incongruous little troop was impossible. I would have sent three quarters of my men to their death only to lose the entire line one hour later.

The road cut the countryside in two. Descending in a wide curve, it crossed the river on the white arc of the undamaged bridge, climbed back up the hill behind the houses, crossed the fields, and entered a forest across from us.

The Soviets had been put on the defensive near the water. I was still hoping that the retreating troops coming from Noo would come out of the woods to the southwest. Together we would then have been able to flatten the enemy in the valley. But the survivors told us that it would be impossible for the forces at Noo to retreat, that the enemy was everywhere.

We had to warn General Wagner immediately. Did he know? In any case, nothing was coming from Dorpat.

A soldier found a telephone wire. The artillerymen had everything needed to hook up an extension. I got the command post, then the general, utterly amazed to learn what was going on and that I was there. I knew as he did that the fate of Dorpat hinged on my hill. He didn't have to explain very much to me. I promised that, as long as I lived, the Reds wouldn't get through.

I could be overrun, however. The Soviet tanks could arrive from one minute to the next. We needed men and tanks quickly and in force.

"Hold on! Hold on!" General Wagner yelled into the telephone, pouring out floods of "Grosse Scheisse! Grosse Scheisse!" more suitable than ever to the occasion.

* * * * *

I organized my men without delay.

Finally, with all the runaways I had scooped up, I had a good hundred men. I formed them into two platoons which I positioned across the road. The left wing was commanded by a young supply officer who had been caught in the whirlwind when, without a care in the world, he was strolling in the mid-morning to take hundreds of loaves of bread to Noo. He had never fired a gun at the front. A German adjutant commanded the right wing.

I sent two patrols fairly far to the east and west to hide in the thickets and the hazel woods protecting our flanks.

I emptied the trucks and appropriated their machine guns and munitions. My soldiers had regained their confidence. I went from one to another, encouraging them in jargon half-French and half-German. Most of them had seen my photo in the newspapers, and they were getting used to the idea that the affair was taking an original turn.

The Reds were machine-gunning us steadily. I planted myself on the parapet of the trench so that none of my boys would lose his head. My life wasn't worth two cents there, but there are days when one knows for certain that this isn't the day when one is going to die. This was my case. They could shoot as much as they liked, and they would miss me every time. I didn't have a shadow of a doubt.

I had picked up an Estonian officer. I would have liked to use him to command his compatriots scattered among my troops, but he was consumed by panicky fear. He turned green hearing the bullets whistle past, and lay down flat against my boots, as stiff as a board. One bullet, instead of hitting me in the foot, struck him full in the face, went through him from one end to the other, and came out between his buttocks.

He twisted about like a worm, spat, cried, defecated. It was too late. He had digested the bullet too quickly. Ten minutes later he was dead.

* * * * *

The Reds were getting more and more reinforcements, arriving from the birch groves of the southeast in little groups, six men, seven men, eight men, stealing along the river. I had forbidden unnecessary shooting. We had to save our ammunition for a close combat about to begin at any time. Suddenly, at eleven o'clock in the morning, I saw something come out of the woods in the south. A Panzer!

I wanted to think that it was a German Panzer escaped from Noo.

Behind it a second Panzer was coming on. Then another. Soon there were eight. Russian? German? We couldn't tell at that distance.

We held our breath. The tanks were moving down the hillside. We would soon know what to think. If the Soviet infantry massed in the basin fired on them it would prove that they were German tanks.

The tanks reached the first house behind the water. Not a gunshot! They were Soviet tanks.

Chilling seconds! I had only my two miserable cannon. I let the tanks approach. They were obviously sure of themselves. Only when they were right under my nose on the road in full sunlight, and the first Red tank was a few meters from the bridge, did I order my two artillery pieces to shoot full into the column.

The lead tank, struck in the first minute, was stopped instantly. The others fled across the little farms as dozens of shells fell on them. One of them did a gorgeous flip and landed with its gun stuck in the mire. I didn't stop firing down at them until it was clear that the disoriented enemy was only looking for refuge. And even then I let fly a last volley of shells onto the houses to show that we had ammunition to spare.

In actual fact, I had exactly twelve of my hundred and twenty projectiles still left. I had played the rich man. If solid help didn't come soon, it looked as though we were lost.

* * * * *

Of course I was receiving reinforcements. At Dorpat, where the news of these happenings had the effect of a V-1, the Staff Office was assembling in all haste everything that wore a uniform and sending it on to Riga. I inherited an apopleptic collection of old veteran majors, supply officers, barrack-keepers, cellarers, one-day marchers, service corps. They squeaked in their uniforms, dripping with sweat under their loads, dead-tired to have done eight kilometers on foot. A throng of bespectacled clerks and orderlies scurried around them. For all that, they were all very courageous and very worthy, asking only to do their duty. In spite of this, I couldn't very well imagine these specialists in paper-pushing stopping the six tanks growling across from us.

Thanks to these recruits I strengthened by flanks. I sent them to occupy the most distant line possible so as to avoid being taken from behind by the Soviet infantry.

I harried General Wagner on the telephone.

"Panzers and Stukas, for God's sake!"

"We're doing all we can to help you, but we need time. Hold on! Hold on!" he yelled back at me.

Of course we'd hold on.

But when the twelve last shells had been fired, what would happen then?

It was 12:30. I had been standing on the parapet for five hours, marching back and forth, encouraging my Germans and Estonians. I stared at the several little farms in the valley. The Reds had had more than an hour, enough time to notice that we couldn't be very strong.

A Soviet tank emerged near the first farm, carrying about twenty soldiers. The other five tanks followed. I had just time to shout over the telephone to General Wagner, "That's it! The Russian tanks are coming!" There they were. They crossed the bridge at full speed and climbed the hillside. At thirty meters from us the enemy infantry jumped to the ground. It was the final assault.

There was nothing left to do but to fire all the ammunition we had left, then die. Just as my last shells were bursting, a fearful roar shook the sky. German Stukas suddenly appeared. Forty Stukas! Forty dived screaming toward the earth. Everything flew up into the air. We were thrown in all directions, for the enemy tanks were upon us, and the Stukas were bombarding the pack like demons. Three Soviet tanks went up in flames. The others took off, climbed back up the opposite slope, and fled into the woods. Those of our machine guns which had escaped the hurricane mowed down the routed Soviet infantry. We yelled like crazy men. We had won the match.

* * * * *

German panzers, enormous Tigers, arrived in their turn. During the evening the flower of all the sections was there. A German colonel relieved me. I was called to General Wagner's command post. We had had a narrow escape. The generals, right to the top of the ranks, had breathlessly followed our duel, upon which the fate of Dorpat, the Embach, and Estonia depended.

At midnight a telegram from the Fuehrer's Main Headquarters announced that Hitler was awarding me the Oak Leaves.

Thus ended a casual drive on the highway from Estonia to Latvia on 23 August 1944.

## The Embach

What had become of our three anti-tank weapons and the Wallonia platoon which operated them in the set-to at Noo? We presumed those boys and those tanks lost. A lone survivor had reached us on the barrier at Lemnasti, having bolted in the middle of a horrifying hand-to-hand battle.

Nevertheless, our men had not been overwhelmed. They had good machine guns and were redoubtable with their three anti-tank guns at point-blank range. At dawn on the 24th Lieutenant Gillis, who commanded them, let me know that his men and his cannons had broken the Soviet encirclement and that they were in position before the River Embach at the west of Dorpat.

They were very proud of their exploit and were only awaiting the opportunity to accomplish another. They were quickly gratified. At four o'clock in the afternoon, ten of the heaviest-tonnage Soviet tanks, ten Joseph Stalins, went for them. Such tanks were almost invulnerable. Gillis, old fox of the Russian front, let them approach to within twenty meters. His cannon were well camouflaged. The Soviets thought themselves already masters of the Embach passage. When they were almost iron against iron, our three weapons fired.

It was a savagely violent combat. The Russian tanks pounded our combat groups. One of our anti-tank guns was blown-up. Then the second blew up amidst the mangled corpses of our men. Lieutenant Gillis was grievously burned. But he kept shouting orders. Clinging to the last weapon, the survivors fired, enraged, determined to sell dearly the few lives still remaining.

Tanks don't like prolonged shoot-outs with anti-tank guns. Two Joseph Stalins caught fire, a great loss for the enemy. The other tanks broke off the combat and headed westward. We didn't have a single cannon left. Most of the operators were on the ground, killed or wounded. But our honor was intact. The Soviet panzers hadn't conquered.

When Gillis came out of the hospital several months later, his eyes shielded by huge black glasses, he was wearing round his neck the Knight's Cross, which Hitler had awarded him for his exploit.

* * * * *

As far as thirty kilometers to the north of Dorpat, life had become infernal. The Soviet Air Force, non-existent in earlier days, was now master of the skies. They had American planes in abundance. Their squadrons swarmed through the country like wasps, swarming ferociously over every road. Everywhere there was nothing but fires, the wreckage of munitions or gas trucks, and miserable peasants' wagons smashed amid horses swollen like balloons.

The smallest village would be attacked ten times a day. Even far from the roads in our modest town of Maria-Magdalena, we spent more time flat on the ground than standing. The planes swooped acrobatically around the steeple, diving like arrows shot from the sky, loosing bursts of incendiary bullets, then climbing vertically back up, as quick as swallows in a marvelous holiday sun.

We could tell where the villages were for a radius of twenty kilometers just by watching the enormous gray and black columns rising straight up against the blue sky. We were so harrassed and there were so many obstacles that movement was practically impossible. We had to cross sheets of flame. Hundreds of shells obstructed the road around the riddled and reddening trucks.

With difficulty I reached General Wagner's command post. His staff trucks were camouflaged in a fir grove behind Dorpat. I realized that the situation was going from bad to worse, for the "Grosse Scheisse! Grosse Scheisse!" were falling like piles of dishes.

I was quickly brought up to date. The Soviet tank attack that had been broken in the afternoon by the epic resistance of our anti-tank platoon had resumed four kilometers farther west. There was an important bridge there on the Embach, guarded by more than a thousand Estonians. Two columns of Joseph Stalin tanks had suddenly appeared. The thousand men fled without even destroying the bridge. The enemy tanks had crossed the river. At seven o'clock in the evening they were already occupying a crossroads five hundred meters north of the Embach. Two Soviet infantry battalions followed them, and from then on formed a protective square around them.

I was ordered to restore the situation. I was supposed to reach the crossroads by night, supported by several German tanks, send my men to the bridge, and blow it up.

"The bridge must be blown up! Understand? Blown up!"

"Grosse Scheisse! Grosse Scheisse! Grosse Scheisse!" repeated General Wagner in a monologue, his eyes redder than ever.

* * * * *

It was easier said than done. I had to return to Maria-Magdalena, alert the battalion, in the midst of its second day of reorganization, and load it onto trucks (which had been promised for ten o'clock in the evening). Only then could our column leave for the west. It would be hard to make contact with the enemy before midnight or one o'clock in the morning. Where would the Reds be then?

Some time before dusk two battalions and about fifteen Soviet tanks had reached an essential crossroads five hundred meters beyond the Embach. That was absolutely all we knew.

The topographic map of the region made it easy to imagine what followed, however. A road ran through a fir forest in our direction for ten kilometers and through several towns. From seven o'clock in the evening until midnight, the enemy would certainly have improved his position by boldly seizing these woods and the villages and towns, which could serve as a defensive line if need be. It was essential for them to conquer this safety zone as early as possible, so as to allow the passage of men and heavy equipment en masse during the whole night.

I chanced a question to General Wagner. "Has anyone done anything yet to stop the Reds? Are there friendly forces which are preventing them from enlarging their bridgehead toward the forest?" The only answer I got was a new flood of "Grosse Scheisse!" The breach was a gaping hole. The Reds were doubtless not wasting any time back there in the great fir forests.

* * * * *

At nine o'clock in the evening our battalion was reunited. Many of its men were rookies, but they had a fierce desire to join the fray. The veterans passed the sacred fire of inspiration to the new men. That night morale was particularly electric.

I had a rather special way of starting a combat, which dumbfounded the Germans who accompanied us to operate the radio and maintain liaison. First of all I held a meeting. Our men massed on the plain. The day was dying, but everywhere the flames from the burning villages rose like huge red gladioli against the sky. From the top of the bank I exhorted my comrades to be worthy of our old Legion. "The Russkies are going to see what a Walloon counterattack looks like."

Once again we were about to charge into a hand-to-hand battle. This time it would be in the middle of the night, across rolling countryside we knew nothing about, in darkness in which you couldn't see a thing. The column of trucks started off, and we saw immediately that it wouldn't be an easy job.

## The Night of Noela

An attack is never an easy operation. While our trucks rolled westward to the village of Noela, I tried to lay out my battle plan. I was in absolute ignorance of what had happened since the end of the day. Where was the enemy poking about? What was his strength now? Total mystery.

The Soviet Air Force interrupted my reflections. It dropped a string of luminescent parachutes all along the road dotted with our big trucks. It was light as day. We had ten seconds at the very most to throw ourselves flat on our bellies in the fields. Hundreds of bombs fell, wounding men, damaging vehicles. Clearly, our movement had been discovered.

We saw identical parachutes swaying over the whole region. Explosions shook the countryside. Villages burned, outlining the roof beams against dancing backgrounds of red and gold.

By eleven o'clock in the evening we met the half-dozen German tanks which were to sustain our assault at a fork in the road. I also found an aide-de-camp there, very short of breath, whom I had sent to reconnoiter the terrain. He had come upon the Soviets, who had already progressed more than ten kilometers beyond the Embach bridge. They had come clear through the great fir forest and occupied the three villages along the way. Their tanks, very numerous, were moving by night. They had appeared without warning in the village of Noela, right in front of us. The only thing still holding back the drive was the presence of mind of the operators of an anti-aircraft battery on the road exiting the village, who had immediately lowered their guns and fired on the tanks.

I had a very advanced radio truck. Telegraphing this remarkable news to the staff office of the *Kampfgruppe,* I received shortly afterwards the inevitable response, "Attack! Attack immediately!"

My four companies, each sixty men strong, positioned themselves at the entrance of the village. I explained to my officers the immediate objectives. First of all we had to retake Noela. Then we would have to take the road which lead to the second village. This route entered right into the forest. The officers would set the tone and lead the charge at the head of the men. It had to be done quickly.

We attacked.

It was one o'clock in the morning. Backed up by our six Panzers, our men bowled over the first enemy contingents. The Reds' tanks fell back, not really knowing the strength of the counterattack. With their usual speed our companies thrust into Noela, seizing the houses with a grenade attack and taking numerous prisoners.

They were gargoyles with gerbil heads, mostly sixteen years old, exhausted by their marches and the lack of sleep. They had come from Pskov on foot, crossing two hundred kilometers in four days, struck with the commissars' rifle butts as soon as they slowed their steps. They looked vicious. Most were wearing motley German army raincoats. They had slyly put them on to mislead the soldiers of the Reich. The treachery was flagrant, but they were youngsters and very much afraid. I told them to sleep. They dropped like puppies in a heap.

Our Panzers hammered the enemy tanks hard. Several of them went up in flames. The others took off at top speed. We had to make the most of the confusion. I gave the order to move on to the second phase of the combat, to capture the forest road.

The Red infantry had a firm hold on the edge of the woods. It was frightfully dark. We could just discern the machine guns which were spitting their silver and pink jets from all the thickets.

Shouting, our soldiers charged the enemy. One of my junior lieutenants, a platoon leader whom I had reprimanded the day before, had replied to me, "I swear to you I'll make that up." He was a giant with a brick-red complexion, downy hair, and big blue eyes. He rushed forward like a meteor, broke through everything, and swooped down like a conqueror onto a Soviet machine gun in the blackness. But he was riddled like a sieve, hit in the arm, the chest, and in the legs. He had kept his word and opened the breach through which his men now poured. Groping, I fastened the Iron Cross to his jacket, all sticky with blood.

The Reds were fleeing. Our men advanced on the run on both sides of the road. Our tanks, assured of their flanks, cleared the road for a long way. At three o'clock in the morning we reached the second town, swept through it, and dislodged its defenders.

We had retaken two villages out of the three and captured half the terrain from the Soviets. Five kilometers more of effort, one village more to occupy with submachine gun and grenade, and we could attack the bridge.

It could just be done if we exploited our success promptly, but it would require at least five hundred men. I had already lost eighty in two hours. I had scarcely more than a hundred and fifty left. Twenty Panzers would also be required. I had had six to begin with. One of them had blown up during the scuffle at Noela, and we were coming to bigger obstacles.

This nocturnal combat had succeeded only because the enemy, who had arrived after a long exertion, had been repulsed in the course of the charge.

Although we were only a handful, we might nevertheless have attained the objective which had been originally set. Our goal, in effect, was not to annihilate the enemy. It was to pass through it and get to the bridge, if only with twenty men, if only with ten men. At this point each of our platoons was to make the attempt by itself, no matter what happened to the others. I gave them the mines necessary for the demolition.

We knew perfectly well that we were being sacrificed in this task. We were ready. There were ten times more volunteers among us than were necessary for the final bold stroke. The fury of battle, the darkness, the effect of surprise, or the enemy's panic could somehow bring us through.

Unfortunately we got temporarily stuck on the way out of the village. Several Soviet anti-tank guns were posted there. They blasted us. We had to wage a determined hand-to-hand battle at the threshold of the fir forest with its thousand booby traps. Half our officers fell. The others brought up the troops for one more go. For half an hour, it was a dramatic free-for- all. The Soviet tanks loomed up everywhere. A second German tank exploded. The German Command had become very miserly with its equipment. The Panzer commanders had orders to be cautious. To succeed here now we had to be ready to risk and probably lose the four tanks that we still had left. Only then could a few of our men perhaps succeed in getting to the bridge and blowing it up.

We saw with consternation the four German tanks retreating, still firing. Our dead were strewn everywhere on the road, our wounded dragged themselves along without a whimper.

The Reds, seeing the retreat of our tanks, took heart again. After the child-soldiers of a while ago, we now had to face a special battalion of convicted murderers, death-dealing giants with shaven heads.

Nevertheless, our boys, obstinate as mules, wouldn't have folded before the likes of those. But the Soviet tanks roared up, their savage cadence thundering in the air. Again they entered, fifteen of them, the burning village.

The German tanks gave no reply. They paused not at all as they left the village. They hastened toward Noela, wanting to get off the long and perilous road carved between the firs as soon as possible. Already the predawn glow was beginning to whiten the firebreaks.

Our soldiers, whom the enemy tanks had overrun by a long way, had the greatest difficulty in getting back through three kilometers of pine woods to the village from which our assault had started. The four German tanks panted there, doing all they could to contain the thrust of the Red tanks. Near them I built a makeshift blockade.

We had failed. I had only a hundred and ten men left. Our four German tanks constituted our only heavy force. I questioned prisoners from diverse enemy battalions. They eagerly reported that more than thirty Soviet tanks had crossed the River Embach during the night.

Some fifteen of them blew up the houses beside which we were fighting one by one, as if they were playing skittles.

## Thirty-Two

The day of 25 August 1944 was the most dramatic of the battle for Dorpat. It was only four-thirty in the morning. Despite our noctural counterattack, the men and the equipment of the Soviets had won. They were now meting furious battering-ram blows ten kilometers north of the Embach. Dorpat lay on the southern bank of the river.

Everything pointed to unusual difficulties. How were we, a hundred men on our improvised Noela line, going to resist? And even if we resisted, wouldn't we be outflanked? Other roads emerged from the forest, far to our right.

I sent radio messages signaling our critical situation to General Wagner. No response, and for good reason. The Soviets had just crossed the Embach again, to the east of the sector this time. At nine o'clock in the morning Dorpat, the center of resistance, had been taken in a flash by the Soviets. The Reds charged without stopping to the other side of the river.

We ourselves were plunged into a fray so brutal that we almost didn't have time to think of the rest of the front. My command post blew up twice in two hours. I got out of it with nothing more serious than plaster showered on my helmet, but my radio equipment was demolished. My car was useless, all four tires riddled with punctures.

I set myself up in a field, no longer able to direct the remnant of my company except by means of messengers who scuttled along the length of the hedges and firs.

I saw my poor boys go past one after another, wounded, maimed, covered with blood, but smiling nevertheless. The Dorpat-Reval road unrolled behind us. They dragged themselves there and climbed onto the trucks which were fleeing by hundreds in gray whirlwinds.

Each company formed a cheval-de-frise* to brake the progress of the Reds. They worked like demons, dragging the anti-tank guns through the firs by hand to install them in our rear.

The essential for us was to block the main routes. An army doesn't haul its heavy equipment through pine woods and ravines. Only two Soviet tanks were able to get by. They came out like elephants to our left, twenty meters away. We let them go without getting too upset, content to isolate them. After cutting off the road from Dorpat for a little while, they were finally destroyed.

Afternoon came. We were still fighting all along the ridge controlling the road out of Noela, backs against the Dorpat-Reval road. A messenger brought me an urgent order to report to General Wagner's command post.

The spectacle that I found a kilometer behind our positions was apocalyptic. As far as the eye could see there was the most horrible panic. All the Estonian soldiers were fleeing along the sandy roads. Thousands of men had taken off their shoes and were milling about. Thousands of peasants' carts were mingled among the trucks. The road was on fire everywhere. The women were crying and beating their cows, who could go no further, with sticks. The roadside was strewn with ammunition bags, bundles, zinc pans, tubs, dead sheep, bird cages. Through this jumble the haggard human river—civilians, soldiers, Estonians—flowed screaming toward Reval.

Army Corps generals bustled about like young company commanders to regroup the last German contingents still able to offer resistance.

At General Wagner's, a new dousing was waiting for me. In addition to the resistance of Noela, I was instantly to organize a Parna-Lombi-Keerdu line on the plateau of Dorpat. The Soviets from the west and those from the east were trying to link up. Everyone found at the depot was to be put into action on this plateau that very evening.

I had no one left but the walking wounded and the office personnel. We rushed to Maria-Magdalena along beautiful blue lakes sparkling with all the fires of the summer, insensible to the rout spreading alongside. I wanted only volunteers. All our brave old comrades of the administrative services came forward. For that matter, what use was there for an administration at the moment? The accountants closed their ledgers. Legionnaires more than sixty years old, who had been cutting sausages and counting loaves of bread since 1941, left their cleavers and their books to take up panzerfausts.

Their quiet courage brought tears to my eyes. All our wounded who still could walk lined up in front of the rectory. Of the only two officers left to me, one had had his arm shot through by a bullet, the other had been hit by a grenade in the chest. But both stepped to the first row of this heroic little troop.

There were sixty in all. I led them away. Two hours later they were in contact with the Soviets, hastily digging fox holes, hiding themselves behind haystacks. Night was almost here. They were ready.

In the afternoon everything foretold a quick and total collapse on the ridge of Noela. After enlisting our wounded, our quartermaster-sergeants, and our accountants, I rushed in all haste to the hill where we had had such a terrible morning. My soldiers of the line, frightfully decimated, were still holding on.

Darkness came. Our barrier remained unshakable. In the meantime the Command had been able to send fresh troops to our two wings. From Reval everything that the capital of Estonia held in the way of German combatants rushed up in trucks.

In the night the situation incontestably improved. The Soviets themselves seemed exhausted. Certainly there was no longer any question of our making it to the famous bridge of the Embach, but a catastrophe had been averted.

The struggle had cost everyone dearly, the Reds who had been mowed down in heaps, the Germans, and our soldiers, who had contained the enemy only by letting themselves be mauled for more than twenty hours.

* * * * *

What was left of my four companies at Noela clung on for eight days and nights atop this hillside. At last only thirty-two men remained, thirty-two men out of the two hundred sixty whom at one o'clock in the morning on 25 August I had dragged to the assault through the treacherous night.

It was impossible for the positions of the machine-gunners and riflemen to be overrun during the day. They had faces the color of earth, bristling with hair as hard as darts. They were dug into holes full of hay gleaned from neighboring haystacks during the darkness; one might have said nests peopled with frightening nocturnal birds.

The general commanding the Army Corps, amazed at their exploits, awarded them all, en masse—a gesture almost unique at the front—the Iron Cross.

Crawling all along the ridge, I carried it to them one rainy night. I slipped into each hole. The man would be on watch, shivering in the wet straw. The Reds were ten meters away. I fastened the ribbon and the cross. I kissed the bristly cheeks. They would whisper in my ear that they would hold on as long as necessary, that I didn't have to worry, that the Reds wouldn't get past.

Ten kilometers away the other crippled company of wounded, old cooks, supply clerks, and accountants, down to the strength of a little platoon, kept watch with the same faith and with the radiant eyes of men who have conquered others but who, above all, have conquered themselves.

## Rommel and Montgomery

At the end of a hard battle, generally, the one who will win and the one who will lose are both close to falling on their knees. He wins then who clenches his teeth with the greatest energy, who strains his nerves in a last effort.

It was thus on the plateau of Dorpat in the last days of August 1944. The Bolsheviks had taken the village; they had crossed the Embach; they had occupied an area some ten kilometers deep to the north of this river. But this wasn't the objective of their campaign. Their goal—their propaganda tracts had proclaimed it often enough—was to storm into Reval, to skirt the front of Narva, to throw the German armies unceremoniously into the sea or to force them to surrender. During the day of 25 August 1944 all this had been possible. The Estonian troops had given ground and scattered in a memorable stampede. The Soviet tanks swarmed. Thousands of Red soldiers were climbing the hills, reaching the communications centers. They were winning by a long chalk.

Nevertheless, in fact, they lost—because they were blocked. They had to deal with an incomparable German Command, absolute master of itself, never making a move in haste, never flagging for an instant, despite its meager resources.

At the headquarters of General Wagner no one had slept for a week. The staff trucks were ranged under the the firs. The enemy was half a kilometer away. Volleys of rockets from the "Stalin's organs" were falling everywhere around the command post.

The trucks stayed.

The general stayed.

And finally victory stayed, in the hands of the most intelligent and the most tenacious.

* * * * *

The German forces were numerically weak, but of a very high quality. The infantry units, now skeletal, were scattered like us and, like us, exposed to brutish assaults. Admirably operated heavy equipment seconded us.

Panzers and armored reconnaissance cars had been in combat day and night throughout the whole week, racing eastward, returning to the northwest, in contact ceaselessly in little groups of four or six against fifteen or twenty adversaries.

Half of the German armored equipment had been destroyed or put out of action by rolling from peak to valley. But the other half didn't leave an instant's respite to the less prudent, less skillful adversary, whose losses had been enormous. The battlefield of Dorpat was littered with the blackened carcasses of Soviet tanks. The enemy's armored units were completely scattered and disorganized. That counted for a lot in the defeat of the Soviets.

Our dauntless men still hadn't had enough. They loved jumping onto the German tanks, slicing their way through the Soviet positions, and wiping them all out with grenades.

The cautious crews of the Reich's Panzers and the dynamic Walloon infantrymen shared a great comradeship: the Germans all knew that the Walloons were the most ardent volunteers on the Eastern front. They made themselves understood to one another with droll mimicry, held long discussions about girls and rogues. They jabbered fluently, using an improbably Russo-Germanic Volapuek,* the new Esperanto of the Eastern front.

Each combat reinforced this fraternal amity.

* * * * *

While every kilometer of the Dorpat front was holding out, fairly considerable German forces had been able to come down from the north.

We had to hold out for another week. Then the counteroffensive was ready and passed us by. Fresh troops knifed through the Soviets, pushing them back within a few days to the River Embach. They drove the Soviet bands back across the water in full flight. Despite their initial success, the Reds had well and truly lost the battle of Dorpat.

Later the Germans evacuated Estonia on the order of Hitler, who wanted to regroup his overly dispersed forces. But they retreated at their leisure, taking a month to re-embark divisions and heavy weapons destined for the Reich front and the Lithuanian front.

The *Kampfgruppe* Wagner gave way to new units. It had fulfilled its mission gloriously, saving Estonia at a moment when its sudden fall—with an attendant capitulation of troops and loss of equipment—would have been an overwhelming reverse for the German Army.

There wasn't much left, alas, of our heroic companies of the beginning of August. Looking for the last time at the Dorpat plateau, the low firs, the fields turning gray, the still-smoking town with its broken spires, I saw only a handful of comrades still at my side. I had lost eighty percent of my soldiers in killed and in wounded evacuated to the hospitals, without even speaking of the numerous superficially wounded who had refused to be taken to the rear. In fact, in a few weeks ninety-six percent of our men had been hit by enemy fire.

Their courage had covered our name with honor. Colonel-General Steiner, who during these epic weeks had cited them three times in the order of the day of the Army Corps, had awarded them almost two hundred Iron Crosses. He wanted to decorate the troops himself. He ended his speech with this solemn declaration: "A Walloon is worth a thousand other soldiers." It was a bit overstated. But for four hundred and fifty men, our volunteers had done a mighty work.

They didn't pride themselves on it. They had only done what the

Walloons on the Donets, at Kharkov, on the Don, in the Caucasus, in the Crimea, and at Cherkassy had done.

Already forgetting their suffering and their glory, they were playing pranks like children, asking General Steiner if he knew the names of the two last soldiers that he had just decorated. One was named Rommel. The forebears of the German marshal had originated in our great Low Countries. Their monument, bearing their arms of the Lion of Flanders, is still at Bruges. The other one was named Montgomery, like the English marshal. They were the two celebrities of the hour in the Legion, Rommel and Montgomery, Walloon volunteers, receiving the Iron Cross Second Class side by side at the Eastern front.

* * * * *

Our soldiers went back down toward Reval. The newspapers of Estonia were full of their exploits. They were loaded down with bottles of champagne, which they happily drank on the boat as they sailed back to the Reich.

Hitler summoned me to receive the Oak Leaves from his hands, as well as the gold Insignia of Close Combat, the highest infantry honor, accorded to holders of fifty hand-to-hand combat accreditations.

I took off in a little Fieseler Storch near Toila. I saw—final adieu—the white cliffs and the pale blue waters of the Gulf of Finland shining in the dawn. The sad and infinite pine woods, the silver flames of the birch groves, the broom thickets, the great menhirs, the cabins lost in the green and russet landscape, and the wooden shingles of a few solitary farms slipped away under the tiny plane. Sometimes a big brown spot and a metallic carcass recalled the tormenting presence of the enemy fighters. The airplane flew low, hopping across the little hills like a hare.

Then it was Riga, the Fuehrer's plane, the curve around the coasts of a Lithuania almost entirely occupied by the Soviets, and finally, the airport of the Main Headquarters.

Back there, at the far end of the Baltic countries, our dead remained, to bear eternal witness that in the tragic, life-and-death struggle for Europe the sons of our people had done their duty, asking nothing and expecting nothing.

We had no land to win, no material interests to assure back there. We were misunderstood by many, but resolute and happy. We knew that a pure and burning ideal is a marvelous good, for which a young man with a strong heart should know how to yearn, to struggle, and to die.

# Chapter Eight
# THE SAFETY VALVE OF THE ARDENNES

In August and September 1944, while the battle for Estonia was raging, the entire Western front had crumbled. At our little field posts we listened to the radio bulletins: Battle of the Seine; the capture of Paris; the drive of the American tanks toward the Somme and Reims. Then Belgium had been hit: Tournai, Mons, Brussels. Every one of our soldiers thought of his home. What had become of our families back there?

Then Liege was overrun. When I came before the Fuehrer the Allies were massing in Holland, in Alsace-Lorraine, and before Aachen. I found everybody expansive nevertheless. Himmler made jokes at the table, and during the ten minutes precisely which it took him to eat a spartan dinner and a few pretzels, washed down with a glass of water in one gulp, he concerned himself with three dozen points of detail.

The Fuehrer's lieutenant, Martin Bormann, round, plump, and pasty-faced, debated noisily with General Sepp Dietrich of the SS, who had arrived in a glider from the Western front. His legs set wide apart, his face red as a turnip, Sepp expatiated at length on the strength of the Anglo-American air force and on the ravages of the *Tieffliegers.** But he wasn't especially worried. He gave everyone great thumps on the back, drank cognac with every breath, and went back to his room at five o'clock in the morning, vigorously supported by four giants of the guard.

Himmler was preparing some twenty new divisions of Waffen SS. He gave me the command of the Wallonia Division—the 28th SS Division—which would include, besides our shock brigade, thousands of Rexists who had fled the Allied occupation and were wandering around the Reich.

In general, Hitler's entourage agreed that the withdrawal in the West had been hard. A counterstroke was being prepared in secrecy and silence.

That evening Himmler withdrew to do his interminable nocturnal work and receive the fifteen or twenty persons who waited—sometimes until morning—their turn for an audience. Then the superior officers conversed with me in low voices about the surprises in store from the new weapons.

They stuck to affirmations like, "Two or three months from now, Germany will strike a great blow." The atmosphere was one of faith.

* * * * *

I was particularly surprised to see how Hitler had regained new vigor in six months. His step was calm and assured, his features rested and astonishingly young. Since the war he had grayed a lot, and his back had become bent. But everything about him radiated life, a moderate and disciplined life.

He decorated me. Then he guided me toward a little round table. He gave the impression that no sharp or urgent worry agitated him. Not a disillusioned word led one to infer that he had the slightest doubt in the world of a final rectification. He quickly left military considerations and passed to the question of bourgeois liberalism. With a marvelous lucidity he explained to me why its fall was inevitable.

His eyes shone with good humor. He threw himself with passion into a debate on the future of socialism. His face, admirably cared for, quivered. He made simple but ardent gestures with his slender and perfect hands, lively companions to the orator.

This discussion gave me confidence. If Hitler was haunted by social problems to the point that he lived them and expounded on them with such clarity for an entire hour of the afternoon, it was because he had serious assurances about everything else. Nevertheless, that week Churchill's airborne divisions tried to set foot in Holland near Arnhem.

Just as he was leaving, as if he wanted to engrave a more personal remembrance forever in my heart, Hitler came back and took my hand in both of his. "If I had a son," he said to me slowly and affectionately, "I would want him to be like you." I looked into his clear eyes, so sensitive, with their simple and radiant flame. He went away under the firs by a road strewn with twigs. I looked after him for a long time.

## Coup de théatre

In the flat and muddy villages of Hanover, thousands of Belgian refugees who had fled before the Anglo-American tanks had been installed after a fashion. I had seen to it that my new division did its training in this province of the Reich so that each of my soldiers could give, besides his service, a maximum of comfort to his family in exile.

Suddenly there was a sensational development. I had just spoken to the final session of the Congress of the European Press at Vienna. A week earlier I had met lengthily with the foreign minister, von Ribbentrop, who, particularly cordial, had confided to me in a mysterious tone, "Remember well what I say to you. Never have we been so close to victory."

I thought he was joking. There was nothing at all that would lead one to expect an imminent change in the situation. I remembered, certainly, what I had been told in the entourage of the Fuehrer two months earlier. But winter was here. It was snowing. What new development was likely?

On my return from Vienna I put up at the Hotel Adlon at Berlin. That evening I ran across a high official from the Ministry of Foreign Affairs. He was radiant.

"You don't know?" he said to me. "We're right in the midst of an offensive."

"Offensive? An offensive where?"

"Why, at your home! In Belgium! Our troops are already in the middle of the Ardennes."

* * * * *

The next day the centers of Berlin officialdom were in an extraordinary effervescence. Unbelievable details were being given out: Liege had fallen. Eight thousand new German planes were attacking.

I was brought a telegram from Himmler. It was an order to leave for Belgium with my division that very instant. We passed under the tactical command of Marshal Model, who directed the offensive, and of General Sepp Dietrich of the Waffen SS, who commanded an army group.

It was officially forbidden to send us into combat on our own territory. We were going in order to avoid the errors of the German occupation of 1940-44. Flemings and Walloons would have the task of reorganizing Belgium.

My car rolled all night. In the morning trucks from Hanover loaded a first contigent of soldiers, who were to accompany me immediately toward the frontier. The rest of the division would follow in express trains.

Our refugees rushed to their doorsteps, crying with happiness at the thought of returning to their country soon. Poor people! What condition they would find it in six months later!

At dawn we rode through Cologne.

## Christmas in Belgium

In the month of December 1944, there was nothing left of Cologne but a field of ruins. I met Gauleiter Grohe inside a bunker on the outskirts of town in a park where trees had been ravaged and hacked into a thousand pieces. The optimism in these undergrounds was less lively than at Berlin in the Wilhelmstrasse.

"The Anglo-Americans? Why, they're thirty-two kilometers away!"

And it was exactly so. The Allied pocket of Aachen extended to a few kilometers west of the Rhine. The Gauleiter stuck to reality. Another thrust in his sector, and the Yankee tanks could very well be in front of his little concrete staircase that same day.

Everyone thinks the threshold of his doorway is the threshold of the whole world. Nevertheless, if the Allied jeeps were thirty minutes to the northwest of Cologne Cathedral on 4 December 1944, the Americans and British were also sweeping in from the west and southwestern Rhineland in the direction of the Meuse and the Semois rivers.

The Gauleiter told us where Sepp Dietrich's command post was to be found, almost at the edge of the Belgian frontier. Our hearts thumping, we began our march. We had only brief glimpses of the sun. We could hear the purring motors of the British *Tiefflieger,* but, sheltered by the overcast sky, we made good time toward the southwest.

We approached the Eifel hills. The route glided through a ravishingly beautiful valley. The towns along the stream with their old houses, their medieval walls, their massive gates and watchtowers were still relatively intact. The little public squares, squeezed between the corbelled cottages displaying signs with long gilded scrolls, were dignified by town halls with thick arcades of bold hewn stone.

In the hollows of the valleys shone violet slate roofs and blue clock towers. The snow was clean and shining in the fields. Every hill dominating the road was topped with powerful anti-aircraft batteries. We were favorably impressed. The columns of trucks advanced without trouble.

At four o'clock in the afternoon we arrived at Sepp Dietrich's. He was returning from inspection. Sepp was far from confirming the dazzling rumors which were running through Berlin like will-o'-the-wisps. Liège had definitely not been retaken, but the German tanks had reached Libramont and Saint-Hubert. They had taken La Roche and Marche. Well beyond these towns, having cleared the Ardennes, they were within a few kilometers of Namur and Dinant. They had crossed the whole Ardennes plateau in three days. The Ourthe had been crossed without firing a shot. The rush toward the Meuse had been as quick as in May, 1940.

I slept in an ice-cold house, above which the long red-tailed comets of the German V-1 rockets kept passing constantly, with a sinister whine.

There had been a hard frost. I attended Christmas Mass at ten o'clock in the morning. We came out all intermingled, elderly farmers, kids with red noses, daydreaming soldiers. We barely had time to throw ourselves down in the snow. Anglo-American fighters were circling around the stepple. The bombers were streaking the cold air with long white trails over the humble country cottages, crushing the families. Farms were burning. Women and little girls, yellow with plaster and dripping with blood and dirt, were being dug out.

The Allied counterattack had just begun. Not on the ground, but in the sky, in a crystalline light. For the next ten days the same royal sun would shine from dawn until dusk. The nights were limpid, sharply lining every wall and every cottage in bright cubes, white as clean laundry drying in the meadows.

The sun would be more deadly for the Germans than two thousand tanks mounting a counteroffensive. Thanks to it, thousands of Allied planes could systematically pound the roads, the villages, the crossroads, and the anti-aircraft weapons which tried to stop them.

* * * * *

On Christmas Day Sepp Dietrich's command post moved off between Malmedy and Saint-Vith. We, too, got underway. The sun had been up for only a few hours. Already the devastation was incalculable.

Certainly most of the bombs fell beside their targets, resulting only in enormous gray craters in the snowy fields, or flattening lines of firs. Nonetheless so many bombs were falling that hundreds were hitting the right places anyway. Automobiles were going up in flames. Gaping holes had torn up the road along the cliff. Houses, folded up like accordians, completely barred the road.

The bombing had been anticipated. Flocks of Russian and Italian prisoners had been sent to all the critical points. They cleared the rubbish and filled in the holes, but it took time. The columns of trucks were immobilized. *Tiefflieger* dove down on them, setting fire to numerous trucks, which added even more to our troubles. From that day on we had to figure that transports couldn't be made without difficulty.

I was using a big all-terrain command car. It was especially powerful, climbing over everything like a tank, but it drank seventy liters of gas to a hundred kilometers. In an argument to get a can of benzine at a filling station, I lost five minutes. The delay saved my life. Without it I would have been in Saint-Vith just at the instant when the whole town blew sky-high.

I was still about three hundred meters from this beautiful little city. I was coming out of the woods, descending the hairpin curves of the steep slope when I saw the Allied squadrons in the airspace above us. It might have been four-thirty in the afternoon.

It looked like a scene from the end of the end of the world. A flare had scarcely been shot when all of a sudden an entire street blew into the air. Not a house. No geysers of debris. But the whole street, all at once. It rose up in a block, then fell back down in a horrible roar.

For twenty minutes the squadrons followed one another. In the distance men were galloping through the fields, little blue points in the snow. Then the great humming turned away toward the setting sun, which was just skimming the tops of the firs.

Feet, heads, and torsos of women or soldiers could be seen sticking out of the jumbled beams. Whole lines of houses lay on the ground like lines of cards flicked over.

We managed to saw off several big trees that had fallen across the pavement opposite the first houses, but it was soon clear that our efforts were in vain. Everything had collapsed into a jumbled wreck. It was impossible for anybody, no matter who, to get through. My all-terrain car had to give up like the rest. These twenty minutes had so ravaged the town of Saint-Vith that it would remain impassable for the whole offensive.

* * * * *

We tried to go around these apocalyptic ruins through the fields. My automobile bounced through the hedgerows, toiling in the snow. I ended up at a trench on the west ridge of Saint-Vith. There was a row of young Americans there, dead. They were still perfectly lined up. They still had the handsome bronze complexion of well-fed boys who have been tanned by the open air. They had been mowed down by tank fire. Two of their faces had been flattened like envelopes, but these two-dimensional faces still had an impressive nobility.

There was not an empty space in the trench. Every one of these boys had stayed firmly at his post in spite of the wave of fifty or a hundred tanks charging them; the chain tracks could still be traced in the thick snow.

We wanted to reach the northern road out of Saint-Vith to get to Malmédy, but all the exits were blocked. The *Feldgendarmes* were overwhelmed, and didn't know a single secondary road by which the columns could be detoured. We spent the night using forest paths encumbered with trucks under cover. The delay seemed endless.

Only at dawn did we finally arrive in a lost hamlet at the end of a valley about eight kilometers from Saint-Vith. The little church, built on a knoll, was surrounded by simple peasants' graves marked with beautiful blue crosses carved from slate.

The northern front was close. We could hear the violent roar of the cannon. In the night American artillery came and fired from the edge of the woods.

Sepp Dietrich was in an isolated white house above the town. I met Marshal Model there. He was a stocky, lively, red-faced little man with sprightly eyes. His courage was legendary. He committed suicide in 1945 so as not to survive his country's defeat.

The resistance in the north, from Malmedy to Monschau, turned out to be tough. The famous Colonel Skorzeny, who had freed Mussolini in August 1943 and borne him off in an airplane, had tried to enter Malmédy by surprise with a few hundred men he had specially trained for hard fighting. He lost a great number of his soldiers in this fray, without much results, and was wounded. He was grazed across the forehead. A horrible black eye gave an even more macabre look to his battered face, seamed with duelling scars.

The V-1's screamed past tirelessly day and night, unfurling their long tails of red fire. One of them turned twice above the village in a fit of madness, then, disgusted with it all, dove nose-first into a neighboring field.

On the maps, the situation hadn't evolved much in three days. It was always the same names: Bastogne, Saint-Hubert, Marche, Dinant, Ciney. The German plans were on a large scale. They might have completely reversed the situation in the west, at least for several months.

It was a triple maneuver. Moving rapidly to the Meuse and the North Sea was not its only aim, although that was one of the planned operations. A second operation aimed to take from behind and encircle the Allied forces which were concentrated to the east of Liège, in the bridgehead of Aachen. This would be the task of Sepp Dietrich's forces, aligned to the north of the Ardennes. A third operation consisted of subduing the Allied army in Alsace.

There also the German front was ready for the assault. Himmler was at the Rhine in person, awaiting the success of the thrust to Liège and Sedan in repeating the maneuver of 1940 at the Maginot line.

The push toward Liège (operation number two) had known no decisive success in the first days. The line from Liège to Aachen had resisted.

Sepp Dietrich's forces were going to repeat the operation further upriver on the Meuse. The river had to be crossed at Huy. Only after that would the real battle take place, which would cut the two hundred thousand Anglo-Americans of the Aachen region off from their rear troops and encircle them with their equipment.

Sepp Dietrich showed me the Tongres-Saint-Trond area on the map, west of Liège. "See! he said, "It's here that I'll corner them!" Then, with glittering eyes, he put his big thumb under the name of Aachen, the holy city of the Empire. "Aachen!" he exclaimed, "Aachen! In the month of January I will be in Aachen."

That very evening the shock divisions of the Waffen SS slipped toward the northwest and spread out opposite Barvaux and Lierneux. The command post of Sepp Dietrich was installed in the mill of a large village on a secondary road between Houffalize and La Roche.

* * * * *

We were at the match as excited as spectators. We passed through our two Ardennais villages with their white farms, on whose walls "REX" could still be read in tall letters, painted in the vibrant days of our great political combats.

We went down as far as the village of Steinbach, a few kilometers to the northeast of Houffalize. An ancient castle was there, frigid and deserted, at which we halted our little column. The Ardennais farmers came out of their houses and welcomed us with a touching simplicity. Everyone remembered my grandparents, who had lived in this region, or recalled the meetings I had given. They took us to eat in their low-roofed farms lit by ancient gas lamps. Potatoes fried in lard were steaming on pretty flowered plates, as at the meals of our childhood.

These hard and noble faces, shaped by the work of the fields, were the beloved faces of our own people. We breathed freely. Our spirits were radiant. In the warm farms, full of shadows, near the wood fire crackling around the andirons, we surrendered ourselves to the sweetness of having found our land again and our people again.

## The Lost Routes

A fabulous sun continued to pour out its golden light onto the little white valleys and the big russet, blue, and violet woods which climbed the flanks of the hills. The Allied air force came to pound every country road, every narrow crossroads with ever-increasing violence. The bombers maneuvered by the hundreds, glistening like fish.

The German Army had made a sensational breakthrough, but it hadn't seized either of the two principal lines of communication to the north and south, the roads from Aachen to Liège and from Trier to Arlon.

The nine hundred tanks and the three hundred thousand men who took part in the German offensive had made a drive straight ahead by secondary roads, fairly slow for traffic. These routes had been torn up by the treads of the tanks, then covered up by very heavy snow. Crossing the little villages was difficult. There were numerous bends between the cottages, piled almost atop one another. Thousands of bombs fell onto these roads, making a hundred holes in them and demolishing them at every slope.

Then the villages and the adorable little Ardennais towns were blown up. Houffalize, which had remained absolutely intact at the back of its steep valley among the great rocks near its singing river, was twice attacked and crushed. After the first raid the principal street could still be used. The houses were gaping holes, but trails through the ruins had been cleared fairly quickly. The Allied bombers returned another morning, and the carnage was total. The road which came down from the east in a curve high above the valley was swept from the rock. It hung above the precipice.

In the hollow of the little valley, an isolated cottage surrounded with fabulous shell-holes had had its roof covered with earth like a garden. The firs had become gray and dirty. Houffalize was flattened. It was no longer possible to get through it.

At La Roche the fleeing American troops had left the bridge intact. The Allied planes came afterward to correct this small oversight. Their bombs turned the ravishing town into a monstrous heap of ruins, with mounds of dead civilians beneath them.

The Ardennes was flattened in a few days. Not a town on a road to somewhere else, not a crossroads escaped.

It was a terrible way to wage war, at the expense of women and children crushed in their cellars. But this means, which the Anglo-Americans used without any restraint, quickly proved to be decisive. At the end of a week all roads used by the columns of the Reich had become almost impassable.

Immense columns of rations, munitions, and gas had to take their chances on logging roads, narrow roads where the trucks skidded in the snow, causing endless bottlenecks. In one night the columns advanced five or six kilometers.

The Germans lost the battle of the Ardennes, not on the approaches to the Meuse or at Bastogne, but in these fir and beech woods crowded with thousands of blocked vehicles. An army can triumph only when the equipment, food, munitions, and fuel follow rapidly and regularly.

* * * * *

A first defeat illustrated this elementary truth, right at the beginning. The tanks which had penetrated toward Dinant and which should have conquered the town easily had to stop at the village of Celles, eight kilometers from the Meuse, not, as the ridiculous story goes, because a scold wearing glasses stopped them, but because they ran completely out of gas. The German tanks waited two days. Their radios sent appeal after appeal in vain. Not so much as a drop of gasoline came. In the end they had to set fire to their magnificent Panzers.

Every day the problem got worse. Taking advantage of the surprise, they should have broken through like Rommel in 1940. The fruit was ripe. The Allied rear was empty: there wasn't a single barrier, once past the Ardennes. The tanks of the Reich would have taken Sedan and Charleroi in forty-eight hours.

The gas didn't come even though there was an overabundance of it at the border. There were depots of several millions of liters not far from Saint-Vith. The victorious spearhead divisions found themselves isolated and deprived of fuel because the dazzling sun which flooded the Ardennes from morning til night for ten days let a fantastic flotilla of American bombers crush all the centers of communication.

Ten days of fog, which is normal in the misty Ardennes, would have been enough for the Germans to change their bad luck. The food, the munitions, and the millions of liters of fuel would have got through. But luck had abandoned the Reich. And an August sun never left the snowy landscapes of December

* * * * *

Even communication by messenger and isolated transports had become virtually impossible during the day. Scarcely was one on a road before *Tief-*

*flieger* would dive at the vehicle. They would prowl in pairs, followed by two more, then two more again to finish the work. Every kilometer of road was watched. The routes were littered with burned trucks and automobiles. It was a frightful sight.

Having had no news from the German command for several days, I tried to reach the command post of General Dietrich by road. I barely had time to behold the marvelous blue, brown, and white panorama of the plateau of the Ardennes, half-way between Houffalize and Baraque-Fraiture, when a *Tiefflieger* came down on us, charging almost at head-height. Two bullets as big as my thumb passed through the motor; another slashed my helmet; a fourth punctured my documents, passing exactly between my ribs and my left arm. A truck which we met did a crazy pirouette on the bank and turned into a torch.

We were able to pull one soldier out of the wreckage more or less whole. The others, crushed under the weight of the car, were burned alive. We could see their thighs crackle. For a quarter of an hour the *Tiefflieger* kept coming back and forth with ferocious hatred, hitting us with incendiary bombs at point blank range each time.

All along the roads it was the same hunt of man and vehicle.

## Days of Waiting

We passed New Year's Eve among our Ardennais at Steinbach.

Everywhere my soldiers were part of the family. The farmers called them by their first names. They shared everything.

These worthy men asked only one thing, peace. To be allowed to work! Not to hear any more about politics! To be left in peace at home to take care of their family, their animals, and their fields! They were quite right, and were just repeating in their own soft drawling tongue the complaints and aspirations of all farmers since antiquity.

I went to eat New Year's Eve waffles with them. Everyone kissed at midnight without ceremony, rough kisses of tanned farmers and womenfolk with whiskers.

But I watched my companions singing with a heavy heart. I was thinking of the snows where men were fighting back there before Bastogne, all along the Ourthe, in the Lierneux and Stavelot woods. I thought of the Ardennes, torn and burning in the white and pink night.

Where would this new year lead us?

* * * * *

The next day we had to give our icy castle to a field hospital that didn't know where else to go. The wounded flowed in from the Bastogne sector. We moved to a village three kilometers away named Limerle.

Theoretically I was to have taken over the administrative reorganization of these regions. The commander-in-chief of military operations, Marshal Model, had officially transferred to me in writing all political power in the Belgian territory retaken from the Allies.

But everywhere the civil authorities had fled. The parish priests had done the same. Terrorized by the Anglo-American bombardments, the families had been living since the beginning of January as best they could, most often burrowed in the back of their cellars. This was not the moment to make decrees and reform the constitution.

All I did was to give the inhabitants of Limerle and Steinbach the consolation of the Mass. Our SS chaplain, a holy Trappist of the abbey of Forges-les-Chimay, the Reverend Father Stockmans, was with us. And, despite the *Tiefflieger,* the village church bells rang to gather civilians and soldiers in the same love at the foot of the altar of the God of peace and mercy.

* * * * *

I had sent couriers in all directions to inform themselves of the situation in the districts, to set our imprisoned compatriots free, and to gather files of the *Moniteur*[1] and other newspapers.

The reports of our freed comrades made our blood run cold. They described to us the savage treatment that thousands of men and women throughout Belgium had been made to endure in the name of "democracy": incarcerated in abominable conditions, jeered at, beaten, tortured, loaded down with infamy, as well as murdered, because they had different political ideas than those of the "liberators" of September 1944.

The newspapers of Brussels, Liège, and Arlon which our emissaries brought back to us were nothing more than hate-filled and savage appeals to the lowest instinct of mobs. They delivered up as fodder to their readers interminable lists of decent people locked in the cells of the victorious politicians only for having once shared our opinions, whether closely or from a distance, or for having subscribed to our papers. They were crowded pell-mell into prisons and barracks in the number of about a hundred thousand and handed over to the bellowing brutalities of frenzied guards. Totally illegally more than half a million Belgians were thus officially persecuted.

The most moving spectacle that it was given to us to witness then was the arrival of about fifteen very young boys escaped from the penitentiary at the town of Saint-Hubert. This house of correction for criminals and juvenile delinquents had a sinister reputation throughout the Ardennes. It was there nevertheless that a certain number of children of Rexist families were infamously locked up. The fathers and mothers were thrown into prison. The children were torn from the family environment, treated as mentally retarded children, and sent to mingle with the most vicious delinquents.

Having political ideas different from the ideas of those in power had become a crime punishable by persecution and death. Young women were herded into jail to be shaved, beaten, and often raped. Mothers of large families were torn from their children and savagely thrown into overcrowded jails. Old men were thrown into cells for the crime of paternity and perished there of want and grief. But it was the children who were punished in the most iniquitous way. In the name of democracy vengeance was taken on the families by trying to turn their children, who knew nothing of politics, into dirty, corrupt, and vicious creatures. All that in the name of justice and civilization!

We could have risen against this outrage and made them expiate these crimes, which cried out for retribution. But we swear before God, we were above anger. We didn't spill a single drop of blood during these weeks when, nevertheless, our souls were roiling with indignation. Everything that smear artists may have told since then about alleged executions carried out in the Belgian Ardennes by us or with our consent point to a police plot and the most repugnant calumny.

We witnessed the suffering of our compatriots crushed beneath Allied bombardments and surrounded by fighting. We didn't want to add to so much misfortune.

We knew also that nothing great can be built on vengeance. We wanted to reconcile the diverse elements of our people, to calm the hatreds instead of prolonging them by bloody reprisals. Not a single one among us violated these orders of fraternity.

## One Morning

The essential thing for the Germans at the end of December 1944 was to cut off, promptly surround, and crush Allied military potential on the Western front. The battle of annihilation eluded the German command by the end of a week.

Sixty hours had been enough for the motorized troops of the Reich to achieve a stunning penetration through the whole Ardennes plateau. They had reached the great Luxemburg-Brussels railroad line at Jemelle. Facing west, they had crossed the forests and the mountains from one end to the other. The German divisions had poured into the vast plains of Condroz and La Famenne.

The Allied rout was still at its height after three days. If the Germans had been able to resupply their Panzers and their machanized divisions with fuel and munitions, they could have easily followed up their advantage at full speed.

Even at the end of 1944 these divisions were remarkably equipped. Of course there were fill-in units for the ordinary work, notably stop-gap troops of gray-uniformed Mongols who were mowed down in confusion in the snows of Bastogne.

The tanks of General Manteuffel, however, which had advanced to the threshold of Dinant, the Tigers of Sepp Dietrich, the brand new trucks of the motorized troops: all were still capable of bringing off a daring and sensational raid.

There were only nine hundred assault tanks in all, it is true. But how many did Rommel have at Abbeville in 1940 and at El Alamein in 1942? How many did the British-Americans have upon entering Brussels and Antwerp on the 3rd and 4th of September, 1944?

The surprise of the Allies in the Ardennes had been total. The roads were wide open. Fifty thousand mechanized troops thrusting on Namur, Andenne and Huy on the 6th or 7th of December would immediately have been able to assure the crossing of the Meuse.

It was at precisely this time that the Allied air force, under a blistering sun, smashed the possibility of massive movements and transport of fuel into the earth.

The difficulty got worse every day. Germany lost the use of her motors. She could no longer even manage to assure sufficient provisions to the troops sent a hundred and fifty kilometers ahead of the Siegfried line. The situation of these divisions would very rapidly become desperate.

If Sepp Dietrich hadn't been able to crush the northern pocket in his iron fist, neither had General Manteuffel been able to clear his left flank to the south of Bastogne. They would have had to occupy Arlon and Virton without striking a blow, to enlarge the security zone.

There, as at Malmédy, were found several thousand obstinate Allies who faced them with a courage to which every soldier is sensitive. Instead of fleeing, he takes example from the many others. They let themselves be surrounded, withstood the blow, and won the days they needed.

The resistance at Bastogne burdened the entire left wing of the Reich's offensive. Bastogne, like Malmédy, could have been taken easily if the armored divisions, resupplied in time, had been able to exploit the initial thrust, to move far, sowing confusion, seizing depots, eliminating potential regroupment and counterattacks. Because the sun put the Germans in a disastrous situation from the third day onward, Malmédy and Bastogne, isolated points of resistance which would have been doomed in the normal course of events, were able to play a dominant role.

By the end of scarcely a week, life had become absolutely untenable for Marshal Model. His divisions were engaged in the southwest at the end of a passage a hundred and fifty kilometers long, which could be supplied only by secondary roads, now being methodically pounded, or by snowy trails which were indescribable bottlenecks. Along the sides of this deadend far behind the lead German troops, the Anglo-American Malmédy-Bastogne vise was gripping tighter every day.

The Allied plan for a double lateral counteroffensive in the near future was visible to the naked eye. There was no longer any doubt as to the outcome of the duel.

Germans are realists. The withdrawal movement began immediately.

It was accompanied by the meticulous precision and perfect calm which always characterized the orders of the Reich's High Command.

The Waffen SS Divisions were placed on both flanks at the most disputed points while the victors of Christmas disengaged methodically, in stages, from the Mosane region, then from Saint-Hubert and Marche, then from the valley of the Ourthe.

The American forces coming up from the south and the British forces coming down from the north were drawing closer and closer together, continually threatening to cut in two, right in the middle, the ribbon of three hundred thousand retreating German soldiers that stretched from the Ourthe to the Eifel.

At the beginning of the second week of January only a corridor about twenty kilometers wide remained between the two waves of assailants, the British and the American forces.

At last only a single road remained by which the German maneuver could continue.

We lived through days and nights of unbearable tension. But the feeling which dominated us was admiration. Not one battalion became dispirited. The troops, schooled in the incomparable ethic of discipline of the German people, accepted this withdrawal with the same even disposition that they had shown two weeks earlier in the drive past the banks of the Ourthe.

Through the glacial nights, while the countless Yankee and British artillery boomed all around, thousands of German soldiers slipped eastward. Watchful tanks were posted at each branch of the road like huge guard dogs in the dark. Panting, they shot their tongues of fire to the rear. The columns advanced in the snow, bent over, silent, orderly.

It was over.

We had tried. We had failed.

The soldiers left as they had come, toward new battles, God alone knew where, toward new suffering, God alone knew how great.

Not a murmur was heard.

Duty was duty. *Dienst ist Dienst.*

* * * * *

While Marshal Model was maneuvering his excellent Wehrmacht and Waffen SS divisions in the Ardennes, other equally seasoned and equally well-equipped divisions waited in vain across from Alsace for the order to march through the eastern part of the French territory.

Himmler held to this plan. He stuck to it until the last, even after the retreat from the Ardennes had begun. For every disturbance of the adversary's plans, even at great price, every disorder in the elaboration of his projected offensives offered an incalculable advantage for the Reich, now more than ever. If we could win two or three months' respite, we might still be able to make and use the new weapons in time to turn the situation around. With a superhuman heroism, Germany tried everything, driven by this last hope.

Thus the Alsace offensive stayed on the program. Its launching was set for mid-January, 1945. At this very moment a tidal wave of Soviets leaped over Warsaw and hurled themselves against Danzig, Posen, and Breslau. Berlin was in mortal danger.

The great dream of liberating the West crumbled. And the divisions returning from the Ardennes, as well as those waiting for action in Alsace, left hastily for the atrocious carnage of the East.

We stayed at Limerle until the Allied tanks were near. For the last three days, the German command had been reinstalled on the Reich's territory.

As for us, it was our native soil that we had to leave, our country, our people. We couldn't tear ourselves away from this last village. Nevertheless, there was absolutely nothing left for us to do there. All hope of rescuing the situation was dead.

We wandered around the house in the snow to look at the whitening fields, the smoke rising in the distance from the roofs of the little farms, the slate steeple, like the blue steeples of our childhood.

We had to make the decision. We kissed the good old Ardennais *maman* who lodged us. It was the last kiss of our country. We went around one more long pink farm and along the black firs. The border was close. Sons of Europe, we were also the sons of our own little fatherland. Our hearts torn, we closed our eyes so as not to see any more.

# Chapter Nine
# FIGHT TO THE DEATH IN POMERANIA

The powerful Soviet drive in mid-January 1945 marked the end of the war in the West. There was still fighting. There were desperate struggles between Aachen and the Rhine when the Allies, recovered from the memorable shove of December 1944, advanced forward again. But the danger to the east was such that the German High Command had to choose. It sacrificed the Western front, which it stripped of its strongest divisions and an important part of its tanks.

There was nothing left on the left bank of the Rhine but a curtain of troops. Everything that counted was thrown into the merciless struggle being waged between the Vistula and the Oder.

The Soviets had never sent such a force into battle, nor such a prodigious amount of equipment. Everything cracked like rotten wood at their passage. Lodz fell. Posen fell. The Russian panzers rolled by the thousands toward Bromberg and Breslau. East Prussia was crushed. The remains of President Hindenburg were hastily saved before the famous Tannenberg monument was blown up.

Everywhere the tidal wave expanded. Thousands of villages burned, and the savage growl of the tanks resounded even inside the territory of the Reich, sowing terror.

The winter was particularly hard that month. Before the Communists, whose cruelty every German feared, the inhabitants of the threatened regions fled in millions. Survivors who had seen the beginnings of the Soviet occupation recounted the abominations that had been committed to villages as yet untouched. Entire provinces fled.

The populations of the large centers were loaded onto all the rolling stock still left in the stations. Tens of thousands of women and children had to stay out in the storm for days and nights at a time, fifty or eighty persons standing on flatcars. Many died of cold on the way. In every convoy babies froze against the breasts of their mothers. The banks of the railroad lines were strewn with stiffened corpses, thrown from the trains to make a bit of room for other gasping runaways.

On one line near Bresleu a train had been abandoned. One hundred forty-two bodies of little boys and girls lay frozen on the uncovered wagons.

The ghastly caravans which had been on the road for a week or two were taken past Berlin by the outer highway so as not to terrify the population of the capital.

* * * * *

At the end of January 1945, our division also received the order to leave for the Eastern Front via Stettin.

The great *Autobahn* from Berlin to Stettin was nothing but a gigantic trail of suffering. There were perhaps two or three hundred thousand women and children on it, disheveled, their faces ravaged by the biting cold.

The columns of thousands of carts could use only the right side of the highway, for a war was going on. It was going on to such an extent that ferocious squadrons of Soviet airplanes kept constantly coming to scourge these pitiful ranks, disregarding their obvious defenselessness.

The carts were so close together that every stick of bombs caused a sickening massacre. The horses floundered among the overturned carts, their hot intestines scattered in the snow. Women and youngsters clung to the debris, brown holes in their backs. The blood fell in big drops onto their black stockings. Blood-red eiderdown fluttered through the air.

These martyred people were about to descend from month to month into the very depths of the worst of tragedies, more horrible than any the world had known.

They had endured years of privations and incredible bombarding. They had learned of the death of a son, of two sons, of their father, fallen who knows where in the Russian snows. Now they were being hunted into the roads by millions, having lost everything, freezing to death. Now bursts of incendiary bullets finished the work of tracking them down, persecuting them, mutilating them.

If only they had at least come to the end of their suffering. But as we watched their tragic procession spreading endlessly, we thought of the thousands of Soviet tanks hot on their heels. We knew that one day or another they would end up falling into the hands of the barbarians just the same, that these young girls, so clean and healthy, would be raped, soiled, contaminated, that thousands of babies would die for lack of milk, that these grandmothers who struggled against the north wind would one day be only lifeless black bundles at the end of all misery and privation.

What good did it do to run? You had to stop and wait, wait for the Soviet savage who would force your legs open, wait to see your roof burning.

The instinct for survival, however, drove them stubborn and crying into the chaotic roads.

I crossed the Oder and took the road east on the right. Above the banks and the hills kilometers of trenches were being feverishly built in sand that immediately caved in. Trucks were unloading thousands of new shovels to thousands of mobilized women.

I began to pass my soldiers, detrained at Stettin Station, who were making their own way to Stargard. And a very poor way it was. They drew their vehicles like draft animals. Our horses had not arrived in time. The troops had taken their courage in both hands, yoked themselves up, laughing, and that way covered the thirty-five kilometers of snow that still separated us from the enemy.

The soldiers cheered my Volkswagen as I passed, happy to arrive at the fighting and knowing I was with them.

I followed along Lake Madue, which extended quite far toward the south, then saw the majestic towers, square and red, of the churches of Stargard. The ancient gates of the city, also in brick, had a magnificent grace and majesty.

The city dated from the High Middle Ages. This whole country of Pomerania had a charm that was profound, strong, and sad, with its lovely weathered walls, its dappled sky, its fir-covered moors, its pale ponds where boats splashed.

The whole population was in the process of fleeing. Stargard was like a humming marketplace. People were rushing everywhere.

I ended up in a school at the command post of the general charged with defending the region. "There you are!" he cried.

In all, he had two tanks, the leftovers of some ill-assorted troops and a few battalions of elderly gentlemen of the *Volkssturm*.[1] That morning the Soviets were fifteen kilometers away.

## Before Stargard

In the second half of January, 1945, the armies of the USSR burst into the German province of Pomerania with the violence of a hurricane. We thought them still at Bromberg when one of their reconnaissance tanks, pressing madly ahead, appeared at the Schneidemuehl Station.

The Soviet attack had three spearheads, soon thrust like lances into the ancient Pomeranian soil: one toward the east to separate Danzig from the Reich; another toward the celebrated city of Kolberg, on the Baltic; the third toward Stettin.

Stargard was the last large town still to be captured on the Stettin route, only thirty-six kilometers from the lower Oder. When we arrived at Stargard on the morning of 6 February 1945, the situation was almost desperate. The Soviet tanks had penetrated deeply to the south, southeast, and southwest of the town.

The defense was just about nil, having been put into the hands of the courageous old "papas" of the *Volkssturm*, who did everything they could, but garnered more of bronchitis than of victory.

It was important to plug the gaping hole in the south. We were immediately sent to Kremzow and Repplin, towns situated ten kilometers from Stargard on the Arnswalde road.

This road crossed a stretch of very gently rolling meadows only a few kilometers wide and populated by six villages between the two Ihna Rivers—the regular Ihna which went stodgily along its way without a single burst of spirit, and the much more likable Lazy Ihna, which daydreamed along the way and made gracious curves, either out of absent-mindedness or because it had noticed a little spot prettier than the others. Despite their diversity of character the two Ihnas came back together at the end of their course like a couple reconciled late in life. The single Ihna then flowed through Stargard and then through the northern forests to empty itself into the Stettiner Haff.

I had received explicit orders. They were counting on us. In a few days the German tanks would be there. In the meantime Stargard had to be saved. If we were to yield, the Soviet tanks would sweep into the village within the hour.

From the very first minute I sent men to the extreme limit of the sector at the village of Repplin. A Soviet detachment arrived there shortly after we did.

The position was good for both them and us, for it dominated all its surroundings. A patrol of Communists was supposed to have secured it several hours earlier, while the town was still empty. Thus the enemy contingent strolled up confidently. Our men let the vehicles and the troops penetrate deeply into the hamlet, then attacked them from every direction. A single Red soldier got away across the cemetery.

This first skirmish got my daredevils into shape and gave us forty-eight hours to organize ourselves.

The fog became thicker. It began to rain. A mud like mastic stuck and sucked at our boots. We barricaded ourselves into long silos of beetroots to avoid the water collecting in the foxholes.

The Communists were making dangerous progress in the southwest, occupying large villages on our right wing. The fires made dirty pink splotches in the rainy nights.

The audacity of the Soviet panzers was unbelievable. Returning from Stargard where I had gone for orders, I saw one bearing right down on me. Now at this moment I was seven kilometers behind our positions. The tank had come cross-country right to our paved road. It was advancing in the open, absolutely alone. A German who was luckily carrying a panzerfaust hid himself in a thicket and blew it up as it passed.

In the wallet of the young Russian officer who had perished with the tank I found a letter which he must have only just written. He wrote triumphantly to his family, "These last days I've crushed lots of Fritzes under my treads. Soon the Red flag will fly over Berlin!" Then he added this moving conclusion, "Then we can go back to our villages."

A few German Panzers finally arrived in our sector. It was decided that at daybreak on Friday, 9 February 1945, a counter-attack would take place between Lake Madue and the Ihna River.

Our mission was to cross the lazy Ihna, to send one of our battalions in a southwesterly direction, and to take by assault first the hills, then the crossroads of Lindenberg through which the columns of enemy tanks regularly passed.

At five thirty in the morning, in an absolute silence, we set out.

## Lindenberg

The Soviet hordes which swept across Pomerania and tried to force the passage of Stargard had powerful arms and thousands of courageous soldiers, inspired by incessant victories.

The counterattack of 9 February 1945 had only a limited objective—to break the Reds' momentum, to regain a few kilometers of terrain, and to retake the crossroads at Lindenberg.

We had to cross ploughed fields near the village of Strebelow. As for the German tanks, going from Lake Madue to the northwest, they would take several villages by assault before rejoining us at the crossroads.

Protected by little groups of machine-gunners who, according to our method, had infiltrated into the enemy lines before dawn, we could climb fairly easily up a long clay cliff from which we could see the fir woods covering the crossroads of Lindenberg two kilometers ahead.

The enemy was hidden in the copses to the left, but the lightning style of the Walloons had always been a decisive element in an attack. Our artillery roared. Our young company commanders plunged ahead of their units, deployed as in the charges of yesteryear. I was armed only with a baton. Out of bravado, my officers imitated me. The work didn't lag. Despite the mud, we were masters of the traffic circle by nine thirty-five. The Soviet tanks, hammered by our anti-tank weapons, disengaged and fled to the south.

I led the first assault wave at the extremity of the pine woods. I sent two combat groups on beyond the crossing and hastily posted my anti-tank guns. The enemy would be contained and we would be protected from a Soviet tank thrust if the German Panzers, victorious, drove them back in our direction.

The patrols came back promptly. Some thickets eight hundred meters away from us concealed a park full of enemy tanks. Our men had noticed an intense activity. That didn't presage anything particularly peaceful.

The crossroads wasn't badly situated. The roads crossed behind us and ended near a quarry. The terrain was raised, bordered on the west by a steep ravine. The entire knoll was covered with firs. To the southeast, the ground was marshy.

Unluckily, apart from this wooded knoll there was no cover. Everything around was bone bare. If we were pushed out of the pine woods our only path of retreat would be the four kilometers of muddy plain by which we had come.

Such a withdrawal, in daylight, followed by enemy tanks, would be impossible. Now that we were there we had to stick to the Lindenberg knoll and wait for the German tanks to arrive.

* * * * *

We had taken the terrain very early. We followed excitedly the bitter combat of the Reich's panzers coming from the north.

They had reached the village nearest to our crossroads. The Stukas were diving in screaming ranks onto the Soviet tanks and artillery. These felt themselves to be in terrible danger. They were cut off from the normal retreat by the southeast. They didn't try to go back in our direction. The tanks were already ranging themselves on a route straight to the south, snorting, firing. The Stukas pounded the village with fantastic violence. Everything was burning.

There were two or three pauses of several minutes, during which we thought that the Germans had finally crushed the resistance. Each time the combat started up anew.

At noon the fighting raged with the same fury. With our binoculars we could see the tanks moving about in the red and gold storm of the village on fire. The enemy anti-tank guns never stopped firing. The column of Soviet tanks, outside the village, gave us immoderate hopes by retreating, then returned to the attack.

At eleven o'clock in the morning two enemy tanks came out of a grove in the southwest and fired on us. One of our men stole up with a panzerfaust and hit one of the tanks. The skirmish ended.

One hour later we heard the ever-distressing rumble of treads. Between the firs we saw five tanks rushing toward us, quickly followed by three more. At the same time some "Stalin's organs" began to pour a rain of rockets onto our little woods, mowing down branches by the hundreds with their explosions. Wounded men were moaning. The tanks were shelling us point blank. It was almost impossible to raise our heads, but we had to fire just the same and fight back with panzerfausts. Otherwise the tanks would go around or through the grove and surround us.

I ran from one group to another to pull up from the ground those who had flattened themselves nose to earth, terrified by the deluge, or who were huddled in trenches rolled up like hedgehogs.

The firs, strong and densely packed, partially protected us. Thanks to them the tanks couldn't come right up to us and crush us under their weight. Our anti-tank guns fired continuously.

Four times the enemy tanks arrived within a few meters of our holes at the edge of the firs. Four times they had to go back. Two Soviet tanks took direct hits. One of our anti-tank guns was demolished. Numerous dead and wounded lay about, but we had been neither cut off nor surrounded.

We had to keep calm. To the left stretched the muck of the marshes. To the right the cliff dropped away twenty meters. To fall back was to die.

At three o'clock in the afternoon the noises died away in the direction of Lake Madue. The village, two kilometers northwest of our Y crossing, hadn't been taken. The German Panzers had occupied the station and part of the town, but the Reds were resisting fanatically and blocking the road. Our link-up was becoming more and more problematical.

Our success was of consequence only if the whole front advanced with the tank victory and secured a new line. But if we had to remain in a vacuum, left to ourselves on our solitary knoll, we would sooner or later be surrounded and annihilated.

A fine rain was falling, freezing us to the bone, and night was coming. The field telephone crackled. It was the general at Stargard. Their attack having failed, the German tanks would be unable to meet us, and were going to withdraw under cover of darkness. At 11 P.M. we were silently to regain our positions of the morning.

We had scarcely effected this return after struggling through the sticky fields when I received the order to send one of my companies to the village of Kruessow, situated on our right flank and occupied by a few meager *Volkssturm* units.

This town straddled the Lindenberg-Stargard road. A thrust was to be expected there. The enemy was emboldened by the previous day's victorious resistance. Our boys arrived at Kruessow just at the same time as the Soviet tanks, who knocked them about, then threw them across the Ihna river. It was an unfortunate affair.

The company commander organized the defense on the right bank. He couldn't help it if he had been sent to Kruessow much too late.

The village was important, though. Our officers didn't take failure lightly. They were proud. Without much ado, but with a heavy heart, our young company commander put his formation in order. He telephoned his plan to me, then alone he ran along the road to Kruessow and died before its walls.

A gratuitous death, but a death for the glory and honor of his flag.

* * * * *

With a dozen tanks and all available Stukas the German command tried in vain to retake Kruessow the next day. All attempts failed. The castle burned. The village blew up. And the enemy stayed glued to their anti-tank guns, near their tanks, hidden in the ruins.

In the meantime the important town of Dammitz fell. The news was getting worse. I was called to Panke, to the train where the Army staff office was. Its commanding general was none other than Colonel-General Steiner, our former chief at the Estonian front of Narva and Dorpat.

In confidence he told me of an impending attempt to turn the situation around. A huge German offensive in the East was ready. On the appointed day two enormous pincers would advance, one from Pomerania, the other coming up from the Slovakian border. Sepp Dietrich was ready and waiting below Breslau. As for the army group to which we belonged, they would be under the personal command of Himmler.

Several armored divisions were going to arrive at our sector. Their first objective would be to make a daring thrust from Stargard to Landsberg. A second operation was to take us from Landsberg to join the offensive from the Slovakian border.

I left devoured by a burning ardor. Certainly, we were going to risk everything. But our High Command was reacting with such will power! Harassed from every direction by overwhelming fire it replied with military science and iron will. How sensational if the coordinating armies in the north and south could link quickly and succeed in surrounding and wiping out the main Soviet force just as in the summer of 1941.

The move was kept as well hushed up as the Ardennes offensive.

Goering came to visit the advanced positions in the capacity of an enthusiast—not without some daring. He made a big hit with our soldiers, whom he addressed with a truculent geniality. He was quite voluminous, covered in layers of coats of an astonishing yellow-brown, and looked like an enormous wet-nurse dressed up as a Serbian general. He drew forth from his bosom cigars as big as baby bottles.

Everyone stocked up from this illustrious source.

On the night of 15-16 February 1945, it became suddenly obvious that great operations were imminent. Three armored divisions arrived on our narrow launching pad in an uninterrupted flow of tanks, guns, and trucks.

Until that moment our Wallonian regiments had known nothing of the offensive plan. The soldiers looked at one another at first, tongue-tied and goggling. What was going on? Then, soon, a happy fervor animated all of them. At dawn the tanks went on ahead. It was an offensive!

## The Last Offensive

The German High Command sent all that was left of its mobile forces, notably its tanks, into the counteroffensive of 16 February 1945 on the Eastern Front.

Himmler addressed a dazzling proclamation to the troops, in which he repeated forcefully, "Forward! Forward through the mud! Forward through the snow! Forward by day! Forward by night! Forward to free the soil of the Reich!"

Upon reaching Landsberg we were going to take the enormous Soviet army, which had already reached and crossed the Oder opposite Berlin, from behind. If Sepp Dietrich's offensive behind Breslau were to succeed, if, to make a long story short, all of us made our junction in Poland near Lodz, the repercussions of this winter victory would be incalculable.

Himmler wanted to succeed here with the operation which had failed on the western front at the end of December, 1944. In place of the Ardennes-Alsace pincers, this would be the Pomerania-Slovakia pincers.

General Steiner, whose army was to deliver the most powerful battering-ram blow, was exultant on the eve of combat. "This year we will be on the Dnieper again!" he kept repeating to me, while giving me great affectionate thumps.

The difficulties could be better glimpsed in the staff offices. The atmosphere was that of Montmirail[2] when Napoleon hurled his last thunderbolts, the most thrilling, but also the most ephemeral. The technicians didn't dwell too much on such reflections. But everyone, specialist or not, felt that we had to throw our last cards on the blood-smeared table.

No longer motorized, the Walloons were not to participate in the initial shock. We were to let the assault wave pass by and give a hand in case of a lateral counterattack by the enemy.

On the western flank of the jumping-off point the German High Command feared a Soviet reaction aiming to cut off the Reich's armored divisions after they started their attack at the southern end of the corridor. To ward off this danger, on the night of the great attack we received orders to enlarge the security zone and in particular to reoccupy the ridge at Lindenberg, which we had taken by assault at dawn on 9 February and evacuated the following night.

The operation succeeded a second time. A reinforced company installed itself firmly on the knolls. It was commanded by a hero of the Estonian front, First Lieutenant Capelle, a young giant with a ruddy complexion, tenacious, modest, radiating the highest ideals.

Our flank guards too had moved to the southwestern end of the roadbed and retaken a strategic point from the enemy two kilometers beyond our main line.

Our objectives had been speedily attained by ten o'clock in the morning. I could then go south to Repplin, where the motorized divisions were to have started.

I had a bad impression right from the start. The assault hadn't taken place at 5:00 P.M., as the orders specified: only at ten o'clock had the tanks started off.

I was installed in one of our machine-gun nests, and I didn't miss a single detail. The German tanks still had great style. They were more sparing of their equipment, but magnificent in the harmony in which they worked.

The enemy had an enormous number of anti-tank guns. Several of our tanks burned, looking like flowering fruit trees, before they reached the woods covering the opposite slope. But other Panzers were advancing on the flanks. They crossed the forest. The moment had come for the infantry to move forward with the same vigor.

The infantry proved soft. These were no longer the crack troops of the past. Several million men had fallen in the East. We had had to fill holes in divisions that had been bled white, not very satisfactorily, by dumping in streams of barracks wardens and reserves who didn't have the health, the vigor, the faith, the technical training of the victors of the first summers. The outstanding noncoms of 1941 and 1942 were no longer there to command and lead the newcomers.

We had to wait until two o'clock in the afternoon for the first village to fall, Brallentin, which should normally have been taken by storm as early as dawn. Due to such dithering we lost the effect of surprise.

Ever since the middle of the night, rumbling with the noise of the German tanks under way, we had been intercepting Russian radio messages urgently asking for help. Hours had passed, permitting the enemy to regroup.

* * * * *

Interrogating the prisoners also gave us something to think about. According to them the first Soviet barrier at Brallentin was backed by two other equally powerful tank barriers spaced twenty kilometers apart. The whole country in front of us was bristling with Soviet tanks. "There are hundreds of them," said the prisoners. They gave the names of the villages where they were concentrated and supplied precise details which confirmed their truthfulness.

I couldn't very well see the reserves of this morning manhandling all that.

We had numerous Panzers. Sixty of them had left in the general advance from our sector. In Pomerania another two hundred and fifty German Panzers had penetrated through the Soviet lines at the same time. But the Soviets were going to bring two or three times as many against them if they were given the time to recover.

They were the strongest in terms of equipment by a long way. They could be beaten only by speed, and this battle was beginning badly.

Two more villages fell before night. The thrust thus penetrated about ten kilometers to the south. It was an achievement.

But already the headquarters was reporting very sharp enemy counterattacks. The Reds had entered the third village in force, where a furious duel was taking place.

As soon as it got dark the Soviet Air Force was sent to the center of the offensive, to Stargard. At 2200 hours, by the light of dazzling parachute flares, the pounding began. Soon huge fires were breaking out. A warehouse containing eight hundred thousand bottles of schnapps, the famous Mampe schnapps, burned. Then a stock of a hundred million cigarettes caught fire. Then all the streets. The aerial bombardment continued without letup, wave upon wave, for hours.

We could feel the earth under our little posts, ten kilometers to the south of the town, vibrating like a drumhead. The sky was red above our heads to the right. The whole countryside was lit up.

At two o'clock in the morning I was called to the command post of the Army Corps and had to drive through the roaring blaze in my Volkswagen. The general was established in a villa above Stargard. I received my orders.

I went out by way of the garden. Beneath me the city was like an immense ship in flames. The ancient square towers of the medieval churches stood out dark and straight above the gigantic torches. They held out in the this hurricane as though wanting to send up one more appeal toward the sky from the civilized centuries that were dying in the fire.

They were pathetic, black against a red and gold background. Never had they been so beautiful. Never had they borne such solemn testimony. Poor towers of Stargard, blackened masts of the burning ship which for five hundred years had flown the noble flag of Christian Europe.

This Europe which was being burned alive was the country of every one of us. These austere square towers of the East were sisters to the great grey towers of Saint-Rombaut of Malines and the belfry of Bruges. All our countries of Europe answered to one another, as did the clock towers. I could hear the great dirge of these disasters resounding in my heart. And I couldn't keep myself from crying, alone on the reddening terrace, facing that ancient city being engulfed, facing those proud towers still standing so black and strong in their misfortune.

* * * * *

The day of 17 February 1945 would be decisive. If the Soviet retort had been so quick and savage in the sky, we dared not lose another minute on the ground. Either we would exploit our half-success immediately and to the limit, or we would get a shock in return.

The German tanks which had attacked from Lake Madue had also achieved some progress. According to the plan of the offensive, the tanks from the northwest should have made their junction with the Reich's tanks coming from the southeast on the first evening. Thus all the Communist forces between the Ihna and Lake Madue would have been surrounded without having had the time to react.

In fact the partial success of the day before had been a failure, since the maneuver of encirclement had been telegraphed before completion. The enemy had had the whole night to set up a barrier in both directions.

The tardy attack would certainly be more difficult, but the game wasn't lost yet. The order to make the junction at whatever price was given to the units.

Dawn was breaking when the duel reached its apogee. Dozens of tanks were flaming on the battlefield. The Stukas were passing in great squadrons, then diving in front of us like arrows from the sky.

## Defeat

Normally the Soviet troops and equipment, threatened by the two enormous armed paws closing in behind them, must immediately have withdrawn from the Stargard pocket, which was already almost closed.

The Soviets' exit corridor had been cut in half the day before. It was now less than twenty kilometers wide at the maximum. These twenty kilometers would doubtless be cut off by the morning of the second day of the offensive.

Throughout the night our watchmen had strained their ears to catch any indications of an enemy retreat. The Soviet tanks that had been engaged at Kruessow as well as the heavy equipment would certainly go back under cover of darkness.

In fact, the nocturnal traffic was very heavy, but the noises that we heard indicated intentions which were the exact opposite of our expectations and our desires. The traffic was moving from the south toward the east. Instead of pulling out, the Soviets were bringing reinforcements into the near-*Kessel.*

They were going to reply to the German threat at their rear by threatening the Germans to their own rear. By the end of the night they attacked, with terrible violence, fifteen kilometers behind the assault divisions of the Reich. It was our unfortunate base at Lindenberg which would receive the hardest blow.

* * * * *

That was to be expected. Whoever held the ridges of Lindenberg held several of the region's lines of communication under control. The Reds, dislodged from this hill, must have been thinking that it would soon serve as a point of departure for a second attack, whose objective would be to slice up the *Kessel* once it had been closed off in the south.

The two adversaries were both running the very greatest risks as though for the pleasure of it: the attackers, in concentrating all their efforts on the southern extremity; and the defenders, in reinforcing to the east, right in the middle of a sector three-quarters surrounded.

This Soviet display would not have been displeasing to the German command had they felt certain of success. What they wanted was to destroy and capture a maximum of troops and equipment. At dawn the Soviet troops and equipment were still in the half-*Kessel,* to such a degree that we could see them driving down on us, thundering and screaming.

There was no question of giving up. Russians and Germans both gave their utmost throughout the day. The winner would be the one who could send forth the last tank and the last man.

The German Command of Stargard realized that the fate awaiting our hundred and seventy boys stuck on the Lindenberg ridge would be particularly cruel. There were no Panzers to back them up. All the tanks, all the anti-tank guns, and all the artillery were in the south. To bring back equipment for defensive operations on the flanks would be to reduce the chances of closing the *Kessel* and to play the enemy's game.

On 17 February I had by way of heavy weapons only two armored trains of the Luftwaffe. They couldn't go any farther to the south, for the railroad line was cut. They had been put at our service. They helped us very effectively, even though they were marked and plastered with hundreds of rockets by the "Stalin's organs." But they couldn't stop the inevitable.

The Soviet tanks hounded our comrades from every direction. At the end of a few hours it was impossible to supply them. Huge mud-holes stretched out behind them and on their flank. The rare practicable passageways were totally dominated by Stalin tanks. The morning's wounded were brought in only with great difficulty, dragged through the muck under a ceaseless machine-gun fire.

We tried to send reinforcements. Only half a dozen men were able to get past the barrage of Soviet fire. The rest were cut down or pinned in the swamps.

Lieutenant Capelle maintained a perfect calm. Every fifteen minutes he radioed a brief picture of the situation to us. The Soviet tanks were skillfully keeping out of range of the panzerfausts. They were pulverizing our positions meter by meter. There were a great many deaths, but the resistance of our comrades was incredible.

Capelle had received orders to stay on the ridge for twenty-four hours, the twenty-four hours that must decide the success or failure of the general operation of encirclement.

The Soviet tanks caused so much destruction that volunteers had to leave the marksmen's holes and crawl along out in the open, armed with panzerfausts, to face the enemy tanks.

One of our young officers gave a sublime example to the troops. Twice wounded and knowing himself lost, he preferred to sacrifice himself rather than to wait for death. He dragged himself, streaming with blood, right up to a Joseph Stalin and fired his panzerfaust, but the projectile didn't pierce the armor of the tank, which in turn blasted our hero down.

Come night, Capelle was holding unshakeably. Two enemy tanks had been hit. But the other tanks had crushed and occupied several of our positions.

In the south the German pincers had still not closed.

The Reich's Panzers had made some progress. But the Joseph Stalins were almost invulnerable.

One as big as a baobab tree, all by itself, stayed for an hour barring the way out of a conquered village. It took its stand right inside a building and no one managed to dislodge it.

The Stukas had to intervene. The whole road out of the village was bombed. Everyone was certain that this time the score had been settled with the Joseph Stalin. The cloud of dust fell back to earth. And what did we see? The ruins quivered, and the Stalin extricated itself and snorted. Covered with the debris of walls and roofs, it advanced along the route. We poured shells onto it. It continued on its way unharmed and disappeared into a grove to the south.

By night there were still four kilometers remaining to cross.

Only four kilometers.

But four kilometers just the same.

The German tanks took up the assault ten times, twenty times, coming from the east and from the west. The Soviet tanks, anti-tank guns, and infantry didn't yield an inch. We had to stop and once again put off the final skewering until the next day. The German tanks were not going to help.

The day of the eighteenth passed in desperate striving.

Instead of crossing the last four kilometers and finally closing the circle, the two German spearheads lost ground from dawn.

The enemy reinforcements had had enough time to hasten up. In forty-eight hours the Soviet tanks and anti-tank guns had arrived in force. They overwhelmed the exhausted Germans and pushed them out of several of the villages they had taken at great cost.

Not only did we have to give up the assault on Landsberg, but even the first phase of the attack, the initial *Kessel,* hadn't materialized. The vise was coming unscrewed. Henceforth the operation was doomed to failure.

* * * * *

On their muddy spur at Lindenberg, our unfortunate companions had grimly obeyed orders. Not one among them would have tolerated anybody's being able to say someday that they had failed to make the extreme sacrifice in order to allow their German comrades, struggling in the south, to have one more try.

Our wounded fought like the others, bleeding, but preferring to die in combat rather than be assassinated with blows from a rifle butt or spade.

Lieutenant Capelle still had seventy men. They were slaughtered where they stood from dawn until three o'clock in the afternoon. Capelle calmly notified us by radio of the last phases of the death agony. The Soviet tanks were everywhere. Little islands of men were fighting obstinately. Finally only the islet of the command post was left, surrounded by a screaming horde of butchers.

When the hand-to-hand combat was ended, Capelle, grievously wounded but still firing his revolver, stood up as best he could, facing the Reds who were driving down upon him. When they were one and a half meters straight ahead of him, he blew his brains out.

Four wounded men only, sunk up to their necks in the slime, watched the last minutes of the drama. They dragged themselves through the horrible mud during the night. Two of them died of exhaustion. The other two were found by a patrol, almost dead.

This total sacrifice by the Walloons at Lindenberg aroused great feelings among the German divisions of Pomerania. An order of the day praising their heroic act was read to the troops of the whole army. They were cited in the communique of the Main Headquarters.

Capelle was proposed for a posthumous Knight's Cross.

Modestly, obscurely, like the six hundred Franchimontois of Belgian history,[3] they let themselves be cut down where they stood for the honor of obeying and being faithful.

* * * * *

In the south the defeat proved irreparable. The last German attempt to re-establish the Eastern Front had failed. Nevertheless, we could always hope that the enemy's losses of equipment would slow his attack against Stargard.

This hope proved fallacious. The destroyed Soviet tanks were replaced by an even greater number of tanks. They would quickly overwhelm our muddy positions.

On the other hand the armored divisions of the Reich left as quickly as they had come. The plan to penetrate toward Landsberg having been abandoned, the trucks and tanks disappeared the following night. They were needed at Kuestrin. They left us with deep ruts, empty artillery emplacements, and a gaping menace to the south.

The German communique scarcely alluded to this failed offensive which had been the last hope of the Eastern Front. It was vaguely reported in a few lines like a local counterattack.

We resumed our former trenches. In our rear, the ravaged and mangled town of Stargard was as gloomy as a cemetery in ruins.

## The Flood

The only prize remaining from the German offensive of 16 February 1945 in the direction of Landsberg, from the procession of tanks, trucks, and cannon which we had witnessed for days, was the modest village of Brallentin and a few hamlets.

Practically speaking, the war had become untenable. In the west the great Ardennes-Alsace endeavor had failed. No other possibility of recouping was even envisaged on the western front. In the east the counteroffensive conceived by Himmler experienced an identical defeat. The definitive proof had been made that any project to cut off the Soviet forces was vain.

The Communists were ten times stronger than we in men, and especially in equipment. Henceforth, barring the use at the very last minute of a superweapon, the victory had been won by the Communists and their Anglo-American backers.

The Reich was now holding a tiger by the tail. The west had been emptied of troops. The east had been completely dismantled. A few armored divisions were still running about here and there from Stettin to Kuestrin and from Kuestrin to Dresden, risking everything. Apart from them, the front was no longer made up of anything but troops that had been bled white, knocked about every day, with no tanks or ammunition to speak of.

An extremely stringent telegraphic order forbade me, like all the division commanders of the Pomeranian front, to use more than six shells a day, or ten, depending on the caliber of the weapons. In the case of a Soviet attack our cannon would fire for a few minutes, and then would have to be silent until the next day.

The troops, cut to pieces by incredible machine-gun fire, had to endure the blows of enemy troops that were almost at full strength and surrounded by tanks five times, ten times, or twenty times as numerous as ours.

In every sector the duel was fought in the same conditions. A few hundred men, deprived of everything, exhausted, in the mud, had to face an avalanche of adversaries clambering on countless tanks, roaring, smashing, crushing everything in their way.

* * * * *

After the defeat of the last offensive, we found ourselves more alone than ever.

Our sector was shaped like a long fishbone. The tail was at Stargard, the head in the villages of Kremzow and Repplin in the south. Our left flank (east) was bordered by the main Ihna and the highway from Stargard to Schoeneberg. The right flank (west) was bounded by the Lazy Ihna, the villages of Strebelow, and the hamlet of Kollin.

Both these last towns had been pounded constantly since the ridges of Lindenberg had fallen back into the hands of the Soviets. The roofs were smashed in, the last animals dead in the stables.

The liaison roads were almost impassible. They were starred by hundreds of craters. We had to race our Volkswagens at ridiculous speeds when firing riddled the road.

The Reds were reinforcing more and more. We could see it. We could feel it, but we knew nothing precise. We hadn't taken a single prisoner in a week. The Reds, spurred on by their successes, well protected by their tank columns, had become uncatchable.

During the last weeks of the war in the East in 1945, we had to lose more soldiers to capture a Mongol than it took to conquer a province of the USSR in 1941, but each round-cheeked Mongol, each sallow Kalmuk, or each Siberian convict was indispensable to the command.

So it was we received orders from the army corps to mount a large-scale expedition in complete darkness in which two hundred of our men would be engaged with no other aim than to seize a single Red.

A large farm called Carlsburg, situated to the west of Strebelow, was assigned as our objective, a vast quadrilateral brick building with long stables and outbuildings where the enemy was strongly entrenched.

We were to take the Reds from behind and drive them out in hand-to-hand combat, losing ten or twenty men if necessary, in order that one or two dazed, shaggy prisoners, stinking like martens, might come and tell headquarters what plots were hatching across the way.

* * * * *

The operation took place one evening at nine o'clock. One part of our troops at Kollin got underway with the coming of darkness. They crawled through the marshes. West of Carlsburg, that is to say in the enemy's rear, they had to move in complete silence. By this time the rest of the forces participating in the assault would have completed a similar movement by way of the north.

Our anti-aircraft guns would first fire directly at the farm, with the aim of setting it on fire and panicking the enemy. Ten minutes before nine o'clock one of our companies, which was before Kruessow, started a diversionary operation.

The Walloons were without peers anywhere on the eastern front for these impossible strikes. They threw themselves at the enemy, as quick as cats. Success was almost inevitable.

At 2045 hours our anti-aircraft weapons opened fire on the Carlsburg horde. A barn caught fire. The wind was extremely strong that evening. The storehouses, which contained enormous quantities of wool, began to glow a fabulous red. The wind sent millions of golden sparks flying high into the sky.

Then our men charged from the north and west to drive the enemy toward our lines. He defended himself fanatically in the furnace. The bright bursts from the submachine guns could be seen flashing all around the buildings. Silhouettes were running, leaping, and falling.

At 9:45 a green flare went up, announcing that some prisoners had been taken and that our men were going to return to our lines.

We had suffered relatively high losses. Then again we could have taken nothing at all and seen our attacks break before the enemy position. Only the ardor of our men and their irresistible momentum had permitted us to bring it off. As well as a funny incident. Two Mongols, despite the fire, the noise of the anti-aircraft weapons, and the volleys of shots, were still soundly sleeping at their guard post in front of the farm. We had to wake them up to start them off toward our positions.

Carlsburg burned the whole night long, as a storm swept across the horizon.

* * * * *

I went to the commanding general of the Army Corps to deliver the prisoners he needed so badly. The interrogations were conclusive. They informed the German Command that the assault on the town of Stargard was ready and the blow would be struck mainly to the east of the Ihna.

The very next day in fact the Reds overwhelmed Brallentin and Repplin, which were defended by German and Dutch SS. They crossed the main Ihna and approached near Schoeneberg, about twenty kilometers southwest of Stargard.

How could the front have held, deprived of any heavy defense? Scheoneberg fell. A few German Panzers, lost in this thirty kilometer breach, tried in vain to stem the flood. It poured through. The Soviet tanks ripped open the entire sector to the east of our positions and set off on the Schoeneberg-Stargard highway as if they were at an auto rallye.

We were separated from them only by the main Ihna and a gentle slope. The muddy enemy tanks deployed themselves before our eyes and reached the same height as our command post, one after another.

From the second day, the fight was waged behind us. We had to turn back toward the northwest to follow the progress of the Soviet tanks. Our fortifications at Kollin, in the southwestern corner, had held out despite the storm. The battered village, the deserted streets strewn with heaps of debris smelled of disaster and death. But our men hadn't let themselves be pushed out of the demolished houses, nor from their machine-gun nests.

All the same, it was wishful to think we might be able to retrieve the situation. We received orders to evacuate Kollin and Strebelow and to bring the forces from behind these villages back to Kremzow, the bridgehead which protected the second Stargard road.

I put the defense of the position into the hands of one of our most popular veterans of the Donets and the Caucasus, Commander Jules Mathieu. Against all odds he held out with his regiment in this large town, so severely choked off.

The enemy wanted to go around Kremzow by way of the fields to the west. We dug our positions there in great haste, completely out in the open. Ten times they were overrun, broken up, and sliced to pieces. Ten times they were retaken in hand-to-hand fighting. Corpses were lying everywhere in the mire, shapeless and heavy as lead.

Only tanks could have relieved us.

I finally arranged with the Army Corps that four German Panzers—four! —would come to lend a hand. We had to furnish all the gas we still had left beforehand. They were scarcely in position at Kremzow when two were taken away again. The other two had four shells apiece.

As it happened they didn't have occasion to use them, as they too were recalled, along with their meager ammunition, leaving us to manage on our own.

They were withdrawn because the gap on the Schoeneberg road was hourly becoming more dangerous. Everything was falling apart. From our command post, we didn't miss a single detail of the show. The Soviet tanks were advancing past some houses and a cemetery.

When they were several kilometers beyond our sector we were given the order to abandon Kremzow and to more or less align ourselves. Illusory alignment. . . . For not only were the Soviet tanks thundering in our rear, but shots also were crackling. The infantry accompanying the enemy tanks had just crossed the main Ihna by night.

There was hardly any more doubt that we would be surrounded in a very short time.

## Stargard in the Hands of the Soviets

Saturday, 3 March 1945 saw the collapse of Stargard. Between the ancient Pomeranian city and our makeshift line there was nothing left but a large village, Vittichow, and the crossroads at Klutzow, where a sugar factory stood.

Two weeks earlier the courtyards and storehouses of this factory had been swarming with German tanks that were there for the offensive. Now it was just an empty space, crossed only by my little Volkswagen, racing from one place to another according to the situation.

That morning the enemy tanks started off toward the southeastern suburbs of Stargard. The Soviet infantry crossed the Ihna a second time, very close to the city, and cut off the gravel road to Vittichow in our rear.

I sent a company immediately. Too late. The road was lost. Bullets by the hundreds whistled about us. One of them passed through the collar of my overcoat and grazed my neck. Everywhere we fought in close combat.

Our men's faces were gray and lined with exhaustion and worry. They machine-gunned the enemy, braced against the sticky banks or the gravel of the road or half buried in the musty-smelling yellow and gray beetroot silos.

The enemy swarmed out of the mud wallows by the hundreds, like clouds of croaking brown and violet amphibians.

The soul of the resistance at Vittichow was a former officer of the Belgian Army, Major Hellebaut, then head of the staff office of our division, brave and totally dedicated.

Son and grandson of two Belgian generals who were both Ministers of War, he wore the Military Cross, which he had won at the Yser in 1918, beside the Iron Cross First Class on his grey uniform.

Inspired by his bravery, our soldiers to the south of Vittichow didn't flinch, although they were only eight kilometers away from the walls of Stargard, which the enemy tanks had been battering since morning. The last ones left in the southern and southeastern sector, they clung to the terrain, which was totally overrun to the east and incessantly threatened in the southwest.

Stoically the companies endured extermination, one by one. Hit in the belly by an exploding grenade, the second provost of the Rexist Youth suffered in the mud. He was 2nd Lieutenant Paul Mezetta, poet, passionate soul who gave of himself like a true knight and who, despite terrible wounds received in the Caucasus, had again wanted to take his place in the fight.

Of the Dierickx Battalion, barely a hundred men were left in all. They cursed, fired, counterattacked, rolled in the bloody muck with the Kirghiz and the Mongols. Nothing could make them give in.

* * * * *

From the noises of tank combat, we realized that the Reds must be fighting now at the very gates of Stargard.

Our situation was unbelievable. Here we were, an isolated defensive unit in the south, under a more and more direct threat of encirclement, and we hadn't received any information or any orders from the division command post since the beginning of the afternoon.

Five o'clock came. We could hardly fail to fall into the hands of the Soviets. I couldn't imagine that we would be abandoned this way. I jumped into my Volkswagen to go find the general.

Never imagining for a single minute that everything was over, I entered Stargard. I had just the time to jerk my steering wheel around and race for the suburbs. Soviet tanks had just forced their way into the streets. Clusters of dead women lay amid their suitcases near the station bridge, mowed down by the tank fire. To the northwest of the city the Soviet tanks were arrayed in battle formation on both sides of the Stettin road.

I learned at Army Corps, several kilometers from there, that the Stargard headquarters, to which we were subordinate, had been submerged by the enemy wave during the afternoon. The general had disappeared as though into thin air. Corps had sent us late orders to withdraw, but the motorcyclist must have been kidnapped on the way.

I dashed back across the countryside in the direction of Vittichow. I was lucky enough to locate one of our telephone wires. I cut in, hooked up a portable phone, and was thus able to direct the retreat of my forces in time.

Starting from the southwest, they would perform a huge circular movement by the west and northwest along Lake Madue in order to escape the enemy grasp. From there they would turn back in the direction of Stargard and take up positions to the northwest of the city.

Worn out by these ten days and nights of fighting, the poor fellows would have to march twenty-five kilometers in the darkness, through sticky mud or quicksand, threatened with being cut off or caught by the stalking enemy at any minute.

* * * * *

One of the platoons, which had struggled with the sandy Vittichow road until nightfall, hadn't quite understood the verbal order or realized the situation. Preferring to take a shortcut, they naively headed for Stargard itself, just as I had done at the end of the afternoon. They marched in ranks, their weapons on their shoulder straps, through the town, which had been in the hands of the Soviets for several hours.

It was rainy, and the darkness was opaque. Red soldiers were posted above the railroad bridge. They took our men for Soviet troops. Ours took them for Germans. They went through the entire city and out again on the northwest without anyone's questioning them. Then they saw the line of flames from the enemy tanks' exhaust. They went around them by compass bearings through the black fields of mud.

* * * * *

I arrived in our new sector at nine o'clock in the evening to find the whole region in a state of anarchy. Two battalions of the Todt Corps, sent to the site to construct a new line, fell back, violently agitated. "The Russians are here! The Russians are here!" the shovelers cried at the top of their lungs.

A German Panzer, returning from the east, had been taken for a Soviet tank. It was the target of massive firing. Getting information was very complicated. The Soviets must indeed have overrun a wide area northwest of Stargard.

I had two men with me in all, plus a motorcycle messenger. I set up my command post according to the orders I had received and posted my motorcyclist on the deserted route three kilometers before the village so that he could hide, belly to the ground, and notify me of the arrival of any enemy tanks.

At dawn the road was still deserted. Our men were arriving from the west in unrecognizable groups, filthy from head to toe, swaying like metronomes, no longer knowing anything or understanding anything. Army Corps insisted that I put them in position within the hour.

I might just as well have lined up pebbles atop the knolls.

These men weren't capable of fighting even for a minute any more. I settled them in the empty farms. "Eat, drink, sleep, and don't worry!" Soon the entire legion was snoring, sounding like a squadron of Junkers. I placed several non-commissioned officers facing the southeast as a symbolic measure.

The enemy must have been dead-tired too, since until nightfall nothing moved.

The next day at eight o'clock in the morning, I pushed our men toward their watch posts somewhat refreshed. They didn't have any time to grow bored. A wave of fifteen Soviet tanks, then another twenty-one, stormed down upon us.

## Pursued by the Tanks

On 5 March 1945 we were thus still on the Ihna. Instead of being south of Stargard on the muddy moor that separated the two arms of the river, we were now posted to the north of the lost city astride the reunited Ihna. A chilly sunshine had returned.

Two villages, Luebow and Saarow, faced each other on either side of the water. The left bank, partially tree-covered, dominated the river. The right bank was bare. Only a railroad embankment beyond the houses of Luebow cut the monotony of the brown, gently rolling land.

The first wave of Soviet tanks appeared at the threshold of this town. I was in the process of checking our positions at Saarow when all hell broke out. We had only a skeleton battalion on each bank. There was not a single German tank in our sector.

The fifteen big enemy tanks immediately charged across Luebow. Our men defended themselves from house to house. A hundred meters away from them on the other side of the water, I had all our mortars at Saarow start firing to contain the Soviet infantry which followed the tanks.

After half an hour our men had been thrown back into the plain beyond the farms. We could see them running, trying to reach the railroad embankment to organize a new line of resistance. But the tank shells blasted the terrain all around them. Two or three men would be left behind every time, green splotches stretched out on the reddish earth.

Some other Walloons, cornered at the edge of the water, embarked as a last resort in some washerwomen's tubs. Their improvised flotilla managed to come ashore on our side.

* * * * *

Now twenty-one Soviet tanks suddenly appeared at the entry to Saarow. In the time it took to watch the walls tumbling down around us, the monsters were in the center of town.

One of our men, hidden in the partially open door of the church, saved the situation for a few seconds by blowing up the lead tank with a panzerfaust.

But what could we do? Only those who lived through those frightful weeks at the end of the war in the East can imagine the butchery that took place. There wasn't any more armored equipment worth talking about. Our Army Corps, the 3rd Panzer Corps, once famous for its hundreds of tanks, had thirty and would end up with only a dozen. Day and night these few Panzers had to cover a sector of more than seventy kilometers.

In contrast, the Soviets were preceded by four thousand tanks on the Pomeranian front alone. That Monday, just for our two hamlets, thirty-six came. And to stop them, nothing—nothing, that is, except panzerfausts and human chests.

Panzerfaust duels are all very well in the movies. In actual fact, however, successes are rare. You have to wait until the tank is at point-blank range before pulling the trigger.

If the tank is alone and the projectile hits it by chance at a vital spot, it's perfect, but often the tank doesn't blow up.

Besides, tanks almost always come in waves and sweep the terrain beforehand. The five-meter-long flame betrays the presence of the marksman. Even if he gets one tank, another tank will machine-gun him into little bits half a minute later.

Every unit had magnificent heroes who struck down Soviet tanks with panzerfausts up until the last day. They had to, for we no longer had anything else. But the man who risked himself at this duel was almost certain to die.

* * * * *

The orders were of a draconian severity. They took no account of any sentimental, psychological, or political considerations. All that counted was the brutal fact: hold out.

We couldn't give in. Even if we were overrun from every direction we had to hold the field, cling to it, get massacred. A general who gave ground was demoted or even arrested. In one month of battle in Pomerania the command was changed eighteen times.

Commanders of armies, army corps, and divisions flew through the air like tennis balls. We ended up losing our bearings, no longer knowing whom to depend on. But every general, feeling the instability of his position, sent implacable orders, whether they were feasible or not.

My battalion at Luebow, chased by tanks and half exterminated, was blockaded on the right bank of the Ihna. I had no more than a hundred and fifty men who had retreated from Saarow and not a single tank in support.

My command post was in a village immediately to the northwest of the two invaded towns. This village was indefensible with the handful of soldiers I had left. The orders nevertheless were to defend it.

The plain was littered with our wounded. We watched their slaughter, livid with sorrow and fury. The Soviet footsoldiers advanced between the tanks and smashed in the heads of our unfortunate comrades with trench shovels. One of them waved a white handkerchief above his head in vain. He had his face bashed in like the others by the slaughterers.

There were still a few German cannon in my sector. I put them in position at the entry to the village and, according to my old custom, ordered them to wait until the very last minute to unleash their fire at point-blank range into the enemy tanks.

Under this tornado of iron, the Reds' tanks scurried back to cover in an oak grove and started pounding the town. The houses fell in on my staff officers and telephone operators.

Our men built a makeshift barrier at the southeastern entry to the village. Their morale was unbelievable, despite the gravity of their condition. They kidded one another and joked when I sent them all the sluggards in the area, whatever their nationality. They adopted them and shared them among themselves.

I regularly informed the new staff officer of the march of events. He was a rather cunning man to whom we had just been linked—probably for a few hours. He jealously hung on to the twelve tanks allocated to the southeastern and southern sector. He gratified us with magnificent and categorical assurances over the field telephone: "There are no more Soviet tanks across from us. Everything is fine."

But while he was talking I could see our wounded men with my own eyes being pursued ferociously by tank shells. They threw themselves onto the ground and tried to crawl, but the shelling wouldn't let up. If the enemy could waste so much ammunition at these cruel games, what would happen later?

To the staff officer in question I sent one of my young aides-de-camp, the severely disabled and very sharp-witted Lieutenant Tony Gombert. Theoretically he was to serve as liaison agent, but in fact he would mainly listen and keep his eyes open.

As I was receiving a telephone message that we didn't have to worry, the German observation planes had just notified the staff officer that a column of forty-one tanks was rumbling toward us.

Forty-one! Our officer jumped onto his motorcycle and hurried to warn me. But we were already fighting amidst the rubble of fallen houses. The tanks were on us from all sides.

We had just been overwhelmed by another surprise. Trying to establish liaison with our right wing, one of our patrols had found nothing left but an empty space. Our neighbors had vanished. The Reds were breaking through this gap in the southwestern front.

To the east, our left wing, too, had been completely overrun by a battalion of Soviet infantry which had crossed the Ihna River fairly far behind our line at the fall of night.

It was in these conditions that we received the rumbling mass of the forty-one enemy tanks. In ten minutes they had broken our barrier in twenty places. Split into lots of small groups, our men fired their last panzerfausts while trying to reach the western part of the forest amid the firing.

The Reds charged through the streets of the town. On the telephone, the staff officer kept endlessly repeating, "You are responsible for the village! You've got to hold on!"

With the coming of darkness we witnessed an amazing spectacle. The Soviet tanks switched on headlights, just like cars on the highways before the war. They started straight for the forest to which the German artillery batteries had fallen back several hours earlier.

The enemy conducted a demons' dance in the village. They had occupied all the farms. There was only fifteen of us left. We were clinging to the northern exit of the village at the edge of the woods. Somehow I managed to save my telephone.

I called amid the ruckus. "The Soviet infantry is flooding in from every direction. The front has broken completely. Believe it or not, but there are forty-one tanks here, and we have only one cannon left to bar entry to the forest. The tanks are going to come through whenever they like. Do you realize this?"

The only words I got in reply were, "Hold on!"

Hold on! And stop forty-one heavy tanks with a puff of air!

* * * * *

At eight o'clock in the evening there were still four of us. My telephone, too, had just died. All contact had been completely cut off.

Several tanks rushed at us to be first across the barrier to the forest road. We sacrificed the last panzerfaust we had left. We were hit right back. A shell felled one of my survivors and wounded another.

I had to make every effort to regroup my soldiers, who had been driven under the pines. My driver dragged the wounded man and the dead one to my Volkswagen, which was hidden in a copse. I rejoined them, firing as I came. Through the forest, crackling with gunfire, we reached a village in a large clearing five kilometers to the northwest.

We didn't see any military post at any of the anti-tank barriers along the route. There were no defenders, nothing to block the gaps.

The village extended one or two kilometers in length. It was full of the field-hospital and staff equipment of units which had been dispersed or wiped out. No one seemed to be the least bit worried.

At each farm everybody ate with an excellent appetite. The soup was steaming on the table. I still wanted to hope that the Soviet tanks wouldn't undertake the crossing of this vast unknown forest in the middle of the night.

Outside, snow had begun to fall in thick flakes. What was happening to my soldiers? How would they escape the hunters? Would they reach the town of Augustenwalde, on the other side of the forest, in time? I had given orders to my officers to regroup their men there if we were cut off by the tanks in the darkness. I imagined them stealing through the maze of fir trees, several dozen kilometers deep, by compass bearings.

Then I saw the tanks again in my mind with their enormous headlights. Where were they?

## Augustenwalde

It was 11 P.M. The battle was making a tremendous racket, but it was hardly the first busy night we had ever had.

We wanted to rest for a few hours before reaching Augustenwalde at dawn, then Altdamm, where according to the orders I had just received from Army Corps, we were to re-form the debris of our division.

Snow fell thicker and thicker. The driver came in several times to say that bullets were bouncing off the wall.

Suddenly a frightful rumbling broke out right near our house. How well we knew this roar! Only tanks made these short raucous clatters. I leaped to the door. At the road into the village flames were spurting like red tongues from the muzzles. The tanks had already crossed the five kilometers of forest.

Nocturnal floral bouquets could be seen sprouting everywhere. The country was in flames. Hundreds of trucks were rushing in both directions. A German transport column coming from the highway was advancing straight into the enemy tanks. Another column was trying desperately to go against the stream of traffic. The road was narrow. Bullets were slamming or richocheting against the walls or the metal panels of the trucks. The lights from fires and explosions made it almost as bright as day.

The whole caravan was going to be cut to pieces, there wasn't a shadow of a doubt. The Soviet tanks were driving right into us. Terrible screams arose.

We managed to push my battered Volkswagen into the snowy fields. Rolling through everything, we reached the highway before the Soviets. Behind us was nothing but red torches, screams, the crash of Soviet tank fire, and explosions. What kind of opposition could there be from this confused horde of doctors, truckers, mess orderlies, and clerks, all running about helter-skelter in the night?

The big trucks from Army Corps Headquarters had felt which way the wind was blowing and disappeared a quarter of an hour earlier. The rest were hopelessly lost. I wouldn't have given a red cent for the hundreds of vehicles piled up in the basin with the Soviet tanks pouring in on them furiously.

The procession of woe spread out on the highway, more and more horrible. Tens of thousands of women and children had come to a standstill in their small carts, covered with fresh snow. Haggard, some watched the flaming sky. They were waiting. The enemy tanks were going to overtake them, but they seemed no longer to understand. Their eyes were empty. The horses, their eyes half-closed, stood still.

I lay down in an abandoned house a few kilometers away amidst an inchoate swarm of soldiers. At dawn I went back as far as I could toward the enemy in order to help any of my soldiers who might have had an accident. Everything was quiet on the highway. Surely the Soviets must have turned aside and continued their advance by a shortcut through the forest.

But the forest paths were certainly impassable. I had a hard time imagining that tanks would have dared to advance under the trees along narrow, sandy paths that a few anti-tank guns could block off.

The Soviet tanks had to be somewhere, however, and they weren't on the highway.

At ten o'clock in the morning I arrived at Augustenwalde. This large village was at the northwestern extremity of the forest about a dozen kilometers east of Stettin. It seemed so well protected by the woods that the officers from Army Corps had withdrawn to it the preceding evening.

I stopped by the general's. His chief of staff, Colonel von Bockelsberg, made despairing signs to me as he hunched over his telephone. As he received the reports he pointed out on the map, "Twenty tanks here! Fifteen tanks here! Thirty tanks here!" He wiped his forehead for a minute. "They're everywhere, they're coming from everywhere."

Since the Dnieper, we were familiar with days when everything falls apart. The Army Corps trucks were there, so it wasn't particularly catastrophic. I regrouped part of our men and their officers in the village. Poultry, carefully trussed, was already stewing in the best military tradition. We cheerfully set ourselves to its enjoyment.

* * * * *

A few bullets bounced off the building's facade.

Another broke a windowpane and landed in the partition. "They're killing chickens," Major Hellebaut remarked imperturbably.

Thirty or forty bullets later I added: "I think they're killing a lot of chickens."

Everyone went on chewing.

Now volleys of shells shook the whole building.

I pressed my point. "They're even killing the chickens with tanks." And I passed my neighbor a platter of delicious fruits taken from a jar found in the fugitive proprietor's cellar.

I looked outside. Men were running about everywhere. We went to the doorstep where we saw a phenomenal uproar. The big Army Corps radio trucks were leaving without even taking down their ten-meter-high aerials. People were shooting every which way. Soldiers yelled to us as they passed, "They're here! There are forty tanks!"

To tell the truth, they had run right through the forest. The Soviet tanks hadn't met a single obstacle across thirty kilometers.

As quick as squirrels our men leaped onto the trucks of the army corps. The enemy had already reached the station to the southwest. They were sweeping the road on which all the equipment stored at Augustenwalde was being rushed up. The automobiles kept stopping suddenly, throwing the staff officers clinging to the roofs headfirst into the muddy snow.

It was impossible to improvise a resistance. There wasn't a German tank, anti-tank, or anti-aircraft gun around. The whole region had been overrun. The Augustenwalde-Stettin road itself had been cut. We had to go south to the Stargard road. From there we went to Altdamm, where the greater part of our soldiers were waiting for us.

The retreat was skillfully accomplished. Few were lost in the course of the night.

Our division was in a lamentable state. Already at Stargard our two infantry regiments had had to be combined. Now the two battalions of this combined regiment didn't number more than about four hundred men. Many officers had been killed. Not one company was still operative.

The enemy had achieved an impressive breakthrough. Now it would take a few days before their equipment could cross the forest. Counterattacks were starting from Altdamm. Thus, there would be a little respite.

I obtained a week to reorganize my crippled forces and amalgamate them with the reinforcements that had just arrived at the Stettin station. I wanted to keep only the tough ones with me. I assembled all the men and thanked them for their magnificent conduct. Bluntly I told them of the situation and the grave combats still awaiting them. "Everyone is free either to return to the firing line or to stay with a safer company." All had come to the Legion as volunteers. There was almost no hope left. I wasn't going to accept their blood unless it was offered freely. It would not be said that in the final struggle a single Walloon fell against his wish.

Eighty men preferred not to return to combat. I treated them with as much affection as before. I wasn't a slave trader. Besides, most of these boys were at the end of their strength. I had them lodged and fed with care thirty kilometers northwest of the Oder.

With the other six hundred, the survivors of this terrible month and the newcomers, I re-formed an assault battalion. Before dawn on the sixth day we started off, singing, toward the docks and bridges of Stettin.

The commander of this battalion of heroes was Major Dierickx, an extraordinary man who had come from the virgin forest of the Congo to the snows of the steppe. His kepi on the nape of the neck, after the fashion of the pioneers, he was the bravest of the brave, a kind of "Captain Conan"[4] by way of Katanga. He had the heart of a child and gave his loyalty with a sincerity and emotion which often brought tears to his eyes.

The front where I led his battalion had shrunk singularly in the last week.

The front guarded part of the Stettiner Haff northeast of Stettin, running along the highway west of Augustenwalde, covering Altdamm and extending beyond the big concrete bridge of the autobahn.

We took position in about the center of the front before Finkenwalde, a long cluster of houses which prolonged the suburbs of Altdamm toward the south.

The enemy occupied numerous ridges on the right bank of the Oder, overlooking our line. They had set up more than a thousand pieces of artillery there, which crushed the positions, the houses, and the streets of Altdamm and Finkenwalde, as well as the three bridges, with a continuous fire. Never since 1941 had we witnessed such a pounding.

## The Bridge of Stettin

In mid-March 1945 life had become absolutely untenable at the bridgehead of Stettin on the right bank of the Oder. The houses of Altdamm and Finkenwalde had collapsed and crumbled all over the streets. The poles for the tramway lines had fallen. The trees were hacked to pieces or lopped off to mere stalks. We were stopped by shell-holes everywhere. The Soviet artillery pounded every street and followed our every move.

To get to our positions we had to cross the airfield, where there was nothing left but the blackened carcasses of planes. We could still climb a staircase littered with broken glass to the terrace of the terminal building, from which we could look out over an incredible panorama. We could see each of the Red tanks lined up at the edge of the woods to the east, each of the enemy batteries perched on the ridges.

The European forces no longer occupied any of the area north of Altdamm at the highway bridge except for a long ribbon of terrain only three or four kilometers wide. The Reds attacked frantically in order to cut us off and push us into the Oder.

Even at night contact with the troops was practically impossible due to the thousands of falling shells. Every company command post, quickly spotted by all the coming and going, was the object of an unbelievable pounding. The streets were strewn with the bodies of soldiers.

The orders were incredibly strict. Runaways were hanged on the spot. They were strung up at the entry to the bridge joining Altdamm and Stettin by the *Feldgendarmes.*

It was horrible to see the stiffened corpses of these handsome German boys who, physically crushed by these weeks of horror, had had a momentary weakness. Their bodies dangled with a placard around their necks saying: "Coward." Pallid, their tongues hard and blue, they did a sinister dance at the end of their ropes, shaken by the innumerable explosions which brought down the cables of the tramway lines on them.

Every soldier knew what was waiting for him if he balked. It was better to stay out in front under the machine-gun fire and amid the roaring of the tanks.

* * * * *

The losses were frightening. In three days, sixty percent of the defenders of our sector were killed or wounded. Entrenched in their foxholes with only the head and arms protruding, they would be wounded, most likely in the face, by the bursts of shells and grenades.

They would run up to my little post with a monstrous bloody hole instead of a jawbone. Often their tongues would still be panting, feverishly pink and hanging from the wound.

Twenty-five or thirty wounded would arrive at once. Some who had been hit while running had steel shrapnel buried in their sexual organs. They shivered horribly, their complexions blue.

I still had to command and see to everything, amid the smells of coagulated blood and smeared excrement among all the sweaty linens.

The shelters were flattened one by one. On the very first day, my command post was hit head on and reduced to dust only two minutes after I had left it. The freezing cellar at Finkenwalde where I passed the last night directing the combat by the light of a candle was hit by a shell which went right through the ceiling and landed in the middle of the onlookers without exploding.

I hurried to our little forward posts, for at one o'clock in the morning the Soviets had just broken the line on our right wing. Our men were fighting admirably, clinging to the bank of the railroad line. They wouldn't give up. Three German tanks of a very old model, but operated by heroic crews, hurried along beside us. Only the muzzle of their cannon protruded above the bank. In half an hour they demolished five of the Soviet tanks which had come from the other side of the railway line. A person could have shouted from one tank to another. We were utterly blinded by the silver lights of the muzzle flash.

* * * * *

At the end of that night the general who commanded the defense assigned me another cellar in Finkenwalde as a command post, closer to his, but situated right at the southern end of the Walloon positions. Nose to nose with the Reds, I would have lots of complications making contact with my other company command posts.

I immediately sent messengers to find a staff office, telephone operators, and a radio. Bullets were coming from every direction. First I saw the autobahn bridge blow up. Then the Soviets stole through Finkenwalde to my right. They got as far as the Oder. Their machine guns, their anti-tank guns, and their tanks were holding our line of retreat under their fire.

The general who had his post five hundred meters behind mine an hour earlier was no longer exhibiting any signs of life. He was no longer answering his telephone. I was left alone and inoperative, wondering what was going on. I stuck to my orders, but they very nearly cost me my life.

I was saved at the last minute only by the presence of mind of a Flemish motorcyclist. Passing the general, who was withdrawing, he boldly reminded him that I still had to man my outpost. The general exclaimed loudly. He had forgotten me in all the tumult. The motorcyclist pushed back through it all and took me up behind him. Numerous German soldiers were lying face down in the sand on the little road, shot down as they withdrew. Under machine gun and cannon fire from the tanks, we reached the general's refuge in the nick of time to learn that he had just been relieved of his command.

* * * * *

That morning it seemed that all was lost. Nevertheless we received orders from our new chief to hold on to the remaining terrain.

He was wise. A massive withdrawal under an open sky and under that kind of pounding would only have brought on a massacre. The commander's posts were all to remain on the right bank. The general himself remained there.

The railroad bridge blew up in its turn. Now only the bridge to the city of Stettin itself was left. The Soviet artillery blasted it and swept it without letup. Shells ricocheted on the road across the bridge. Others sent up enormous sprays around the arches or shook the hanged men as if they were mannequins.

The Soviet air force plastered us with hundreds of bombs. The squadrons dove, come back, and grazed the roofs. Whole sides of buildings collapsed. Behind us the Red Cross field post caved in. The horrible screams of the wounded, who had been buried alive, rose from the heaps of rubble.

At the crest of the Finkenwalde railway line our soldiers, supported by several tanks, were holding out with a heroism comparable to that of their German comrades clinging to the ruins of Altdamm.

As always when the game was desperate, the Walloons distinguished themselves by their determination and their good humor. They stole past the sheds in the enemy sector. Some had been taken prisoner, taken by the Communists to some wooded hills. They took advantage of a violent bombardment by the German artillery to get away. They all made it back to our lines, all except one who was killed on the way.

The NCO's gave the most extraordinary examples.

We had a pale and slender young officer in the Dierickx Battalion, Lieutenant Leroy, from Binche, a volunteer at sixteen years old, who had lost his right arm and his left eye a year earlier at the time of the Cherkassy combats. He had absolutely insisted on coming back to the anti-Soviet front. He fulfilled the functions of liaison officer. The presence of this severely disabled soldier among the troops was as moving as could be.

One of Leroy's brothers was a platoon leader. He was killed on the bank at Finkenwalde three days before the end of the battle of Oder. Our young amputee, instead of letting himself be overwhelmed with grief, immediately asked to take the place of the dead man. I accepted. And we saw the admirable spectable of this terribly disabled man, his torso all twisted, fighting hand-to-hand battles for three days and three nights, shooting a submachine gun which he handled quite skillfully with his left hand.

One of our Belgian nurses, an admirable widow, had her three sons on combat duty. They all died with equal heroism. The mother, stabbed by such sorrow, never for an instant accepted the idea of abandoning her work. On the contrary, wanting to dedicate herself on the very spot where her boys had fallen, she begged me to let her carry on her apostolate in the front lines. In the hurricane of machine-gun fire, she helped our wounded with such extraordinary courage that she earned the Iron Cross.

* * * * *

The tenacity of our men was such that when the right bank of the Oder was evacuated it was the Wallonian volunteers who had the honor of ensuring the safety of Finkenwalde during the last night. They had to hold on three hours after everyone else along the railroad embankment, while the three divisions withdrew. These divisions no longer numbered more than a thousand men in all.

The struggle for Stargard and the Oder had lasted five weeks. During those thirty-five days the Reds had had to launch a hundred attacks, lose an enormous amount of equipment, and sacrifice more than four hundred tanks in order to cross the thirty-five kilometers which separated them from Stettin.

The night of the retreat was especially pathetic. Helped by two tanks, our volunteers feigned a particularly aggressive action. The counterbatteries of the Reich sent a hurricane of shells into the enemy from the left bank of the river.

Under this protection the survivors of the three divisions, with all their equipment and all their weapons, slipped toward the Oder and reached the first bridge in silence. They took up their positions on the other side of the water, hidden among the enormous wooden storehouses which covered the first peninsula.

Lighted by the fires, the eight- or ten-story concrete docks of the great port were still standing, studded in vain by Soviet shell holes. In their dusky cellars, where the command post was set up, thousands of Russian and Polish civilians were sprawled on old rucksacks, men and women all jumbled together.

The Oder divided into five arms upon entering Stettin. Only the bridge over the first arm, the widest, was going to be blown up at the end of the night.

At 3:00 A.M. every unit was in place in its new sector. Our last platoon of volunteers, who until that moment had maintained contact three kilometers beyond the river, climbed onto the two tanks which had stayed shoulder-to-shoulder with them until the last, and disengaged at top speed. They burst across the great steel bridge, which fell into the seething water behind them with a terrible crash.

* * * * *

It was dawn. Nearby the sturdy rust-colored hulls of large ships which had been burned were lying in dry-dock. On the other side of the gulf, several lovely brick clock towers were still standing in Altdamm. Clouds of smoke were rising.

Some German latecomers who had slept in the ruins of Finkenwalde and didn't know about the retreat showed up on the other bank, shouting loudly. The Soviets were following close behind them. They threw themselves into the water. Some managed to swim over to us, but the others were swept away by the current.

We could see the Reds approach the Oder in little groups, as though they were afraid of an ambush. Nevertheless the battle was all over. A few hours later the artillery on both sides ceased fire. It was sunny.

The Haff brought us the aroma of the sea.

At the entry to the bridge, three hanged men that the explosion hadn't dislodged were still outlined at the end of their steel beams, green and sinister in the glaring light.

Between the enemy and us, they alone remained, with their white placards, their glazed eyes, and their distorted, bloated purple tongues.

# Chapter Ten
# THE AGONY OF THE BALTIC

The end of March 1945 saw the final break-up of the Western Front.

At that time the divisions in Pomerania were re-forming between Stettin and Pasewalk, sheltered by the Oder, a mass of mighty waters already stirred by the tides. The two armies were temporarily still.

We listened to the radio with growing anxiety. The Rhineland had fallen; the Rhine had been crossed; the Ruhr had been overrun; the American tanks were driving toward Kassel.

We still had numerous Walloon soldiers in Hanover, recruits under instruction and convalescent wounded. Moreover, seven hundred men from our artillery regiment and two hundred men from our battalion of engineers under instruction in the Prague area had apparently been set en route toward our depot.

I wanted to gather all these men together promptly. I left my men to rest and hurried to look over our base in Hanover. I didn't find the region in much of a fever.

The coming of the Allies seemed to the population to be only a distant possibility about which, furthermore, it would have been indecent to speak. The *Kreisleiter* of Springen was tranquilly preparing for his marriage, set for Saturday, 31 March. But on the 29th the American tanks made a spring of a hundred and ten kilometers. That evening they were forty kilometers from the Weser. Another leap and they would be hammering the streets of the villages of Hanover.

At Gronau, an industrial city where our regimental barracks was located, it proved impossible to evacuate our wounded. I took it on myself to demobilize all the convalescents without delay.

From there I hurried southward near Holzminden where, on an order from the Kommandantur of Hanover, two hundred young Walloon recruits had been put in position armed with panzerfausts. These boys had enlisted to fight against Communism and didn't have to be sent out to meet the Americans.

Their withdrawal was decided only after an entire day of discussion. I was able to put them on the train which at the very last minute had just brought my two hundred engineers and my seven hundred artillery men into the Gronau station. I immediately dispatched the complete convoy to Stettin.

Already the roar of the Allied tanks, trying to force a passage over the Weser, could be heard. We could no longer expect the Reich to hold out in the West.

Between the Americans and Berlin everything was totally deserted. The front had vanished. Nothing came out to meet the Yankees any longer. The highways were empty.

On the other hand, the Eastern Front would be defended right up to the very end. The German High Command had decided to fight there with grim resolution.

I hastily rejoined my soldiers near Stettin. The Oder glistened in the sun like a great sleeping serpent. The front was quiet. The farms had been evacuated. The game ran in the beautiful brown fields. The air was soft and warm, filled with the songs of birds.

The death struggle was approaching in a moist perfume of China asters, cowslips, and ranunculi.

The Allied tanks flooded Bavaria at the beginning of April, 1945. They reached the Elbe and turned up toward Bremen and Hamburg.

Across from us the Red Army lay low. The battle of Pomerania had cost the Soviets dearly. They had had to take all their men out of the Kuestrin sector to the south of Stargard at the time of the German counteroffensive in mid-February, 1945. For five weeks they had waged very hard battles to dig us out and take the right bank of the Oder around Altdamm. At present they were licking their wounds and getting their equipment ready for action.

Stettin had been organized as an autonomous bridgehead eighteen battalions strong. The 3rd Germanic Corps, to which we belonged, had been given the Penkun region as its zone of action. The sector that we would have to defend was as always far too long.

But the High Command hadn't given up daydreaming. In mid-April, 1945, three weeks before the capitulation, Colonel-General Steiner announced the complete reorganization of my division. I was going to receive as reinforcements an artillery regiment and an infantry regiment appropriated from German units. My division would attain its maximum strength.

Furthermore it had been decided for the near future to form an Army Corps, the "Occident," comprising the Charlemagne (France), Wallonia, and Flanders divisions. I would receive the general command.

I remained skeptical. I liked to stick to realities. With my survivors from Pomerania, my cannoneers without cannons, and my engineers without pontoons, I still had just barely enough men to re-form a serious infantry regiment.

I integrated the rest of my division into a second regiment, a depot regiment composed of the sick, the temporarily disabled, and old legionnaries who couldn't be used on the front lines.

This unit also temporarily took in about a hundred compatriots who had been working in the factories of the Reich and whom a sullen bureaucrat had sent to us in a moment of lunacy, all dressed in field grey, their wishes in the matter not having been consulted.

We were a legion of volunteers. At no price would I have wanted to send decent fellows into the fray, or even keep them in uniform, if they didn't share our beliefs and hadn't come of their own free will. I made them a little speech and told them they were free to go.

I had them all given provisions for three days and some cigarettes. One of my officers conducted them back to the rear provided with demobilization orders.

A bit later I decided to evacuate the sick and those with minor wounds. The Reich's resistance was nearing the end of its rope. It was better to save those who could only weigh us down during the final battles and take them out of the way of the Soviet abyss in time. It wasn't in the regulations, but I disregarded that and signed a sheaf of marching orders. Two hundred unfit men thus took the road to Rostock, the ancient port on the Baltic Sea.

Discreetly, but in every way possible, I discarded dead weight and tried to limit the final casualties.

## Berlin, 20 April

I trembled to think of the fate which awaited the division's thousand or more survivors who, fit for combat, stayed at my side near the Oder. We were at the far end of the Eastern Front. In a couple of days of unlucky fighting, we could be crushed or surrounded by the Soviets.

The Americans and the British, moreover, were coming closer and closer to our rear. The German command in our sector watched their progress with a sympathetic eye. It even thought they were too slow. They still had the most astonishing illusions, and more than one German general imagined with touching faith that the Anglo-Americans were going to make war against the USSR at any minute. When the Allies arrived on the Oder everything would work out magnificently for sure.

At any rate, the High Command made no provisions at all for covering itself. Colonel-General Steiner even talked about setting up huge placards behind our lines facing to the west bearing the inscription: "Anti-Soviet Front!"

I was not as sanguine as these German officers. Taking advantage of the sector's temporary tranquillity, I hurried to Berlin one morning to badger the Minister of Foreign Affairs, Ribbentrop, into asking through a neutral state or the International Red Cross for particulars about the fate intended for our volunteers, should they fall into the hands of the Anglo-American armies as they pushed eastward.

I received the official response at my command post one week later. It was clear. If our soldiers were taken prisoner by the British or the Americans, they would be treated exactly like prisoners of war. That would be true for Vlassov's troops and for all European volunteers of the Eastern Front.[1]

That was normal. This news reassured our boys.

Thus, at the time of the disaster a certain number among them relied in all good faith upon the honesty of the Anglo-American Military Command. Alas! They weren't treated like soldiers at all. These heroes of the Russian front, most of whom had been wounded one or several times in combat, were all delivered up to the terrible Belgian political police, held up to public scorn, thrown into dungeons or into concentration camps like international common criminals.

Hundreds were condemned to death and several thousand to dozens of years in prison by emergency tribunals whose imbecility and blatant prejudice amounted to madness.

They had been heroic soldiers. They had been only soldiers. Almost all wore war decorations which they had gloriously and painfully earned. They had fought cleanly and honorably for a pure ideal with total lack of self-interest. The Allies' delivery of these heroes to political torturers was morally base and militarily dishonest.

* * * * *

On the eve of the final Soviet assault our legion received a double mission. Our first battalion, six hundred and fifty men strong, had been temporarily removed from my command and put in a flanking line six kilometers west of the bombed highway bridge over the Oder. It occupied a little village lying between the hills. If required it would support a German regiment posted on the left bank of the river.

I had been given the command of the second line of defense fifteen kilometers to the west of the Oder. This line ran for four leagues above a wide swampy hollow. To occupy it I only had my second infantry battalion and a regiment of Flemish volunteers detached from their division and placed under my orders.

Toward mid-April the Soviets threw themselves into the final assault.

The northern sector—ours—from Stettin to the Hohenzollern Canal remained strangely silent for several days yet.

But Saxony had been penetrated, and the breakthrough was widening before Berlin.

On the Army Corps's maps at Colonel-General Steiner's I saw the Soviet progess toward the capital of the Reich. If the barrier were broken—and it was—how could the thousands of Soviet tanks be prevented from forcing their way into Berlin?

On the evening of 19 April 1945, General Steiner showed me the extent of the disaster. The Red tanks had nearly reached the *Ring,* the famous highway which circled the city.

A certain number of our comrades were on mission in Berlin. There, on the very eve of the encirclement, with extraordinary coolness, they were still publishing our daily French language newspaper, *L'Avenir.* I jumped into my Volkswagen to let them know just how grave the danger was. Berlin was an hour and a half away from my command post. Going back past the wretched columns of refugees who were fleeing in every direction, I entered the ancient Prussian metropolis at nine o'clock in the evening.

The Hotel Adlon was still operating in spite of the bombs and the shells falling right in the streets. In the brilliantly lighted restaurant tuxedoed waiters and maitres d'hotel in tails continued solemnly and impassively to serve purple slices of kohlrabi in the huge silver platters for state occasions. Everything was ordered, distinguished, without a strident word or a sign of haste.

Tomorrow or the day after the building would probably go up in flames. Or else some large-pawed barbarian would burst into the gilded hall. But *bon ton* was still *bon ton.*

It was impressive. The German people's comportment, their self-mastery, and their self-discipline right down to the most minor details and until the last moment will be a noble memory of mankind for all those who lived the end of the Third Reich.

No least sign of panic was shown in Berlin during the collapse.

Nevertheless, who could still have doubted the outcome of the combat? The defensive fortifications in the suburbs were ridiculous. The infantry forces were tiny. The number of tanks was insignificant.

The real bulwark had been built opposite Kuestrin. It had been broken. The road was open.

I drove around the bombed city that night. I even went as far as Potsdam. Not a trace of pillaging. Not a shout of panic. The old men of the *Volkssturm* and the boys of the Hitler Youth were waiting for the enemy, panzerfausts in their hands, as solemn as the great Teutonic Knights.

In the morning the electrical current was cut off and the telephones stopped working. Hundreds of enemy planes flew over the roofs, tracing multiple white streaks. Shells were falling from everywhere. The thousands of Soviet artillery weapons were creating a mad din. The tanks roared at the gateway to the city.

I got my comrades underway.

At one o'clock in the afternoon I left the Adlon. One of my German friends, a man severely disabled, who had taken twenty-one bullets in the body at Moscow in 1941, had come to make his adieus under the machine-gun fire. He was accompanied by some ravishing girls from Berlin, loaded with the poetic harvests of spring. They decorated the whole front of my little Volkswagen with red tulips and hundreds of golden-centered purple pansies. They smiled, simple and courageous. The Reich was disintegrating; Berlin was falling; the worst humiliations lay in wait for every one of them, but fervent, delicate, and beautiful, they were still bearing flowers.

I reached the ancient route from Prenzlau to Stettin only with great difficulty. The highway had already been cut off by the Soviets. The enemy tanks were hitting hard. The confusion of the thousands of carts of refugees was indescribable. They were lost. The Russians were hastening up.

When I approached Bruessow, where my command post was located, I saw great clouds of smoke rising toward the sky across an area thirty kilometers wide. The last intact sector of the Eastern Front had just received the final blow.

Just across from our marshes the Russians were coming out across the sands of the left bank of the Oder.

## Good-Bye to the Oder

On 20 April 1945, Hitler's birthday, at six o'clock in the morning, the Soviet artillery opened up an unprecedented fire on the German positions defending the ruins of the old highway bridge to the south of Stettin.

For the last three days we had been noticing an extraordinary activity on the right bank of the Oder. The Soviets had set themselves up on an island around the first arch of the destroyed bridge. They had brought heavy equipment there with the help of boats, pontoons, and old mud-lighters. An attack was certain.

The troops defending this especially threatened sector were composed of nothing but policemen. More than a thousand enemy weapons suddenly concentrated their fire at them. They just couldn't hold off the powerful Soviet commandos who, exploiting their initial advantage, sent several shock battalions to the other side of the water in little boats.

Since it was unhealthy to announce defeats, the police commander felt it preferable not to make the defeat of his forces known any sooner than necessary. The result: by the time the division was informed of the tragedy the Communists were already well to the west of the river and had made several more landings.

The disaster occurred before seven o'clock in the morning. Many infantry battalions, which formed the divisional reserves, were called only at two o'clock in the afternoon. At three o'clock they were sent to the counterattack.

* * * * *

Studying the terrain before April 20th, my officers and I had arrived at the conclusion that if the left bank of the Oder were lost, a counterattack would almost certainly be doomed to failure if it weren't organized extremely promptly.

Indeed, beyond the hills of the Oder's left bank, the terrain descended toward the west in wide, sandy moors without folds or natural obstacles. Charging across this wasteland to drive out the enemy posted on the ridges would be rushing into a massacre.

Then, by three o'clock on the afternoon of 20 April 1945, several thousand Reds had settled on the left bank, crossed the sandy zone, and reached the foothills six kilometers to the west.

Tactically, this battalion of Walloons no longer belonged to my division. It received very hard orders from whitewashers who didn't have my reasons for being sparing of the men. They were to go to the attack of these lost kilometers in mid-afternoon across the bare terrain and re-occupy the left bank of the Oder.

Our brave boys, without a word of discouragement, obeyed with their customary fidelity. Until the last day it would be seen that their oath had not been mere empty words.

The counterthrust should at least have been facilitated by a preparation of heavy artillery fire. But how could they fire? With what ammunition?

At Stargard, two months earlier, we could no longer fire more than six to ten rounds per weapon per day. For this last battle of the Oder the orders that we had just received were even more draconian. Firing was limited to one shell per day per muzzle.

One shell! Only one!

The restrictions were almost as severe for the heavy mortars: two shots a day! For the light mortars: one shot per day!

In actual fact: zero.

The enemy opposite possessed a thousand pieces of artillery and an unlimited quantity of munitions. The front zone was absolutely drowned by the cataclysmic Soviet machine-gun fire. We had nothing left to oppose to it but a few lifeless heavy weapons.

Our battalion had to wage its battles with personal arms alone. At the beginning of the action only a half dozen friendly tanks supported the thrust—but at a distance and cautiously.

That didn't prevent the enemy from being dislodged. Three kilometers of terrain were retaken in hand-to-hand fighting in less than an hour.

Our losses were already extremely high.

Our battalion approached the dunes of the Oder. The combat lasted until night. The Soviets had had time to place machine-gunners' nests on every knoll. Our comrades were crushed by the full brunt of their artillery fire.

I hurried to the battalion command post just to encourage our men. Alas! They had been removed from our unit. During the course of the evening I saw more than a hundred wounded men drag themselves to us. Many of our non-commissioned officers had perished. In spite of that the attack continued with a furious determination.

One of our companies finally reached the village overlooking the Oder. Our soldiers were able to hang on atop the sandy ridges two hundred meters from the water. They had reached the river just the same, fanatically carrying out their orders.

But what could the poor fellows do alone near this steep river bank? Several thousand men would have had to be brought up behind them and, above all, the enemy batteries, as well as the new Soviet troops which were continually landing, would have had to be pounded by artillery and aircraft.

On the sandy trails to their rear several Latvian companies were coming along toward the river. But what could these meager reinforcements do? For that matter, the Soviet planes were harrassing them. All the crossroads were blazing. Gray and red torches rose up in the twilight from every village in the area. The machine-gun fire was falling like a hailstorm.

We no longer even knew where to shelter the wounded.

Every street was smashed by shell holes. Every house was riddled with shrapnel as far away as six or seven kilometers from the battlefield.

* * * * *

That night the enemy crossed a huge mass of troops and discharged boatloads of supplies and equipment. They had virtually free passage of the river. Our artillery without munitions and our aircraft without fuel could react no longer.

When dawn came up the Soviet tanks, long as alligators, were on our side of the water, still cautious, not yet advancing, but forming a frightening barrier in front of the abutments of the wrecked highway bridge.

During the night's combats the company that had climbed to the ridges above the Oder had lost four-fifths of its forces. Every meter of sand had received a shell or a grenade.

The orders were nevertheless implacable. They must counterattack again!

It was madness!

In order to succeed in that way, out in the open, the support of powerful artillery fire, Panzers, Stukas, and a half dozen shock battalions would have been more necessary than ever.

But we weren't going to disobey after four years of obediance.

Our companies charged once again and were horribly decimated each time. Captain Thyssen, the unforgettable Thyssen of the Cherkassy *Kessel,* one of our most outstanding specialists in hand-to-hand combat, was hit by three bullets. He succumbed atop a pile of Soviet corpses. Lieutenant Regibeau, already wounded seven times on the Eastern Front, was wounded numerous times by exploding shells. His whole body streamed with blood. Lieutenant Albert Verpoorten, a dynamic young writer full of humor, was stopped cold in mid-leap. His forehead was wounded but he didn't realize the rest. He wanted to sponge it off. "I don't have an arm any more!" he screamed, horrified. Then he collapsed.

Six times in the course of this terrible day of 21 April 1945 the Walloons received orders to remount their attack against the left bank of the Oder. Six times they charged into the inferno.

Nothing will tell their heroism better than this frightful figure: Out of the six hundred fifty men engaged since the day before in the hand-to-hand fighting in these dunes, only thirty-five remained unhurt on the evening of 21 April.

The other six hundred fifteen who were killed or wounded—in other words ninety-four percent of the battalion—were struck down for a cause that all then knew to be essentially lost.

But they believed in the immortality of their ideal. They wanted to obey right up to the end, to be faithful to the end—and the last fighters, if necessary, on ground that wasn't even theirs.

* * * * *

I had passed the day trying to maintain the second line, twenty kilometers wide, that I had to defend to the east of Bruessow, but the sector was soon pretty well empty. Company by company, all our comrades in the Flemish regiment were taken from me to be thrown in their turn onto the corpses of our Walloon soldiers near the Oder.

Thus a second line of defense became absolutely illusory. All we had left to close off twenty kilometers of terrain to an enemy that was now landing in fleets was one last battalion of battleworthy Wallonian volunteers.

A bridge had been thrown up over the Oder by the Russian engineers. Hundreds of tanks and pieces of artillery, as well as entire divisions, were passing over like a hurricane. Furthermore, several kilometers upstream the Soviets had established two other bridgeheads even wider than that of the autobahn.

Who now could stop the cataclysm?

The German command was still sticking to the stringent orders: hold on!

But tens of thousands of Russians were overrunning our marshes! The whole country was in flames around us!

We maintained our position unshakeably on the Bruessow line on the 22nd, 23rd, 24th, and 25th of April, since those were the orders.

The Soviet Air Force exercised an absolute dictatorship in the sky. Cleaving the ash-filled air, the starred planes dove crackling down upon us, smashing walls, partitions, and doors. The command post was continually riddled with gunfire. On the 25th an entire wing of the building went up in flames. Then the center of Bruessow went up in flames. The animals screamed. Women shot through by long incendiary bullets writhed on the ground, their fingers yellow, their nails clenched like cock's spurs. Every quarter hour the machine-gun fire would begin again.

At five o'clock in the evening a motorcycle messenger arrived. The Army

Corps was relinquishing any further use of the Bruessow defense line, which the enemy had passed by a long way on both wings. We were to fall back to new positions to the northwest of the city of Prenzlau.

I immediately put my men on the march, but life had become untenable. A plane fired on my Volkswagen and burst three tires. I repaired it hastily, while crazed pigs from some burning sties ran in all directions.

The Soviets were swarming everywhere, like lemmings.

The flood-gates were wide open.

How would we keep from being drowned in the final maelstrom?

## Toward Luebeck

Prenzlau was an ancient city with brick churches as massive as dungeons, but made light and airy by admirable slender Gothic arches. When we crossed through it on 25 April 1945, the death agony had just begun for it, too. For several days the Soviet air force had been battering the streets. Crumbled houses blocked traffic. Flocks of haggard civilians were fleeing.

Three thousand officers of the Belgian Army had just left the Prenzlau barracks, where they had been interned following the capitulation of 28 May 1940. They puffed and sweated on the road. Rubicund generals with their kepis askew would sponge themselves on the embankments or, like fat, flushed nannies, would push baby-buggies over-filled with belongings. Great feats of endurance were not to be expected of them. The Russians would soon pluck them up.

We were to take position several kilometers to the northwest of Prenzlau. I set up my command post in the Holzendorf castle, where flocks of shivering refugees swarmed. Most of them had been evacuated from the Rhineland toward the east. Now the Communists were attacking and chasing them back toward the west.

They were exhausted by so much emotion. The expressions of many of the women were disturbing. One of them had three little blond kids clinging to her skirts. She was expecting a fourth baby, and was being jostled about. That evening she went mad. Lying flat on her back, she cried and gasped, refusing all attention. The Soviet planes would drive her out at dawn, dazed, joining the terrified human flood that was expanding indefinitely toward the north and west.

* * * * *

From then on Flemish volunteers were jumbled with Walloons in the final venture. The next day I tried to rejoin the German staff officer to whom we were, one and all, tactically subordinate. I found him far to the west in an ugly brick castle hidden in the depths of a forest.

The orders, apparently, were to hold on. That was all I could find out. I got back to my command post at Holzendorf by going alongside flaming Prenzlau. Immense pale gray columns of smoke were rising straight up against the golden twilight.

At nine o'clock in the evening the noise of the battle in the southwest became particularly violent. Our window panes fell out. The Soviet tanks were baying at the entrance to Prenzlau. The city was barely defended. It didn't hold out more than an hour.

In the morning our observers notified me that enemy tanks were driving about far to the southwest, several kilometers beyond our line.

I had been promised a van that could receive and transmit by radio. It hadn't come. I didn't know any of the decisions of the High Command. Finally at eleven o'clock in the morning a German motorcyclist brought me an order to withdraw dated the evening before at 2000 hours. The messenger had wandered behind enemy lines and gotten lost. He had arrived fifteen hours late. We had been well and truly outflanked since last night. It wouldn't be easy to extricate ourselves from the wasps' nest now.

Our people had fought since daylight with a marvelous heroism once again. They had made desperate counterattacks to get free from the enemy thrust. One of our young officers had charged into a house which the Soviets had converted into a bunker all by himself with his submachine gun. He caused a terrible massacre there and in the end had one of his arms cut all to pieces.

Rather than persisting against this stubborn resistance, the Reds side-stepped and advanced deep on both wings. It was no longer possible to fall back to the west. The enemy was ten kilometers west of Prenzlau.

We took a northerly direction, which seemed the least threatened. Already the towns had filled the anti-tank barriers. So much the worse for the wretches who, like us, were fighting as rear guards. We had a terrible time getting around the heaps of rubble to get our last Volkswagens through, our only means of liaison amid the enemy tanks roaring at our heels.

The German commander notified me in his order for retreat that he was moving his command post to the edge of a forest twenty kilometers west of Prenzlau. I arrived there at three o'clock in the afternoon, after endless detours and adventures.

Naturally there was no one left at the appointed place except the Soviet tanks advancing along the outskirts of the forest. The motor of my little automobile was hot enough to burst from having toiled through fields and embankments for hours. We hadn't received a drop of gas for the last week. I could go on only by emptying cans of potato alcohol obtained in the region into my tank, a poor and asphyxiating fuel. Hidden behind a thicket, we had to wait for a quarter of an hour to repair the fan belt while the motor cooled off.

The Soviet tanks were coming on straight and fast.

We reached the Scarpin intersection by little dirt roads. There, five hundred French volunteers with beautiful blue, white, and red badges were standing firm, in very high spirits although they had nothing but rifles to oppose the waves of tanks of the USSR.

The staff office for which I was looking seemed to be nearby. I found it that night after great difficulty. New withdrawal orders were waiting for me. This time we had to cross fifty kilometers in a single jump to the north of the Neustrelitz-Neubrandenburg line.

I knew that my men were worn out, but we would have to gather all our strength. North! North! Escape from the Soviets! My liaison officers didn't need to have the problem explained to them twice.

Groups of young women in flight stayed with us. What could we do! There was no longer anything to keep them from falling into the hands of the Bolsheviks. Their youngsters were exhausted. They were dying of hunger and thirst. The young mothers, still beautiful in their ordeal, knew what awaited them.

* * * * *

It was 28 April 1945. The crowds on the road had become prodigious. Thousands of political deportees mingled their blue and white striped uniforms with the throng of trucks and carts, the hundreds of thousands of women and children, and the columns of soldiers with the most diverse weapons.

Our two last infantry battalions went forward with difficulty. But they passed nevertheless through the gigantic scramble.

At eight o'clock in the evening the town of Neustrelitz exploded in huge orange flames across a sky of bedlam behind us. In four years we thought we had seen the greatest in the way of catastrophes. But Neustrelitz broke all the records that night. No expense was spared for the final fireworks of the war. Stupendous explosions burst forth amidst a din like the end of the world.

We went out onto the jetty of a little gray lake, streaked by the burning reflections of the spectacle. A black bark was drifting there. The darkness smelled of moss, of forget-me-nots, and of new leaves. It was an admirable spot, just made for murmuring poetry to a lady with silken hair. But this was a universe on fire that was spewing its life to the skies, to fall back in vertiginous cataracts, shaking this spring evening to infinity.

The enemy would be here in the morning.

Our orders came. We were to draw back still more towards the northwest and cross sixty more kilometers in a single march. Our limbs were heavy with exhaustion. But danger gave everyone enough strength to manage another effort.

We shook our old Volkswagens into life, though they had been hit twenty times over by shrapnel.

In the southwest the whole sky was afire and getting redder and redder.

We had to reach the town of Waren in Mecklenburg the very next day, pass beyond the big lakes of the region, and temporarily take up position in the Tottiner Huette sector.

Many refugees collapsed for the night on both sides of the pavement. Tens of thousands of women, children, and wretched old men rolled up in blankets were huddled one against another in the fog under the firs.

Three lines of vehicles hurried along in tight ranks, often led by very dedicated French prisoners who visibly felt themselves to be a part of the German families crowded onto the carts.

My soldiers were in a good position. They lost no time as they slipped nimbly among the bottlenecked teams, keeping perfect good humor.

I advised everyone to step along in double time. I hadn't any illusions at all. I held a little battery-operated radio between my legs in my Volkswagen. The British transmissions obligingly announced from hour to hour what the situation was.

Now, the British front in Germany had started moving again two days ago. The Tommies had crossed the Elbe to the southwest of Hamburg. There wasn't a shadow of a doubt that they were heading for Luebeck. If they reached this Baltic port first, we would be throttled by the Soviets.

We had to extricate the troops at any price, keep our eyes open, and get to Luebeck in time. Afterwards, we would see. We had to be careful not to give up in despair, to surrender spinelessly like the dull flocks who were collapsing all along the roads and waiting with ashen faces for the unconditional law of the conqueror.

From Luebeck we might perhaps be able to move up further to the north. I pushed my men as much as I could, but we were still far from the Baltic and events were rushing forward.

On 30 April 1945, at eight o'clock in the morning, I heard some amazing news from Radio London: "Himmler is negotiating an armistice!" The talks were taking place, it seemed, in the area of Luebeck.

The commander of the Flemish division rejoined me at Tottiner Huette. He and I had been trying to re-establish contact with the Army Corps for two days, in vain. The retreat was rushing headlong at such a speed and on roads so choked that liaisons had become impossible for the first time in the war, despite all the calm of the High Command. It was absolutely impossible to know what our divisions should do, or even where the Army Corps staff officer was to found. The radio trucks had disappeared. Not a messenger could return against this flood of carts and refugees. We had been left entirely to our fate.

Fascist Italy had just been disintegrated. Mussolini had been assassinated with abominable sadism. His corpse was hanging in the middle of the city of Milan, fastened by the feet like a dead animal.

I made careful preparations, to give maximum help to my endangered soldiers. Before leaving Berlin on 20 April, I had had several thousand foreign workers' cards delivered to me in case the worst should happen. The time had come to act for our survival.

On the morning of 30 April, I had the cards confidentially distributed to my unit commanders. Thus if certain companies found themselves scattered at the time of the final blow, those men who didn't want to surrender could still slip on old clothes,disguise themselves as transported workers, avoid the military internment camps, and, thanks to those providential papers, get back to the house of a friend either in Belgium or in the Reich or find refuge abroad, as more than three thousand of them did.

* * * * *

For the last hundred hours our volunteers had marched day and night. I gave them no respite. It was essential not to yield, not to lose our heads, but on the contrary to cling to the possibilities for survival, to try to reach Denmark, then the Norwegian glacis, where perhaps the struggle might continue—in any case to try everything possible to spare our soldiers a gloomy collapse into the anonymity of defeat.

We could no longer hope that a miracle might stem the Soviet flood. Our resistance had finally come to an end. To hang on anymore would be suicide.

I drew up orders for withdrawal to Luebeck for my regiment and battalion commanders. They were to use every means of transport to carry the troops.

I set up my Wallonian *Feldgendarmes* at all the crossroads to guide our comrades from stage to stage, spur on the loafers, and save them from any complications.

I had decided to see Himmler whatever the cost, to obtain clear orders from him for my division and for the Flanders Division, to remind him of the existence of tens of thousands of foreign volunteers, the bravest of the brave. Would they still be remembered in the discussions at Luebeck? Or would they be left to sink into the abyss?

As long as there was a chance of saving my boys, I wanted to take it. Cutting through the fields, speedily overtaking everyone in front of me, I raced my Volkswagen toward Luebeck and Himmler.

## "Hitler is Dead"

The Luebeck road gave an exact picture of the situation on 30 April 1945.

As far as Schwerin the flood of civilians and armies from the east flowed on, immense, tumultuous.

The fatal confluence was at Schwerin. Solitary above slate-colored waters, the castle of the dukes envinced the serenity of stones which have seen men and centuries pass. The rest of the town was swamped by the throngs from east and west.

It was there that the imminence of the end of the war in Germany became a blinding reality for us. A human river descending from Waren gathered momentum as it fled the Soviet tanks. Another human river poured down from the Elbe, fleeing the British. The two Allied offensives were coming closer and closer together, like double doors closing.

The proximity of the British was being written in the sky. From Schwerin on, squadrons of *Tiefflieger* patrolled all the roads with savage determination. The British planes would dive onto the columns, and instantly ten or fifteen clouds of thick smoke would rise from them. The fuel tanks burned. The tires burned. The baggage burned.

Fire was everywhere, thick, almost opaque, stitched by explosions.

The clothing of fleeing women lay about the broken carts. Endless columns had been abandoned. My Volkswagen and that of my chief of staff picked their way with extreme difficulty among the heaps of debris and the fires. We had to dive down the embankments every five minutes while the guns of the *Tiefflieger* rattled above our heads.

The wounded soldiers made the most tragic spectacle. The hospitals of the region had been evacuated in haste, but there weren't any more ambulances. Hundreds of men with casts on their arms or chests had been put out on the roads, their heads covered with bandages.

Many walked on crutches.

They had to get to the Baltic that way on foot, under the machine-gun fire, through the flaming trucks and the general panic.

I finally arrived in Luebeck in the afternoon, at the staff office of Grand Admiral Doenitz.

One of his close associates took me into a corner of the office—it was 30 April 1945, at five thirty in the evening—and whispered a secret which made my blood run cold.

"Listen, the death of the Fuehrer will be announced tomorrow."

Was Hitler really dead? Were they trying to gain time before announcing this terrible news? Or was something else being prepared?

In any case, one whole day before the historic declaration of Grand Admiral Doenitz: "Today, May 1st, at two-thirty in the afternoon, the Fuehrer died a hero in the course of the battle of Berlin," the news of the death of Hitler was whispered in my ear right in the staff office of the Grand Admiral.

I was even more convinced that the end was near when I reached the Waffen SS staff office to the north of Luebeck on the shore of the rain-streaked gulf. "Hurry and see Himmler," I was told. "It's only a matter of hours now." But no one knew exactly where the Reichsfuehrer SS was to be found.

They could only show me on the map the castle where his command post was supposed to be. To reach it I had first to come back to Luebeck, then go back up the eastern road along the Baltic for about forty kilometers in the direction of Wismar.

In the inky night it was very difficult to make progress against the flow of the thousands of trucks pressing toward the northwest. We were constantly in danger of being crushed by these monsters.

At two o'clock in the morning, when we were coming into the Kladow region, I was struck by an astonishing phenomenon. The long white gleams of a searchlight were lighting the neighboring slope and sky. It had to be Himmler's airfield. But if they were displaying lights like that, it had to be because the enemy tolerated them.

I imagined Himmler flying at this hour in the dark night. Which he was, in fact.

The castle was almost deserted when I reached it. It was a gloomy building in imitation Gothic, circa 1900, perfect decor for a suspense movie. The dimly lighted corridors and stairs were sinister. Hanseatic flags hung, drawn tightly, as in a funeral chapel. In the refectory were modern paintings showing all the categories of eaters, involuntarily caricatured in the style of Picasso. All along the red-brick battlements and under the aspens in the park, police were on guard, their faces long, ravaged and ashen.

I found no one in the depths of the buildings but the head of Himmler's special train, an ever-obliging bon vivant, his face speckled with hundreds of little gray spots, as if a colony of flies had used it for a testing bench. He conducted me to the office of a colonel with pale tired eyes.

I saluted him with the habitual "Heil Hitler!" No "Heil Hitler!" came in reply. I thought this omission bizarre. Cautiously, I inquired. Everyone seemed quite embarrassed. From all the evidence Hitler had become a forbidden subject of conversation in these cavernous halls. No one could tell me when Himmler would come back. He had left by plane "for the north."

He reappeared in the morning like a whirlwind, but he stayed for only a few minutes. We didn't even have time to see him. When we arrived at the staircase he had already left again, pallid and unshaven. All we saw were three automobiles jolting down the sandy road.

In any event, Himmler had unhesitatingly signed the order which I had had drawn up that night for the withdrawal of the Wallonia and the Flanders Divisions toward Bad Sedeberg, a town in Schleswig-Holstein, to the northwest of Luebeck. He had said he wanted to see me. I was to look for lodgings in the area and wait for his return.

I immediately sent my chief of staff off in one of our two Volkswagens, carrying the official order, to meet the Walloon and Flemish troops on the Schwerin road. At the same time I sent my second aide-de-camp to Bad Sedeberg with the second car so that suitable quarters would be ready to welcome our exhausted soldiers. In addition this officer was to inform the posts of the *Feldgendarmes* and the commandant of Luebeck of Himmler's orders.

I found myself alone once again. I took lodgings in a blacksmith's little house on the Wismar road. I got a chair and went out onto the doorstep as I used to do in the evenings when I was young and living with my parents in the town of my birth.

Hundreds of trucks were passing by. More than ever, the *Tiefflieger* dominated the roads. Gunfire would crackle to the east, north, and west above endless lines of red and gray fires.

I fell to daydreaming. My eyes wandered in space as if the world in which I had so intensely lived had already stopped breathing and was dissolving into melancholy puffs of smoke.

The Baltic Sea was half an hour away, at the end of some ploughed fields where the April wheat was sprouting. At dusk I went out there and sat on a big brown rock. The evening was tinged with pink. Nothing could be heard of the tumultuous traffic. From time to time a German plane would fly along the sea, skimming the waves to avoid detection.

Was my dream, too, dying like this pale sky invaded by the night?

I stood up and came back through the sown fields. At the house I lay down fully clothed in the darkness.

At 2:00 A.M. there was a terrible racket at the door. I hurried to open it up.

The modest room was lighted in big patches by a candle.

A young German colonel sent by Himmler was holding himself stiffly erect before me, his features drawn.

I understood before he said a word.

I stood to attention.

"The Fuehrer is dead," he whispered.

Neither of us said anything. The blacksmith, too, was silent.

Then two tears, the tears of a pure heart, ran down his old tanned cheeks.

## Malente

The German colonel who told me of the death of Hitler added that Himmler would leave the area that same night and establish himself north of Luebeck in the direction of Kiel, at Malente. This sticky name had all the flabbiness of fever. Himmler asked that I go to him there at three o'clock on the afternoon of 2 May.

I spent the rest of the night thinking about Hitler.

I didn't know the terms of Admiral Doenitz's declaration, which was largely false. Thus no doubt about the death of the Fuehrer could have occurred to me then.

I saw him again, a simple, sensitive heart, full of genius and power. His people had loved him and followed him until the end. During the entire war, no blow had shaken the admirable fidelity of the German masses to a man whose honesty, unselfishness, public spirit, and sense of Germanic greatness they all knew.

It was a fact almost unique in the history of the world. Bruised, crushed, delivered up to the most frightful suffering that a people has ever had to endure, this people didn't make a murmur against the leader who had started and kept them on this terrible path.

I was sure that in every house and in every cart on the roads people were crying or praying at this moment. But I was certain that none was breathing a word of reproach. No one felt sorry for himself. It was for Hitler that they felt sorry.

He disappeared in an apotheosis of vanquished gods, amid an uproar like the end of the world, which seemed to burst forth in a Wagnerian chorus. To end thus was to be resuscitated already in the imagination of the peoples, with a superhuman intensity, cast in an epic which would never be extinguished.

* * * * *

But what would happen tomorrow? What would the first day affected by such a void be like?

The Fuehrer gone, Berlin was lost.

In the south, the Reich was on its knees.

The north was swept by a prodigious tidal wave.

The armies were no longer fighting, not because they lacked courage or discipline, but because there was no longer any front, any Panzers, any ammunition, or any liaison. The roads were kilometers of suffering, hunger, and blood. The death of Hitler meant the end of the struggle in Germany.

At five o'clock in the morning my little Volkswagen stopped in front of the sign of the forge. Back at Bad Sedeberg, my second aide-de-camp had heard the announcement of the death of Hitler on the radio. Instantly he had understood that everything was about to fall to pieces. He had turned back and, for a second time, had gone against the tide of retreat through the night to save me. After eight hours of striving he succeeded in making the forty kilometers.

I started out immediately.

Thousands of trucks had collided on the roads.

The closer we came to Luebeck, the harder it was to move. The Allied tanks were pushing at our backs like madmen.

Ten kilometers from Luebeck the road went through a forest before coming to the town. Everything was snarled up. Columns of huge blue and white Swedish Red Cross trucks were trying to move toward the east to help the freed political prisoners who were hurrying away from Waren and Schwerin. They, too, were fleeing the troops of the USSR.

With everyone wanting to get through, no one could get through any longer. I took extraordinary measures and hoisted my Volkswagen to the top of a local tramway embankment which passed nearby. Thus we crossed the last kilometer like tightrope walkers, bumpety-bump along the ties and the rails.

* * * * *

The sun shone in Luebeck. The proud Hanseatic city had suffered relatively little from the bombardments.[2] Its noble houses of weathered brick and its Gothic buildings from the glorious centuries when the ocean-going ships of the Teutonic Hansa whitened the waters of the Baltic and the North Sea were still standing against the brilliant sky.

At every crossroads my *Feldgendarmes* awaited the Wallonian and Flemish volunteers to direct them toward Bad Sedeberg. I found a first contingent of them at the Luebeck barracks. As soon as the greater part of the troops rejoined us, we would form a solid square at Bad Sedeberg for whatever purpose it might be needed.

For I had made a firm resolution. Either the fate of the anti-Bolshevik volunteers would be precisely settled at the time of the armistice or, as a foreign unit, we would not consider ourselves bound by the German negotiators. We would fight like hell as long as possible until we had been guaranteed a humane and honorable surrender. To help toward this solution, since I was the founder of the Legion, I decided to give myself up to the Belgian political police—but on the condition that my blood, offered as a tribute to hatred, would buy the salvation of my companions of the Eastern Front. Otherwise we would continue to fight with all we had after the armistice.

My soldiers weren't ciphers. Our last stand would be memorable.

Alas! A few hours later the gathering storm smashed my plans. I tried to achieve them again at Copenhagen and even at Oslo, but a typhoon was now blowing us all away.

* * * * *

I stayed at the Luebeck barracks until the beginning of the afternoon.

I sent a first detachment of officers and soldiers to Bad Sedeberg. I would join them later after my meeting with Himmler. Then I left for Malente.

The softly rolling countryside was cool and harmonious: pine groves, birch woods, broad deep green pastures, blue and black lakes bordered by villas and hotels. I went first through the lovely little town of Eutin. I found Himmler's command post in a farm at a distance from Malente.

Himmler wasn't there. The news was particularly catastrophic. The British had taken Schwerin and cut off the army returning from Mecklenburg. The atmosphere of the house was macabre.

High police officials, their backs bent, were pacing and whispering in the rooms of the farm. They gravely explained to me that Himmler had gone, no one knew where, and that no one knew whether he would ever return.

I got back into my Volkswagen. We Walloons were now on our own. And I started off again toward the south by the Luebeck and Bad Sedeberg roads.

* * * * *

It was four o'clock in the afternoon.

I had just come through the thickets at Malente and reached the Eutin highway when I saw more problems. Every kilometer had been blasted with orgiastic fury by the British *Tiefflieger.* Wretched women and little girls with their legs twisted, tibias broken by horrible incendiary cartridges, lay in the embankments and at the thresholds of the houses vainly waiting for help.

It was an apocalypse from Luebeck to Eutin. Hundreds of refugees' carts and hundreds of military trucks were in flames. There was nothing left of the highway but a column of fire. All the drivers of vehicles were flat in the embankments or running in the fields.

You could read the area's roadmaps just by looking at the sky. The *Tiefflieger* were diving in ranks of six at a time, firing, making a wide turn, and beginning their devil's work once more.

I went forward until the minute the *Tiefflieger* began their dive. Then I drove my Volkswagen between two trucks on fire. It was the best place. The vehicle was more or less hidden in the whirlwind of flames and smoke. Once the firing stopped I jumped into the car again and gained five hundred meters before the new attack swooped down.

A German driver told me that the British were at Luebeck. I didn't believe him. The German troops were still occupying Hamburg that morning. No, it was nonsense. It wasn't possible.

We came to the fork of the Bad Sedeberg road. The machine gun fire there was terrifying. Soldiers were coming from the side roads running like madmen.

I moved up close to a major who was questioning them. They all had trucks on fire nearby. They all reported the same news. Luebeck had surrendered at four o'clock in the afternoon without a single shot being fired. There were more than twenty thousand wounded in the hospitals of the town. The bridges had fallen intact. The British tanks were coming, just ahead of us.

"And Bad Sedeberg?"

That was the final blow. Bad Sedeberg too had fallen.

Hamburg had been declared an open city that very morning. The British tanks had crossed through it immediately and gone on to the north for more than a hundred kilometers without any fighting. The *Tiefflieger* were devastating everything in front of them. Bad Sedeberg had been occupied during the course of the afternoon.

I was stunned. At noon I had been with my comrades who had escaped from Mecklenburg. Within hours we were torn apart. I could not save them or endure these hours of anguish with them. I had no one left except two officers and a soldier. Everything had fallen in. The catastrophe had hit me like a tower collapsing on a passer-by. There was nothing left but to escape the advancing storm.

* * * * *

In spite of everything I hoped to find some of my boys in Denmark.

Two hundred of our men had been sent to Rostock in time. Surely they had been able to take to the sea from there.

Others who hadn't been able to get to Luebeck in time must also have reached the coast. My men had become masters of resourcefulness. Where no one else got through, they always got through. But I was four hundred kilometers from Copenhagen. The Volkswagen was shaky, with only thirty liters of potato alcohol in reserve, and the road was ablaze.

As long as I was alive I resolved to hope and fight. I headed north.

The gunfire of the *Tieffliger* threatened to destroy my little car. Several bullets had passed through it already without damaging anything vital.

Hundreds of burning trucks blocked the road. Speer, the minister, whose automobile was caught in the confusion, was trying to clear the way himself. He was surrounded by the members of the Todt staff office, all wearing stunning pistachio and gosling green uniforms, like Mardi Gras revellers. A weird touch in a chaotic scene.

I drove along the side field and made a few kilometers through the furrows. Suddenly a long black car came out of a side road. A very pale man with intense features wearing a leather helmet was at the wheel. I recognized him. It was Himmler.

I raced after him.

## Kiel-Copenhagen

I wouldn't have been able to stay with Himmler's powerful car, but I had spotted his direction. He was going to Malente. My wobbly Volkswagen made it to the courtyard of the SS Reichsfuehrer's villa just as some police officials were getting into their cars.

Himmler was giving orders to two SS generals. I recognized one of them as a very good friend, the famous Professor Gebhart, doctor to the Belgian king, Leopold III. As I approached, Himmler behaved in the most friendly manner toward me.

His self-control was impressive. Everything was lost, especially for him, but he showed remarkable calm. I asked him what he planned to do. "I am German," he replied. "I will not leave German soil." He kept his word.

Somewhere along a road near Lueneburg his body lies in the embrace of that German earth today.

He advised me to get to Copenhagen immediately and to regroup my soldiers there. The German governor of Denmark, Dr. Best, was close to him. He had given him all instructions on this matter.

His bright little eyes blinked in the half-light of the dusk. He, who had always been so curt and so discreet about his feelings, took my hands forcefully. "You have been among the faithful, you and your Walloons," he said. "You were the last to stay by our side through the fighting and the misfortune. One day Germany will remember."

He gave some brief orders and took the wheel. Just as he was starting he suddenly rolled down the window and hammered out these words, "Degrelle, you will be needed one day. Everything will change quickly. Gain yourself six months. You must live."

He started off. Some fifteen big cars fell in behind his, going north.

* * * * *

One hour later I caught up with his entourage again. The road was broken by a hundred shell holes. People were turning back toward the south. Four kilometers in front of us a large aerial fleet was over Kiel.

Himmler directed the cars to a little side road. Bombs poured down on the harbor.

There was a halt. The column started off again. A new wave of Allied bombers appeared. We were at the threshold of the town. We had to leave the cars on the pavement and throw ourselves into the muddy gardens. Himmler's two secretaries, one a lanky dark-haired girl with thin legs, and the other small and heavyset, were scurrying about among the generals and the police. The poor girls had apparently lost their shoes in the muck. To restore some order into the expedition Himmler exhorted, "Discipline, men, discipline!"

He ordered his people back into the big cars. They left once again in search of shelter. They didn't return. I had parted with Himmler forever.

* * * * *

The pounding of Kiel went on for several hours. Bombs fell by the hundreds very close to us. The earth resounded like a raging sea. Gigantic flashes lit the sky. Finally we were able to slip through the heaps of rubble, the torn-up tram lines, and the crowd coming out of the shelters in sepulchral silence.

We crossed the great bridge of Kiel. My Volkswagen began to backfire repeatedly. It had seen too much and done too much. In the end it stopped, in dead earnest, its rods seized. It was about three o'clock in the morning.

The Allies had to be advancing on all the roads. Would we be beaten by a breakdown?

Lacking a map of the region, we had gone astray in the darkness. We found ourselves on a little deserted road. Luckily an automobile passed at daybreak. We climbed up on the fenders. My poor Volkswagen stayed sadly on the road, having lost the war, waiting for the British.

During the morning we arrived at Flensburg, where a general gave me another Volkswagen. By one o'clock in the afternoon we were in Denmark, among rich and golden pastures with clumps of trees, mills, and white farms with little blue, green, and bright red shutters outlined in the distance.

* * * * *

In Denmark, as well, we could sense that the end had come.

The retreating German troops were absolutely forbidden to cross the German-Danish border. We had been blocked for an hour by the customs officers. It had taken a telephone call from Marshall Keitel to convince the officers to let us continue on our way.

In front of us a line of Swedish Red Cross cars were transporting hundreds of political prisoners freed from the German concentration camps. In every town an enormous crowd pushed forward to cheer them. Our little SS automobile, at the tail of the procession, didn't exactly enjoy such brilliant success. The men showed us their fists and the women flipped up the back of their skirts.

We were the only ones in uniform, mingling quite involuntarily with these continuing demonstrations. It was impossible to pass the convoy. We had to pass through grassy Jutland that way, cross the little Belt over the magnificent bridge of Fredericia and then go across the whole island of Fyn as far as the port of Nyborg.

The town of Nyborg was already virtually in a state of siege. The German troops were keeping themselves behind thick curtains of barbed wire, as if they wanted to intern themselves.

We now had to cross the Great Belt by boat. The atmosphere was terribly electric. Numerous German ships loaded with tens of thousands of refugees from the Reich were waiting in the port, but didn't risk disembarking their people.

They began by loading the Swedish Red Cross trucks onto a first ferry. The freed prisoners were cheered and covered with flowers. The crowd sang hymns. We ourselves expected to be chucked into the Great Belt from one minute to the next.

The wait lasted four hours. Finally we made the crossing. The crewmen were extremely surly. The night was very dark when we disembarked at the island of Sjaelland.

The countryside was infested with guerillas. We still had more than a hundred kilometers to cross before reaching Copenhagen. It was two o'clock in the morning when we passed by the barbed wire fences which prevented access to the German buildings of the town square.

My calculations had proved exact. A group of Walloon soldiers who had come by sea were already in Copenhagen. We met one another with great shouts of joy.

We had an understanding with General Panke, commandant of the SS in Denmark, that as our men arrived they would be sent to Norway, where we would regroup and face events.

There the last anti-Communist front was to be found. The three hundred thousand German soldiers who were massed there were well armed and supplied. They would be able to fight for a long time. Their surrender would be the last and would probably have the benefit of better conditions.

I fixed all the details for the transfer of my men. It was understood that the departure of the Walloons for Oslo would begin the very next day.

These preparations calmed us. The sun was hot. We leaned on our elbows in the windows. The town square of Copenhagen swarmed with activity. It was market day. Jugglers were circulating, clowning. We watched the colorful spectable with the amused eyes of tourists.

* * * * *

The SS general had offered to put me up at his country house, Viking House, by the sea on the way out of town. The house was vacant. I would be able to rest a bit. The next morning a plane would take me to Oslo.

The afternoon was marvelous. The villa was in perfect taste. At the end of the lawn the sea stretched out blue-gray and peaceful, with tiny wavelets.

That evening we were served a copious dinner. In spite of the war Denmark lived well: pastries, butter, cream, eggs, bacon, the most diverse delicacies were all plentiful.

My mind was on alert, however. I listened to the radio. It was perhaps nine-thirty. In a German transmission there was talk about the capitulation of Denmark. I rushed from set to set and finally heard the fateful sentence, "The Armies of Denmark have surrendered unconditionally. They will lay down their weapons tomorrow morning at eight o'clock."

I tried to telephone the SS office. I could hear nothing on the phone except the howling of a delirious crowd assaulting the buildings. All the bells in town were ringing.

A lot of good it had done us to run!

The mousetrap had shut.

## Partisans and English

It was the evening of Friday, 4 May 1945.

We drew up the balance sheet, my two aides-de-camp, the driver, and I. The surrender of the armies of the northern Reich and Denmark was a fact. We were alone at the far end of Copenhagen in an absolutely unknown district. We were occupying the villa of the SS general, which would certainly not better our situation.

The youngest of my officers was jumpy.

"Tomorrow," he kept repeating, "it will be too late. We have to find a solution immediately. I'm going to the German staff office."

He took the driver and planted a submachine gun between his knees. A quarter of an hour later in the center of the town, he fell into a frenzy of riots. They were attacking isolated soldiers who hadn't got out of the way in time. The officer, the driver, and the automobile were struck down in this obscure tragedy.

At eleven o'clock in the evening the balance sheet was even clearer. There were only two of us. We didn't have a car any more. We didn't have anyone's address.

* * * * *

A key grated in the lock. The door opened. A man entered.

It was a German civilian in convalescence at Copenhagen. He was lodging—we hadn't known it at all—in the same villa as we were.

This fellow had been gone since noon to take a walk along the sea. He was coming back in to sleep. The war was over? That was none of his business. He was no soldier. Therefore he would await events philosophically.

He got undressed, put on some pale green pajama pants and went on to eat the hors d'oeuvres we had left.

We brought him back to reality. Our case seemed to him a bit more complicated than his own.

"Don't you know a single person who might live in the area?" we asked him.

He slowly chewed an egg with mayonnaise, pausing again. "Yes," he said, "the German governor of Denmark lives five minutes from here."

We didn't make him repeat it. My last aide-de-camp put on civilian clothing and immediately left for Dr. Best's property. We found him slouched in his kitchen behind nineteen suitcases and quite desperate. He couldn't see a single way left for getting us out of the wasp's nest of Copenhagen.

"I'm going to try everything," he said. "If it's still possible, a naval officer will come for you in an hour and try to put you on a boat."

We waited all night lying in the vestibule. No one came.

In the morning red and white flags were flying at the tops of poles on all the villas in the neighborhood. A motor boat was patrolling in front of our terrace a hundred meters out to sea. Trucks packed with helmeted "partisans" with machine guns in their hands were passing like whirlwinds down the boulevard. Everyone pointed out Viking House.

We would certainly be attacked before too long.

* * * * *

The servants had gone for information. The town was in full-fledged riot. Germans had been murdered by the populace. Several thousand guerrillas were masters of the streets. The German offices at the center of Copenhagen had been surrounded by a furious mob.

We almost envied our comrades who were besieged back there. They at least were together and could unite until the arrival of the British troops. We two were liable to be lynched at any moment.

From the town came violent noises of combat. There was machine gun fire and even cannon fire. It was a rather noisy surrender. We asked ourselves when and how we would be engulfed.

Suddenly a blue limousine with Danish plates stopped in front of the door. A man hastened up.

"Get into civilian clothes right away and jump into my car."

In a few seconds we had put a pair of trousers and a civilian jacket on over our uniforms.

"We're going to try to go through town," the driver, a very stylishly dressed gentleman two meters tall, said to us.

"And if we're attacked?"

"Then there's nothing to be done. You'll have to leave all your weapons here, even your revolvers. The troops of Denmark have capitulated. We have to respect the word of the Reich."

We emptied our pockets.

The car started off down the avenue.

* * * * *

Our driver was an officer in civilian dress. Dr. Best had loyally done everything to save us. He was risking a lot. Some German ships were still occupying a corner of the Copenhagen harbor. We were going to try to get to them. We would have to drive through the entire town before reaching them.

We had scarcely started into the boulevards when we encountered the first barriers. Six partisans with leveled machine guns were cutting off the way from one crossroads to the next.

Our guide pretended to stop, then gave a friendly wave of his hand to the sentinels. These thought they had to do with one or another of the big chiefs of the partisans. Taking advantage of their surprise, our German officer immediately stepped on the accelerator. We passed a half dozen barriers that way.

The further we went into the center of town, the more intense was the congestion. All Copenhagen was in the streets. The car went forward only with great difficulty. People gave us strange stares.

We veered off on several side streets and ended up coming back to the boulevard fifty meters away from a snarling crowd which was attacking a building. They were dragging civilians out onto the ground. Groups of partisans were blocking the way.

We had only a second to rush into a side alley. When the car had swung into it, it was too late to go back. We had entered right into the courtyard of a barracks occupied by the "Resistance."

Our driver, unflappable, drove straight in, made a dazzling turn, scaled a concrete tank trap, and exited the lair with perfect ease. We passed near the delirious crowd and headed into the neighboring lanes at full throttle.

* * * * *

Our driver knew Copenhagen admirably. He succeeded in nearing the harbor district, driving from side to side street.

From time to time we would find ourselves confronted by a huge throng pillaging the house of a "collaborator." They would load the half-stunned civilians into vans. Each time we had to swerve suddenly to avoid falling into the middle of the pack.

Unfortunately we had to pass over a Copenhagen station to reach the harbor. How would we keep from being trapped when we tried to cross one of the long guarded bridges which straddled the lines?

It was then that my former good luck once more ruled my destiny. Heavy machine-gun fire had broken out just that minute. The Danish Communists had tried to seize the harbor petroleum depot a few hundred meters away. The Germans had violently resisted with all the weapons at their disposal, including anti-aircraft guns. There was a desperate scramble. Civilians, terrorists, and partisan sentinels fled, rushing into the houses. God's second! Our automobile raced forward, crossed the thirty or forty meters of narrow bridge like an arrow, made a wide curve, came down again, and stopped in front of a gate. We were saved. We were at the entrance to the harbor.

* * * * *

Even there Danish partisans with revolvers in their hands and disarmed German soldiers mingled one with another. Discreetly I showed my decoration, with its Oak Leaves, which I held hidden in the palm of my hand, to a naval officer. With an innocent air, he had me sit down in a boat which took us, my aide-de-camp and I, to the ship of a commander of eighteen minesweepers.

The Copenhagen anchorage was a moving spectacle. Facing this town gone mad, a whole German fleet, comprising magnificent ships like the *Prinz Eugen,* was moored in the blue bay. The flags of the *Kriegsmarine* still flew proudly atop the masts. Twenty thousand men were aboard.

But these splendid boats, already chained to fixed moorings, would be prey for the Allies this evening or tomorrow. Had I escaped the terrorists to be swept up now at the anchorage by the British?

The commander of the minesweepers was a determined officer.

"Our Norwegian armies weren't included in the capitulation," he repeated. "Perhaps there is a chance to get there."

But the admiral, consulted, replied that any idea of leaving for Norway had to be abandoned.

* * * * *

The town glittered in the sun. At three o'clock in the afternoon the commander showed me a radio-telegram. A British airborne division was going to land. A quarter of an hour later a British airplane passed above our masts, turned, and landed before our eyes at the Copenhagen airport.

At five o'clock in the evening the sky was filled with an immense rumbling. Hundreds of British transport planes were landing at the airport a few kilometers away from us.

Six o'clock in the evening.

Motorcycles and jeeps were unloaded from the vast cabins. The Tommies took off toward the town. The crowd cheered them deliriously. Any minute we would see them come out onto the quays.

My commander's eyes were glittering. He took me fraternally by the shoulders.

"No, no," he exclaimed, "It will not be said that Germany abandoned you."

He hailed the young commander of a minesweeper.

"You're going to break a passage through," he said to him. "I want you to get to Oslo with Degrelle."

A handsome warship approached, as grey as the water and as narrow and slender as a hare. I put on a big sheepskin coat and passed to starboard.

At six-thirty in the evening, right in front of the British, who were showing off on the streets and docks, we set sail at full speed toward the coast of Sweden, then straight north.

## Oslo, 7 May 1945

On the bow of the warship on which I was escaping from Copenhagen *in extremis,* I found a reviving balm in the sharp aroma of the sea.

On the Swedish coast the reflections of twilight were dying out. The shore was very close. I looked at the whitewashed walls, the tall pink chimneys, and the darkening hills. On the Danish coast the green roofs of Elsinore[3] were outlined against the twilight, more romantic than ever.

The sea was nothing but a wide river now. I was in a hurry to get out of this bottleneck and reach the Kattegat, to see the colors of the hostile sky melt away.

Evening came without our having been caught by British planes. The breeze was brisk. I leaned on my elbows right at the bow to dream, to catch the rough caress of the north wind and the spray, and to watch the lights of a million stars. The sea shimmered, glimmered, and shone to infinity. It was tranquil and soothing.

Our warship was fast. If we wanted to escape a massive air attack we had to reach the fjords of Norway early in the morning.

No one on board was authorized to sleep, for we might run into some mines at any minute. But the sea was wide. There was enough room for both the mines and us. We didn't hit a single one.

Three times during the night Allied planes came prowling above the masts. The sailors told us the harrassment at sea was as fierce as on land.

The night was clear.

The British planes contended themselves with coming down quite low, almost to the water level. We carefully refrained from showing any reaction. They must have been wondering what we were doing in the Kattegat when the war in Denmark was over, but they didn't insist. We were polite and imitated their discretion.

At eight o'clock in the morning we saw the big brown and black rocks of Norway. We came into the dazzling Oslo fjord. Not a boat on the horizon. The water was icy blue and smooth as metal. On the banks villas built of wood and painted blue, brown, white, or dark green were half hidden in the firs. I thought about the Reich's landing fleet, advancing on an equally luminous morning in April 1940, as the fjord's black rocks glistened in the shining water.

We advanced for two hours.

Past the harbor entrance, roofs, church towers, docks, cranes, and elevators emerged.

Oslo.

It was ten o'clock in the morning. A siren answered us. We drew up alongside two pocket submarines, hardly bigger than canoes and yellow like drying tobacco leaves.

The city of Oslo is set at the end of one of the most radiant inlets in

Europe. The town was still sleeping. It was Sunday. An occasional tram would pass. We telephoned, and an automobile came for us. It took us toward the mountains which lined the Oslo fjord on the southwest.

The weather was perfect.

Thousands of girls with splendid figures outlined by light pajamas in shimmering colors were riding bicycles along the creeks, the grey and brown rocks, and the black firs. They were heading toward the wooded hills.

We stopped twice to ask the way. The bicyclists stared at us. Every head shook "no." In spite of the countryside, the blond locks, the coquettish red or blue trousers of these charmers, in spite of the sun and the brilliance of the spring, the war and its surliness came through first.

We came to Crown Prince Olaf's castle on top of a mountain, where I was to meet the German governor of Norway, Dr. Terboven. He received me immediately, his face non-committal, his little eyes blinking like those of Himmler.

I explained my plan to him. I wanted to join the northern front of Norway promptly. As long as the war against Communism continued, we wanted to affirm the presence of our Legion in the struggle. Other Walloons would rejoin us without delay.

Dr. Terboven must have received particularly discouraging news. He shook his head. He talked to me of Sweden and Japan. I had been thinking in terms of Narvik and the North Cape.

He had an old French cognac brought out and offered me some very satisfying sandwiches. From the castle terrace the view extended over the gulf, an immense, unforgettable symphony of dark blues, whites, browns, and greens. With the world so beautiful why did so much fury ravage the hearts of men?

Dr. Terboven had reserved an apartment for me in Oslo. He would keep me informed of events. I went back down into the iridescent valley. I could no longer see how I was going to get out of it.

* * * * *

I took a bath and listened to the radio. The Allies were exultant, but I was exhausted and fell asleep.

The next day, Monday, 7 May 1945, I heard the warriors of Radio London baying. They trumpeted the end of the hunt. The general surrender of the Reich was arranged. It was no longer a matter of hours, maybe only of minutes.

The Norwegian Prime Minister, Quisling, whom I hadn't yet met, had invited me to the Royal Palace.

I arrived at eleven-thirty, after a stroll in the streets. The palace was nothing much. Two large and attractive tapestries hung in the white marble grand staircase. The royal furniture was worn. In front of the palace a classic thundering monarch, speckled with bird droppings, was riding a massive green bronze stallion.

Quisling seemed crushed by fate. We made small talk for half an hour. Terboven had asked me to calm him, which eliminated most subjects of conversation. He gave the impression of being devoured from within. His face was puffy, his eyes wandered in every direction, his fingers tapped the table. The man felt lost.

I was his last visitor. That afternoon he hurried to the Swedish border, was turned back, and returned to Oslo that night, no longer knowing into which fjord to throw himself. He was shot a few months later.

* * * * *

These events hadn't shaken the hotel's burgundy. I drank a delectable bottle of it at lunch, but the radio kept me from fully enjoying it. At two o'clock in the afternoon it announced a statement from the Reich's new Minister of Foreign Affairs.

A speech by this man in such circumstances? I guessed every paragraph of it before a single word had been spoken. The surrender outside the Reich was complete: in Bohemia, in Lithuania, in Crete, at the French ports of the Atlantic Ocean. The three hundred thousand men of Norway were giving themselves up like the others. Why should Germany have gone on fighting and have sacrificed German lives now that the last meters of her soil were conquered from Schleswig to the Sudetes?

The troops of the Reich in Scandinavia were treated correctly—repatriated and liberated. The German forces in Crete even obtained the honors of war. They went back to their country armed.

But for us, the last foreign volunteers, it was the abyss.

I stayed at the window the whole afternoon. What was the good of feeling sad? I had done what I could. I had held on right to the end, obstinately, without flinching. There was no point in going north again. The North Cape, too, had capitulated.

The crowd was massing in the streets, more dignified than in Copenhagen. The girls were waving flags. German soldiers were still moving about without any Norwegian attacking them. The brawls, executions, and suicides began only with the arrival of the partisans, who came down from the neighboring mountains the next day.

I waited for news from Dr. Terboven. At six o'clock in the evening he had me called to the palace of Prince Olaf.

* * * * *

Dr. Terboven welcomed me in company with his friend, General Reedis. They were heroically calm. Nevertheless they would both be found the next morning, exsanguinated, revolvers in their icy hands, neither one having wanted to turn Norway over to the victors.

We gazed again, together, at the dazzling landscape. A headwaiter in tails served drinks as if we were at a garden party on an innocent spring afternoon.

Dr. Terboven then said to me in a grave voice, "I have asked Sweden to give you asylum. She has refused. A submarine could perhaps have taken you as far as Japan, but the capitulation is absolute. Submarines can no longer leave."

"At the airport at the foot of the mountain there is still a private plane. It belongs to Minister Speer. Do you want to take your chances and try to reach Spain tonight?"

We made some calculations. From Oslo to the Pyrenees was about twenty-one hundred and fifty kilometers in a direct line. In theory the plane had a range of twenty-one hundred kilometers.

By flying very high to save fuel it wasn't impossible to get there.

I had no choice.

I accepted.

I had risked my life every day for two weeks. I would risk it one last time.

* * * * *

Once more I went back to Oslo, swarming with a huge multitude.

The hotel had completely emptied. All the doors were wide open. Even the staff had disappeared.

I had to wait; we couldn't take off before it was completely dark. I would have to get into the airfield secretly.

At eleven o'clock in the evening a magnificent frizzy-haired pilot with hands as big as flippers, decorated with the German Gold Cross, brought a little automobile up in front of the hotel. Together with my last officer I got in.

The crowd was demonstrating everywhere in the streets. I was still in the uniform of a Waffen SS colonel, and I was wearing the Oak Leaves and the Knight's Cross ribbon around my neck. Tens of thousands of tall blond boys and girls with perfect features crowded the streets, but they moved aside smiling to let the car pass.

Not a single anti-tank barrier had been constructed outside of Oslo. Our pilot brought us up under the wings of the plane in the darkness without anyone's noticing us.

The aides took their places.

One minute later we were in the sky.

# Chapter Eleven
# "ALEA JACTA EST."

My first feeling when the airplane left Norwegian soil was one of relief. In taking off we had cut the last mooring ropes of uncertainty. Now everything was clear. When the airplane landed either we would have succeeded or we would be irremediably lost.

*Alea jacta est.*[1] Life or death! We would soon know which definitively. We didn't have to do any more thinking, planning, and weighing.

It was almost midnight. The war had in fact been over since the German radio transmission at 1400 hours. Nonetheless the capitulation would not be officially in force until the next day, 8 May 1945.

We were between war and peace, as between earth and sky. We flew for a time above the Skagerrak. From this time on, only the compass on our instrument panel and the marvelous skill of the pilot would guide us in the storm. Naturally we couldn't take our bearings from the radio. We didn't even have a map of Europe.

All in all our aviators had a magnificent map . . . of Norway.

One of them had in addition a minuscule map of France which came from a pocket atlas. It lavishly displayed three rivers: the Seine, the Loire, and the Rhone.

We climbed to 4,000 meters in order to save fuel, but a storm quickly forced us to fly fairly low.

* * * * *

Obviously an isolated plane launched thus across 2,000 kilometers of occupied territory without any protection would run twenty times the risk of being brought down. Our only chance of salvation lay in the monster celebration which had been going on all afternoon in the Allied camp.

On all the airfields in the West the victors were in the process of swilling rivers of champagne and whiskey. Thousands of British and American combat pilots, freed from the worry of nocturnal missions, would be on the edge—or in the depths—of inebriation at the hour our Heinkel was crossing their surveillance zones. Of all nights, this was the one to pull it off.

Besides, who would imagine that a solitary plane still proudly bearing its swastikas would dare fly over Holland, Belgium, and the whole of France, now that the war was over? Above all, who would imagine that one of the Reich's planes would come out of the North Sea from along the coast of Scotland? We had taken care, in truth, to use this stratagem, heading first straight toward England, then approaching the European continent as if we were coming from British shores.

I watched the dark lands beneath. Automobiles were hurrying along with their headlights on. Little towns shone like boxes of burning matches. Everywhere people would be singing and drinking.

It was perhaps one-thirty in the morning when I noticed a disturbing phenomenon. A big searchlight had been turned on behind us and was scanning the sky.

My heart began to beat faster.

* * * * *

In spite of the celebrations on the ground, we had been spotted. Searchlights were now probing at out altitude. Others were lighting up far in front of us. The airfields were outlined in great squares of light. The runways shone like white sheets.

Our machine flew as fast as it could to escape those accursed lights, but always other searchlights lit up and rose toward us as though to seize us.

Glimmers of light spattered our wings.

The radio began to crackle. The Allied observers called us: "Who are you? What are you doing?"

We didn't reply. We fled, pushing harder and harder.

* * * * *

Belgium was below me. Antwerp was there, shining in the first night of the return of peace. I thought about our rivers, our roads, about all the towns where I had spoken, the plains, the hills, the ancient houses that I loved so much. These people who were there under the plane, these people I had wanted to raise, to ennoble, to bring back to the paths of glory. To my left I saw the lights of Brussels, the big black splash of the Soignes forest which had long been my beloved home.

Ah! The wretchedness of being beaten and seeing one's dream die! I gritted my teeth to keep from shedding tears. It was in the night and the wind, pursued by a bitter fate, that I had my last rendezvous with the sky of my homeland.

We had not passed Lille. Always the airfield searchlights harassed us.

But the further south we penetrated, the more hope we had of cheating death.

We approached Paris, which our Heinkel flew over at a very low altitude. I could make out the streets and the squares, silvery as doves.

We were still alive. We flew over the Beauce, the Loire, the Vendee. Soon we would reach the Atlantic.

The pilots, however, were exchanging worried looks. Certainly we now ran less risk of being brought down by the Allied anti-aircraft guns or night fighters. But the fuel was running low.

The night was terribly dark.

I searched the ground anxiously. The luminous hands showed five o'clock in the morning. An ephemeral glow eased the darkness. I recognized it instantly. It was the Gironde estuary. We were on the right route.

We followed along the sea.

We could just make out the leaping line of the waves at the edge of the beach. To the east, at the very end of the sky, the horizon shimmered almost imperceptibly.

We were running lower and lower on fuel.

By the bluish lights on the instrument panel I scrutinized the drawn features of the pilots.

The plane slowed and descended.

We passed opposite Arcachon. I had once lived there under the aromatic pines. The harbor was lit up as if for Bastille Day.

From a distance we followed the black mass of the Landes, broken by the gleaming lake of Biscarosse.

The Heinkel misfired a number of times.

One of the pilots brought us life jackets. The fuel gauge showed empty. We might fall into the sea at any moment.

With a tension that ate at my nerves I studied the probable line of the Pyrenees. Daybreak was glimmering feebly.

The peaks of the mountains ought to be visible. We couldn't see them.

The plane was misfiring more and more loudly.

To the southeast a distant blued curve hemmed the sky. The chain of the Pyrenees was there.

But could we stay in the air as far as the Spanish coast?

Because of the storm we had flown almost twenty-three hundred kilometers. We had to list the airplane onto the left wing, then onto the right wing, to make the last liters of fuel from the tanks flow into the motors.

I knew the region of Biarritz and Saint-Jean-de-Luz. I could barely make out the whitening bend of the Pyrennes at the mouth of the Bidassoa.

But the plane wanted no more of it and had come down almost to water level. We were going to die twenty kilometers from the Iberian coast.

We had to shoot the red shipwreck flares. Two military patrol boats headed towards us, coming from the French coast.

What a tragedy! And to think that a searchlight was now blinking in the distance, a Spanish searchlight!

It was strange to see the white-capped crests of the waves and the sea lapping close beneath us, ready to swallow us up. We still hadn't fallen in. The coast was coming closer, pushing its reefs and rocks toward us and its green and black peaks, barely detached from the shadows.

Suddenly the pilot stood the plane up vertically, almost turning it completely over, and revving the motor so as to catch the last drops of benzine. Then he charged over a rocky hill and, with an awful racket, grazed several red roofs.

We no longer had the time to think.

We had seen a short ribbon of sand in a clearing. The Heinkel, which hadn't lowered its landing gear, slid on its fuselage at two hundred and fifty kilometers an hour. I saw the right motor explode, glowing like a ball of fire. The machine turned, lunged toward the sea, went into the waves, and crashed.

The water flooded into the back cabin and rose up to our waists. I had five fractures. On the beach at San Sebastian the civil guards with black two-cornered hats rushed back and forth in agitation. Some Spaniards as naked as Tahitians swam out to our wrecked plane.

They pulled us up onto a wing of the twin-engine, then into a canoe. An ambulance came alongside.

This time the war was really over.

We were alive. God had saved us.

My injuries themselves were a blessing.

I spent months in a hospital bed, but I had kept my strength and my faith.

I hadn't experienced the bitterness of falling uselessly into the hands of my enemies.

I remained, a witness to my soldiers' deeds. I could defend them from the lies of adversaries insensible to heroism. I could tell of their epic on the Donets and the Don, in the Caucasus and at Cherkassy, in Estonia, at Stargard, on the Oder.

One day the sacred names of our dead would be repeated with pride. Our people, hearing these tales of glory, would feel their blood quicken. And they would know their sons.

Certainly we had been beaten. We had been dispersed and pursued to the four corners of the world.

But we could look to the future with heads held high. History weighs the merit of men. Above worldly baseness, we had offered our youth against total immolation. We had fought for Europe, its faith, its civilization. We had reached the very height of sincerity and sacrifice. Sooner or later Europe and the world would have to recognize the justice of our cause and the purity of our gift.

For hate dies, dies suffocated by its own stupidity and mediocrity, but grandeur is eternal.

And we lived in grandeur.

# GLOSSARY

*Abteilungen*: Government bureaus, or sections.

bashibazouks: 19th century Ottoman irregulars, notorious for their brutality.

cheval-de-frise: Originally a spiked obstacle for horses; here it denotes a close-knit formation for defense on all sides.

*Dienststelle*: In the German Army, an office or department.

droshky: An open, four-wheeled, horse-drawn carriage.

*Feldgendarmes*: The military police of the Prussian, then German, Army, from 1866-1945.

*Feldpost*: The German Army postal service.

*isba*: a Russian or Ukrainian peasant's cottage.

*Intourist*: The Soviet organization which controls tourism and tourists.

*Kessel*: A pocket resulting from complete encirclement.

*kolkhoz*: Abbreviation for Russian *kollektivnoye khozyaynstvo*, Soviet-controlled agricultural community and enterprise, nominally a collective. Produce belonged to the state, as did capital; pay was supposed to be based on labor; small garden plots were allowed the collectivized farmers.

*Landsknecht* (pl. -e): A type of professional soldier, first recruited by the emperor Maximilian I in the late 15th century, which flourished in the 16th century. Until the foundation of a standing imperial army around 1620 the *Landsknechte* formed the backbone of the forces of the Reich, and became celebrated for their military exploits and lusty way of life.

*mamka*: "Little mother"; affectionate Ukrainian diminutive.

*muzhik*: A Russian peasant.

Pak: Abbreviation for *Panzerabwehrkanone*, German for an anti-tank gun, which typically was long-barreled, with a high muzzle velocity, and fired armor-piercing shells.

*pan*: Ukrainian for "Mr." or "Sir."

panzerfaust: The light panzerfaust ("mailed fist") used as an anti-tank weapon by the Walloons and the Germans was an individually fired tube which discharged a rocket-propelled hollow-charge projectile. The tube was discarded after use.

*politruk* (pl. -y): Soviet political officer, charged with a number of functions among the troops, including political supervision and agitation. Commonly translated as "commisar."

*shapska*: Variant of Russian, Ukrainian *shapka,* "cap."

*sovkhoz*: Soviet state farm, similar to the *kolkhoz*, but generally originating in the Soviet seizure of a single large estate.

*Stabsfeldwebel*: German non-commissioned officer corresponding roughly to a U.S. Army Sergeant or Major. Usually a career soldier.

Stuka: Abbreviation of *Sturzkampfflugzeug*, "dive bomber." The most famous, and most effective, was the Junkers 87.

*Sturmgeschuetz* (pl. -e): Cannon or howitzer used for infantry support, primarily against armor. Originally drawn by horses or a truck, it was later mounted as a "self-propelled gun" on an armored, treaded vehicle.

telega: A crude Russian cart, lacking springs.

*Tiefflieger*: German for "strafing plane."

uhlans: Heavy cavalry, or lancers. The word, from the Turkish for "boy, lad," was first used to denote Polish cavalry units in the 16th century. From 1734 there were Prussian uhlan regiments; after 1918 the division of the German cavalry into light (dragoons, hussars, mounted rangers) and heavy (curassiers, uhlans) units was abolished. Cavalry units were employed by many nations in World War II.

Volapuek: An "international" language invented by the German preacher J.M. Schleyer in 1879 under the delusion that a common language for humanity would foster peace and tolerance.

*Volksdeutsche*: Name for persons of German stock, language, and culture outside the boundaries of the German Reich, for the most part living in communities in Eastern and Central Europe. They made an immeasurable contribution to the culture and economy of the lands in which they dwelt. In the 20th century the great majority of the *Volksdeutschen* were driven from their adopted homelands, either into exile in the Central Asiatic "republics" of the Soviet Union or back to the western rump of the German Reich (the German Federal Republic.).

# FOOTNOTES

## Foreword

1. Berchtesgaden was the site of Hitler's mountain chalet, the Berghof, 1,700 feet high in the Alps, near Salzburg and the Austrian border.
2. Wallonian is the dialect spoken in most of the French-speaking parts of Belgium. The word came from a Germanic word designating foreigners, originally the Celts, later the more or less Romanized population of countries from Dacia (now roughly Romania) to Britain. The designation of a territory as Wallonia occurs no earlier than 1858.

## Chapter 1

1. Although Degrelle underscores the Russian role in the plot against the lawful government of Yugoslavia, there is now no doubt that Great Britain's and the United States's secret and not so secret agents, including "Wild Bill" Donovan, first head of the U.S. Office of Strategic Services (OSS), played a more important role in organizing the putsch. See *The Last European War,* John Lukacs; *The Shadow Warriors,* Bradley F. Smith; *The Fall of Yugoslavia,* Iliya Jukic; etc.
2. Lemberg is the German name of the great city, capital of Galicia, variously known as Lvov (Russian), Lviv (Ukrainian), and Lwow (Polish).
3. The kulaks, the farmers of Russia and the Ukraine who owned their own farms and were able to employ farm laborers, were systematically "liquidated" (that is, deprived of their property, deported to forced labor camps, and starved to death) in huge numbers at Stalin's order in the early 1930's. The details of this crime, and the massive famine which resulted from it (deaths are estimated at several millions) have received little attention in the West.

## Chapter 2

1. Abbreviation for *Gosudarstvennoye Polititsheskoye Upravleniye,* or "State Political Administration." The literal meaning expresses the key function of this organization in the USSR far better than the usual over-quick designation as the Soviet secret police; it fulfills that role and much more. At the time of the Second World War, it had become known as the NKVD. Several more name changes and reorganizations have resulted in its present designation as the KGB; its role and function remain unchanged.

2. Hungarians and Romanians have nursed a centuries-old rivalry over Transylvania, a large area, now in Romania, flanked to the north, east, and south by the sweeping curve of the Carpathians. The pusztas are the great steppes of Hungary.

3. The Borinage was formerly an important mining area of Hainaut, on the French border of Belgium. Its coal mining has been rendered uncompetitive by unfavorable geological conditions, and the Borinage has been economically depressed for decades.

4. Rosa Luxemburg was a Jewess born to a wealthy merchant's family in Zamosc, Poland, in 1870. A Marxist revolutionary who harbored a general contempt for the European nations, and for the Germans in particular, her revolutionary peregrinations brought her at length to the Reich. While attempting to subject a prostrate Germany to Bolshevist terror and revolution after the First World War, she was captured and shot by German nationalists during the anarchy reigning in Berlin in 1919.

## Chapter 3

1. The reader will remember that these events took place at around 49 degrees of latitude north. There was no "daylight saving" in the Soviet Union.

2. The Brandenburg Gate was designed and built by Carl Langhans in 1788–1791 at the entrance to the great avenue Unter den Linden in Berlin. Langhans imitated the Propylaea, the great gate to the Athenian Acropolis. The massive quadriga, or four-horse chariot, on top of the gate was modeled by Georg von Schadow after the vehicles in which Roman generals were drawn in triumph through Rome. The approach to the Brandenburg Gate is now mockingly barred by the wall constructed by the regime of the "German Democratic Republic."

3. The Iron Cross, established as a decoration for bravery during the German War of Liberation by King Frederick William III of Prussia in

1813, was renewed in the Franco-Prussian War, the First World War, and the Second World War. When Adolf Hitler, who was awarded both the Iron Cross 1st and 2nd Class in the First World War, re-established the medal in 1939, it was divided into four grades, the third of which had five levels: the Knight's Cross of the Iron Cross; the Knight's Cross of the Iron Cross with Oak Leaf; the Knight's Cross of the Iron Cross with Oak Leaf with Swords; the Knight's Cross of the Iron Cross with Golden Leaf with Swords and Diamonds. The last was awarded to one man only, the intrepid Stuka pilot Hans-Ulrich Rudel. Degrelle, who was eventually to be awarded the Knight's Cross with Oak Leaf, was the only non-German so honored.

## Chapter 4

1. "Capuan" for Capua, the Etruscan-founded city in Campania, proverbial in classical antiquity for its luxury.
2. Artaban was a character in the Gascon La Calprenide's novel *Clēopatre* (1647), famous for his hauteur.
3. Vatel was a celebrated French chef, the great aristocrat Condé's maitre d'hotel, who became legendary by his suicide after several minor lapses at a banquet he had prepared at his master's request for King Louis XIV in 1671.
4. The *Vieux grognards* ("old grumblers") were the veterans forming the core of Napoleon's armies, including the Imperial Guard.

## Chapter 5

1. Meant are the *blancs becs* (literally "white beaks"), very young troops who served as dragoons in the regiment of Prince Charles Joseph de la Ligne in the Seven Years' War. They particularly distinguished themselves at Prague, Kolin, and Leuthen in 1757 against Frederick the Great's Prussians, and were styled *blancs becs* by the Austrian marshal Daun for their lack of moustaches. They received a banner from Empress Maria Teresia embroidered with a tender rose ringed by thorns and the device "*Qui s'y frotte s'y pique*" ("Who vexes me pricks himself").

## Chapter 6

1. The *Leo belgicus* ("Belgian lion"), like the Lion of Flanders, is a heraldic symbol of the nation.
2. Napoleon's embattled crossing of the Beresina, 27-28 November 1812,

while dogged by three different Russian armies, with 10,000 stragglers and wounded left behind to be butchered by Cossacks, encapsules the disaster of his Russian campaign.

## Chapter 7

1. Several hundred thousand workers from Belgium were employed in German industry. Many had come voluntarily before the war to take advantage of the Hitler boom; many more were drafted to work in the mines and factories of the Reich after the conquest and occupation of Belgium.
2. The ancient capital of Estonia is called Tallinn ("Danish fortress") by the Estonians, Reval by the Germans.
3. The German Hansa (*Hanse*), or Hanseatic League, was the great Germanic trading confederation of the High Middle Ages, with member cities radiating from Luebeck up the Baltic to Reval, down into the Rhineland and as far east as Cracow. The Hansa flourished until finally superseded by England and the Netherlands in the seventeenth century.

## Chapter 8

1. *Le Moniteur* (The Monitor) was a war-time Rexist newspaper.

## Chapter 9

1. The *Volkssturm* was raised by the last military draft in Germany during the Second World War, and formed in late 1944 from all able-bodied men aged sixteen to sixty. Most fought as well as they could.
2. The reference is to the Battle of Montmirail, 11 February 1814, in which Napoleon, fighting brilliantly but hopelessly in the Campaign of France, defeated two numerically superior armies, one Prussian, one Russian.
3. The six hundred men of Franchimont, castle and headquarters of the prince-bishops of Liège, sallied forth in 1468 to defend their ancient liberties against King Charles XI of France and Charles the Bold of Burgundy, who were dickering over the annexation of their country. They were captured and slaughtered to a man. Liège fell to Burgundy but their example lived on as an inspiration to Lowlands patriots.
4. Indeed Robert E. Howard's Conan, whose adventures were as avidly read by the American and European youth of the 1930's as they are seen by today's teenagers at the movies.

## Chapter 10

1. General Andrei Andreievich Vlassov, commander of the 2nd Soviet Shock Army, was captured by the Germans in 1942. Leader of a German-sponsored "Russian Committee" from 1942, Vlassov was able to raise two divisions from Russian POWs in German captivity in 1945. He and his troops were captured by the Americans at the end of the war and handed over to the Soviets shortly thereafter. Vlassov and doubtless most of his men were executed.

2. Although Luebeck was heavily damaged by a British incendiary attack on 24 March 1942 its characteristic skyline with its seven church towers and its massive gate was relatively unscathed, preserving a good deal of the city's traditional aspect.

3. Hamlet's Elsinore is called Helsingor in modern Danish.

## Chapter 11

1. "The die is cast." Gaius Julius Caesar's famous dictum as he led his legions across the Rubicon River, the dividing line between the Roman province of Cisalpine Gaul and the territory of the Republic proper, in violation of the Republic's laws, in his quest for *imperium.* Now a tag for any decision momentous and irrevocable.